"It was a joy to read this excellent and useful book. In this volume, Joel Beeke—one of our best ambassadors for warm, winsome, experiential, solid, orthodox, passionate, evangelistic Calvinism—introduces us to a healthy, well-rounded view of the Reformed tradition—Calvinism as it really is. It presents us with the basics of the history of Calvinism and confessionalism, as well as the mainstream Calvinistic teaching on salvation, piety, growth, the church, preaching, evangelism, marriage, family, work, politics, ethics, doxology (the idea of living all of life for God's honor—from which this book gets its title), and more. The total picture presented here will help strengthen in our time confessional, experiential Calvinism—the great, central, Reformed tradition flowing out of the best of British (Puritan and Scottish) and Dutch (Further Reformation) Calvinism."

—J. LIGON DUNCAN III
Senior Minister, First Presbyterian Church, Jackson, Miss.
President, Alliance of Confessing Evangelicals

"There seems to be a popular misconception afoot that Calvinism is an impressive intellectual structure, but that Reformed people must find resources elsewhere for practical piety. At the heart of Joel Beeke's ministry has been a burden to show the opposite conclusion, and this book has the same goal. Covering many important aspects of Calvinism, its practice as well as its faith, the book is written in a warm, pastoral, and engaging way."

—MICHAEL HORTON
Professor of systematic theology and apologetics,
Westminster Seminary California

"Finally—a book about Calvinism that covers the broad scope of the Calvinistic or Reformed movement. Calvinism affects the whole man: his head, his heart, and his hands. It has an intellectual or doctrinal dimension, as well as spiritual and practical dimensions. It influences not just the church but the culture. It is not confined to the Lord's Day, but impacts daily life. Calvinism is not a dead historic phenomenon, but a living view of God, man and Christ, sin and grace, time and eternity, and church and society. I hope this book will contribute to a revival of biblical, God-centered, and practical theology—that is, of Calvinism."

—PIETER ROUWENDAL
Writer and editor
Kampen, The Netherlands

"*Living for God's Glory* is a very helpful and insightful introduction to Reformed Christianity. It demonstrates that Calvinism is not narrowly doctrinal, but broad and profound, speaking to every aspect of Christian life. It will inform and inspire Christians in biblical faithfulness."

—W. ROBERT GODFREY
President, Westminster Seminary California

"Dr. Joel Beeke has once again performed a great service for the church of the Lord Jesus Christ. This book will profit every class of reader, from the new convert to the most mature believer. Dr. Beeke's style embodies the characteristics of experiential Calvinism on which he writes: every chapter is clear and addressed to the heart. I particularly found the chapter 'Applying the Word' to be a needed word for Calvinistic preachers in our day. Buy a copy for yourself and a number to give away."

—JOSEPH A. PIPA JR.
President, Greenville Presbyterian Theological Seminary
Greenville, S.C.

"*Living for God's Glory* is solid Christian truth in all its fullness, beauty, and strength. To study what is given so pleasantly here in these pages is to take a firm step toward becoming a clear-sighted and well-equipped student of theology. It will satisfy the appetite of believers, young and old. I wish I had had such a book in my hands when I was a young believer starting out on the journey to learn theology."

—MAURICE ROBERTS
Minister, Free Church of Scotland (Continuing)
Inverness, Scotland

"This book is rooted in the conviction that Calvinism is a gospel-centered, biblical theology for all of life. Drawing from his wide knowledge of Reformation and Puritan thought, and using his gift for illustrating biblical truth, Joel Beeke shows how God's grace is glorified in the believer's mind and heart, not only in the church, but also in the world."

—PHILIP GRAHAM RYKEN
Senior minister, Tenth Presbyterian Church, Philadelphia

LIVING

for

GOD'S GLORY

AN INTRODUCTION TO CALVINISM

JOEL R. BEEKE

WITH CONTRIBUTIONS FROM: SINCLAIR B. FERGUSON • JAMES GRIER •
MICHAEL A. G. HAYKIN • NELSON KLOOSTERMAN • RAY LANNING •
ROBERT OLIVER • RAY PENNINGS • DEREK W. H. THOMAS

℞

Reformation Trust
PUBLISHING

A DIVISION OF LIGONIER MINISTRIES · ORLANDO, FLORIDA

Living for God's Glory: An Introduction to Calvinism
© 2008 by Joel R. Beeke

Published by Reformation Trust
a division of Ligonier Ministries
400 Technology Park, Lake Mary, FL 32746
www.ligonier.org   www.reformationtrust.com

Printed in Harrisonburg, Virginia
R.R. Donnelley & Sons Company
December 2009
Second printing

Cover design: Tobias' Outerwear for Books
Interior design and typeset: Katherine Lloyd, The DESK, Colorado Springs, Colo.

All Scripture quotations are from The Holy Bible, King James Version.

Library of Congress Cataloging-in-Publication Data
Beeke, Joel R., 1952-
Living for God's glory : an introduction to Calvinism / Joel R. Beeke ; with contributions from Sinclair B. Ferguson ... [et al.].
   p. cm.
Includes bibliographical references and index.
ISBN 978-1-56769-105-4
1. Calvinism. I. Ferguson, Sinclair B. II. Title.
 BX9422.3.B44 2008
 284'.2--dc22

                                         2008020854

To three faithful, seasoned friends:

Dr. Robert Johnson

Word-centered elder, physician of physicians, tender counselor, assistant editor,

Dr. James Grier

Christ-exalting preacher, seminary mentor, wise counselor, servant leader, and

Rev. Ray Lanning

loyal colleague, walking encyclopedia, exegetical counselor, ruthless proofreader.

CONTENTS

ABBREVIATIONS

CO	*Opera quae supersunt omnia* (Calvin's writings)
Commentary	Calvin's Commentaries
Inst.	Calvin's *Institutes of the Christian Religion* (Battles' edition)
Inst. (Bev.)	Calvin's *Institutes of the Christian Religion* (Beveridge's edition)

FOREWORD

*W*ith all of my heart, I believe that the Reformed faith, or "Calvinism," is biblical Christianity—or the closest thing to it in the history of the church. This conviction rises out of thirty-four years of reading the Scriptures and church history.

It is not the conviction I had when I began my pilgrimage as a Christian. From February 1974, when I was converted as a philosophy student at the University of Toronto, through the next seven years, I was deeply involved in the charismatic movement. I was also enamored with the vision of the Christian life expressed by some of the church fathers and John Wesley, their eighteenth-century student. Wesley was definitely not a Calvinist, though at some points in his life, by his own admission, he was within an inch or two of it.

I suspect it was Augustine who helped change my theological outlook. Augustine's stress on the sovereignty of God's grace in salvation, described in his *Confessions*, won me when I first read the book in the mid-1970s. But I was still ignorant of some important issues. When I applied for a teaching position in 1981, I was asked what I thought about the five points of Calvinism. Though I had a doctorate in church history, I could not say what those points were. However, within a year of being asked that question, I was on my way to embracing a Calvinistic worldview. Arnold Dallimore's two-volume life of George Whitefield; the first volume of Iain Murray's life of "the Doctor," Martyn Lloyd-Jones; John Owen's study of the mortification of sin in believers; and some students helped open my eyes to Calvinism as the best expression of biblical Christianity. By 1985, I was committed to the five points of Calvinism.

As time went on, however, I came to see that Calvinism cannot be limited to soteriology but affects all church issues, especially worship and spirituality. Indeed, as does Christianity itself, Calvinism applies to all of life, including politics and economics, art and architecture. As Abraham Kuyper said, there is not one square inch of this universe that does not belong to Jesus Christ. In stating that, Kuyper reflected the New Testament, which affirms that Christ upholds and sustains all things by the word of His power (Heb. 1:3; Col. 1:17). Calvinism is a worldview that shapes and informs one's approach to all of life.

The chapters in this volume examine the main areas of Christian thought and life from the vantage point of Calvinism, showing how it makes sense of the Scriptures and Christian experience. The chapters in Part Five look at some of the broader aspects of society through the lens of Calvinism. Other areas of human life could have been examined through this lens with satisfying results. But the areas discussed are sufficient to show how Calvinism speaks to all spheres.

Such universality is what one should expect. Calvinism resonates deeply with biblical truth; it speaks to every area of human life and thought. If you, the reader, are not convinced of this, let me encourage you to read what others have found in Calvinism. If you are already convinced, may the chapters that follow help edify and mature you in thought and experience as you explore Calvinism.

—*Michael A. G. Haykin*
Dundas, Ontario
January 2008

PREFACE

or many years, I have searched for a book that would cover the intellectual and spiritual emphases of Calvinism, the way it influences the church and everyday living, and its ethical and cultural implications. The book I had in mind would explain for today's reader the biblical, God-centered, heartfelt, winsome, and practical nature of Calvinism, and would clearly convey how Calvinism earnestly seeks to meet the purpose for which we were created, namely, to live to the glory of God. By doing so, it would serve as a corrective to the many caricatures of Calvinism that still exist in North America and beyond.

I searched in vain. Over the years, I have frequently used H. Henry Meeter's *The Basic Ideas of Calvinism* and Leonard Coppes's *Are Five Points Enough? The Ten Points of Calvinism*, as well as a number of smaller books on the five points of Calvinism. But none of these, good though they are, covered all the emphases I had in mind. After giving a number of addresses on Calvinism for Malcolm Watts' conference in Salisbury, England, for the Puritan Project in Brazil, and for a conference in Adelaide, Australia, I realized more acutely the real need for the kind of book I envisioned. I wish to thank these groups for the warm fellowship I received from them, and I am glad that I can finally respond to their requests to publish these addresses as part of this introductory volume on Calvinism.

Greg Bailey of Ligonier Ministries pushed me to do the book myself with a commitment that he would edit it and that Ligonier would publish it through its Reformation Trust Publishing imprint—provided that I could complete it early in 2008 to be available in time to commemorate the 500th anniversary of Calvin's birth in 2009. So, in the end, I felt compelled to undertake the task myself. Looking back, I thank Greg for the early deadline and for his capable handling of my manuscript.

My first outline included fifteen chapters, but by the time I finished, the book had doubled in size. I apologize for that and hope the length won't be a hindrance to anyone who wants to learn more about Calvinism. I do have some justification, however, for expanding this book. In the 1980s, my doctoral dissertation adviser, D. Clair Davis, often said that Calvinism is so comprehensive that it is hard to get one's mind and arms around it. He would then say, a bit tongue-in-cheek, that this comprehensiveness is one major difference between Lutheranism and Calvinism. Lutheranism could neatly bring all of its confessional statements under one cover in 1580 and call it *The Book of Concord*.[1] But the Calvinistic faith is so rich that at least three families of confessional statements developed in the sixteenth and seventeenth centuries: the English-Scottish family, the Dutch-German family, and the Swiss family—none of which contradicted the others but built on and complemented them.[2]

This diversity is reflective of John Calvin himself. His theological work was comprehensive and, as a result, it has significant ramifications for a host of areas of human life, society, and culture. He was intent on bringing every sphere of existence under the lordship of Christ, so that all of life might be lived to the glory of God. That is why Calvinism cannot be explained simply by one major doctrine or in five points, or, if we had them, even ten points! Calvinism is as complex as life itself.

The breadth of Calvinism, earnestly and zealously lived out, is most clearly manifest in Puritanism. Therefore, I have held the Puritans up as examples in a number of areas, including sanctification (chapters 14 and 15), evangelism (chapter 21), and marriage and family life (chapters 23 and 24). The Puritans have much to teach us today about how to live with one eye on eternity and the other on this world, dedicating our entire lives to God's glory.[3]

The target audience for this book is laypeople and ministers who are interested in learning the basics of Calvinism. I hope it also will serve as a stimulating summary and refresher course for those who are already avid Calvinists, much as Steven J. Lawson's *The Expository Genius of John Calvin* from Reformation Trust excites those of us who are already familiar with much of its content.[4] I have worked hard to keep this book simple, clear, and non-technical, in the hope that you might hand it to others to help them understand how you think as a Calvinist.

I called on some of my friends to cover certain areas of Calvinism. I owe a great debt to Ray Pennings for writing so helpfully on three of the most challenging areas of Calvinism: its comprehensive nature (chapter 22), vocational Calvinism (chapter 25), and political Calvinism (chapter 26). I asked James Grier to summarize philosophical Calvinism (chapter 11), Derek Thomas to present ecclesiastical Calvinism (chapter 16), Ray Lanning to explore liturgical Calvinism (chapter 17), Robert Oliver to work on expositional Calvinism (chapter 18); and Nelson Kloosterman to examine Calvinist ethics (chapter 27). Each of them ably and graciously fulfilled my requests; their chapters were a joy to edit. I also asked my dear friend and mentor, Sinclair Ferguson, to provide the capstone on doxological Calvinism (chapter 28), which, astonishingly, he wrote in one afternoon, on the final due date. I am grateful for his moving conclusion to this book.

I also thank Michael Haykin, a dear brother and great church historian, who eagerly and faithfully read the entire manuscript; offered numerous valuable suggestions; and contributed a preface, a chapter on Calvinistic spirituality (chapter 12), and the first draft of the study questions. I am also deeply grateful to Phyllis TenElshof, Martha Fisher, Kate DeVries, and Ray Lanning for their proofing and editorial assistance. Thanks, too, are due to Jay Collier and Fred Sweet for tracking details on a number of stubborn endnotes.

I thank our pastoral flock, the Heritage Netherlands Reformed Congregation of Grand Rapids, and our staffs at Puritan Reformed Theological Seminary and Reformation Heritage Books for their encouragement and patience when I am in a book-writing mode. Particular thanks go to my colleagues, Gerald Bilkes and David Murray, who never hesitate to go the extra mile at my request. I could not work with better colleagues or have better staff.

My dear, faithful wife Mary is a constant source of inspiration, and I thank her for allowing me to work late at night on this book. I am grateful for my loving children, Calvin, Esther, and Lydia, whose kindness to me is unsurpassed.

Most of all, I am grateful to the holy, gracious, beautiful triune God, who makes Himself increasingly lovable to me the older I grow. Though I fall short of my goal dozens of times every day, I can say that my consuming desire is to live to His glory, and I believe what we call Calvinism is the system of biblical truth that best enables us to do that by the gracious Spirit of God.

I am keenly aware that my friends and I have addressed only tiny segments of Calvinism. Many more areas could have been examined, but the basics are here.

As for the various sections of this book, I wish to express gratitude to God for the following people: for "Calvinism in History," I am most grateful for Iain Murray and the Banner of Truth Trust's books and conferences, as well as the teaching of Dr. Ferguson, Rick Gamble, and D. Clair Davis at Westminster Seminary in the 1980s.

For "Calvinism in the Mind," I am indebted to the teaching of Rev. J. C. Weststrate, who was my first and primary theological seminary instructor in the 1970s. I was privileged to work with Rev. Weststrate on translating into English Rev. G. H. Kersten's *Reformed Dogmatics*, which profoundly influenced me. More recently, I am thankful for Richard Muller's friendship and writing, and for Dr. Grier's friendship and teaching. And, of course, I have been influenced by the opportunity to have taught systematic theology for more than twenty years, first with Dr. Ferguson and Mike Bell at the Center for Urban Theological Studies (CUTS) in inner-city Philadelphia, then at the Netherlands Reformed Theological School and at Puritan Reformed Theological Seminary since 1994.

For "Calvinism in the Heart," I am deeply indebted to my departed father's numerous conversations with me about how the Holy Spirit works in the hearts of sinners, and to the preaching and teaching of Rev. W. C. Lamain, under whose ministry I was reared and who later gave me what he called "practical lessons for ministry" every six weeks during my seminary years. Then, too, I owe a huge debt to Rev. Arie Elshout and Rev. Cor Harinck, whose ministries God used to bring me to more experiential liberty in Christ Jesus. Perhaps I profited most of all from ransacking my father's bookcase as a teenager, reading his Puritan tomes night after night. Forty years later, the Puritans still speak powerfully to my soul. I have also been influenced by preparing a course on Reformed experiential preaching, which I have taught in several seminaries around the world.

For "Calvinism in the Church," I am grateful for the three congregations I have been privileged to serve over the past thirty years in Sioux Center, Iowa (1978–81), Franklin Lakes, N.J. (1981–86), and Grand Rapids, Mich. (since 1986). All three churches have treated me well, and many individuals have influenced me greatly by their humility and godliness. Despite ministerial pressures and failures, I cannot imagine a greater joy in life than serving as a pastor of God's sheep in a Reformed church that yearns to live by the whole counsel of God as deposited in the Scriptures.

For "Calvinism in Practice," my greatest influence has been the afflictions that my sovereign God has sent my way and that I hope and pray have been sanctified to me. I am afraid to consider who and where I would be without God's loving, paternal, chastening hand. This I know: if God had not broken me deeply many times in His sovereign wisdom, I would be more prideful than I am. What a glorious Father He is, not only in the first person of the Trinity, but also as the Son of God, who is called "everlasting Father" (Isa. 9:6), and as the Holy Spirit, whose fatherly patience with our backslidings is stupendous. Humanly speaking, I am most thankful for my wife's kindness and integrity, and my mother's prayers and godliness. Other friends over the years have greatly moved me as well; I think of

Bert Harskamp and Henry Langerak, former elders with whom I worked in love, who modeled Calvinistic humility so poignantly for me. I also must express my gratitude for Dutch writers, including Wilhelmus à Brakel (whose *Christian's Reasonable Service* I was privileged to edit for six years) and Herman Bavinck, as well as the teaching of Robert Knudsen at Westminster Seminary.

For "Calvinism's Goal" (doxological Calvinism), nothing has moved me so much as Samuel Rutherford's *Letters,* a copy of which I have kept on my nightstand for decades and turned to often for inspiration to praise my sovereign God, to whom darkness and light are both alike (Ps. 139:12).

Finally, in addition to my brothers, John and James Beeke, my fellow ministers and members in the Heritage Reformed and Free Reformed denominations, and the alumni and students of Puritan Reformed Theological Seminary, I wish to thank the following friends and colleagues for stimulating intellectual and spiritual fellowship on matters related to Calvinism: Tom Ascol, Karl Boonzaayer, John Brentnall, Flip Buys, Walter Chantry, Scott Clark, Robin Compston, Curt Daniel, Ben Dowling, Heinz Dschankilic, Ligon Duncan, George Ella, Edwin Elliott, Arnold Frank, W. Robert Godfrey, Ian Hamilton, Peter Hammond, Christo Heiberg, Paul Helm, Martin Holdt, Michael Horton, Irfon Hughes, Erroll Hulse, Sherman Isbell, Mark Johnston, Theocharis Joannides, Hywel Jones, Ronald Kalifungwa, David Lachman, Anthony Lane, John Lawler, Robert Letham, Peter Lillback, Sam Logan, Wayne Mack, William Macleod, Jerry Marcellino, Leo Markwat, Albert Martin, Peter Masters, Mike Mathis, Bill May, Gary Meadors, R. Albert Mohler, John J. Murray, Adrian Neele, Tom Nettles, Stuart Olyott, Kerry Orchard, Joseph Pipa, John Piper, Lance Quinn, Maurice Roberts, Hal Ronning, Phil Ryken, Calvin Rynbrandt, Carl Schroeder, David Schuringa, Tom Schwanda, Changwon Shu, Denis Shelton, Don Sinnema, R. C. Sproul, John Temple, John Thackway, Geoff Thomas, Carl Trueman, Tim Trumper, Tom VandenHeuvel, Arie VanEyk, Bernie VanEyk, Anthony VanGrouw, Ray VanGrouw, Fred van Lieburg, John VanVliet, Douglas Vickers, Brian Vos, Cees Vreugdenhil, Sam Waldron, Malcolm Watts, Donald Whitney, Andrew Woolsey, and William Young.

I have taken the liberty to modernize spellings in quotations from antiquarian books. In chapters of historical interest, endnotes containing additional source material are supplied. In more practical chapters, I have been more sparing in the use of endnotes.

It is my hope that this book will help those who are already Calvinists to know, appreciate, and live the historical truths of Calvinism. If we do not *know* our Reformation heritage, ignorance will lead to indifference, and indifference to relinquishment. I urge you to study Reformed thinking. Immerse yourself in the writings of solid, renowned Calvinists. Read sixteenth-century classics such as Calvin's *Institutes*. Try Henry Bullinger's *The Decades*, which teaches the doctrines of the Bible in fifty messages on a somewhat simpler level than the *Institutes*. Read seventeenth-century classics, too, such as John Bunyan's *Pilgrim's Progress* and John Flavel's *The Fountain of Life*. Pick up eighteenth-century works such as Wilhelmus à Brakel's *The Christian's Reasonable Service* and Jonathan Edwards' *Religious Affections*. From the nineteenth century, read Octavius Winslow's *Work of the Holy Spirit* and Charles Spurgeon's *The Treasury of David*. From the twentieth century, read D. Martyn Lloyd-Jones' *The Sermon on the Mount* and John Murray's systematic theology (*Collected Writings*, vol. 2).[5] If we do not *appreciate* our Reformation heritage, our faith will lack authenticity. No one will be jealous of us, for we will be sorely lacking in true peace, joy, and humility. And if we don't *live* our Reformation heritage, we will not be salt in the earth. When salt has lost its saltiness, it is good for nothing but to be cast out and trodden under the feet of men (Matt. 5:13).

If God uses this book to clear away some of the serious misrepresentations people have about Calvinism and to stir in many souls the faith and conviction to believe that all of life must be lived to His glory, my efforts will be more than amply rewarded.

—Joel R. Beeke
Grand Rapids, Mich.
February 2008

NOTES

[1] Robert Kolb and Timothy Wengert, eds., *The Book of Concord: The Confessions of the Evangelical Lutheran Church,* trans. Charles Arand et al. (Minneapolis: Fortress, 2000).

[2] See chapter 2 below.

[3] For two helpful sources that show the breadth of Puritanism's Calvinist vision, see Leland Ryken, *Worldly Saints: The Puritans as They Really Were* (Grand Rapids: Zondervan, 1986), and *The Journal of Christian Reconstruction: Symposium on Puritanism and Law,* 5, no. 2 (Winter, 1978–79). The bulk of the latter source is devoted to the Puritan approach to various spheres of life.

[4] Steven J. Lawson, *The Expository Genius of John Calvin* (Lake Mary, Fla.: Reformation Trust, 2007).

[5] All of these books, and several thousand more of solid Reformed persuasion, are available at discount prices from Reformation Heritage Books, 2965 Leonard N.E., Grand Rapids, MI 49525; 616-977-0599; orders@heritagebooks.org; www.heritagebooks.org.

PART ONE

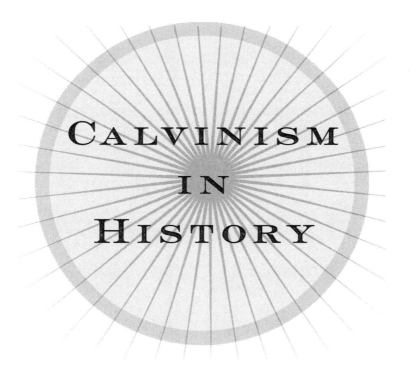

CALVINISM

IN

HISTORY

CHAPTER 1

THE ORIGINS OF CALVINISM

The spread of Calvinism was unusual. In contrast to Catholicism, which had been maintained by civil and military force, and Lutheranism, which survived in becoming a religion of politics, Calvinism had, for the most part, only its consistent logic and its fidelity to the Scriptures. Within a generation it spread across Europe.[1]

—CHARLES MILLER

*C*alvinism is rooted in the sixteenth-century religious renewal in Europe that we refer to as the Protestant Reformation.[2] But this great movement was not an isolated phenomenon. It did not simply begin with Martin Luther's (1483–1546) act of posting his Ninety-five Theses on the church doors of Wittenberg on Oct. 31, 1517, even though those theses were soon translated into numerous languages and distributed to the masses. In one sense, the Reformation originated in Luther's so-called "tower experience," which probably predated his theses by a few years. Through this experience, Luther came to grasp the definitive doctrine of the Reformation: justification by gracious faith alone. But in another sense, the Reformation flowed out of earlier attempts for renewal, the most notable of which were led by Peter Waldo (ca. 1140–ca. 1217) and his followers in the Alpine regions,[3] John Wycliffe (ca. 1324–1384) and the Lollards in England,[4] and John Hus (ca. 1372–1415) and his followers in Bohemia.[5] Lesser-known divines, such as Thomas Bradwardine (ca. 1300–1349)[6] and Gregory of Rimini (ca. 1300–1358),[7] came even closer to what would become known as Protestant theology. All these men are properly called forerunners of the Reformation rather than Reformers because, although they anticipated many of the emphases of the Reformation, they lacked a complete understanding of the critical doctrine of justification by gracious faith alone.[8]

These forerunners of the Reformation were morally, doctrinally, and practically united in their opposition to medieval Roman Catholic abuses. This opposition is critical to note, since the Reformation began primarily as a reaction to the abuses of Roman Catholicism. Luther did not set out to destroy the Roman Catholic Church and to establish a new church. His initial intent was to purge the Roman Catholic Church of abuses.

Reformed theology thus cannot be fully understood apart from its reaction to problems in the church, such as:

• *Papal abuses.* The medieval papacy was rife with abuses in theology and practice. Immoral conduct was lived out and condoned even by the popes, and grace became a cheap, commercialized religion throughout the church via a complex system of vows, fasts, pilgrimages, masses, relics, recitations, rosaries, and other works. The papal imperative was "do penance" (as translated in the Vulgate) rather than "be penitent," or "repent," as Jesus commanded.

• *Papal pretentiousness.* Biblical and historical study by the Protestant forerunners led them to question papal claims to apostolic authority as head of the church. For example, the Reformers concluded that the rock on which the church was built (Matt. 16:18) was the content of Peter's faith rather than Peter himself, which meant that the bishop of Rome possessed no more than a position of honor. Though the Protestants initially were willing to accept a Reformed papacy that would honorably serve the church, the cruel opposition of the popes to reform eventually persuaded many of them to regard the pope of Rome as Antichrist (cf. Westminster Confession of Faith, 25.6).

• *Captivity of the Word.* Protestants taught that the Roman Catholic Church held Scripture captive, withholding it from the laypeople and thus keeping them in bondage to church councils, bishops, schoolmen, canonists, and allegorists for interpretation. The Protestants worked hard to deliver the Bible from this hierarchical captivity. As Malcolm Watts writes:

> The Church of Rome degraded the Holy Scriptures by alloying the purity of the Canon with her apocryphal additions, by supplementing the inspired records with an enormous mass of spurious traditions, by admitting only that interpretation which is according to "the unanimous consent of the

Fathers" and "the Holy Mother Church," and, particularly by diminishing the role of preaching as their "priests" busied themselves with miraculous stories about Mary, the saints and the images, and magnified the importance of the Mass, with its elaborate and multiplied ceremonies and rituals. It was thus that preaching deteriorated and, in fact, almost disappeared. The Reformers vigorously protested against this and contended with all their might for the recovery of God's Holy Word.[9]

• *Elevation of monasticism.* Protestants opposed the Roman Catholic concept of the superiority of the so-called religious life. They did not believe that monasticism was the only way to spirituality or even the best way. By stressing the priesthood of all believers, they worked hard to eliminate the Roman Catholic distinction between the "inferior" life of the Christian involved in a secular calling and the "higher" religious world of monks and nuns.

• *Usurped mediation.* Protestants also rejected the Roman Catholic ideas of mediation by Mary and the intercession of saints, as well as the automatic transfusion of grace in the sacraments. They opposed all forms of mediation with God except through Christ. They reduced the sacraments to two, baptism and the Lord's Supper, thereby stripping priests and the church of mediating power and the sacramental dispensation of salvation.

• *The role of good works.* Protestants rejected the ideas of Semi-Pelagianism, which says that both grace and works are necessary for salvation. This theological difference was at the heart of Protestant opposition to Roman Catholicism, though it was largely through moral and practical corruption that the issue came to the fore.

The Protestant response to Roman Catholic abuses gradually settled into five Reformation watchwords or battle cries, centered on the Latin word *solus*, meaning "alone." These battle cries, expounded in chapter 10, served to contrast Protestant teaching with Roman Catholic tenets as follows:

Protestant	*Roman Catholic*
Scripture alone (*sola Scriptura*)	Scripture and tradition
Faith alone (*sola fide*)	Faith and works
Grace alone (*sola gratia*)	Grace and merit
Christ alone (*solus Christus*)	Christ, Mary, and intercession of saints
Glory to God alone (*soli Deo gloria*)	God, saints, and church hierarchy

The first of these battle cries deals with the fundamental issue of authority, the middle three deal with the basics of salvation, and the final one addresses worship.

In early Protestantism, both Lutheran and Reformed believers embraced these five watchwords. Regrettably, Luther and Ulrich Zwingli (1484–1531), the early leader of the Swiss Reformation, parted ways in October 1529 during the infamous Marburg Colloquy, when they could not reach agreement on the nature of Christ's presence in the Lord's Supper.[10] From that time on, Protestantism divided into two traditions, Lutheranism and Calvinism—the latter being the Reformed tradition as understood and expressed in the writings of John Calvin and his fellow Reformers.

THE SPREAD OF THE REFORMED (CALVINISTIC) FAITH

The Reformed tradition has its earliest roots in Switzerland with Zwingli and Heinrich Bullinger (1504–1575), who established and systematized it after Zwingli's death.[11] Calvin (1509–1564), its greatest representative and most influential exponent, established Geneva as a model Reformed city.[12] In many respects, Geneva was the most important Protestant center in the sixteenth century. This was not only because of the presence of Calvin, but also because the seminary Calvin established sought to train and educate Reformers for all of Western Europe. Amazingly—somewhat to the chagrin of some of the Genevan populace—the town became the Protestant print capital of Europe, with more than thirty houses publishing literature in various languages. Because of Zwingli's premature death on the battlefield, the fact that Bullinger's works[13] were not as easily accessible by the later Calvinist tradition, and Calvin's able work in systematizing Reformed Protestantism through his *Institutes of the Christian Religion*, commentaries, sermons, and leadership, the terms *Reformed* and *Calvinism* became virtually synonymous. Calvin himself preferred *Reformed* because he was opposed to having the movement called by his name.

The Reformed movement then spread to Germany. The city of Heidelberg, where the Heidelberg Catechism originated, became an influential center of Reformed thinking. Nonetheless, much of Germany remained staunchly Lutheran. A minority of Lutherans in Germany were affected by Calvin's thinking, most notably Philip Melanchthon (1497–1560), a close associate of Luther who was unkindly referred to by his peers as a crypto-Calvinist.[14] Eventually, a number of Melanchthon's followers, estranged from the Lutherans after Luther's death, joined the Reformed Church in Germany.[15]

Calvinism also took hold in Hungary,[16] Poland, and the Low Countries, particularly the Netherlands, where it penetrated the southern regions about 1545 and the northern about 1560.[17] From the start, the Calvinist movement in the Netherlands was more influential than its number of adherents might suggest. But Dutch Calvinism did not flower profusely until the seventeenth century, cultivated by the famous international Synod of Dort in 1618–1619 and fortified by the Dutch Further Reformation (*De Nadere Reformatie*), a primarily seventeenth- and early eighteenth-century movement paralleling English Puritanism.[18] The Dutch Further Reformation dates from such early representatives as Jean Taffin (1528–1602) and Willem Teellinck (1579–1629), and extends to Alexander Comrie (1706–1774).[19]

The Reformed movement also made substantial inroads into France.[20] By the time Calvin died in 1564, 20 percent of the French population—some two million people—confessed the Reformed faith. In fact, this 20 percent included half of the aristocracy and middle class in France. For a while, it seemed that France might officially embrace the Reformed faith. But Roman Catholic persecution and civil war halted the spread of Reformed teaching. In some ways, the French Reformed movement has never recovered from this blow of persecution and attack in the sixteenth century. On the other hand, God brought good out of evil—the Reformed believers who fled France, known as the Huguenots, injected fresh spiritual vitality and zeal into the Reformed movement everywhere they settled.[21]

The Reformation spread rapidly to Scotland, largely under the leadership of John Knox (1513–1572), who served nineteen months as a galley slave before he went to England and then to Geneva. Knox brought the Reformation's principles from Geneva to Scotland and became its most notable spokesman there.[22] In 1560, the Scottish Parliament rejected papal authority, and the following year, the Scottish Reformed "Kirk," or church, was reorganized. In ensuing generations, many Scots became stalwart Calvinists, as did many of the Irish and the Welsh.

In England, Henry VIII (1491–1547) rebelled against papal rule so that he could legally divorce, remarry, and hopefully produce a male heir. He tolerated a mild reformation but established himself as the Church of England's supreme head, even as he remained essentially Roman Catholic in his theology.[23] During

the short reign of his young son Edward VI (1547–1553), who, together with
his council, had a great heart for true reformation, some gains were made, especially by Archbishop Thomas Cranmer (1489–1556) through his book *Homilies*,
his *Book of Common Prayer*, and his Forty-Two Articles of Religion. All of this
seemed to be reversed during the bloody reign of Mary Tudor (1553–1558),
who reinstated the Latin Mass and enforced papal allegiance at the cost of nearly
three hundred Protestant lives. But the blood of those martyrs, including Cranmer, was to be the seed of the Protestant cause in England.

When Mary's half-sister Elizabeth (1533–1603) succeeded her, many Protestants harbored fervent hopes that the reforms begun under Edward VI would
grow exponentially. Elizabeth, however, was content with the climate of British
Protestantism and strove to subdue dissident voices. Those who fought too much
for reform in matters of worship, godliness, politics, and culture were persecuted
and deprived of their livings. Elizabeth's cautious, moderate type of reform disappointed many and eventually gave rise to a more thorough and robust Calvinism
that was derogatorily called Puritanism.

Puritanism lasted from the 1560s to the early 1700s. The Puritans believed the
Church of England had not gone far enough in its reformation, because its worship
and government did not agree fully with the pattern found in Scripture. They called
for the pure preaching of God's Word; for purity of worship as God commands in
Scripture; and for purity of church government, replacing the rule of bishops with
Presbyterianism. Above all, they called for greater purity or holiness of life among
Christians. As J. I. Packer has said, "Puritanism was an evangelical holiness movement seeking to implement its vision of spiritual renewal, national and personal, in
the church, the state, and the home; in education, evangelism, and economics; in
individual discipleship and devotion, and in pastoral care and competence."[24] Doctrinally, Puritanism was a kind of vigorous Calvinism; experientially, it was warm
and contagious; evangelistically, it was aggressive, yet tender; ecclesiastically, it was
theocentric and worshipful; and politically, it sought to make the relations between
king, Parliament, and subjects scriptural, balanced, and bound by conscience.[25]

Presbyterians, Episcopalians, and Congregationalists were all part of the
Calvinist movement. Some Puritans seceded from the Church of England during the reign of King James I (1603–1625). They became known as separatists or
dissenters and usually formed Congregationalist churches. Puritan conformists
remained within the Anglican fold.

Eventually, Calvinism crossed the Atlantic to the British colonies in North America, where the New England Puritans took the lead in expounding Reformed theology and in founding ecclesiastical, educational, and political institutions.[26] The Puritans who settled in the Massachusetts Bay Colony continued to sanction the Church of England to some degree, whereas the Pilgrims who sailed to America in the Mayflower and settled in Plymouth (1620) were separatists.[27] Despite these differences, all Puritans were zealous Calvinists. As John Gerstner observes, "New England, from the founding of Plymouth in 1620 to the end of the 18th century, was predominantly Calvinistic."[28]

Four more streams of immigrants brought Calvinism to America. Dutch Reformed believers, from the 1620s, were responsible for the settlement of New Netherlands, later called New York. The French Huguenots arrived by the thousands in New York, Virginia, and the Carolinas in the late seventeenth century. From 1690 to 1777, more than two hundred thousand Germans, many of whom were Reformed, settled mostly in the Middle Colonies. The final stream was the Scots and the Scotch-Irish, all Presbyterians. Some settled in New England, but many more poured into New York, Pennsylvania, and the Carolinas. "As a consequence of this extensive immigration and internal growth it is estimated that of the total population of three million in this country in 1776, two-thirds of them were at least nominally Calvinistic," John Bratt concludes. "At the outbreak of the Revolutionary War, the largest denominations were, in order: Congregationalists, Anglicans, Presbyterians, Baptists, Lutherans, German Reformed, and Dutch Reformed. Roman Catholicism was tenth and Methodism was twelfth in size."[29]

With the exception of the migrations to America, all of this spreading of the Reformed faith happened by the end of the sixteenth century.[30] The most extensive and enduring strongholds of the Reformed movement became the Netherlands, Germany, Hungary, Great Britain, and North America.

It is noteworthy that all of these Reformed bodies shared the conviction that Christianity in many parts of Europe prior to the Reformation was little more than a veneer. As these Reformed believers surveyed Europe, they saw what they could regard only as large swaths of paganism. The planting of solidly biblical churches was desperately needed. This explains in large measure the Reformers' missionary focus on Europe.

In time, the Reformed movement developed into two very similar systems of theology: the Continental Reformed, represented primarily in the Netherlands by its Three Forms of Unity—the Belgic Confession, Heidelberg Catechism, and Canons of Dort; and British-American Presbyterianism, expressed in the Westminster standards—the Westminster Confession of Faith, the Larger Catechism, and the Shorter Catechism.[31] These two systems were not opposed to or entirely separate from each other, however. For example, British Puritans profoundly influenced the Dutch Further Reformation in the seventeenth century. Likewise, the Italian-Swiss Francis Turretin (1623–1687) profoundly affected American Presbyterianism.[32] Turretin's systematic theology was taught at Princeton Seminary until the 1870s, when it was replaced by that of Charles Hodge.

CALVINISM AND THE LUTHERANS

Both systems of Reformed theology parted ways with Lutheranism. By the end of the sixteenth century, Calvinism differed from Lutheranism in the following areas:

• *Approach to the Lord's Supper.* Lutherans maintained the doctrine of consubstantiation, which holds that Christ is physically present in, with, and under the elements in the Lord's Supper. They resisted any attempt to explain Jesus' statement "this is my body" as a metaphor, saying that such efforts opened the door to allegorizing away the gospel itself. Furthermore, they said, if all that is offered in Communion is a spiritual Christ, the sacrament presents a truncated gospel that offers no comfort to believers whose bodies eventually will die. Lutherans would be satisfied only with a concrete, historical Christ.

The Reformed leaders said that the incarnate, historical Christ is now risen and ascended, and therefore is not present in the Supper in the way He was prior to His ascension. Furthermore, the concept of Christ's spiritual presence does not mean something less than complete; rather, it refers to His ongoing work through His Spirit. The Reformed believed they were affirming all that the Lutherans wanted to protect, but in a clearer, more biblical manner.

• *The primary function of the law.* Luther generally regarded the law as something negative and closely allied with sin, death, or the Devil. He believed that the dominant function of the law is to abase the sinner by convicting him of sin and driving him to Christ for deliverance.

Calvin regarded the law more as a guide for the believer, a tool to encourage him to cling to God and to obey Him more fervently. The believer must try to follow God's law not as an act of compulsory duty, but as a response of grateful obedience. With the help of the Spirit, the law provides a way for a believer to express his gratitude.

• *Approach to salvation.* Both Lutherans and Calvinists answered the question "What must I do to be saved?" by saying that Spirit-worked repentance toward God and faith in the Lord Jesus Christ and His substitutionary work of atonement are necessary. But Lutherans had a tendency to remain focused on the doctrine of justification, whereas Calvinists, without minimizing justification, pressed more than Lutherans toward sanctification, which asks, "Having been justified by God's grace, how shall I live to the glory of God?" Calvinism thus became more comprehensive than Lutheranism in explaining how salvation works itself out in the life of a believer.

• *Understanding of predestination.* In the late sixteenth century, most Lutherans moved away from Luther and the Calvinists, who asserted the predestination of both the elect and the reprobate rather than the predestination of the elect only. Reformed theologians believed this shift in thinking was at odds with the content of Romans 9 and similar passages, as well as with the comprehensive sovereignty of God.

The Calvinists were convinced that election is sovereign and gracious, and that reprobation is sovereign and just. No one who enters heaven deserves to be there; no one who enters hell deserves anything different. As Calvin said, "The praise of salvation is claimed for God, whereas the blame of perdition is thrown upon those who of their own accord bring it upon themselves."[33]

• *Understanding of worship.* Luther's reform was more moderate than Calvin's, retaining more medieval liturgy. Following their leaders, the Lutherans and Calvinists differed in their views of how Scripture regulates worship. The Lutherans taught that we may include in worship what is not forbidden in Scripture; the Calvinists maintained that we may not include in worship what the New Testament does not command.

CALVINISM TODAY

Calvinism has stood the test of time. Most Protestant denominations that originated in the Reformation were founded on Calvinistic confessions of faith, such as the Thirty-nine Articles (Anglicanism), the Canons of Dort (Reformed), the

Westminster Standards (Presbyterianism), the Savoy Declaration (Congregation-alism), and the Baptist Confession of 1689 (Baptist). All of these confessions essentially agree, with the major point of disagreement being the doctrine of infant baptism.

Reformation theology prevailed, for the most part, in Protestant evangelical-ism for many decades, but was diluted in the nineteenth century because of several influences, such as the Enlightenment in Europe and Finneyism in America. By the mid-twentieth century, Calvinistic theology had declined dramatically in the Western world, having been assaulted by nineteenth-century liberal theology and revived Arminianism.

About two centuries ago, William Ellery Channing, the father of Ameri-can Unitarianism, wrote: "Calvinism, we are persuaded, is giving place to better views. It has passed its meridian, and is sinking to rise no more. It has to con-tend with foes more powerful than theologians; with foes from whom it cannot shield itself in mystery and metaphysical subtleties—we mean the progress of the human mind, and the progress of the spirit of the gospel. Society is going forward in intelligence and charity, and of course is leaving the theology of the sixteenth century behind it."[34]

Channing was a false prophet. Today, even though the world in general is becoming more anti-God and wicked than ever, Calvinism is being revived, although, sadly, it is still a minority position. A fresh hunger for Calvinism's biblical doctrine and spirituality is causing the roots of Reformed theology to spread throughout the entire world. In recent decades, a significant num-ber of Calvinistic churches and denominations have been birthed around the world. Today, Reformed churches exist in the Netherlands, Germany, Hungary, Poland, Italy, the United Kingdom, North America, Brazil, South Africa, Aus-tralia, New Zealand, Singapore, South Korea, China, the Philippines, Russia, Egypt, Pakistan, India, Israel, and various additional African and Asian coun-tries. Also, since the 1960s, there has been a resurgence of interest in Calvinistic literature. Calvinistic conferences are being offered in numerous countries; in many of these nations, the number of Calvinists is steadily growing in our new millennium.

Calvinism has a bright future, for it offers much to people who seek to believe and practice the whole counsel of God. Calvinism aims to do so with both clear-headed faith and warm-hearted spirituality, which, when conjoined, produce vibrant living in the home, the church, and the marketplace to the glory of God. It confesses with Paul, "For of him, and through him, and to him, are all things: to whom be glory for ever" (Rom. 11:36). That, after all, is what Scripture, Calvinism, and life itself are all about.

DISCUSSION QUESTIONS

1. What are the historical roots of Calvinism?

2. What are the main geographical areas where Calvinism spread in the first two centuries after the Reformation?

3. How does Calvinism differ from Lutheranism?

NOTES

1   Charles Miller, "The Spread of Calvinism in Switzerland, Germany, and France," in *The Rise and Development of Calvinism*, ed. John H. Bratt (Grand Rapids: Eerdmans, 1959), 27.

2   For Reformation history, see Owen Chadwick, *The Reformation* (Harmondsworth, Middlesex: Penguin Books, 1972); Hans J. Hillerbrand, *The Reformation: A narrative history related by contemporary observers and participants* (Grand Rapids: Baker, 1978) and *The Protestant Reformation* (New York: Harper Perennial, 2007); Bernard M. G. Reardon, *Religious Thought in the Reformation* (London: Longman Group, 1981); Lewis William Spitz, *The Protestant Reformation, 1517–1559* (New York: Harper & Row, 1985); Andrew Pettegree, *The Early Reformation in Europe* (Cambridge: Cambridge University Press, 1992) and *The Reformation World* (London: Routledge, 2000); Carter Lindberg, *The European Reformations* (Cambridge: Blackwell Publishers, 1996) and *The European Reformations Sourcebook* (Oxford: Blackwell, 2000); Diarmaid MacCulloch, *Reformation: Europe's House Divided 1490–1700* (London: Penguin, 2003); Heiko Oberman and Donald Weinstein, *The Two Reformations: The Journey from the Last Days to the New World* (New Haven: Yale University Press, 2003); and Patrick Collinson, *The Reformation: A History* (New York: Modern Library, 2004).

    For Reformation theology, see Timothy George, *Theology of the Reformers* (Nashville: Broadman Press, 1988); Carter Lindberg, *The Reformation Theologians: An Introduction to Theology in the Early Modern Period* (Oxford: Blackwell, 2002); and David V. N. Bagchi and David Curtis Steinmetz, *The Cambridge Companion to Reformation Theology* (Cambridge: Cambridge University Press, 2004).

    For helpful encyclopedias on the Reformation, see Hans Joachim Hillerbrand, ed., *The Oxford Encyclopedia of the Reformation*, 4 vols. (Oxford: Oxford University Press, 1996), and *The Encylopedia of Protestantism*, 4 vols. (New York: Routledge, 2004).

    For bibliography and research on the Reformation, see Roland H. Bainton and Eric Gritsch, *Bibliography of the Continental Reformation*, 2nd ed. (Hamden, Conn.: Archon Books, 1972); Steven E. Ozment, *Reformation Europe: A Guide to Research* (St. Louis: Center for Reformation Research, 1982); William S. Maltby, *Reformation Europe: A Guide to Research II* (St. Louis: Center for Reformation Research, 1992) and David M. Whitford, ed., *Reformation and Early Modern Europe; a guide to research* (Kirksville, Mo.: Truman State University Press, 2008).

    For Reformation historiography, see Lewis Spitz, ed., *The Reformation: Basic Interpretations* (Lexington, Mass.: Heath, 1972).

3   For studies on Waldo and the Waldensians, see Gabriel Audisio, *The Waldensian Dissent: Persecution and Survival, ca. 1170–ca. 1570* (Cambridge: Cambridge University Press, 1999); Peter Biller, *The Waldenses, 1170–1530: Between a Religious Order and a Church* (Aldershot, U.K.: Ashgate, 2001); Euan Cameron, *Waldenses: Rejections of Holy Church in Medieval Europe* (Oxford: Blackwell, 2000); Giorgio Tourn, et al., *You Are My Witnesses: The Waldensians Across 800 Years* (Torino: Claudiana, 1989); J. N. Worsfold and B. Tron, *Peter Waldo, The Reformer of Lyons: His Life and Labours* (London: John F. Shaw, 1880); and J. A. Wylie, *The Story of the Waldenses* (Altamont, Tenn.: Pilgrim Books, 1995).

4   For books on Wycliffe and the Lollards, see Ellen W. Caughey, *John Wycliffe: Herald of the Reformation* (Ulrichsville, Ohio: Barbour Publishing, 2001); G. R. Evans, *John Wyclif: Myth & Reality* (Downers Grove, Ill.: IVP Academic, 2005); Anthony John Patrick Kenny, *Wyclif in His Times* (Oxford: Clarendon Press, 1986); Ian Christopher Levy, *A Companion to John Wyclif: Late Medieval Theologian* (Leiden: Brill, 2006); G. H. W. Parker, *The Morning Star: Wycliffe and the Dawn of the Reformation* (Grand Rapids: Eerdmans,

1966); and Fiona Somerset, Jill C. Havens, and Derrick G. Pitard, *Lollards and Their Influence in Late Medieval England* (Woodbridge, U.K.: Boydell Press, 2003).

5 For books on Hus and the Hussites, see Poggio Bracciolini, *The Trial and Burning of John Huss: An Eye-Witness Account* (Toronto: Wittenburg Publications, 1991); E. H. Gillett, *The Life and Times of John Huss: Or, The Bohemian Reformation of the Fifteenth Century* (New York: AMS Press, 1978); *The Letters of John Hus* (Manchester: University Press, 1972); Matthew Spinka, *John Hus, a Biography* (Westport, Conn.: Greenwood Press, 1979); and Jarold Knox Zeman, *The Hussite Movement and the Reformation in Bohemia, Moravia, and Slovakia (1350–1650): A Bibliographical Study Guide (with Particular Reference to Resources in North America)* (Ann Arbor, Mich.: Michigan Slavic Publications, 1977).

6 See Heiko A. Oberman, "Archbishop Thomas Bradwardine: A Fourteenth-Century Augustinian" (Ph.D. dissertation, Utrecht, 1957), and Gordon Leff, *Bradwardine and the Pelagians* (Cambridge: Cambridge University Press, 1957).

7 See Gordon Leff, *Gregory of Rimini* (Manchester: Manchester University Press, 1961).

8 For a good study of those who were forerunners of the Reformation together with some of their writings, see Heiko A. Oberman, *Forerunners of the Reformation: The Shape of Late Medieval Thought Illustrated by Key Documents*, trans. Paul L. Nyhus (New York: Holt, Rinehart, & Winston, 1966).

9 Malcolm Watts, "What is a Reformed Church?" *Banner of Sovereign Grace Truth*, 16, no. 3 (March 2008): 73.

10 For Luther, see the classic studies by Roland H. Bainton, *Here I Stand. A Life of Martin Luther* (Nashville: Abingdon Press, 1950); James M. Kittelson, *Luther the Reformer* (Minneapolis: Augsburg, 1986); and Heiko A. Oberman, *Luther: Man Between God and the Devil*, trans. Eileen Walliser-Schwarzbart (New Haven: Yale University Press, 1989). For a succinct study, see W. Robert Godfrey, "Martin Luther: German Reformer," in John D. Woodbridge, ed., *Great Leaders of the Christian Church* (Chicago: Moody Press, 1988), 187–196.

11 For Zwingli, see Jaques Courvoisier, *Zwingli: A Reformed Theologian* (Richmond: John Knox Press, 1963); Gottfried Locher, *Zwingli's Thought: New Perspectives* (Leiden: Brill, 1981); G. R. Potter, ed., *Huldrych Zwingli* (New York: St. Martin's Press, 1978); Robert C. Walton, "Zwingli: Founding Father of the Reformed Churches," in *Leaders of the Reformation*, ed. Richard L. DeMolen (Selinsgrove, Pa.: Susquehanna University Press, 1984), 69–98; and W. P. Stephens, *The Theology of Huldrych Zwingli* (Oxford: Clarendon Press, 1986) and *Zwingli: An Introduction to His Thought* (Oxford: Clarendon Press, 1992).

On Bullinger, see especially Cornelis P. Venema, *Heinrich Bullinger and the Doctrine of Predestination: Author of "the Other Reformed Tradition"?* (Grand Rapids: Baker, 2002). Venema's work is a response to J. Wayne Baker, *Heinrich Bullinger and the Covenant: The Other Reformed Tradition* (Athens, Ohio: Ohio University Press, 1980), and Charles S. McCoy and J. Wayne Baker, *Fountainhead of Federalism: Heinrich Bullinger and the Covenantal Tradition* (Louisville: Westminster/John Knox Press, 1991). The work by McCoy and Baker contains their translation of Bullinger's *A Brief Exposition of the One and Eternal Testament or Covenant of God* (1534).

12 For Calvin's life and ministry, see especially François Wendel, *Calvin* (New York: Harper & Row, 1963); T. H. L. Parker, *Portrait of Calvin* (London: SCM Press. 1954, and *John Calvin: A Biography* (Philadelphia: The Westminster Press, 1975); Ronald S. Wallace, *Calvin, Geneva and the Reformation* (Grand Rapids: Baker, 1988); Timothy George, ed., *John Calvin and the Church. A Prism of Reform* (Louisville: Westminster/John Knox Press, 1990); and Alister E. McGrath, *A Life of John Calvin: A Study in the Shaping of Western Culture* (Oxford: Blackwell, 1990).

For an annotated bibliographical guide to Calvin's vast corpus and material on his life and theology printed prior to 1964, see Lester de Koster, "Living Themes in the Thought of John Calvin: A Bibliographical Study" (Ph.D. dissertation, University of Michigan, 1964). For a bibliography on Calvin and Calvinism since the 1960s, see Peter De Klerk and Paul Field's annual articles in the *Calvin Theological Journal.* See also D. Kempff, *A Bibliography of Calvinism, 1959–1974* (Potchefstroom, South Africa: I. A. C., 1975), and Michael Bihary, ed., *Bibliographia Calviniana* (Prague: n.p., 2000). The best list of Calvin and Calvinism resources is available from the database of the Henry Meeter Center, Calvin College Library, Grand Rapids, Mich. I wish to thank the staff there for supplying me with a list of 662 books and 6,081 articles on Calvinism, and for their competent and friendly assistance.

13 Only in recent years has Bullinger's work been recognized as nearly equal in influence to that of Calvin in their own day. See especially Pamela Biel, *Doorkeepers at the House of Righteousness: Heinrich Bullinger and the Zurich Clergy, 1535–1575* (Bern: Peter Lang, 1991); Thomas Harding, ed., *The Decades of Henry Bullinger*, 4 vols. in 2, intro. George Ella and Joel R. Beeke (Grand Rapids: Reformation Heritage Books, 2004); Bruce Gordon and Emidio Campi, ed., *Architect of Reformation: An Introduction to Heinrich Bullinger, 1504–1575* (Grand Rapids: Baker, 2004); and George Ella, *Henry Bullinger* (Eggleston, England: Go Publications, 2007).

14 See Michael Rogness, *Philip Melanchthon: Reformer Without Honor* (Minneapolis: Augsburg, 1969), and Karin Maag, ed., *Melanchthon in Europe: His Work and Influence Beyond Wittenberg* (Carlisle, U.K.: Paternoster, 1999).

15 For a summary of the Reformed church in Germany, see R. W. Scribner, *The German Reformation* (London: Macmillan, 1986), and James N. Hardin and Max Reinhart, *German Writers of the Renaissance and Reformation, 1280–1580* (Detroit: Gale Research, 1997).

16 See Laszló Ravasz et al., *Hungarian Protestantism* (Budapest: Sylvester Nyomda, 1927); Imre Révész, *History of the Hungarian Reformed Church*, ed. G. N. Knight (Washington: Hungarian Reformed Federation, 1956); Gyula Combos, *The Lean Years: A Study of Hungarian Calvinism in Crisis* (New York: Kossuth Foundation, 1960); Alexander Sándor Unghváry, *The Hungarian Protestant Reformation in the Sixteenth Century* (New York: Edwin Mellen Press, 1990); and Graeme Murdock, *Calvinism on the Frontier 1600–1660: International Calvinism and the Reformed Church in Hungary and Transylvania* (Oxford: Clarendon Press, 2000).

17 For a summary of the Reformed church in the Netherlands, see Maurice G. Hansen, *The Reformed Church in the Netherlands* (New York: Board of Publication of the RCA, 1884); Jerry D. van der Veen, "Adoption of Calvinism in the Reformed Church in the Netherlands" (B.S.T. thesis, Biblical Seminary in New York, 1951); Walter Lagerway, "The History of Calvinism in the Netherlands," in *The Rise and Development of Calvinism*, ed. John Bratt (Grand Rapids: Eerdmans, 1959); W. Robert Godfrey, "Calvin and Calvinism in the Netherlands," in *John Calvin: His Influence in the Western World*, ed. W. Stanford Reid (Grand Rapids: Zondervan, 1982), 95–120; J. P. Elliott, "Protestantization in the Northern Netherlands: A Case Study—The Classis of Dordrecht, 1572–1640," 2 vols. (Ph.D. dissertation, Columbia University, 1990); and A. C. Duke, *Reformation and Revolt in the Low Countries* (London: Hambledon, 2003).

18 For English secondary sources on the Dutch Further Reformation, see F. Ernest Stoeffler, *The Rise of Evangelical Pietism* (Leiden: Brill, 1973); Cornelius Pronk, "The Dutch Puritans," *The Banner of Truth*, nos. 154–155 (July–Aug. 1976): 1–10; Martin H. Prozesky, "The Emergence of Dutch Pietism," *Journal of Ecclesiastical History*, no. 28 (1977): 29–37; Jonathan Neil Gerstner, *The Thousand Generation Covenant: Dutch Reformed Covenant Theology and Group Identity in Colonial South Africa, 1652–1814* (Leiden: Brill, 1991); Fred Van Lieburg, "From Pure Church to Pious Culture: The Further Reformation in the

Seventeenth-Century Dutch Republic," in *Later Calvinism: International Perspectives*, ed. W. Fred Graham (Kirksville, Mo.: Sixteenth Century Journal Publishers, 1994), 409–430; Arie de Reuver, *Sweet Communion: Trajectories of Spirituality from the Middle Ages through the Further Reformation*, trans. James A. de Jong (Grand Rapids: Baker Academic, 2007); and Joel R. Beeke, "Insights for the Church from the Dutch Second Reformation," *Calvin Theological Journal*, 28, no. 2 (Nov. 1993): 420–424, and "Gisbertus Voetius: Toward a Reformed Marriage of Knowledge and Piety," in *Protestant Scholasticism: Essays in Reassessment*, ed. Carl Trueman and R. Scott Clark (Carlisle, U.K.: Paternoster, 1998), and "Appendix: The Dutch Second Reformation," in *The Quest for Full Assurance: The Legacy of Calvin and His Successors* (Edinburgh: Banner of Truth Trust, 1999), 286–309, and "Assurance of Faith: A Comparison of English Puritanism and the *Nadere Reformatie*," in *Puritan Reformed Spirituality* (Darlington, England: Evangelical Press, 2006), 288–308, and with Randall Pederson, *Meet the Puritans* (Grand Rapids: Reformation Heritage Books, 2006), 739–823, and "Evangelicalism in the Dutch Further Reformation," in *The Emergence of Evangelicalism: Exploring Historical Continuities*, ed. Michael A. G. Haykin and Kenneth J. Stewart (Nottingham, U.K.: Apollos, 2008), 146-168.

[19] See Jean Taffin, *The Marks of God's Children*, trans. Peter Y. de Jong, ed. James A. de Jong (Grand Rapids: Baker, 2003); Willem Teellinck, *The Path of True Godliness*, trans. Annemie Godbehere, ed. Joel R. Beeke (Grand Rapids: Reformation Heritage Books, 2007); and Alexander Comrie, *The ABC of Faith*, trans. J. Marcus Banfield (Ossett, West Yorkshire: Zoar Publications, 1978).

[20] For the spread of Calvinism in France, see especially Jean-Marc Berthoud, "John Calvin and the Spread of the Gospel in France," in *Fulfilling the Great Commission* (London: The Westminster Conference, 1992), 1–53; W. Stanford Reid, "Calvin's Geneva: A Missionary Centre," *The Reformed Theological Review*, 42, no. 3 (Sept.–Dec. 1983): 65–74; and Mack P. Holt, *Renaissance and Reformation France, 1500–1648* (Oxford: Oxford University Press, 2002).

[21] See Philip Conner, *Huguenot Heartland: Montauban and Southern French Calvinism during the Wars of Religion* (Aldershot, England: Ashgate, 2002).

[22] For the writings of Knox, see David Laing, ed., *The Works of John Knox*, 6 vols. (Edinburgh: J. Thin, 1895). For Knox's life and ministry, see Thomas M'Crie, *The Life of John Knox* (Philadelphia: Wm. S. Young, 1842); W. Stanford Reid, *Trumpeter of God: A Biography of John Knox* (New York: Charles Scribner's Sons, 1974); Richard L. Greaves, *Theology and Revolution in the Scottish Reformation: Studies in the Thought of John Knox* (Grand Rapids: Christian University Press, 1980); Richard G. Kyle, *The Ministry of John Knox: Pastor, Preacher, and Prophet* (Lewiston, N.Y.: E. Mellen Press, 2002); Roger Mason, *John Knox and the British Reformations* (Aldershot, U.K.: Ashgate, 1998); and Douglas Wilson, *For Kirk & Covenant: The Stalwart Courage of John Knox* (Nashville: Cumberland House, 2000).

[23] For a history of the Reformation in England, see W. H. Beckett, *The English Reformation of the Sixteenth Century: With Chapters on Monastic England and the Wycliffite Reformation* (London: Religious Tract Society, 1890); Charles Davis Cremeans, *The Reception of Calvinistic Thought in England* (Urbana, Ill.: University of Illinois Press, 1949); Gordon Crosse, *A Short History of the English Reformation* (New York: Morehouse Gorham Co., 1950); Merle d'Aubigné, *The Reformation in England*, 2 vols. (London: Banner of Truth Trust, 1962); and Rosemary O'Day, *The Debate on the English Reformation* (London: Methuen, 1986).

[24] J. I. Packer, *An Anglican to Remember—William Perkins: Puritan Popularizer* (London: St. Antholin's, 1996), 1–2.

[25] For sources that will introduce you to the Puritans, their Calvinistic theology, and their lifestyle, see Martyn Lloyd-Jones, *The Puritans: Their Origins and Successors* (Edinburgh: Banner of Truth Trust, 1987); J. I. Packer, *A Quest for Godliness: The Puritan Vision of the Christian Life* (Wheaton, Ill.: Crossway, 1990);

Leland Ryken, *Worldly Saints: The Puritans as They Really Were* (Grand Rapids: Zondervan, 1990); Benjamin Brook, *The Lives of the Puritans*, 3 vols. (Morgan, Pa.: Soli Deo Gloria, 1994); Ralph Martin, *A Guide to the Puritans* (Edinburgh: Banner of Truth Trust, 1997); Peter Lewis, *The Genius of Puritanism* (Morgan, Pa.: Soli Deo Gloria, 1997); Erroll Hulse, *Who are the Puritans? And what do they teach?* (Darlington, England: Evangelical Press, 2000); Kelly M. Kapic and Randall C. Gleason, eds., *The Devoted Life: An Invitation to the Puritan Classics* (Downers Grove, Ill.: InterVarsity Press, 2004); Joel R. Beeke and Randall J. Pederson, *Meet the Puritans, with a Guide to Modern Reprints* (Grand Rapids: Reformation Heritage Books, 2006); Francis J. Bremer and Tom Webster, eds., *Puritans and Puritanism in Europe and America: A Comprehensive Encyclopedia*, 2 vols. (Santa Barbara, Calif.: ABC CIIO, 2006); and Charles Pastoor and Galen K. Johnson, *Historical Dictionary of the Puritans* (Lanham, Md.: Scarecrow Press, 2007).

26 For New England Puritanism, see Andrew Delbanco, *The Puritan Ordeal* (Cambridge, Mass.: Harvard University Press, 1989); David Hall, *Worlds of Wonder, Days of Judgment: Popular Religious Belief in Early New England* (Cambridge: Harvard University Press, 1989); Charles E. Hambrick-Stowe, *The Practice of Piety: Puritan Devotional Disciplines in Seventeenth-Century New England* (Chapel Hill, N.C.: University of North Carolina Press, 1982); Perry Miller, *The New England Mind: From Colony to Province* (Cambridge: Harvard University Press, 1939) and *The New England Mind: The Seventeenth Century* (Cambridge: Harvard University Press, 1953); Darrett Rutman, *American Puritanism: Faith and Practice* (Philadelphia: Lippincott, 1970); Alden T. Vaughan and Francis J. Bremer, eds., *Puritan New England: Essays on Religion, Society, and Culture* (New York: St. Martin's Press, 1977); and Larzer Ziff, *Puritanism In America: New Culture In A New World* (New York: Viking Press, 1973).

27 See William Bradford, *Of Plymouth Plantation, 1620–1647*, ed. Samuel Eliot Morison, 2 vols. (New York: Russell and Russell, 1968), and George F. Willison, *Saints and Strangers* (Reynal and Hitchcock, 1945).

28 John Gerstner, "American Calvinism until the Twentieth Century," in *American Calvinism*, ed. Jacob T. Hoogstra (Grand Rapids: Eerdmans, 1957), 16.

29 John H. Bratt, *The Rise and Development of Calvinism* (Grand Rapids: Eerdmans, 1959), 114–122.

30 For the advance of Calvinism during the sixteenth and seventeenth centuries, see John T. McNeill, *The History and Character of Calvinism* (New York: Oxford University Press, 1954), 235–350; W. Stanford Reid, ed., *John Calvin: His Influence in the Western World* (Grand Rapids: Zondervan, 1982); Menna Prestwich, ed., *International Calvinism 1541–1715* (Oxford: Clarendon Press, 1985); and Alastair Duke, Gillian Lewis, and Andrew Pettegree, trans. and eds., *Calvinism in Europe, 1540–1620: A collection of documents* (Cambridge: Cambridge University Press, 1996). See also Richard Gamble, ed., *Articles on Calvin and Calvinism*, 14 vols. (New York: Garland, 1992).

31 For a brief historical summary of these confessions, see the next chapter.

32 For his systematic theology in English, see Francis Turretin, *Institutes of Elenctic Theology*, trans. George Musgrave Giger, ed. James T. Dennison Jr., 3 vols. (Phillipsburg, N.J.: P&R, 1992–1997).

33 Cf. John Calvin, *Institutes of the Christian Religion* (hereafter, Inst.), ed. John T. McNeill, trans. Ford Lewis Battles (Philadelphia: Westminster Press, 1960), 3.24.7–11.

34 Quoted in Bratt, *The Rise and Development of Calvinism*, 134–135.

CHAPTER 2

CONFESSING
THE FAITH

*The Reformed confessions are much more numerous than those of the
Roman, Greek, and Lutheran churches. This is largely because they embrace
several nationalities: Swiss, German, French, Dutch, English, Scottish,
Polish, Bohemian, and Hungarian. Each of these nationalities formulated its
own creed because of its geographical and political isolation. The Reformed
churches allowed great freedom in the development of several dogmas, but
always remained within the framework of the Word of God, to which they
strictly adhered.*[1]

—PETER J. S. DE KLERK

One of the striking features of early Calvinists was their dedication to making confessional statements. Those Calvinists and subsequent Reformed
believers held that confessions have only a provisional character, since they reflect
the limited insights of mere men. Their authority is *derived* and must always be
subordinated to Scripture, which possesses *intrinsic* authority. Nevertheless, they
recognized that confessions make a valuable contribution to the church's primary
tasks: worshiping (the doxological task), witnessing (the declarative task), teaching (the didactic task), and defending the faith (the disciplining task). Reformed
confessions have been particularly effective in helping the church unitedly declare
what it believes, what it is to be, and how it is to be an evangelical testimony to
those outside of its fellowship.

The sixteenth- and seventeenth-century Reformed churches produced several
families of orthodox confessions that promoted the Calvinist faith and

differentiated it from Roman Catholicism and other groups of Protestant churches. The most well-known of these groups of confessions were the Swiss-Hungarian family, represented by the First and Second Helvetic Confessions (1536 and 1566) and the Helvetic Consensus Formula (1675); the Scottish-English family, represented by the Scots Confession (1560), the Thirty-nine Articles (1563), the Westminster Confession of Faith (1647), and the Shorter (1648) and Larger (1648) Catechisms of the Westminster Assembly; and the Dutch-German family, represented by the Three Forms of Unity: the Belgic Confession of Faith (1561), the Heidelberg Catechism (1563), and the Canons of Dort (1618–1619).[2]

Of those Reformed confessions, the seven most diligently adhered to by various Reformed denominations today are the Three Forms of Unity, the Second Helvetic Confession, and the Westminster Confession and Catechisms. They can be called "living" doctrinal standards because they are sanctioned officially by numerous twenty-first century Reformed churches. This chapter provides a basic historical introduction to these standards in the order in which they were composed.[3] It also summarizes the history of two Calvinistic Baptist confessions of the seventeenth century.

BELGIC CONFESSION OF FAITH (1561)

The oldest of the seven living confessions is the Belgic Confession of Faith, the name of which is taken from the seventeenth-century Latin designation *Confessio Belgica*. *Belgica* referred to the whole of the Low Countries, which today are divided into the Netherlands and Belgium. Other names for the Belgic Confession include the Walloon Confession and the Netherlands Confession.[4]

The confession was modeled after the Gallic confession, a 1559 French Reformed statement of faith, which, in turn, followed Calvin's design. Basically, the Belgic Confession follows what has become the traditional doctrinal order of Reformed systematic theology: the doctrines concerning God (theology proper, articles 1–11), man (anthropology, articles 12–15), Christ (Christology, articles 16–21), salvation (soteriology, articles 22–26), the church (ecclesiology, articles 27–35), and the last things (eschatology, article 37). Article 36 addresses the theocratic nature of civil government. Though it follows an objective doctrinal order, the confession has a warm, experiential, personal spirit, which is helped by its repeated use of the pronoun *we*.

The Belgic Confession's chief author was Guido de Brès (1522–1567), an itinerant Reformed pastor. During the sixteenth century, the Reformed churches in the Netherlands experienced severe persecution at the hands of King Philip II of Spain, an ally of the Roman Catholic Church. In 1561, de Brès, likely assisted by fellow pastors, wrote the confession to prove that the adherents of the Reformed faith were not rebels but law-abiding citizens who professed biblical doctrines.

The year after it was written, a copy of the confession was sent to Philip II, along with a statement that the petitioners were ready to obey the government in all things lawful, but would "offer their backs to stripes, their tongues to knives, their mouths to gags, and their whole bodies to the fire, well knowing that those who follow Christ must take His cross and deny themselves"[5] rather than deny the truth expressed in the confession. Neither the confession nor the petition persuaded Spanish authorities to be more tolerant of the Protestants, however. In 1567, de Brès became one martyr among hundreds who sealed their faith with blood. Nevertheless, his work has endured as a convincing statement of Reformed doctrine.

The Belgic Confession was readily received by Reformed churches in the Netherlands after its translation into Dutch in 1562. In 1566, it was revised by the Synod of Antwerp. Subsequently, it was regularly adopted by national Dutch synods held during the last three decades of the sixteenth century. After a further revision, the Synod of Dort (1618–1619) adopted the confession as a doctrinal standard to which all office-bearers in the Reformed churches had to subscribe.

HEIDELBERG CATECHISM (1563)

The Heidelberg Catechism was written in Heidelberg, Germany, at the request of Elector Frederick III (1516–1576), ruler of the Palatinate, an influential German province.[6] The pious prince commissioned Zacharius Ursinus (1534–1583), a 28-year-old professor of theology at Heidelberg University, and Caspar Olevianus (1536–1587), Frederick's 26-year-old court preacher, to prepare a Reformed catechism for instructing young people and guiding pastors and teachers. Ursinus was primarily responsible for the content of the catechism, while Olevianus was probably more involved with final composition and editing. The learning of Ursinus and the eloquence of Olevianus are evident in the final product, which has been called "a catechism of unusual power and beauty, an acknowledged masterpiece."[7] Frederick indicated that many others, including the theological faculty and chief officers of the Palatinate church, contributed to the finished document.

After the catechism was approved by a Heidelberg synod in January 1563, three more German editions, each including small additions, as well as a Latin translation, were published the same year in Heidelberg. The fourth edition has long been regarded as the official text of the catechism. The Dutch translation sanctioned by the Synod of Dort, from which our English text is rendered, was made from that edition.

When the first edition of the Heidelberg Catechism appeared, the German Bible had not yet been divided into verses. Consequently, the Scripture passages listed in the margin included only book and chapter. Moreover, the catechism's questions were not numbered. A Latin translation soon rectified these problems by including verse references and numbered questions. The catechism also was divided into fifty-two sections so that one section—referred to as a "Lord's Day"—could be preached on each Sunday of the year.

The catechism contains more proof texts than most because its authors wanted it to be "an echo of the Bible." The proof texts were to be regarded as an important part of the catechism, as Frederick notes in the original preface: "The Scripture proof by which the faith of the children is confirmed, are such [texts] only as have been selected with great pains from the divinely inspired Scriptures."[8]

The Heidelberg Catechism's 129 questions and answers are divided into three parts, patterned after the book of Romans. After a moving introduction about the true believer's comfort, questions 3–11 cover the experience of sin and misery (Rom. 1:1–3:20); questions 12–85 cover redemption in Christ and faith (Rom. 3:21–11:36), along with a lengthy exposition of the Apostles' Creed and the sacraments; and questions 86–129 cover true gratitude for God's deliverance (Rom. 12–16), primarily through a study of the Ten Commandments and the Lord's Prayer. The catechism presents doctrines with clarity and warmth. Its content is more subjective than objective, more spiritual than dogmatic. It is not surprising that this personal, devotional catechism, as exemplified by its use of singular pronouns, has been called "the book of comfort" for Christians.

In 1563, Petrus Dathenus translated the catechism into Dutch, then published it in his metrical Psalter in 1566. Its experiential and practical content won the love of God's people in the Netherlands. Within months after the catechism was published in Dutch, Peter Gabriel set a precedent for Dutch ministers by preaching from the catechism every Sunday afternoon. The catechism was approved by the synods of Wesel (1568), Emden (1571), Dort (1578), the Hague (1586), and Dort (1618–1619), which officially adopted it as part of the Three Forms of Unity. The latter Synod of Dort also made weekly preaching of the catechism mandatory.

The Heidelberg Catechism has since been translated into all European and dozens of Asian and African languages. It has circulated more widely than any other book except the Bible, Thomas à Kempis' *The Imitation of Christ*, and John Bunyan's *Pilgrim's Progress*. Soundly Calvinistic yet moderate in tone and irenic in spirit, this "book of comfort" remains one of the most widely used and warmly praised catechisms of the Reformation.

SECOND HELVETIC CONFESSION (1566)

The First Helvetic Confession had its origins in 1536 in a concern to harmonize and solidify Reformation teaching by providing a common Swiss confession (*Helvetii* being the Latin designation for the people of East Gaul, now Switzerland). Although appreciated by Martin Luther himself, it foundered because of disagreement over the "real presence" of Christ at the Lord's Supper, an issue later resolved—at least for Calvinists and Zwinglians—in the Zurich Consensus (*Consensus Tigurinus*) of 1549.

The Second Helvetic Confession is of greater significance, but it had more personal origins. It began in the form of a personal confession and testimony written by Heinrich Bullinger in 1562. In 1564, Bullinger contracted the plague when it ravaged Zurich and began revising his earlier work in anticipation of his death. Although his wife and three daughters died, Bullinger survived. Asked by Frederick III, elector of the Palatinate, to provide an exposition of the Reformed faith, Bullinger gave him a copy of the confession. Frederick had it translated into German before his appearance to defend himself against Lutheran criticism at the Imperial Diet of 1566. Following some revision at a conference in Zurich that same year, the confession was agreed to by the Swiss cities of Berne, Biel, Geneva, the Grisons, Mühlhausen, Schaffhausen, and St. Gall. It was thereafter widely approved in Scotland, Hungary, Poland, and elsewhere.

The Second Helvetic Confession is actually a compact manual of Reformed theology, containing thirty chapters and extending to some twenty thousand words. Written against the background of the definitive edition of John Calvin's *Institutes of the Christian Religion* (1559) as well as the Roman Catholic Counter-Reformation assembly at Trent (1545–1563), it summarizes Reformed theology in a comprehensive manner. Beginning with Scripture, it moves through the loci of systematic theology, striking characteristic Reformed and Calvinistic notes: the preaching of the Word of God is the Word of God (chap. 1); Christ is the mirror in which we are to contemplate our election (chap. 10); providence and predestination are separate works of God; and the body and blood of Christ are received not carnally but spiritually—that is, by the Holy Spirit. But practical religious issues are also a major concern: prayer and singing, the question of holy days, catechizing, visitation of the sick, and burial of the dead are discussed (chaps. 23–26), as well as issues surrounding marriage and celibacy, and the role of the magistrate (chaps. 29–30).

The Second Helvetic Confession was thus a mature statement of Reformed theology for the second half of the sixteenth century. Well-received internationally, it was translated into Dutch, English, Polish, Italian, Magyar, Turkish, and Arabic. It stands as a worthy testimony to Bullinger's labors and faith, and it is still used today by the Hungarian Reformed churches.

CANONS OF DORT (1618–1619)

The Judgment of the Synod of Dort on the Five Main Points of Doctrine in Dispute in the Netherlands is popularly known as the Canons of Dort or the Five Articles Against the Remonstrants.[9] It consists of doctrinal statements adopted by the Synod of Dort, which met in the city of Dordrecht in 1618–1619. Although this was a national synod of the Reformed Churches of the Netherlands, it had an international character. In addition to its sixty-two Dutch delegates, it comprised twenty-seven delegates from England, Switzerland, Germany, and five other countries. The French government refused to allow any French delegates to attend the synod, including the foremost French Calvinist theologian of the era, Pierre du Moulin (1568–1658).

The Synod of Dort was held to settle a serious controversy in the Dutch churches initiated by the rise of Arminianism. Jacob Arminius (1560–1609), a theological professor at Leiden University, differed from the Calvinist faith on a number of important points.[10] After Arminius' death, forty-three of his followers presented their heretical views to the States General of the Netherlands. In this document, called the Remonstrance of 1610, and even more explicitly in later writings, the Arminians taught (1) election based on foreseen faith, (2) the universality of Christ's atonement, (3) the free will and partial depravity of man, (4) the resistibility of grace, and (5) the possibility of a lapse from grace. They asked for revisions to the Reformed churches' doctrinal standards and for government protection of Arminian views. The Arminian-Calvinian conflict became so severe that it led the Netherlands to the brink of civil war. Finally, in 1617, the States General voted 4-3 to call a national synod to address the problem of Arminianism.

The synod held 154 formal sessions over a period of seven months (November 1618 to May 1619). Thirteen Arminian theologians led by Simon Episcopius tried to delay the work of the synod and divide the delegates, but their efforts proved unsuccessful. Under the leadership of Johannes Bogerman, the Arminians were dismissed. The synod then developed the canons, which thoroughly rejected the Remonstrance of 1610 and scripturally set forth Reformed doctrine on the debated points. These points, which later became known as the Five Points of Calvinism, can be summarized as unconditional election, particular redemption, total depravity, irresistible grace, and the perseverance of the saints. Though these points do not represent all of Calvinism and are better regarded as Calvinism's five answers to the five errors of Arminianism, they certainly lie at the heart of the Reformed faith, for they flow out of the principle of absolute divine sovereignty in the salvation of sinners. They may be summarized as follows:

1. Unconditional election and saving faith are sovereign gifts of God.

2. While the death of Christ is sufficient to expiate the sins of the whole world, its saving efficacy is limited to the elect.

3–4. All people are so totally depraved and corrupted by sin that they cannot exercise free will toward, or effect any part of, salvation. In sovereign grace, God irresistibly calls and regenerates the elect to newness of life.

5. God graciously preserves the redeemed so that they persevere until the end, even though they may be troubled by many infirmities as they seek to make their calling and election sure.

Although the canons have only four sections, we speak of five points or heads of doctrine because the canons were structured to correspond with the five articles of the 1610 Remonstrance. The third and fourth sections were combined into one because the Dortian divines considered them to be inseparable and hence designed them as "Head of Doctrine III/IV."

The canons are unique because of their role as a judicial decision in the Arminian controversy. The original preface called the canons a "judgment, in which both the true view, agreeing with God's Word, concerning the aforesaid five points of doctrine is explained, and the false view, disagreeing with God's Word, is rejected." Each section of the document includes a positive and a negative part—an exposition of Reformed doctrine on the subject, then a rejection of corresponding Arminian errors. In all, the canons contain fifty-nine articles of exposition and thirty-four rejections of error. Together they form a scriptural, balanced document on specific doctrines.

The canons are the only document among the Three Forms of Unity that was written by an ecclesiastical assembly and the only one that represented the view of all the Reformed churches of the day. All the Dutch and foreign delegates affixed their signatures to the canons.[11] Then they joined in a service of thanksgiving to praise God for preserving the doctrine of sovereign grace among the Reformed churches.

WESTMINSTER CONFESSION OF FAITH (1647)

The confession of faith produced by the Westminster divines has undoubtedly been one of the most influential documents of the post-Reformation period of the Christian church.[12] A carefully worded exposition of seventeenth-century Reformed theology, the calmness of its sentences largely hides the tempestuousness of the political backdrop against which it was written.

The Westminster Assembly was convened in 1643 after years of tension between England's King Charles I and his increasingly Puritan Parliament. Meeting under the chairmanship of the learned William Twisse against the king's express wishes, its vision was to effect closer uniformity of faith and practice throughout Charles' realm. The original task of the mostly Puritan delegates was to revise the Thirty-Nine Articles of the Church of England, but following the signing of the Solemn League and Covenant between Parliament and the Scottish Covenanters in 1643, this developed into the more specific and exacting task of framing theological and ecclesiastical formulas that would bring the Church of England into conformity with the doctrine and practice of the Presbyterian Church of Scotland.

The ministerial delegates from the Church of Scotland, who declined to become members of the Assembly, were the great ecclesiastical statesman Alexander Henderson; the high Calvinistic theologian and exponent of Reformed piety Samuel Rutherford; the extraordinarily gifted young George Gillespie; and the fascinating Robert Baillie (in whose *Letters and Journals* we find snapshots of the Assembly's activities and personalities).[13] The Scots also insisted on sending ruling elders as representatives, thus illustrating their commitment to the government of the church by both teaching and ruling elders.

For all practical purposes, these Scottish delegates constituted the most powerful group among those who gathered in the Chapel of Henry VII and later in the Jerusalem Chamber at Westminster Abbey, London, during the years of discussion and debate. While the majority of the delegates seem to have been of Presbyterian persuasion to varying degrees, Episcopalians and Independents were also represented, the latter group (which included Thomas Goodwin and Jeremiah Burroughs) at times exasperating the Scots.

The various documents composed by the assembly proceeded through a process of committee work in the afternoons, followed by plenary discussion on the floor of the assembly in the mornings. There were also regular additional gatherings for worship, fast days, and the like. Despite disagreements, the divines produced one of the truly monumental documents of church history, which has instructed, directed, and profoundly influenced Presbyterian churches worldwide ever since. Along with the Shorter Catechism, it has shaped Presbyterianism even more profoundly than Calvin's *Institutes*.

The Westminster Confession of Faith represents a high point in the development of federal theology, and its inner dynamic is powerfully covenantal. Divided into thirty-three chapters, it carefully covers the range of Christian doctrine, beginning with Scripture as the source of knowledge of divine things (following the First and Second Helvetic Confessions, the Formula of Concord, and the Irish Articles). It continues with an exposition of God and His decrees, creation, providence, and the fall (chaps. 2–6) before turning to expound the covenant of grace, the work of Christ, and, at length, the application of redemption (chaps. 10–18). While criticism is sometimes voiced that the confession is a deeply scholastic document (e.g., it has no separate chapter on the Holy Spirit), it is now increasingly noted that it was the first confession in the history of Christianity to have a separate chapter on adoption (chap. 12)—perhaps the least scholastic of all doctrines. Careful attention is given under various chapter headings to questions of law and liberty, as well as to the doctrine of the church and sacraments (chaps. 25–29) and the last things (chaps. 32–33).

While the confession was composed by disciplined theological minds, it also displays the influence of men with deep pastoral and preaching experience. It is an outstanding expression of classical Reformed theology framed for the needs of the people of God.

WESTMINSTER SHORTER CATECHISM (1648)

The Westminster Assembly also produced two catechisms. The shorter of these contains 107 questions, to which, generally speaking, single-sentence answers are provided. The pattern followed is broadly that of the Confession of Faith, but here the theological definitions are compact and concise.[14]

The most notable and famous feature of the catechism is its brilliant first question and answer: "What is the chief end of man? Man's chief end is to glorify God, and to enjoy him for ever." But equally important, if less often recognized, is its stress that this goal is to be accomplished by conformity to the Word and will of God. Hence, careful attention is given to the exposition of the Decalogue (questions 41–81). Far from being an indication of actual or incipient legalism, this emphasis was seen by the Westminster divines as an essential lesson in Christian living. For them, the knowledge of God's will lay largely in living for Christ in the power of the Spirit as the heavenly Father revealed in Scripture.

WESTMINSTER LARGER CATECHISM (1648)

The Larger Catechism shares the theology and many of the characteristics of its better known companion, but it covers more ground in greater detail. It contains 196 questions and answers, many of the latter extending to complex sentences of more than one hundred words.[15]

The usefulness of the Larger Catechism lies less in its memorizability than in its value as a teaching aid framed in the catechetical form. Philip Schaff expressed the opinion that its intended function might have been to promote the kind of catechetical preaching common in the Continental Reformed tradition. While such a purpose is unsubstantiated and quite unlikely, it is true that the Larger Catechism serves well as a guidebook for preaching doctrinal themes. It identifies the key elements and issues that ought to be addressed in such preaching.

Following five opening questions indicating that it is from Scripture that we learn who God is, how we may know Him, and what He requires, questions 6–90 teach us what we are to believe about Him. Questions 91–196 spell out the duties of the Christian life.

As is the case with the Shorter Catechism, this emphasis on the obedience of the Christian is set within a strong and full grasp of God's grace in Christ. The divines set out to provide a well-structured guide to applying the Word of God in the practical context of everyday life. While few may have the mental energy to memorize the Larger Catechism, it is a valuable guidebook to Christian thinking and living.

W. Robert Godfrey rightly concludes: "The Puritans of the 17th century were some of the most careful, faithful, and profound students of the Bible in the history of the church. The Westminster standards represent a summary and distillation of their labors."[16]

All seven of these living confessions have recently been printed in a single, harmonizing volume, together with an annotated bibliography of Reformed doctrinal works.[17] One cannot avoid being amazed at the remarkable unity of Calvinist theology in the sixteenth and seventeenth centuries.

TWO CALVINISTIC BAPTIST CONFESSIONS

By the mid-1640s, there were at least seven Calvinistic Baptist congregations, all having a Puritan background and all located in London.[18] Among the key leaders of these churches in the early years were John Spilsbury, William Kiffin, and Samuel Richardson, who later wrote what would come to be known as the First London Confession of Faith.

Owing to their commitment to the baptism of believers, Calvinistic Baptists were thought to be Anabaptists. To dispel this confusion, to dispute other charges against them, and to demonstrate their solidarity with Calvinists throughout

Western Europe, the Calvinistic Baptists issued a statement of faith in 1644. It was issued as the Westminster Assembly was meeting and on the eve of the publication of the Presbyterian-leaning Westminster Confession of Faith.

The First London Confession of Faith went through at least two printings in its first year of publication. It was reissued in a slightly amended edition on Nov. 30, 1646 (four days after the Westminster Confession was completed, though not yet published). Two more editions appeared in the early 1650s.[19] As historian Barrie R. White has shown, this confession gave early Calvinistic Baptists a clear and self-conscious sense of who they were, what they were seeking to achieve, and how they differed from other Puritan groups.[20] It also helped to satisfy many that Calvinistic Baptists were not guilty of heterodoxy.

By the 1670s, though, this confession was out of print and new challenges had arisen, most notably the emergence in the 1650s of the Quakers, who supported separating the written Word from the Holy Spirit. Also, a key Calvinistic Baptist leader, Thomas Collier, had defected from the faith. Then, from 1660 to 1688, the Puritan cause struggled for its life while a resurgent Anglicanism, with the help of the state, sought to eradicate the Puritans. Calvinistic Baptists wanted to present a united front with fellow Puritans, such as the English Presbyterians and the Congregationalists, then called Independents, against this vicious persecution. Therefore, a new confession was issued in 1677 that was based on the Westminster Confession and the Congregationalist Savoy Declaration (1658), which had been drawn up by John Owen and Thomas Goodwin.

Although this new Baptist confession was published anonymously (it would henceforth be known as the Second London Confession and would be the most influential of all Baptist confessions), it probably was prepared by two London Baptist pastors, William Collins and Nehemiah Coxe. Collins had studied in France and Italy, and had earned a divinity degree in England. He resisted conforming to the Church of England and in 1675 accepted a call to pastor Petty France Baptist Church in London. Coxe originally had been a member of John Bunyan's church in Bedford, had been imprisoned with Bunyan for preaching the gospel, and was ordained to the ministry at the same church meeting that called Bunyan to be pastor of the church.

Collins and Coxe used the Westminster Confession and the Savoy Declaration in preparing the Second London Confession. Nevertheless, they did not reproduce these confessions without modification. As the pastors stated in the preface, "Some things, indeed, are in some places added, some terms omitted, and some few changed." These changes were in subjects such as baptism and church government, but also in less-obvious matters. Yet, as Robert Oliver notes: "These differences must not be allowed to obscure the overwhelming agreement between the Second London Confession and those of Westminster and Savoy. The Baptist Confession can be clearly seen to be in the stream of evangelical theology, which flowed from the Westminster Assembly."[21]

The confession was reissued in 1689 at the first national meeting of the Calvinistic Baptists after persecution ceased with the accession of the Dutch prince, William of Orange, to the throne of England. Hence, this confession is often known as the 1689 Confession.

These confessions and catechisms from the early days of the Calvinistic movement provided a magnificent legacy of doctrinal truth for those who followed in the Reformed tradition. Today, they still are powerful tools Reformed churches may use to instruct believers in the faith, to reach out evangelistically, and to defend the church against error.

DISCUSSION QUESTIONS

1. What are the main confessions that the Reformed tradition has produced?

2. Why are confessions of faith important?

3. Identify the origins and the leading features of the following confessions:
   a. The Belgic Confession
   b. The Heidelberg Catechism
   c. The Second Helvetic Confession
   d. The Canons of Dort
   e. The Westminster Standards
   f. The Calvinistic Baptist confessions

NOTES

[1] Peter J. S. De Klerk, "Confessions and Creeds," in *Encyclopedia of Christianity*, ed. Philip E. Hughes (Marshallton, Del.: National Foundation for Christian Education, 1972), 3:94.

[2] James Dennison is issuing an edited version of a large number of Reformed confessions, to be printed as *Reformed Confessions of the 16th and 17th Centuries in English Translation* (Grand Rapids: Reformation Heritage Books). The first volume, expected to cover the period 1523–1552, is scheduled to be printed in 2008.

[3] Most of this chapter is adapted from the "Historical Introduction of the Reformed Confessions" in *Reformed Confessions Harmonized*, ed. Joel R. Beeke and Sinclair B. Ferguson (Grand Rapids: Baker, 1999), ix–xiii.

[4] For helpful literature on the Belgic Confession, see Nicolaas Hendrik Gootjes, *The Belgic Confesion: Its History and Sources* (Grand Rapids: Baker, 2007); Henry Beets, *The Reformed Confession Explained* (Grand Rapids: Eerdmans, 1929); Peter Y. De Jong, *The Church's Witness to the World* (Pella, Iowa: Pella Publishing, 1960); and Daniel R. Hyde, *With Heart and Mouth: An Exposition of the Belgic Confession* (Grandville, Mich.: Reformed Fellowship, 2008). For a short summary article, see Cornelis Venema, "The Belgic Confession," *Tabletalk*, 32, no. 4 (April 2008): 10–13.

[5] Cited in Gootjes, *The Belgic Confession*, 13–32.

[6] For historical material on the Heidelberg Catechism, see Lyle D. Bierma, *An Introduction to the Heidelberg Catechism* (Grand Rapids: Baker, 2005); Fred H. Klooster, *The Heidelberg Catechism: Its Origin and History* (Grand Rapids: Calvin Theological Seminary, 1981); and James I. Good, *The Heidelberg Catechism in Its Newest Light* (Philadelphia: Publication and Sunday School Board of the Reformed Church in the United States, 1914). For a listing of sermon expositions of the catechism, see bibliographical references under "Article 20 – Justice and Mercy in Christ," in Joel R. Beeke, *A Reader's Guide to Reformed Literature: An Annotated Bibliography of Reformed Theology* (Grand Rapids: Reformation Heritage Books, 1999), 47–49. For a full listing of Heidelberg Catechism printings and expositions in various languages, see Eric D. Bristley, "*Bibliographica Catechismus Heidelbergensis*: An Historical Bibliography of Editions, Translations, Commentaries, Sermons and Historical Studies of the Heidelberg Catechism 1563" (unpublished paper done for an independent research course at Westminster Theological Seminary, Philadelphia, 1983). For a short summary article, see Lyle D. Bierma, "The Heidelberg Catechism," *Tabletalk*, 32, no. 4 (April 2008): 14–17.

[7] *The Westminster Dictionary of Church History*, ed. Jerald C. Brauer (Philadelphia: Westminster Press, 1971), 391.

[8] *The Catechism*, trans. William Turner (London: Richard Johnes, 1572).

[9] For books on the Canons of Dort, see *Crisis in the Reformed Churches*, ed. Peter Y. De Jong (Grand Rapids: Reformed Fellowship, 1968); Thomas Scott, *The Articles of the Synod of Dort* (Harrisonburg, Va.: Sprinkle, 1993); Gordon Girod, *The Deeper Faith* (Grand Rapids: Reformed Publications, 1958); Homer C. Hoeksema, *The Voice of Our Fathers* (Grand Rapids: Reformed Free Publishing, 1980); Henry Peterson, *The Canons of Dort: A Study Guide* (Grand Rapids: Baker, 1968); Cornelis Pronk, *Expository Sermons on the Canons of Dort* (St. Thomas, Ontario: Free Reformed Publications, 1999); Cornelis P. Venema, *But for the Grace of God: An Exposition of the Canons of Dort* (Grand Rapids: Reformed Fellowship, 1994); and Donald W. Sinnema, "The Issue of Reprobation at the Synod of Dort (1618–19) in Light of the History of this Doctrine" (Ph.D. dissertation, University of St. Michael's College, 1985). For a short summary article, see R. Scott Clark, "The Canons of Dordt," *Tabletalk*, 32, no. 4 (April 2008): 18–21.

[10] For Arminius' corpus, see *The Writings of James Arminius*, 3 vols., ed. Carl Bangs (Grand Rapids: Baker, 1986). For secondary sources, see Carl Bangs, *Arminius: A Study in the Dutch Reformation* (Nashville: Abingdon Press, 1971); Richard A. Muller, *God, Creation, and Providence in the Thought of Jacob Arminius* (Grand Rapids: Baker, 1991); and Nicholas Tyacke, *Anti-Calvinism: The Rise of English Arminianism, ca. 1590–1640*, 2nd ed. (Oxford: Oxford University Press, 1990).

[11] G. H. Kersten, *Reformed Dogmatics: A Systematic Treatment of Reformed Doctrine*, trans. Joel R. Beeke and Jan C. Weststrate (Sioux Center, Iowa: Netherlands Reformed Book and Publishing, 1980), 1:128–130.

[12] The best edition of the three Westminster standards is the *Westminster Confession of Faith* (Glasgow: Free Presbyterian Publications, 1994). For able expositions of the Westminster Confession of Faith, see Francis R. Beattie, *The Presbyterian Standards: An Exposition of the Westminster Confession of Faith and Catechisms* (Richmond: Presbyterian Committee of Publication, 1896); A. A. Hodge, *The Westminster Confession: A Commentary* (Edinburgh: Banner of Truth Trust, 2002); Robert Shaw, *Exposition of the Westminster Confession of Faith* (Ross-shire, U.K.: Christian Focus, 1973); and Joseph A. Pipa, *The Westminster Confession of Faith Study Book* (Ross-shire, U.K.: Christian Focus, 2005).

[13] Robert Baillie, *Letters and Journals*, ed. David Laing, 3 vols. (Edinburgh: Bannatyne Club, 1841–42).

[14] Numerous expositions of the Shorter Catechism have been written over the centuries. Some of the best include Thomas Vincent, *The Shorter Catechism of the Westminster Assembly Explained and Proved from Scripture* (Edinburgh: Banner of Truth Trust, 1980); John Flavel, "An Exposition of the Assembly's Catechism," *The Works of John Flavel* (Edinburgh: Banner of Truth Trust, 1968), 6:138–317; Thomas Watson, *A Body of Divinity* (Edinburgh: Banner of Truth Trust, 1965), *The Ten Commandments* (Edinburgh: Banner of Truth Trust, 1965), and *The Lord's Prayer* (Edinburgh: Banner of Truth Trust, 1965); Thomas Boston, "An Illustration of the Doctrines of the Christian Religion," *The Complete Works of Thomas Boston*, vols. 1 and 2 (Stoke-on-Trent, U.K.: Tentmaker Publications, 2002); John Brown of Haddington, *Questions and Answers on the Shorter Catechism* (Grand Rapids: Reformation Heritage Books, 2006); James Fisher, *The Assemblies Shorter Catechism Explained, by Way of Question and Answer* (Stoke-on-Trent, U.K.: Tentmaker Publications, 1998); A. A. Hodge and J. Aspinwall, *The System of Theology Contained in the Westminster Shorter Catechism* (Eugene, Ore.: Wipf & Stock Publishers, 2004); Alexander Whyte, *An Exposition on the Shorter Catechism* (Ross-shire, U.K.: Christian Focus, 2004); and G. I. Williamson, *The Westminster Shorter Catechism: For Study Classes*, 2nd ed. (Phillipsburg, N.J.: P&R, 2003).

[15] The best works on the Larger Catechism are Thomas Ridgeley, *A Body of Divinity*, 2 vols. (London: for Daniel Midwinter et al., 1731–1733), and Johannes G. Vos, *The Westminster Larger Catechism: A Commentary* (Phillipsburg, N.J.: P&R, 2002).

[16] W. Robert Godfrey, "The Assembly at the Abbey," *Tabletalk*, 17, no. 9 (Sept. 1993): 9.

[17] Beeke and Ferguson, *Reformed Confessions Harmonized*.

[18] For the full story of the emergence of the Calvinistic Baptists from the Puritan-Separatist matrix, see especially B. R. White, *The English Baptists of the Seventeenth Century* (London: The Baptist Historical Society, 1996), and Kenneth R. Manley, "Origins of the Baptists: The Case for Development from Puritanism-Separatism," in *Faith, Life and Witness: The Papers of the Study and Research Division of The Baptist World Alliance 1986–1990*, ed. William H. Brackney with Ruby J. Burke (Birmingham, Ala.: Samford University Press, 1990). I am indebted to Michael Haykin for his help in drafting this material on Calvinistic Baptists.

[19] Murray Tolmie, *The Triumph of the Saints: The Separate Churches of London 1616–1649* (Cambridge:

Cambridge University Press, 1977), 61–65, and B. R. White, "The Origins and Convictions of the First Calvinistic Baptists," *Baptist History and Heritage*, 25, no. 4 (Oct. 1990): 45.

[20] See, in particular, B. R. White, "The Organization of the Particular Baptists, 1644–1660," *Journal of Ecclesiastical History*, 17 (1966): 209–226; "The Doctrine of the Church in the Particular Baptist Confession of 1644," *The Journal of Theological Studies*, n.s., 19 (1968): 570–590; "Thomas Patient in Ireland," *Irish Baptist Historical Society Journal*, 2 (1969–70): 36–48; and *The English Baptists of the Seventeenth Century* (London: Baptist Historical Society, 1983), 59–94.

[21] Robert W. Oliver, "Baptist Confession Making, 1644 and 1689" (unpublished paper presented to the Strict Baptist Historical Society, March 17, 1989), 21.

PART TWO

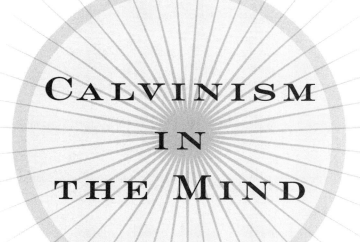

CALVINISM
IN
THE MIND

CHAPTER 3

THE MARROW
OF CALVINISM

There is no true religion in the world which is not Calvinistic—Calvinistic in its essence, Calvinistic in its implications. . . . In proportion as we are religious, in that proportion, then, are we Calvinistic; and when religion comes fully to its rights in our thinking, and feeling, and doing, then shall we be truly Calvinistic. . . . [Calvinism] is not merely the hope of true religion in the world: it is true religion in the world—as far as true religion is in the world at all.[1]

—BENJAMIN B. WARFIELD

*I*f you were to ask theologians in seminaries or people on the street, "What is Calvinism all about?" the answers you would receive would vary widely. Caricatures abound. For instance, on Thanksgiving Day 2007, the *Grand Rapids Press* printed an article by John M. Crisp titled, "Thinking like a Pilgrim on Thanksgiving." It said of the Pilgrims: "Their religious roots reached back to the gloomy tenets of John Calvin, which means—at the risk of oversimplification—that they lived with the nagging fear that they dangled every moment by a thin thread over the fiery pit of hell in spite of their own faith or good works or the outward manifestations of the blessings of God."[2]

Does any Calvinist recognize this as a definition of Calvinism? I wrote back to the *Grand Rapids Press*: "This statement is not an oversimplification. It is a misrepresentation. Calvin and most of the Pilgrims rejoiced in Christ their Savior, and lived joyous Christian lives of spiritual depth with assured faith in the rich promises of God."[3]

Of course, most evangelical Christians and, sadly, even some Calvinists, lack a proper understanding of the real heartbeat of Calvinism. "There is nothing upon which men need to be more instructed than upon the question of what Calvinism really is," Charles H. Spurgeon once said.[4] Whether you are a Calvinist, a non-Calvinist, or an anti-Calvinist, you need to give this question a fair hearing: what really is the marrow of Calvinism?

THE BASIC PRINCIPLE OF CALVINISM

Calvinistic theology includes all the essential evangelical doctrines, such as the deity of Christ, objective atonement, and the person and work of the Holy Spirit. It also includes many doctrines developed by theological giants such as Athanasius, Augustine, Anselm, and Martin Luther. Yet, it is not entirely correct to say, as did "Rabbi" John Duncan, "There's no such thing as Calvinism [because] the teachings of Augustine, Remigius, Anselm, and Luther were just pieced together by one remarkable man [Calvin], and the result baptized with his name."[5]

Calvin's synthesis is far more remarkable than that; he certainly was no midget standing on Augustine's giant shoulders. Calvin's presentation of the plan of salvation, choice of materials, and sense of the interconnectedness of biblical doctrine are unique. He was a genius in organization and systematization. His indebtedness to his predecessors does not detract from his originality, which is clearly evident in his doctrine of divine Sonship; his emphasis on the humanity of the Redeemer and His threefold mediatorial office as Prophet, Priest, and King; his explanation of the inward witness of the Holy Spirit; his development of Presbyterian church polity; and his exposition of how worship should be based on the Second Commandment, which the Puritans would later develop as the regulative principle of worship.

In addition, Calvinists throughout history have not been mere imitators of Calvin. For example, in their development of covenant theology, decretal theology, and the doctrine of assurance of faith, they labored hard to explain the whole counsel of God within the context of all the profundity, harmony, and consistency of Scripture.

Despite these various contributing strains, Calvinism is remarkably consistent and defined. As Valentijn Hepp writes, "Calvinism is the broadest and deepest Christianity; or, if you will, it is the purest Christianity; or, as I should prefer to qualify it, it is the most consistent and likewise the most harmonious Christianity."[6]

But what is at the heart of the Calvinistic system? Over the centuries, many scholars have sought to identify a single concept that governs Calvinism. Herman Bauke, a German Calvinist, lists at least twenty interpretations of the "basic principle of Calvinism." Some of these include:

• *Predestination.* While some scholars say predestination is the core of Reformed truth, that assertion can be misleading if it is understood to mean that everything proceeds from absolute predestination in such a way that what transpires in time matters little. This hyper-Calvinistic view leads to a tendency to move away from biblical revelation into a more rationalistic kind of theology.

• *The covenant.* While the covenantal relationship between God and man is emphasized in Reformed theology, it is not necessarily the controlling concept. All men are indeed either in covenant with God or are covenant-breakers, but Calvin did not structure all doctrines under this important truth.

• *The sovereignty of God.* Sovereignty means "rule"; hence, to speak of God's sovereignty is to refer to God's rule. God's sovereignty is His supremacy, His kingship, and His deity. His sovereignty declares Him to be God, the incomprehensible Trinity who is nevertheless knowable insofar as He chooses to reveal Himself to us. His sovereignty is exercised in all of His attributes, declaring Him to be perfect in all respects and possessor of all righteousness and holiness. He is the sovereignly gracious and omnipotent Jehovah, the Most High who does His will in the army of heaven and among the inhabitants of the earth (Dan. 4:35). He cannot be reduced to special or temporal categories for human understanding and analysis.

Here, at last, we draw near to the true marrow of Calvinism. The Calvinist believes that God is the Lord of life and Sovereign of the universe, whose will is the key to history. The Calvinist believes that He is free and independent of any force outside Himself to accomplish His purposes; that He knows the end from the beginning; that He creates, sustains, governs, and directs all things; and that His marvelous design will be fully and perfectly manifest at the end of the ages.[7] "For of him, and through him, and to him, are all things: to whom be glory for ever" (Rom. 11:36). As Charles Hodge says: "God's sovereignty is to all other doctrines what the granite formation is to the other strata of the earth. It underlies and sustains them, but it crops out only here and there. So this doctrine should underlie all our preaching, and should be definitely asserted only now and then."[8]

God's sovereignty is the marrow of doctrinal Calvinism—provided we understand that this sovereignty is not arbitrary but is the sovereignty of the God and Father of our Lord Jesus Christ. As Duncan wrote: "It is a holy will that rules the universe—a will in which loving-kindness is locked up, to be in due time displayed. It is a solemn thing that we and all creatures are at the disposal of pure will; but it is not merely free will, it is the free will of the sovereign Lord Jehovah, and therein it is distinguished from the abstractness and apparent arbitrariness of mere will."[9] B. B. Warfield wrote in his essay on predestination: "The Biblical writers find their comfort continually in the assurance that it is the righteous, holy, faithful, loving God in whose hands rests the determination of the sequence of events and all their issues. . . . The roots of the divine election are planted in His unsearchable love, by which it appears as the supreme act of grace."[10]

This is balanced, genuine, defensible Calvinism. It is the Calvinism expressed in Isaiah 9:6, which says that the government, or sovereignty, is upon the shoulders of Him who is "Wonderful, Counseller, The mighty God, The everlasting Father, The Prince of Peace." In Christ, the warm and fatherly sovereignty of the God of the Scriptures is vastly different from the cold and capricious sovereignty of other "gods," such as Allah. Fatherly sovereignty, like the incarnation itself, is in perfect harmony with all of God's attributes. The Calvinist finds peace in the conviction that behind God's all-encompassing providence is the full acquiescence of the triune God. The sovereign grace and love that went to Calvary has the whole world in its hands. God's fatherly sovereignty in Christ is the essence of who God is.

THEOCENTRISM

Thus, if we had to reduce Calvinism to one concept, we might be safest to echo Warfield, who said that to be Reformed means to be theocentric. The primary interest of Reformed theology is the triune God, for the transcendent-immanent, fatherly God in Jesus Christ is God Himself. Calvinists are people whose theology is dominated by the idea of God. As Mason Pressly says: "Just as the Methodist places in the foreground the idea of the salvation of sinners; the Baptist, the mystery of regeneration; the Lutheran, justification by faith; the Moravian, the wounds of Christ; the Greek Catholic, the mysticism of the Holy Spirit; and the Romanist, the catholicity of the church, so the Calvinist is always placing in the foreground the thought of God."[11]

To be Reformed is to stress the comprehensive, sovereign, fatherly lordship of God over everything: every area of creation, every creature's endeavors, and every aspect of the believer's life. The ruling motif in Calvinism is, "In the beginning God . . ." (Gen. 1:1).

In His relation to us, God has only rights and powers; He binds Himself to duties sovereignly and graciously only by way of covenant. In covenant, He assumes the duties and responsibilities of being a God unto us, but that does not detract from His being the first cause and the last end of all things. The universe is ruled not by chance or fate, but by the complete, sovereign rule of God. We exist for one purpose: to give Him glory. We have only duties to God, no rights. Any attempt to challenge this truth is doomed. Romans 9:20b asks, "Shall the thing formed say to him that formed it, Why hast thou made me thus?" God enacts His laws for every part of our lives and demands unconditional obedience. We are called to serve Him with body and soul, in worship and daily work, every second of every day.

To be Reformed, then, is to be concerned with the complete character of the Creator-creature relationship. It is to view all of life *coram Deo*, that is, lived before the face of God. As Warfield wrote:

> The Calvinist is the man who sees God: God in nature, God in history, God in grace. Everywhere he sees God in His mighty stepping, everywhere he feels the working of His mighty arm, the throbbing of His mighty heart. The Calvinist is the man who sees God behind all phenomena and in all that occurs recognizes the hand of God, working out His will. [The Calvinist] makes the attitude of the soul to God in prayer its permanent attitude in all its life activities; [he] casts himself on the grace of God alone, excluding every trace of dependence on self from the whole work of his salvation.[12]

The doctrine of God—a fatherly, sovereign God in Christ Jesus—is therefore the center of Reformed theology. R. C. Sproul puts it this way: "How we understand the nature and character of God himself influences how we understand the nature of man, who bears God's image; the nature of Christ, who works to satisfy the Father; the nature of salvation, which is effected by God; the nature of ethics, the norms of which are based on God's character; and a myriad of other theological considerations, all drawing on our understanding of God."[13]

So Calvinists define all doctrine in a God-centered way. Sin is horrible because it is an affront to God. Salvation is wonderful because it brings glory to God. Heaven is glorious because it is the place where God is all in all. Hell is infernal because it is where God manifests His righteous wrath. God is central to all of those truths.

Consider the example of the true reason for the horror of sin. A Christian may say that sin is damaging and leads to wretchedness, but without a God-centered perspective, he will miss the most important emphasis of all. Sin is an affront to God Himself, as David confesses in Psalm 51:4: "Against thee, thee only, have I sinned, and done this evil in thy sight: that thou mightest be justified when thou speakest, and be clear when thou judgest."

The most common word in the epistle to the Romans, the greatest doctrinal text of the Bible, is not *grace*, *faith*, *believe*, or *law*, but *God*. Most of the great theological statements in Romans begin with God:

• God gave them over.
• God will give to each person according to what he has done.
• God will judge men's secrets through Jesus Christ.
• God set Him forth as a propitiation.
• God justifies the ungodly.
• God has poured out His love into our hearts.

As Calvinists, we are enamored with God. We are overwhelmed by His majesty, His beauty, His holiness, and His grace. We seek His glory, desire His presence, and model our lives after Him.

Other Christians say that evangelism or revival is their great concern, and these things must concern us greatly, of course. But ultimately, we have only one concern: to know God, to serve Him, and to see Him glorified. That is our main objective. The salvation of the lost is important because it leads to the hallowing of God's name and the coming of His kingdom. The purifying of society is important because it helps us do God's will on earth as in it is done in heaven. Bible study and prayer are important because they lead us into communion with Him.

THE TRADEMARK OF THE CHURCH

God-centeredness has been the trademark of the church, and especially of Calvin and of Calvinism, through the centuries. Here are some examples:

• *Augustine.* One significant reason the Reformed tradition has held the early church theologian and author Augustine in high regard is his theocentric perspective on life and salvation. Listen to him as he writes about his conversion:

> During all those years [of rebellion], where was my free will? What was the hidden, secret place from which it was summoned in a moment, so that I might bend my neck to Thy easy yoke . . . ? How sweet all at once it was for me to be rid of those fruitless joys which I had once feared to lose . . . ! Thou didst drive them from me, Thou who art the true, the sovereign joy. Thou didst drive them from me and took their place, Thou who art sweeter than all pleasure, . . . who dost outshine all light, . . . who dost surpass all honor, . . . O Lord my God, my Light, my Wealth, and my Salvation.[14]

• *John Calvin.* Calvin's life offers abundant commentary on theocentrism. Despite shortcomings, he strove to live *soli Deo gloria.* That goal bore fruits of godliness in his character. When Theodore Beza broke the news of Calvin's death to the Geneva Academy students, he said, "Having been a spectator of his conduct for sixteen years, . . . I can now declare, that in him all men may see a most beautiful example of the Christian character, an example which it is as easy to slander as it is difficult to imitate."[15]

• *Jonathan Edwards.* Calvin's most noble group of successors, the Puritans, aimed to live all of life theocentrically. That is perhaps best illustrated in Jonathan Edwards, the New England Reformed theologian of the eighteenth century:

> The enjoyment of God is the only happiness with which our souls can be satisfied. To go to heaven, fully to enjoy God, is infinitely better than the most pleasant accommodations here. Fathers and mothers, husbands, wives, or children, or the company of earthly friends, are but shadows; but God is the substance. These are but scattered beams, but God is the sun. These are but streams, but God is the fountain. These are but drops; but God is the ocean.[16]

Then, too, journals of Presbyterians such as Andrew Bonar, the letters of Anglicans such as John Newton, and the sermons of Baptists such as Spurgeon all center on God. These men developed their theology and fulfilled their ministry in adoration of God. Everything flowed out of that passion.

You might be saying that these men had such a God-centered mindset only because they were extraordinary theologians and pastors. If so, listen to these words of Ann Griffiths, a humble Welsh Calvinistic Methodist who was a farmer's wife and who died in 1805 at the age of 29 when giving birth to her first child:

> *Gladly would I leave behind me*
> *All the idols I have known,*
> *Since I bear inscribed the likeness*
> *Of a more exalted One;*
> *Worthy of unending worship,*
> *Love, and reverence is He;*
> *By His precious death were myriads*
> *From the jaws of death set free.*[17]

This kind of God-centered passion has been mostly lost because of our backsliding and the theological errors of our day. In many so-called evangelical churches, the fear of God has been lost and thus, in a real measure, so has a biblical understanding of the love of God. Evangelicalism has become man-centered and, as a result, promotes a view of God that is far less than the reality set forth in Holy Scripture.

But even many who delight in Reformed truth seem to have lost their sense of the awe of God. As in the broader evangelical culture, God-centeredness has given way to man-centeredness in many Reformed circles. We aim too often at giving people what they want instead of following the example of the great Reformed evangelists, whose first objective was to confront men and women with God's greatness and majesty.

Too many of us today present God as more user-friendly than His own Word does. We want to make people feel comfortable, so we avoid telling them anything that will make them uneasy. We are so concerned about losing our young people that we never ask them to gaze on the holiness of God or challenge them to live out that holiness in the childlike fear of God. We condone materialism, worldliness, and triviality because we have so little sense of an ever-present, infinitely holy God.

Our lives seldom testify that we are willing, at any price, to "buy the truth, and sell it not" (Prov. 23:23). Dangerous compromises, subtle backsliding, Ephesian coldness, and Laodicean indifference multiply the "unreformedness" of our lives. How often we esteem ourselves and our reputation above the name of God and His reputation.

But when the Holy Spirit shows us the Father's divine generosity to us in His Son, together with the absolute freeness of His grace, we wholeheartedly yearn to glorify our worthy, fatherly triune God with all that is within us. As Maurice Roberts writes:

> The realization that God has chosen an individual to life and glory, though he was not a whit better than others, leads the mature Christian to cherish the most ecstatic feelings of gratitude to our heavenly Father. With an upturned face the adoring believer confesses to heaven that, apart from eternally given grace, he would never have believed in Christ, nor even have wished to believe. Then, lowering his gaze and covering his streaming eyes, the grateful Christian exclaims: "My Father and my God! To Thee alone be everlasting glory for such unmerited grace!"[18]

Are we true sons and daughters of the Calvinistic Reformation who are enamored with God Himself, and with honoring and obeying Him? If so, we should pray with the psalmist:

By all whom Thou hast made
Be praise and worship paid
Thro' earth abroad;
Thy Name be glorified,
There is none great beside,
Matchless Thy works abide,
For Thou art God.

Help me Thy will to do,
Thy truth I will pursue,

Teach me to fear;
Give me the single eye
Thy Name to glorify,
O Lord, my God Most High,
With heart sincere.[19]

And with Philip Doddridge:

Perish each thought of human pride,
Let God alone be magnified;
His glory let the heavens resound,
Shouted from earth's remotest bound.[20]

DISCUSSION QUESTIONS

1. What lies at the core of Calvinism?

2. Who were some notable believers who held to the central tenet of Calvinism?

3. Can you think of some individuals in the Bible whose lives and thinking reflect what we have seen to be at the core of Calvinism?

4. How does the fatherly sovereignty of God help you in practical ways in your daily walk with Him?

NOTES

1 B. B. Warfield, *Selected Shorter Writings [of] Benjamin B. Warfield*, ed. John E. Meeter (Phillipsburg, N.J.: P&R, 1970), 1: 392.

2 *Grand Rapids Press* (Nov. 22, 2007), A-18.

3 *Grand Rapids Press* (Dec. 3, 2007), A-6.

4 Charles H. Spurgeon, *Metropolitan Tabernacle Pulpit* (Pasadena, Texas: Pilgrim Publications, 1986), 7:301.

5 John Duncan, *Colloquia Peripatetica* (Edinburgh: Edmonston & Douglas, 1870), 9.

6 Valentijn Hepp, *The Reformed Faith Commonly Called Calvinism*, 87.

7 G. C. Berkouwer, *The Providence of God* (Grand Rapids: Eerdmans, 1972), 7ff.

8 Charles Hodge, *Princeton Sermons* (Edinburgh: Banner of Truth Trust, 1958), 6.

9 Duncan, *Colloquia Peripatetica*, 89.

10 B. B. Warfield, *Biblical and Theological Studies* (Philadelphia: P&R, 1952), 301, 323–324.

11 Mason Pressly, "Calvinism and Science," in *Evangelica Repertoire* (1891), 662.

12 B. B. Warfield, *Calvin as a Theologian and Calvinism Today* (London: Evangelical Press, 1969), 23–24.

13 R. C. Sproul, *Grace Unknown: The Heart of Reformed Theology* (Grand Rapids: Baker, 1997), 25.

14 Augustine, quoted in John Piper, *The Legacy of Sovereign Joy: God's Triumphant Grace in the Lives of Augustine, Luther, and Calvin* (Wheaton, Ill.: Crossway, 2000), 57.

15 Quoted in *Selected Works of Calvin*, ed. and trans. Henry Beveridge (Grand Rapids: Baker, 1983), 1:c.

16 Jonathan Edwards, "The Christian Pilgrim," in *The Works of Jonathan Edwards*, ed. Edward Hickman (Edinburgh: Banner of Truth Trust, 1974), 2:244.

17 Quoted in A. M. Allchin, *Songs to Her God: Spirituality of Ann Griffiths* (Cambridge, Mass.: Cowley Publications, 1987), 104.

18 Maurice Roberts, "Before the Omnipotent's Throne," *Tabletalk*, 16, no. 11 (Nov. 1992): 17.

19 *The Psalter* (Grand Rapids: Reformation Heritage Books, 2003), no. 236, stanzas 1–2.

20 From the hymn "God Magnified by Those That Love His Salvation," by Philip Doddridge.

CHAPTER 4

TOTAL
DEPRAVITY

Dr. Martyn Lloyd-Jones was hesitant about preaching on Sundays such doc-
trines as the five points of Calvinism. He was a Calvinistic Methodist and
unashamed of that, but his approach was to permeate all his sermons with
these truths and so to Calvinize people by showing them the greatness of our
Sovereign Lord and his free redemption. However, when Dr. Lloyd-Jones
took part in conferences and discussions he used theological and Calvinistic
terms, but rarely did he do so when he preached on Sundays. People learning
about Christianity must start in the infants' school of trust in Jesus Christ
before getting to the grammar school of election and the design of the atone-
ment. I appreciate that wise response and have tended to take the same
approach myself, but I also think times come when these truths, which are so
preachable, need to be declared clearly. I do believe all five points and I want
every Christian to believe them because they are the teaching of the Bible.
They are historic Christianity. Charles Haddon Spurgeon was different from
Dr. Lloyd-Jones as he asked his invited preachers to speak on the Five Points
at the grand opening of the Metropolitan Tabernacle, one point each evening
for a week. London needed to hear the Five Points as it does today.[1]

—GEOFFREY THOMAS

*T*he Reformation's emphasis on sovereign grace met a great deal of resistance,
not only from the Jesuits in the Roman Catholic Counter-Reformation,
which was initiated especially to roll back the tide of the Reformation, but also, as
we have seen, from James Arminius and his followers. The Arminians (or Remon-

strants) presented five theological challenges to the Reformed faith, stating their belief in:

• *Conditional election.* Election, they said, is based on foreseen faith, meaning that God saw ahead of time which sinners would believe in His Son and elected them on that basis. Strictly speaking, election is neither sovereign nor unmerited.

• *Universal atonement.* Christ's merits are universal—that is, Christ earned salvation for everyone equally—but only believers obtain its efficacy. The atoning work of Christ makes it possible for everyone to be saved, though it does not actually secure the salvation of anyone.

• *Partial depravity.* Man is seriously but not totally depraved; with God's enabling grace, he has the free will and ability to choose salvation in Christ. Everyone chooses to either cooperate or not cooperate with the gospel call to faith and repentance. Sinners are born again by the Spirit only when they believe of their own choice.

• *Resistible grace.* Man can resist God's internal, gracious call to salvation; thus, the Spirit's work is defined and controlled by the sinner's willingness to cooperate. God's grace is vincible.

• *Lapsing from grace.* Arminius and the early Arminians were unsure whether a believer could lapse from grace, but by the time the Synod of Dort met (1618), the Arminians had rejected the doctrine of the perseverance of the saints. They said that unless a believer continues in the faith, he will not ultimately be saved.

The delegates at the Synod of Dort recognized that Arminian teaching threatened two major gospel themes: the glory that belongs to God alone in saving sinners and the believer's security and assurance in God's invincible grace. The rejection of these two themes implies the repudiation of salvation by sovereign grace alone.[2] The synod responded to these challenges both negatively and positively in the Canons of Dort. Negatively, the delegates rebutted Arminianism in its every nuance in their rejections; positively, they expounded the main Calvinistic doctrines of salvation in a constructive way, presenting the marrow of what is called soteriological Calvinism. The word *soteriological* derives from *soteria*, the Greek word for "salvation"; *soteriological*, then, simply implies that which pertains to the truth or doctrine of salvation. Central to that salvation, according to the Canons of Dort, is God's sovereign grace in saving sinners. Simply stated, the canons offer:

- Sovereign grace conceived (unconditional election)
- Sovereign grace merited (particular redemption)
- Sovereign grace needed (total depravity)
- Sovereign grace applied (irresistible grace)
- Sovereign grace preserved (perseverance of the saints).

These five points are integrally linked; they stand or fall together. They are all rooted in two inescapable truths of Scripture: man's complete ruin by sin and God's perfect, sovereign, and gracious remedy in Christ. These parts of salvation fit together to provide us with a biblical, consistent view of grace revealing how God saves sinners to His glory. They show how great God's grace is, how it directs everything in this world, and how salvation is ultimately not dependent on anything that man can offer. The real heart of Calvinism is that God sovereignly and graciously loves sinners fully and unconditionally in Christ.

It is important to note that the five points do not summarize all of Calvinism; that would be a truncated view of the Reformed faith. One of the aims of this book is to show the panoramic grandeur of the Reformed faith's worldview. The Reformed confessions, as well as numerous books, such as Abraham Kuyper's *Lectures on Calvinism*, H. Henry Meeter's *The Basic Ideas of Calvinism*, Leonard Coppes' *Are Five Points Enough? The Ten Points of Calvinism*, and Ernest C. Reisinger and D. Matthew Allen's *Beyond Five Points*, show us that Calvinism is too broad and grand to be encompassed in five doctrines.[3] Richard Muller says the five points are "elements that can only be understood in the context of a larger body of teaching," which includes the necessity of justification by gracious faith alone, thankful obedience, the sacraments as means of grace, and many more. Muller concludes: "When that larger number of points taught by the Reformed confessions is not respected, the famous five are jeopardized, indeed, dissolved—and the ongoing spiritual health of the church is placed at risk."[4]

However, these points do summarize Calvinistic soteriology, which is one of Calvinism's most important theological contributions. The Calvinistic plan of salvation is best defended in some of its most controversial areas by these five points.[5]

The five points are conveniently memorized through the acronym TULIP, which, since the late nineteenth century, has been a common way of summarizing and teaching Reformed soteriology.[6] But the acronym has weak points: it rearranges the order of the Canons of Dort and simplifies them. The canons say a great deal more than is represented by TULIP, and they say it with more vitality and in a better order. Nevertheless, TULIP can be used with profit, provided each point is explained with sufficient nuances, so I will follow its order as I examine the five points.

Some people have attempted to modify the terminology of Calvinism's five points. They prefer *radical depravity*, *radical corruption*, or *pervasive evil*, which suggests that evil is at the root of things, to *total depravity*, which they assume to mean that every man is as evil as he can be, with no good at all. They prefer using the term *sovereign election* rather than *unconditional election* because the first term indicates that God's gracious choosing makes man willing to receive salvation in Christ, whereas *unconditional election* seems to downplay the necessity of repentance and faith. Instead of *limited atonement*, which they say implies that God's love and power are limited, they suggest *definite atonement* or *particular redemption*, which stresses that Christ's death was for particular individuals. They prefer *efficacious* or *effectual grace* rather than *irresistible grace*, which they say conflicts with the human tendency to resist the common work of the Spirit. And they choose to stress *the perseverance of God* or *the preservation of the saints*, which gets at the source of perseverance, rather than *the perseverance of the saints*.

While such revisions, technically speaking, are consistent with Scripture, none is essential. Personally, if I had to change the wording of any part of TULIP, I would choose only to use *definite atonement* over *limited atonement* to avoid misunderstanding. Nevertheless, when rightly explained, TULIP ably sets forth Calvinist soteriology and defends it against its critics and against Arminian theology.[7] Critics often say that TULIP represents a harsh or cruel form of theology, but Calvinism is actually the most loving theology possible, for it is a theology of grace.

This chapter briefly explains total depravity, the first of the five points of Calvinism. The next five chapters will expound the remaining points: unconditional election, limited atonement (two chapters), irresistible grace, and perseverance of the saints.

The Bible tells us that although fallen man is capable of doing some externally good acts, he cannot do anything truly good or pleasing in God's sight (Rom. 8:8) unless he is regenerated by the Holy Spirit (John 3:1–8). From God's standpoint, which is the only true standpoint, natural man is incapable of goodness in thought, word, or deed, and thus cannot contribute anything to his salvation. He is in total rebellion against God.

When Calvinists speak of total depravity, they are confessing our hell-deserving demerit and corruption before God because of our original and actual sins. We can neither erase our demerit nor do anything to merit the saving favor of God. To grasp the full implications of this truth, we must understand five things that lie at the heart of what Scripture presents total depravity to mean.

DEVIANT INIQUITY

First, total depravity is *inseparable from iniquity.* Total depravity is the inevitable result of our sin, and sin is the inevitable result of our total depravity. You can't understand what total depravity is if you don't understand what sin is. The Bible tells us, "Sin is the transgression of the law" of God (1 John 3:4). Thus, sin is any failure to conform to the moral law of God in our actions, attitudes, or nature—either by doing or being what we should not do or be (sins of commission) or by not doing or not being what we should do or be (sins of omission). Sin is unrighteousness, and all unrighteousness is anti-God. In essence, sin is all that is in opposition to God. Sin defies God; it violates His character, His law, and His covenant. It fails, as Martin Luther put it, to "let God be God." Sin aims to dethrone God and strives to place someone or something else upon His rightful throne.

The Bible uses a variety of words for sin. Taken individually, they mean (1) to miss the mark God has established as our aim—that is, not to live to His glory; (2) to be irreligious and irreverent, which is to show the absence of righteousness; (3) to transgress the boundaries of God's law—that is, to violate His established limits; (4) to engage in iniquity—that is, to deviate from a right course, to show a lack of integrity, or to fail to do what He has commanded; (5) to disobey and rebel against God through a breach of trust or a conscious act of treachery; (6) to commit perversion by twisting one's mind against God; and (7) to commit abomination against God by performing acts particularly reprehensible to God.[8]

Every life—including yours and mine—has missed its target and is irreverent by nature. Every life has transgressed the lines of God's prohibitions and engages in iniquity. Every life has disobeyed the voice of God, has rebelled against Him, and is prone to commit perversion and abomination. Isaiah 53:6a says "all we like sheep have gone astray; we have turned every one to his own way," and Romans

3:23 says that "all have sinned, and come short of the glory of God."

Thus, total depravity means that we are lawbreakers at every turn. By nature, we never love God above all or our neighbors as ourselves. We are at "enmity against God" (Rom. 8:7), living in active, frenetic hostility toward Him, and we are "hateful, and hating one another" (Titus 3:3). We are always sinning, for our motives are never altogether pure.

PRIMARY INWARDNESS

Second, total depravity is *primarily inward*—an inwardness that stems from our profound and tragic fall in Adam. When we think of sin, we are prone to limit ourselves to outward actions such as murder, theft, assassination, cruelty, and anything else that is external and observable in human behavior. But the Bible is much more rigorous and far more radical. It looks not simply at what is outward, touched, and heard, it goes into the depths of human life and says that sin and depravity exist there, too—in our thoughts, our ambitions, our decisions, our motives, and our aspirations.

Jesus said that it is not what a man eats or touches that defiles him, but that which comes out from him that defiles him and affects all he thinks and does (Matt. 15:17–20). It is not so much that human actions or speech have missed the target; it is that the *heart of man* has missed the target. The very heart of man is unbelieving, selfish, covetous, sensuous, and always desiring to displace God Himself. Hence, the very desire to sin is sin. John Calvin put it this way: "According to the constitution of our nature, oil might be extracted from a stone sooner than we could perform a good work."[9]

Why is this? Why are we all so inwardly depraved? Why is it impossible for the natural man to produce any righteousness? To answer these questions, we must return to Paradise. There we were affected by Adam's sin in two ways. First, the guilt of his sin was imputed to us, so we are guilty sinners before God, as Paul tells us graphically in Romans 5:18a: "By the offence of one [man,] judgment came upon all men to condemnation." Second, we inherited the pollution of his sin, so we are corrupt sinners before God, conceived and born in iniquity, as David tells us graphically in Psalm 51:5: "Behold, I was shapen in iniquity; and in sin did my mother conceive me." Thus, we are depraved in our inner beings through our fall in Adam, both in our state of guilt and in our condition of pollution. Isaiah said that the best of our righteousness—that is, the best of our best—is as "filthy rags" before the holy God (Isa. 64:6). We are worse than we can imagine. Jeremiah 17:9 says, "The heart is deceitful above all things, and desperately wicked: who can know it?" Calvin declares that no one knows even 1 percent of his sin. And a common ancient proverb says, "If the best man's faults were written in his forehead, it would make him pull his hat over his eyes."[10]

We have two problems in God's sight: we have a bad record and we have a bad heart—and the second problem is by far the greater of the two. When we understand our inner depravity in scriptural terms (read Rom. 3:9–20), we see that this condition—known by the theological term *original sin*—is a far greater burden than our actual sins, for all our actual sins flow from the fountainhead of our original sin and our bad heart. We sin because we are internally depraved, not because we are externally deprived. That's why Calvin writes, "Every sin should convince us of the general truth of the corruption of our nature."[11]

When Paul got a glimpse of the depths of his depravity, he confessed that he was the "chief" sinner among mankind (1 Tim. 1:15). When John Bunyan saw just a bit of his inner depravity, he said that he would trade his heart with anyone in all of England.[12] Luther summarizes our problem well: "Original sin is in us like our beard. We are shaved today and look clean; tomorrow our beard has grown again, nor does it cease growing while we remain on earth. In like manner original sin cannot be extirpated from us; it springs up in us as long as we live."[13]

TRAGIC INCLUSIVENESS

Third, total depravity means that sin is *tragically inclusive*, i.e., it dreadfully impacts every part of us. There is something terribly wrong not only with who we are inwardly, but with every aspect of our being. No element of our personality is less affected by sin than any other. Our intellects, our consciences, our emotions, our ambitions, and our wills, which are the citadels of our souls, are all enslaved to sin by nature. That's why Jesus complained, "I would have gathered thy children . . . and ye would not" (Matt. 23:37).

Total depravity is not absolute depravity. Calvinists have always taken pains to state that total depravity does not mean men are animals or devils, or that they are as depraved as they could be or will be. This world is not hell. Total depravity does not mean that an unbeliever is wholly evil in everything he does, but rather that nothing he does is ever wholly good. Man is not so far fallen that he has lost all awareness of God or conscience; by God's common goodness, he is still capable of showing domestic affection, doing civic good, and performing his duties as a citizen. He is capable of great heroism, of great physical courage, and of great acts of self-denial. Yet he is a corrupt sinner in every aspect of his nature, and as such, he is utterly incapable of performing any spiritual good in the eyes of God.

Total depravity means that when God scrutinizes the human heart, affections, conscience, will, or any part of the body, He finds every part damaged and polluted by sin. Apart from saving grace, every part is alienated from God and actively pursuing sin. If the Spirit teaches us this experientially, we will understand Jonathan Edwards' confession: "When I look into my heart, and take a view of my wickedness, it looks like an abyss infinitely deeper than hell."[14] As D. Martyn Lloyd-Jones writes, "When a man truly sees himself, he knows that nobody can say anything about him that is too bad."[15]

SLAVISH INABILITY

Fourth, total depravity spells *inability*. It means we are active "sin-aholics" by nature. There is no thought, no word, no act, and no area of human life that is not affected by sin. Romans 6:16 says that we are by nature slaves of sin: "Know ye not, that to whom ye yield yourselves servants to obey, his servants [or slaves] ye are to whom ye obey; whether of sin unto death, or of obedience unto righteousness?" Consider this literally for a moment. A slave was his master's property. A slave had no time, property, or wealth of his own. He had no single moment of which he could say, "This moment is mine; my master has no rights over this moment." He was always his master's property; his every movement, his every talent, his every possession was entirely his master's. So, Paul says, you were by nature the slaves of sin (Rom. 6:16). Sin was your master. Sin lorded itself over you. Sin was in control. And yet, sin gave the impression all the while that you were free and in charge of your own destiny.

Total depravity thus entails moral inability. In ourselves, we are unable to do anything about our condition. We are spiritually impotent by nature, unable and unwilling to save ourselves. We cannot appreciate the Christian faith and we are powerless to work toward our conversion. "We can do nothing but sin,"

Calvin says, "until the Holy Spirit forms a new will within us."[16] No matter how much the natural man is urged by the law or the gospel to believe in Christ and turn from sin, he is "not able, by his own strength. to convert himself, or to prepare himself thereunto" (Westminster Confession, 9.3). Charles Hodge puts it poignantly: "The rejection of the gospel is as clear proof of moral depravity as inability to see the sun at noon is proof of blindness."[17] The natural man may want to be free of some sin and of the consequences of sin; he may even expend some effort in that direction. But he is too much a slave to it. He is not simply "going lost" or "dying," he *is* lost and *is* dead in trespasses and sins (Eph. 2:1).

Every person in the world is by nature a slave of sin. The world, by nature, is held in sin's grip. What a shock to our complacency—that everything of us by nature belongs to sin. Our silences belong to sin, our omissions belong to sin, our talents belong to sin, our actions belong to sin. Every facet of our personalities belongs to sin; it owns us and dominates us. We are its servants.

Total depravity is active in us. It is not simply the absence of righteousness, but the presence of corruption. Our depravity is enormously creative and inventive, ever devising new ways of violating God's will. It is a growing cancer within us—a rampant, productive, energetic, and self-propagating entity. It is fire out of control—a living, fierce, powerful force. In the horrors of the Holocaust, the monstrosity of modern-day terrorism, and the dreadful headlines of our daily newspapers, we are shown what our corrupt, active human nature is capable of, given the requisite conditions, if God leaves us to ourselves.

My dear unsaved friend, you are a "sin-aholic." You are a slave this very hour, a slave in your bed tonight—even when you pray. And you will be a slave until God's almighty power raises you from spiritual death, opens your blind eyes, unstops your deaf ears, and breaks the chains of depravity that enwrap you. And even then, until your last breath, you will battle against your addiction to sin, for we remain recovering sin-aholics to the end (Rom. 7:24).

DEADLY ISSUE

Finally, total depravity is a stark reminder of the final issue of sin: *the wages of sin is death* (Rom. 6:23). If you serve sin, you will receive the wages of sin. This is a moral universe. We live and move and have our being in God. Every breath of our lives is in His hands. Sow a seed of sin and you will reap the harvest of judgment. Sow the wind of unbelief and you will reap the whirlwind of destruction. "It is appointed unto men once to die, but after this the judgment" (Heb. 9:27). Judgment is always imminent. There is a moment when God sends in the bill and we have to render account.

The fact of physical death is utterly unavoidable. You and I have a unilateral appointment with death in God's eternal record book. The one absolute certainty about every one of us is the rending apart of our bodies and our souls. But beyond that is spiritual death—the rending apart of our soul from God, so that we lose the image of God and communion with Him, and abide under His curse. Above all, there is eternal death—the rending of soul and body from God forever without any alleviation from common grace. Eternal death is hell—the solemn, awesome reality that the book of Revelation calls "the lake which burneth with fire and brimstone . . . the second death" (21:8). Hell is the cesspool of the universe. It is that appalling cosmic incinerator into which one day God Almighty will gather the refuse of the world, that place that is ever under His undiluted wrath, where the worm of memory dies not, where the false prophet is, where the Dragon and the Beast are (see Rev. 12–13), and where everyone will be unless they deal with their sin. Hell is the logic behind sin. It is the divine response to persistent impenitence and final disobedience. Pollution is the forerunner of perdition. And hell is what God ultimately thinks of impenitent sin and total depravity.

Calvinism teaches the sinfulness of sin and depravity.[18] But it declares that sin and depravity are anomalies. In the final analysis, they are beyond all reason. They cannot be depicted as too heinous and dastardly. They represent the height of spiritual stupidity and insanity. The magnitude of our sin and depravity exhibits the magnitude of our need for God's gospel way of salvation.

Calvinism humbles us and exalts God. Ian Hamilton concludes:

Calvinism challenges the residual pride in human hearts. We are naturally and natively far more comfortable with Arminianism, which allows us to make a contribution to our salvation. To be confronted by the truth of our total inability is deeply humbling, but it is the truth of God's own word, not a notion that John Calvin concocted in Geneva. Becoming persuaded of this and casting ourselves alone on God's mercy in Christ knocks (in large measure) the pride out of us and teaches us to live as men and women who glory in the God of grace. This is simply another way of saying that Calvinism puts God where he belongs and puts us where we belong. This is the test of authentic, biblical Christianity.[19]

DISCUSSION QUESTIONS

1. What is Arminianism and why was it rejected as being unbiblical?

2. What is the doctrine of total depravity?

3. How would you explain the doctrine of total depravity to a person who is not a Christian?

NOTES

1. E-mailed sermon of April 1, 2008, p. 1.

2. Cornelis P. Venema, *But for the Grace of God: An Exposition of the Canons of Dort* (Grand Rapids: Reformed Fellowship, 1994), 14–17. I am indebted to Geoffrey Thomas in this chapter and the next for sermons he preached on depravity and election many years ago.

3. Abraham Kuyper, *Lectures on Calvinism* (Grand Rapids: Eerdmans, 1987); H. Henry Meeter, *The Basic Ideas of Calvinism*, 6th ed. (Grand Rapids: Baker, 1990); Leonard H. Coppes, *Are Five Points Enough? The Ten Points of Calvinism* (Manassas, Va.: Reformation Educational Foundation, 1980); Ernest C. Reisinger and D. Matthew Allen, *Beyond Five Points* (Cape Coral, Fla.: Founders Press, 2003).

4. Richard Muller, "How Many Points?" *Calvin Theological Journal*, 28, no. 2 (1993): 433.

5. For books on the five points of Calvinism, see Horatius Bonar, et al, *The Five Points of Calvinism* (Evansville, Ind.: Sovereign Grace Book Club, 1962); Ronald Cammenga and Ronald Hanko, *Saved by Grace: A Study of the Five Points of Calvinism*, 2nd ed. (Grandville, Mich.: Reformed Free Publishing Association, 2002); Robert L. Dabney, *The Five Points of Calvinism* (Harrisonburg, Va.: Sprinkle, 1982); Herman Hanko, Homer C. Hoeksema, and Gise J. Van Baren, *The Five Points of Calvinism* (Grand Rapids: Reformed Free Publishing Association, 1976); Bastian Kruithof, *The High Points of Calvinism* (Grand Rapids: Baker, 1949); Edwin H. Palmer, *The Five Points of Calvinism* (Grand Rapids: Baker, 1972); William Parks, *Sermons on the Five Points of Calvinism* (London: Sovereign Grace Union, 1929); Duane Edward Spencer,

TULIP: The Five Points of Calvinism in the Light of Scripture (Grand Rapids: Baker, 1979); William D. Smith, *What is Calvinism?* (Philadelphia: Presbyterian Board of Publication, 1908); David N. Steele, Curtis C. Thomas, and S. Lance Quinn, *The Five Points of Calvinism: Defined, Defended, Documented*, 2nd ed. (Philipsburg, N.J.: P&R, 2004); and Ben A. Warburton, *Calvinism* (Grand Rapids: Eerdmans, 1955).

[6] For a study on the late usage of the acronym TULIP, see Kenneth J. Stewart, "What Future for the Five Points of Calvinism?" (a paper delivered for the Evangelical Theological Society annual meeting, 2006).

[7] R. C. Sproul says that changing these terms "seems such a waste of tulips that we will stay with the original acrostic and simply labor the clarifications necessary" (*Grace Unknown: The Heart of Reformed Theology* [Grand Rapids: Baker, 1997], 188).

[8] Millard Erickson, *Christian Theology* (Grand Rapids: Baker, 2002), 586–593.

[9] Inst., 3.14.5.

[10] *Select Proverbs, Italian, Spanish, French, English, British, etc., Chiefly Moral* (London, 1707), 111.

[11] John Calvin, *Commentaries of Calvin* (Grand Rapids: Eerdmans, 1950ff.) on Psalm 51:5. (Hereafter the format *Commentary* on Psalm 51:5 will be used.)

[12] Cf. John Bunyan, *Grace Abounding to the Chief of Sinners* (Choteau, Mont.: Old Paths Gospel Press, n.d.), 88–95.

[13] Quoted in John Blanchard, *The Complete Gathered Gold* (Darlington, England: Evangelical Press, 2006), 144.

[14] Quoted in John Blanchard, *Gathered Gold* (Welwyn, England: Evangelical Press, 1984), 64.

[15] D. Martyn Lloyd-Jones, *Studies in the Sermon on the Mount* (Grand Rapids: Eerdmans, 1984), 58.

[16] John Calvin, *Hebrews and the Epistles of Peter*, trans. William B. Johnston, ed. David W. and Thomas F. Torrance (Grand Rapids: Eerdmans, 1963), 223–224.

[17] Charles Hodge, *An Exposition of the Second Epistle to the Corinthians* (New York: Robert Carter & Brothers, 1862), 84.

[18] The Calvinist Puritans excelled at expounding the heinousness of sin. See Jeremiah Burroughs, *The Evil of Evils* (Morgan, Pa.: Soli Deo Gloria, 1995); Ralph Venning, *The Plague of Plagues* (London: Banner of Truth Trust, 1965); Thomas Watson, *The Mischief of Sin* (Morgan, Pa.: Soli Deo Gloria, 1994); and Thomas Goodwin, "An Unregenerate Man's Guiltiness Before God," in *The Works of Thomas Goodwin*, vol. 10 (Grand Rapids: Reformation Heritage Books, 2006).

[19] Ian Hamilton, "Is Calvinism Hard-hearted?" *Presbyterian Network* (Spring, 2007), 9.

CHAPTER 5

UNCONDITIONAL
ELECTION

To either deny sovereign election or to store it away in some theological closet on shelves labeled "good for nothing" or "harmful" is to rob the people of God of the fullest view of God's glory and to limit the church's worship to the realms of human logic.[1]

—ROBERT B. SELPH

nconditional election is one of the most controversial doctrines in Holy Scripture. Some think it is a doctrine that Satan uses to thwart the church's evangelistic zeal. Others, including Calvinists, consider it a most comforting biblical truth, one without which God would be deprived of His rightful glory in the salvation of sinners. To those who minimize the scriptural record of man's total depravity, election is the primary reason people are in hell. To Calvinists, who accept the Bible's teaching of total depravity, election is the primary reason people are in heaven.[2] Such Calvinists can say with Charles H. Spurgeon: "I believe the doctrine of election, because I am quite sure that if God had not chosen me I would never have chosen him; and I am sure he chose me before I was born, or else he never would have chosen me afterward."[3]

Regardless of their approach to election, few dispute that the Bible teaches it. The debate is not about the reality of election, but the grounds on which some people are elected to salvation and others are not. Basically, there are three views:

• *Merited election.* Pelagianism teaches that God elects those who are good. Election is more of a debt that God owes to good people than a gift He graciously bestows on them. A British monk named Pelagius (ca. 350–ca. 425) popularized the idea that God elects people on the basis of personal righteousness. Pelagianism is diametrically opposite to what Paul teaches in Titus 3:5–7 and is so extreme that it needs no more explanation.

• *Conditional election.* Arminianism teaches that God elects those who are depraved but who He foresees will believe in Christ for salvation. Though people are sinful, they can meet God's condition of believing in Jesus Christ by exercising their free wills.

• *Unconditional election.* Calvinism teaches that God elects those who are totally depraved and are not able to exercise their fallen wills to believe in Christ. God elects them on the basis of His sovereign good pleasure, conquering their wills so that they are made willing to exercise faith in Christ for salvation.

The real debate, then, is between Arminian conditional election and Calvinistic unconditional election. As Sam Storms writes, "The question reduces to this: Does God elect people because they believe in the Lord Jesus Christ [Arminianism], or does God elect people in order that they shall believe in Christ [Calvinism]?"[4]

Conditional election fails on three counts.[5] First, it fails to recognize the primacy of God's election in salvation. According to the Bible, the verb *elect* means "to select, or choose out." The biblical doctrine of election is that long before the foundations of the world were laid, God freely chose to save a number of individuals in Christ (Rev. 7:9–17). He ordained the means by which they would be saved (Eph. 1:4–5), despite their sin. He determined to redeem, bring to faith and repentance, justify, sanctify, preserve, and glorify the elect in and through Jesus Christ (Rom. 8:28–39; 2 Thess. 2:13–14; 2 Tim. 1:9–10), while determining to leave others who persist in unbelief to perish in their sin (Rom. 9). Election is unconditional since God did not choose the elect because of any intrinsic goodness in them (1 Cor. 1:27–31) or because He knew that they would believe one day.

Second, conditional election fails to recognize both the extent of our depravity and the extent of God's sovereignty and grace. By doing so, it robs God of His absolute sovereignty and glory. Unconditional election is a necessary corollary of the doctrines of total depravity and of God's sovereignty and grace. If we are as depraved as the Bible says we are, our salvation cannot originate with us. We are by nature "dead in trespasses and sins" (Eph. 2:1). Our only hope is in a sovereign, electing, loving, fatherly God, who gave His own Son to suffer and die for the elect, for we are all accountable for our sin and deserving of God's eternal wrath.

Without election, no one would be saved. Spurgeon summarizes this well: "From the Word of God I gather that damnation is all of man, from top to bottom, and salvation is all of grace, from first to last. He that perishes chooses to perish; but he that is saved is saved because God has chosen to save him."[6] In other words, God gets all the glory in salvation, but man gets all the blame in damnation.

Third, conditional election really saves no one. In the end, it destroys men, because it bases salvation, at least in part, upon depraved human beings. Unconditional election, on the other hand, does not destroy men but saves them; it is our friend, not our enemy. It does not keep out of heaven people who otherwise would be there, but it brings to heaven people who otherwise never would be welcome there. The wonder is not that God justly rejects some sinners but that He graciously saves any sinners at all. "We may better praise God that he saves any than charge him with injustice because he saves so few," says Augustus Strong.[7] Who can fathom the mystery that God elects sinners like us, not because of our virtues, but in spite of our vices? As J. C. Ryle says, "The believer who knows his own heart will ever bless God for election."[8]

The Bible explains unconditional election in various places, most notably in Romans 8–9 and Ephesians 1. We should carefully study these great, classic chapters of Scripture. In the exposition of election, however, shorter portions of Scripture are often bypassed. Let us look at one such portion—the opening two verses of Peter's first epistle:

> Peter, an apostle of Jesus Christ, to the strangers scattered throughout Pontus, Galatia, Cappadocia, Asia, and Bithynia, elect according to the foreknowledge of God the Father, through sanctification of the Spirit, unto obedience and sprinkling of the blood of Jesus Christ: Grace unto you, and peace, be multiplied.

Peter teaches five major truths about election in these verses:

SINNERS ARE CHOSEN BY
THE FATHER'S FOREKNOWLEDGE

The elect are chosen "according to the foreknowledge of God the Father," Peter says. By "foreknowledge," Peter is not simply referring to God's intellect and omniscience, or to His knowledge of future events, including His awareness that certain people will believe. William Perkins writes, "We are not elected . . . either for our faith, or according to our faith, but to our faith; that is, elected that we might believe."[9] Peter is speaking here of *decretal* foreknowledge, of God's determination of whom He would graciously save from just condemnation. God's foreknowledge is inseparable from His sovereign plan and purposes (Acts 2:23), including His predestination of sinners to be conformed to Christ. As Romans 8:29a says, "For whom he did foreknow, he also did predestinate to be conformed to the image of his Son."

God's election is neither impersonal nor capricious. We know this is so because, in Scripture, the idea of knowledge is often more affectionate than cerebral, and this is particularly true of God's knowledge. For God to truly *know* is for God to truly *love*. In Amos 3:2, God says to Israel, "You only have I known of all the families of the earth." That does not mean God was ignorant of what was happening in Babylon or Egypt. God knows everything in the world, including every sparrow that falls. But God's knowledge is inseparable from His special, paternal love to His chosen people. That love, in turn, is inseparable from His selection and approval. That is why Christ, though omniscient, can say to impenitent unbelievers on Judgment Day, "I never knew you: depart from me, ye that work iniquity" (Matt. 7:23). Of course, He knows all about impenitent unbelievers; He knows them exhaustively, but He does not know them affectionately.

God's election of His people is His seal that He loves them. Because He elects them, He will cherish them in their Savior, Jesus Christ, who is so in love with them that He calls them His bride. Moreover, having gone to the cross to die for His bride, Jesus takes all of her liabilities upon Himself. God's foreknowledge of His people, then, is like a man's love for his wife. God's foreknowledge means that He is so passionately and intimately in love with His people that He offers His own Son to go to Calvary for them.

Thus, God the Father elects His people on the basis of His eternal, overwhelming, sovereign affection for them. Why did He love them? Because He chose to do so. Sovereign, unchangeable love is the ultimate joy and reality of the universe. It is the rock of God's redeeming grace. We cannot get beyond that sovereign love to something else. Love is the ultimate reality of God Himself. God is love.

God's foreknowledge means that God has always been in love with His people. He has loved the elect from all eternity. Just as a Bible-believing Christian cannot conceive of God not existing, not being eternal, or not being triune, so he cannot conceive of God not being in love with His people and not exercising that love through His gracious plan of salvation. Henry Law says, "Eternal love devised the plan; eternal wisdom drew the model; eternal grace comes down to build it."[10]

God's love is voluntary, discriminatory, and gracious. But oh, what glory to realize that this is the way God has always been! He has always loved His bride, the church, and has always been intensely passionate about her salvation. Dear believer, let this amazing truth sink deeply into your soul: God chose us because He has *always* foreknown us, meaning He has always loved us.

SINNERS ARE CHOSEN TO HOLINESS THROUGH THE SPIRIT'S SANCTIFICATION

The elect are called to holiness through the Spirit's sanctifying work. Peter says this, affirming that sinful, depraved people cannot enter into the presence of a holy God and live a holy life unless God, through His Spirit, sanctifies them. Peter says the Spirit does this work of sanctification in those whom the Father elects. The original Greek here indicates that holiness is an ongoing process rather than a one-time act. This ongoing work draws the elect to pursue holiness in dependence on the Spirit. So Peter says to believers later in this chapter, "As he which hath called you is holy, so be ye holy in all manner of conversation" (1 Peter 1:15).

In this, Peter refutes the greatest objection Arminians have about the doctrine of election. "If election is true, men can live as they please," Arminians say. "Therefore election is a dangerous and demoralizing doctrine. If people glean their assurance in any way from election, their holy walk with God will be compromised." Peter replies that the very purpose of election is to make men holy. God's election does not destroy moral effort; rather, as Spurgeon notes, "God's choice makes chosen men choice men."[11] And Thomas Watson says, "Sanctification is the earmark of Christ's elect sheep."[12]

God wants to make His elect holy, for He has predestined them to be conformed to the image of His Son. No one can then say, "I am elect; therefore, I do not need to be Christlike." Rather, as Peter implies, a believer should say, "Because I am elect, I cannot *avoid* being Christlike." God's elect cannot be at peace living in sin; they cannot live under sin's domination (Rom. 6:11–14) or live counter to Christ and His will. If we are elect, God has committed all the fullness and glory of His resources to make us like His Son. As surely as God has determined to save the elect from eternity past and provided the cross of Calvary as the means of that salvation, so He has determined that the effects of that salvation will be holiness, even into eternity.

SINNERS ARE CHOSEN IN CHRIST TO OBEDIENCE WITH THE SPRINKLING OF BLOOD

The Spirit sanctifies the elect to confirm that divine election is "unto obedience and sprinkling of the blood of Jesus Christ," Peter says. Believers were not chosen simply to receive gospel benefits but to be sprinkled with the blood of Christ. They were chosen to have the work and benefits of Christ applied to them so that they can live in obedience to God.

Peter alludes here to Exodus 24:3–8, in which Moses as God's servant confirmed the covenant between the Lord and Israel. Moses sprinkled the blood of sacrifice upon the people, symbolizing the sacrificial blood-shedding of the coming Messiah for the forgiveness of sin. With that act, the Israelites came to see themselves as the covenant people of God and pledged that they would obey Him in everything (Ex. 24:7). When Peter says that we have been chosen to be sprinkled with the blood, He is referring to the blood of Christ, the blood of the new covenant, which is shed for many for the remission of sins. Through Jesus' death, the elect are redeemed (1 Peter 1:18–19; cf. Heb. 9:18–28; 12:24). They are brought into covenant with almighty God to set their faith and hope in God and to obey Him (1 Peter 1:2, 21).

The blood of forgiveness is applied to believers' souls as a fruit of God's gracious election in Christ. Election in Christ and through His blood to obedience is a saving act of God. Election is the parent of faith, John Calvin says. If we are believers, we are elected to faith and salvation, elected to union with Christ, elected to adoption, and elected to participate in the great redemptive provision of God Himself. We have been chosen by God to be Abraham's seed, heirs of Abraham's promise. That promise, says Paul in Galatians 3:14b, is "that we might receive . . . the Spirit through faith." We are born again, we are forgiven, we are made God's children, we are kept by the power of God, and we are glorified—all because of our election in Christ. One day we shall see our Savior as He is. Christ will feed us and lead us by the river of living water at the throne of God. Our election in Christ offers us all the glory of salvation.

In sum, by the sovereign, loving foreknowledge of the Father we are elect to be sprinkled by the blood of Christ unto obedience and to holiness so that we may be conformed to the image of God the Son.

SINNERS ARE PERSONALLY CHOSEN

Peter says in his opening greeting, "Grace unto *you*, and peace, be multiplied" (1 Peter 1:2b; emphasis mine). "You" in 1 Peter 1:2b is specific, definite, and irreversible. There is intense personal choice here, which is never unjust.

The personal nature of election is evident even from the Old Testament, where God says in Malachi 1:2–3: "I loved Jacob. And I hated Esau" (Mal. 1:2–3; cfs Rom. 9:13). God loves one graciously, such as Jacob, and passes by another justly, such as the reprobate Esau. This is the essence of Calvin's view of predestination, which includes both election and reprobation. Calvin teaches that God's election is always sovereign and gracious; none of the elect deserves to be elect and to enter into heaven. At the same time, God's reprobation is always sovereign and just; none of the reprobate will be unjustly damned to hell.[13]

The personal nature of God's election is warm, paternal, and relational. God treats His millions of children as if each were His only child. The minuteness of His loving, fatherly concern is staggering. The hairs of our heads are all numbered. Our names are engraved on the palms of Jehovah's hands and carried in the heart of the Savior, the Lord Jesus. He whispers our blood-bought names into the ears of His Father in heaven as He makes intercession for us.

Personal election is an incredible comfort in today's impersonal, computerized society. Many people feel lonely and insignificant, like creatures clinging desperately to a little planet in a vast universe. But the believing Calvinist finds his identity in the infinite God of this vast universe. He confesses with the psalmist, "The LORD is my shepherd; I shall not want" (Ps. 23:1). He who has chosen us graciously will never abandon us. All things will work out for our good (Rom. 8:28–39).

No Calvinist who has a personal relationship with the God of unconditional election ever need say, "No one cares; I do not matter." Rather, God grants him to say, "God cares for me so much that He has given me His own Son. He loves *me* and gave Himself for *me*" (Gal. 2:20). How wondrous to confess that "Christ gave Himself for me, meeting all the conditions of God's justice for me. He obeyed the law perfectly on my behalf in active obedience, loving God above all and His neighbor as Himself for thirty-three years in this world. For me, Christ became incarnate; for me, He walked perfectly in this world; for me, He suffered immense agony and cruel rejection; for me, He did not come down from the cruel tree, because I was on His heart as He hung under the curse of God. He fully paid the penalty of my sin, even to death, in passive obedience. For me, He declared that salvation is complete (John 19:30). Now He who rose for me lives to make intercession for me" (Rom. 8:34; Heb. 7:25).

How intensely personal is God's election. It involves the great heart of the living God.

SINNERS ARE CHOSEN TO BE ADOPTED INTO A LARGE FAMILY

"Grace unto *you*, and peace, *be multiplied*," says 1 Peter 1:2 (emphasis mine). God has elected believers to be part of a great, invisible church chosen to everlasting life. Peter's "you" is not ultimately singular but wonderfully plural. It refers, first, to the strangers of verse 1, who are scattered throughout Pontus, Galatia, Cappadocia, Asia, and Bithynia. But it also refers to the glorious invisible church, the vast throng that no one can number (Rev. 7:9).

Heaven will not be thinly populated. The living seed of Abraham will be as numerous as the sand on the seashores and the stars in the heavens (Gen. 15:5). Election declares the expansive generosity of God, not His stinginess.

The election of millions of brothers and sisters means that believers will share eternal glory in an incredibly diverse, large family. God's vast election assures us that heaven will be a vast concourse of communication. Heaven will teem with relationships, first with Christ and the triune God, but also with fellow believers and the holy angels.

In addition to the preceding five truths about election drawn from 1 Peter 1:1–2, at least two other aspects of this doctrine bear mentioning:

SINNERS CAN BE ASSURED OF THEIR ELECTION

By means of election, God assures His children that they are adopted into His family and belong to Him. That is why Peter counsels believers to "give diligence to make your calling and election sure" (2 Peter 1:10).

Peter does not deny that our election can be obscured. The people to whom he is writing are characterized as elect according to God's love. But they are also strangers in the world, "scattered throughout Pontus, Galatia, Cappadocia, Asia, and Bithynia" (1 Peter 1:1). They are scattered and stateless; they have no citizenship, no permanent residence. When things go awry in the world, these elect are persecuted and in danger of losing their lives. So here is the paradox: they are loved eternally by God as His dear children, yet they are aliens and strangers in the world.

The New Testament reminds us repeatedly of this paradox. John says to God's adopted sons, "the world knoweth us not, because it knew him not" (1 John 3:1a). Just as Jesus' election by the Father ("mine elect, in whom my soul delighteth," Isa. 42:1) meant earthly poverty, degradation, dereliction, death, and the tomb, so His followers must often walk through this world as suffering strangers. Their status as elected children of God is not impressive to the world. Thus, the election of believers is often obscured by lowly conditions.

How do we know whether we are God's elect? We know it through faith, by having a vital relationship with Jesus Christ. In Christ and His promises in His Word, we find assurance of our election. As 1 John repeatedly tells us, when we possess Christ in His Word, desire Him for His own sake, know Him in our souls, yearn for Him in our walk of life, and love those who love Him, we know that we have passed from death to life as God's elect. Ultimately, then, Christ is our assurance of election. As Calvin writes: "If we have been chosen in Christ, we shall not find assurance of our election in ourselves; and not even in God the Father, if we conceive of him as severed from his Son. Christ, then, is the mirror wherein we must, and without self-deception may, contemplate our own election."[14]

Is Christ the mirror in which you see your election? Do you believe in Christ as your only hope for salvation? Do you see beauty in Christ, finding Him to be the altogether lovely One? Do you desire Christ for His own sake, not merely for the sake of benefits, such as heaven? Oh, then you have Him and the seal of His election. You are the elect of God, for the elect are known by their fruits (Matt.

7:20), and the crowning fruit is to know Jesus Christ, whom to know is eternal life (John 17:3). If you can say, "Less than Jesus would not satisfy me, and more is not needed because more than all in Him I find," you are elect, for that is what saving faith believes. As Ernest Kevan writes, "Nobody ever came to Christ because he knew he was one of the elect: he came because he needed Christ."[15] The great sign of our election is this soul dependence on Christ.

We are not granted assurance of our election by disputing our election. We are assured of our election by the fruits of election that focus us on Christ. In other words, we must focus on repentance and faith in order to come to assurance of election. As Joseph Alleine writes, "Prove your conversion, and then never doubt your election."[16] And William Gurnall says we may know we are elect by a work of grace in us as certainly as if we had stood by God's elbow when He wrote our names in the Book of Life.[17]

Election, then, always brings us back to Christ. Faith in Christ is both the fruit and the confirmation of election. God chooses the elect "in him" (Eph. 1:4), so we must never think of election apart from Christ. As John Blanchard says, "A Christian has been selected to live; to live essentially in Christ, to live effectively for Christ, and to live eternally with Christ."[18]

SINNERS ARE AFFECTED PASTORALLY BY THE GRACE AND PEACE ELECTION BRINGS

Grace and peace, flowing out of a sense of God's electing love, work themselves out pastorally in several ways:

• *Humility.* Rather than promoting pride and elitism, election is a profoundly humbling doctrine for believers. It keeps us from trying to reverse roles with God (Rom. 9:6–23). It persuades us to let God be God by teaching us there are some things that God has not revealed to us because they are not good for us to know, such as who is elect and who is reprobate (Deut. 29:29) or what tomorrow might bring (James 4:14). Election teaches us not to occupy ourselves with matters too difficult for us (Ps. 131).

Election also humbles us by making us realize that we owe everything to God's grace. If our eyes have been opened, we see that our salvation is entirely due to the sovereign love and pity of our God, and not to any merit of our own. Electing grace initiates our salvation, accomplishes it, and preserves it. Peter says in verse 5 that we are "kept by the power of God." Thus, we can boast of nothing. "A 'proud Calvinist' is an oxymoron, a contradiction in terms," Robert Peterson notes.[19]

Dear believer, in electing you, God has given you everything. He has given you His Son, and through Him a new heart, a new status, and a new life. Humble yourself quietly before your electing God, remembering that you owe everything to Him.

• *Encouragement.* Election is profoundly encouraging and comforting for believers. It tells us that God chose us rather than that we chose Him (John 15:16), and that He chose us even when He knew all about our sin. He knew our personalities, our flaws, our hypocrisy, our depression, and our coldness, and yet He loved us and determined to make us like Christ.

Think of Peter, whom Christ knew so intimately. Jesus knew that one night Peter would warm his hands by a fire and swear that he had never known Christ. He knew that one day Peter would stumble again in trying to compromise the gospel in Paul's presence. He knew Peter would struggle with hypocrisy all his life. Yet Christ still chose Peter, setting His love on such a sinner.

Dear believer, Christ continues to choose sinners. That is good news. But the greatest news of all is that Christ chose you and me, knowing our entire life ahead of time and knowing how disobedient we would be. How encouraging this electing love is to help us press on and to be "stedfast, unmoveable, always abounding in the work of the Lord" (1 Cor. 15:58b). Election does not discourage us from well-doing, writes Calvin, but makes us "devote ourselves to the pursuit of good as the appointed goal of election" (Eph. 1:4).[20]

• *Confidence.* Election compels evangelism, for all the elect must be saved by the Word brought to them. When Paul feared to speak in Corinth, God sent a messenger to assure him: "Be not afraid, but speak, and hold not thy peace: for I am with thee, and no man shall set on thee to hurt thee: for I have much people in this city" (Acts 18:9b–10). What an encouragement this was for Paul and for us today to spread the gospel.

We do not know how many people God has elected in our cities. We trust there are many. But many or few, they are the Lord's, and He has given us means to find them. So we must faithfully pray, speak, and visit people, always abounding in Christ's work and always ready to give a reason for the hope that is in us to anyone who asks (1 Peter 3:15).

Election gave courage to the great Calvinist missionaries of the past to press on with the Lord's work, even in danger and self-sacrifice, because they were confident that the Lord would bring in His chosen ones. Election gave courage to David Brainerd, William Carey, John Elias, Adoniram Judson, John Paton, and a host of missionaries who gave their lives for the gathering in of the elect. They believed, as Blanchard says, that "in the Bible, election and evangelism meet with joined hands, not clenched fists" (Acts 13:44–49).[21]

What courage election still brings to evangelism today. It makes us bold for Christ, removing our fears, our shyness, and our indifference. It drives us to prayer, confident that the elect are in God's hands, and He will use evangelism to draw them in. And it makes us patient, reminding us that while evangelism is an urgent work because sinners are dying and going to hell every day, it is not a desperate work, for God, in His way and in His time, will gather in all of His elect.

• *Joy and praise.* J. I. Packer calls the joy election brings to believers their "family secret."[22] Believers have a joyful security that is incomprehensible to the world. For true believers, John Piper says, election is not "a doctrine to be argued about, but a doctrine to be enjoyed. It's not designed for disputes; it's designed for missions. It's not meant to divide people (though it will); it's meant to make them compassionate, kind, humble, meek, and forgiving," and to fill them with joy (Eph. 1:3–14).[23]

Election glorifies God (Eph. 1:6, 12). "The end of our election is that we might show forth the glory of God in every way,"[24] Calvin says. According to the Canons of Dort, the final glorification of the elect is for the demonstration of God's mercy and for the praise of His glorious grace (I, 7).[25] Election makes us praise God for our salvation. As Sinclair Ferguson writes, "Until we have come to the place where we can sing about election with a full heart, we have not grasped the spirit of the New Testament teaching."[26] Election assures us that God is the seeker rather than the sought; thus, all the praise belongs to Him. As C. S. Lewis says: "Amiable agnostics will talk cheerfully about man's search for God. For me, they might as well talk about the mouse's search for a cat. . . . God closed in on me."[27] As Josiah Conder wrote in 1836:

> 'Tis not that I did choose thee, for, Lord, that could not be;
> This heart would still refuse thee, hadst thou not chosen me.

Thou from the sin that stained me hast cleansed and set me free;
Of old thou hast ordained me, that I should live to thee.

'Twas sov'reign mercy called me and taught my op'ning mind;
The world had else enthralled me, to heav'nly glories blind.
My heart owns none before thee, for thy rich grace I thirst;
This knowing, if I love thee, thou must have loved me first.[28]

Election is the Bible's teaching, not man's. It promotes humility, not pride; encouragement, not depression; confidence in evangelism, not paralyzing fear; holiness, not license; assurance, not presumption; God's glory, not our own.[29] Oh, that election would make us cry out with the apostle Paul, "For of him, and through him, and to him, are all things: to whom be glory for ever" (Rom. 11:36).

DISCUSSION QUESTIONS

1. What is the doctrine of unconditional election?

2. What are the biblical reasons for believing the doctrine of unconditional election?

3. How does the doctrine of unconditional election help form Christian character?

4. How does the doctrine of unconditional election encourage evangelism?

NOTES

[1] Quoted in John Blanchard, *Sifted Silver* (Darlington, England: Evangelical Press, 1975), 75.

[2] Sam Storms, http://www.enjoyinggodministries.com/article/what-is-election

[3] Charles H. Spurgeon, *C.H. Spurgeon Autobiography, Vol. I: The Early Years, 1834–1859* (Edinburgh: Banner of Truth Trust, 1962), 166.

[4] Sam Storms, *Chosen for Life: The Case for Divine Election* (Wheaton, Ill.: Crossway, 2007), 22.

[5] See Iain D. Campbell, "Witness to History," *Tabletalk*, 25, no. 3 (March 2001): 12–13.

[6] Quoted in John Blanchard, *The Complete Gathered Gold* (Darlington, England: Evangelical Press, 2006), 161.

[7] Augustus Strong, *Systematic Theology* (Philadelphia: Griffith & Rowland Press, 1909), 785.

[8] J. C. Ryle, *Expository Thoughts on Luke* (Edinburgh: Banner of Truth Trust, 1998), 254 (on Luke 18:1–8).

[9] Quoted in Blanchard, *The Complete Gathered Gold*, 163.

[10] Henry Law, *"Christ is All": The Gospel in the Pentateuch* (Stoke-on-Trent, U.K.: Tentmaker Publications, 2005), 253.

[11] Charles H. Spurgeon, *Cheque Book of the Bank of Faith* (Ross-shire, U.K.: Christian Focus, 1996), 240.

[12] Quoted in Blanchard, *The Complete Gathered Gold*, 164.

[13] Cf. Fred Klooster, *Calvin's Doctrine of Predestination* (Grand Rapids: Baker, 1961), 29–87.

[14] Inst., 3.24.5.

[15] Quoted in Blanchard, *The Complete Gathered Gold*, 161.

[16] Joseph Alleine, *An Alarm to the Unconverted* (Edinburgh: Banner of Truth Trust, 1978), 30.

[17] Quoted in Blanchard, *The Complete Gathered Gold*, 160, 164.

[18] Blanchard, *The Complete Gathered Gold*, 160.

[19] Robert A. Peterson, *Election and Free Will* (Phillipsburg, N.J.: P&R, 2007), 176.

[20] Inst., 3.23.12.

[21] Blanchard, *The Complete Gathered Gold*, 177.

[22] J. I. Packer, *Concise Theology* (Carol Stream, Ill.: Tyndale House, 1993), 150.

[23] John Piper, "Unconditional Election and the Invincible Purpose of God," sermon on Romans 9:6–13, http://www.desiringgod.org/ResourceLibrary/ScriptureIndex

[24] Quoted in Blanchard, *The Complete Gathered Gold*, 163.

[25] *Doctrinal Standards*, ed. Joel R. Beeke (Grand Rapids: Reformation Heritage Books, 1999), 98.

[26] Quoted in Blanchard, *The Complete Gathered Gold*, 161; cf. Sinclair B. Ferguson, *The Christian Life: A Doctrinal Introduction* (Edinburgh: Banner of Truth Trust, 1989), 115–130.

[27] Quoted in John Blanchard, *Gathered Gold* (Welwyn, England: Evangelical Press, 1984), 74.

[28] From the hymn "Tis Not That I Did Choose Thee" by Josiah Conder, 1836.

[29] See Richard D. Phillips, *What are Election and Predestination?* (Phillipsburg, N.J.: P&R, 2006), 9–18.

CHAPTER 6

THE EXTENT OF
THE ATONEMENT

The Arminians say, Christ died for all men. Ask them what they mean by it. Did Christ die so as to secure the salvation of all men? They say, "No, certainly not." We ask them the next question—did Christ die so as to secure the salvation of any man in particular? They answer, "No." They are obliged to admit this if they are consistent. They say, "No, Christ has died that any man may be saved if"—and then follow certain conditions of salvation. We say, then, we will just go back to the old statement—Christ did not die so as beyond a doubt to secure the salvation of anybody, did he? You must say "no"; you are obliged to say so, for you believe that even after a man has been pardoned, he may yet fall from grace, and perish. Now, who is it that limits the death of Christ? Why, you. . . . You are welcome to your atonement; you may keep it. We will never renounce ours for the sake of it. [1]

—CHARLES H. SPURGEON

$\mathcal{S}$ome Christians today are fond of saying, "I am a four-point Calvinist." They accept all of the TULIP acronym except limited atonement because they think it sounds too restrictive to say that Christ died only for the elect. "Christ died for everyone," they say, "and, with the Spirit's help, each person must accept Jesus Christ as Savior and Lord as an act of free will. When that occurs, that person is born again."

Basically, this is popularized Arminian theology, which the Synod of Dort argued against in the Second Head of the Canons, titled "The Death of Christ, and the Redemption of Men Thereby." Since the extent of the atonement was the most contentious issue debated at Dort[2] and is so pertinent to debates among Christians today, I will devote both this chapter and the next one to it. In exposing the faultiness of this line of thinking, I will examine, first, the centrality of the atonement; second, four positions in church history regarding the universality of the atonement; and third, the major theological problems of the Arminian view of the atonement. In the following chapter, I will show how a Calvinist view of the atonement is both biblical and more encouraging than many think, and I will answer some remaining objections to the Calvinist view.

THE CENTRALITY OF THE ATONEMENT

The Christian church always has recognized that the atonement, which Christ accomplished at the cross, is the central theme of the Christian message. To atone is to make "at one." Through Christ's atoning blood, a holy God and sinful men and women are reconciled. The atonement brings unity and fellowship between God the Holy One and man the sinner. This is the central doctrine of Christianity because Christianity is preeminently a religion of redemption.

Against the backdrop of the fall and our ensuing depravity, the gospel brings a message of reconciliation, offering a way of escape from sin and its destructive power and a way of entrance into a reconciled and fellowshiping relationship with God. This way is the way of the cross. God's way of reconciling Himself with sinners was through the redeeming sacrifice of Jesus Christ. Any definition of Christianity that does not have redemptive atonement at its core is fundamentally defective.

The atonement is rooted in the free and sovereign love of God. Think of John 3:16, where the work of Christ as the Priest who brings atonement is traced back to God's love for the world. If we were to ask the questions that come to mind in order, they would go like this: *Why am I saved?* Because I believe and trust in Christ. *Why am I saved through faith?* Because faith unites me with Christ, and in union with Him I receive all the blessings of His atoning work. *Why did Christ come to perform that atoning work?* Because this was God's commission to Him. *Why did God give Christ that commission?* Because of His love for sinners. Here we have reached the ultimate source of the blessings of the atonement; further into the mind and will of God we cannot go.

Up to this point, many Arminians agree with Calvinists. But then other questions arise: What is the place of the atonement in the overall plan of God for human redemption? For whom did Christ die—everyone? Is the atonement universal? What is its extent, or perhaps better, its intent, since the central issue is its purpose or design?[3] Or, as John Murray says: "On whose behalf did Christ offer himself a sacrifice? On whose behalf did he propitiate the wrath of God? Whom did he reconcile to God in the body of his flesh through death? Whom did he redeem from the curse of the law, from the guilt and power of sin, from the enthralling power and bondage of Satan? In whose stead and on whose behalf was he obedient unto death, even the death of the cross?"[4]

It is here that Arminians and Calvinists sharply disagree. In terms of salvation, Calvinists believe that Christ died only for the elect (while not denying the eternal, infinite value of Christ's work or denying that some nonsaving, indirect benefits from Christ's death accrue to unbelievers), whereas Arminians believe that He died for everyone universally.

FOUR VIEWS OF THE ATONEMENT'S EXTENT

There are at least four views of the extent of Christ's atonement. All but the first of these views grapple with the issue of limitation to Christ's atonement. Limited atonement is not a Calvinist invention, and neither is it an exclusively Calvinist dilemma. Anyone who takes seriously the Bible's message about hell and its inhabitants, as well as sin and its wages, must grapple with the question of limitation in some form when studying the death of Jesus Christ.

The first view is *unlimited universal redemption*. This view presumes complete universalism because it believes that God's intent was for Christ to die for all so that all will be saved. Universalism believes in the final restoration of all things to God and hence rejects the doctrine of an everlasting hell. This view was taught by several ancient church theologians, such as Clement of Alexandria (ca. 160–215) and his student, Origen (ca. 185–251). Origen even taught that the devils ultimately would be saved.

Though never popular among those who profess the teachings of Scripture, universalism has lived on throughout the centuries. In 1803, the Universalist Church of America said in its statement of faith: "We believe that there is one God, whose nature is Love . . . and who will finally restore the whole family of mankind to holiness and happiness."[5] By 1961, when the Universalist Church merged with many Unitarian churches to form the American Unitarian Universalist Association, it had close to four hundred congregations with a total membership of seventy thousand.

Universalism directly opposes Scripture, which speaks of hell more than two hundred times. Jesus, in particular, affirmed the doctrine of eternal hell (Matt. 12:32; 13:40–42, 49–50; 25:41, 46; Mark 9:44–48; Luke 12:4–5). No wonder few universalists regard Scripture as infallible or take it seriously. Most succumb to a kind of rationalism that transcends Scripture; they reason that divine love precludes everlasting punishment, regardless of what Scripture says.

The second view has been called *limited universal redemption*. This view teaches that the atonement is universal in design but limited in its accomplishment. The Trinity purposed the salvation of all through Christ's atoning death, but not all are saved in the end. The cross is not directly a satisfaction for sin; it only becomes so when a sinner believes in Christ for salvation. Though all are given sufficient grace to be able to believe the gospel, many refuse to believe it and so do not receive the benefits of the atonement.

This view, common to many evangelicals today, might be called *inconsistent* or *Arminian universalism*.[6] Jacob Arminius (1560–1609) regarded election and the atonement as being conditional on God's foreseeing who would believe. Raymond Blacketer provides an excellent summary of his views:

> For Arminius the work of Christ on the cross does not effect salvation (understood as propitiation, satisfaction or redemption) for any person or group; instead, it only makes salvation *possible*. The cross brings about a new legal situation in which God consequently has the right to enter into a new relationship to humanity, under new conditions that God is free to prescribe. The condition that he prescribes is faith; and it is up to the individual sinner to use the universal grace provided by God to take that step of faith. The determinative factor in salvation is the free choice of humanity, albeit assisted by cooperating grace.[7]

Arminius' followers, known as the Remonstrants, presented the following assertion to the Dutch government in their document "The Five Articles of the Remonstrants": "Jesus Christ, the Savior of the world, died for all men and for every man, so that he has obtained for them all, by his death on the cross,

redemption and the forgiveness of sins; yet . . . no one actually enjoys the forgiveness of sins, except the believer (John 3:16; 1 John 2:2)."[8] That is to say, salvation
depends on human acceptance of it. Arminians often picture salvation as a gift
offered to all men upon the merits of Christ's dying for them, but each individual
must reach out his hand of faith to accept it.

The third view is *hypothetical universalism*. This position, first proposed by
Moïse Amyraut (1596–1664) and known as Amyraldianism,[9] teaches that Christ
died hypothetically for all without exception, but divine grace and election have
ensured that only the elect will believe. Since God knew that all humankind was
so corrupt that no one would believe, He elected some to faith, to whom the
Holy Spirit grants faith and applies salvation. So the intent of the atonement differs from the application of salvation.

George Smeaton says Amyraldianism presents an incoherent system, for it
supposes "a double and a conflicting decree; that is, a general decree, in which
God was said to will the salvation of all, and a special decree, in which He was said
to will the salvation of the elect. To Christ also it ascribed a twofold and discor-
dant aim, viz. to satisfy for all men, and to satisfy merely for the elect."[10]

Both Amyraldianism and Arminianism maintain that Christ suffered for
mankind, not that He paid the penalty for sins. And they both teach, as Robert Letham says, "that this suffering does not intrinsically achieve what it was
intended to do since it is dependent on a response on the part of human beings
which, in very many cases, fails to materialize."[11] The difference between Amyraldianism and Arminianism is that in the former, the limitation is the choice of
God, while in the latter, the limitation is the choice of the one who believes. Iain
Murray says, "Traditional Reformed theology rejected this Amyraldian combination of the universal with the particular, holding that God had only one intent
and purpose in the death of his Son, the actual salvation of those for whom he
suffered."[12]

The fourth view is the Calvinist view of *limited* or *definite atonement*, which,
as codified by the Canons of Dort, "is the belief that the satisfaction rendered by
Christ on the cross was of infinite value and worth by virtue of Christ's incarnation but that its intended object was not sinners in general, or every individual,
but rather those whom God had elected from eternity."[13] The Father sent His
Son to the cross to pay for the sins of the elect, so that Christ died savingly and
personally for all of God's chosen people. His death was a voluntary (Ps. 40:7–8),

ransoming (Matt. 20:28), obedient (Rom. 5:19), vicarious (Rom. 6:23), expiatory (Heb. 10:10, 14), propitiatory (Rom. 3:25), reconciling (Rom. 5:10), redemptive (1 Peter 1:18–19), and victorious (Rom. 8:31–39) act that secured salvation for all those the Father had given Him. All of these words differ somewhat in meaning, but they all indicate that Christ's death is our salvation.

The doctrine of limited atonement is not simply a point of logic in the Calvinistic system of thought; it is an integral point of an exegetical understanding of the work of Christ. In terms of both intent and accomplishment, the extent of Christ's cross work is limited to those who will be saved. The death of Christ is not a provisional measure, but actually secures salvation; it does not just make sinners redeemable, but actually redeems.

Those who believed that redemption was designed for the elect included Augustine (354–430), Prosper of Aquitaine (ca. 390–460), and Gottschalk (ca. 805–869), though they also had differences. Gottschalk, for example, rejected the teaching of Prosper that though Christ's atonement is efficient only for the elect, it is sufficient for all. Peter Lombard (ca. 1100–1160) codified the efficiency-sufficiency view for the Middle Ages,[14] which most Reformation theologians upheld. Calvin never criticized this view, either, though he acknowledged that it did not answer all the questions relative to the atonement's extent.[15] Among other Reformers, Johannes Oecolampadius (1482–1531), Martin Bucer (1491–1551), Peter Martyr Vermigli (1499–1562), and Caspar Olevianus (1536–1587) all taught that Christ atoned only for the sins of the elect.

Scholars have long debated Calvin's view, usually finding support in Calvin for their own positions. James Anderson, Robert T. Kendall, James B. Torrance, Curt Daniel, and M. Charles Bell think Calvin taught either universal redemption or what one might call a *provisional universal atonement* that recognizes that God loves all mankind while yet purposing that only some should be saved.[16] Alan Clifford thinks that Calvin agrees with Amyraut rather than with John Owen and traditional Reformed theology on the extent of the atonement.[17] A. A. Hodge, Paul Helm, Robert Godfrey, Roger Nicole, and Richard Muller assert that Calvin taught an implicit, effective atonement.[18] Tony Lane and Robert Letham say that Calvin was ambiguous or even contradictory on the atonement, but that he maintained its intrinsic efficacy.[19] Hans Boersma and G. Michael Thomas conclude that Calvin did not support either particular or universal redemption, but kept a certain tension in his doctrine of atonement.[20]

Robert Peterson argues that the issue of the extent of the atonement belonged more to the subsequent period of Reformed orthodoxy and was therefore largely anachronistic for Calvin.[21] Pieter Rouwendal shows, however, that the question of the atonement's extent was dealt with in Calvin's day, but the way that it was handled by later Reformers was foreign and anachronistic to Calvin. Theodore Beza (1519–1605) and other later Reformers maintained particular atonement while being critical of the notion of Christ's atonement being sufficient for all. They were unhappy with the word *for* because it implied intent, whereas Christ had no intent to die for all, they said. Thus, Beza's doctrine of particular atonement was somewhat removed from the classical position that maintained the efficiency-sufficiency distinction.[22] I think Rouwendal is correct, though there are indications that Calvin was leaning in the direction of what would come to be called particular redemption. Commenting on the possibility that Christ's propitiation appeased God's wrath even for the reprobate, Calvin said, "Such a monstrous idea is not worth refuting."[23] The unanswerable question, of course, is whether Calvin, if he had lived thirty or forty years later, would have moved from the classical position to embrace Beza's criticism of the efficiency-sufficiency distinction.

In response to the Remonstrants, the Synod of Dort, after considerable debate, maintained the classical position on atonement, albeit with a mild capitulation to Beza and his staunchest supporter at the synod, Franciscus Gomarus (1563–1641). Head II, Article 8 says, "For this was the sovereign counsel and most gracious will and purpose of God the Father, that the quickening and saving efficacy of the most precious death of His Son should extend to all the elect, for bestowing upon them alone the gift of justifying faith, thereby to bring them infallibly to salvation." Though limiting the saving benefits of Christ's satisfaction to the elect, the delegates at Dort also stressed that the doctrine of limited atonement does not suggest any inadequacy in the death of Christ. Because it was Christ who suffered, His death is of infinite value. The Canons of Dort declare unequivocally that "the death of the Son of God . . . is of infinite worth and value, abundantly sufficient to expiate the sins of the whole world" (Head II, Art. 3).

Thus, the canons affirm that although Christ's atoning death is efficient only for the elect, it is sufficient for all. The Dortian divines recognized, however, that the sufficiency of Christ's atonement for all must be carefully defined so that it does not degenerate into a thinly disguised form of Arminianism. They said that

Christ's death was sufficient in itself for all while denying that Christ died with saving intent for all. In other words, they moderated the classic formula of atonement by taking Beza and Gomarus's criticisms into account.[24]

Later Calvinists provided even more clarity here. For example, nearly all Calvinists would agree with Owen, who says that Christ's atonement would have been "sufficient in itself for the redeeming of all and every man, if it had pleased the Lord to employ it to that purpose."[25] But since God did not so purpose it, as Owen goes on to show, the atonement is truly sufficient only for those for whom it is efficient.[26] Even Beza would have accepted Owen's comments here, I believe.

The Synod of Dort rejected the charge that definite atonement had negative implications for the indiscriminate preaching of the gospel and the calling of all people everywhere to look to Christ and live (Head III–IV, Art. 8). Most Calvinists ever since have taught that definite atonement should instill confidence in our preaching and witnessing because we are calling on people to entrust themselves to a Savior who infallibly saves, who has left nothing to chance, who will not lose any of those whom the Father has given Him, and who has fully paid for the salvation of everyone who will trust in Him.[27]

PROBLEMS WITH ARMINIAN UNIVERSAL REDEMPTION

The Arminian view is by far the most popular of the four views of the atonement in the Christian church today. However, serious objections must be lodged against Arminian universal redemption, among which are these:

• *It slanders God's attributes, such as His love.* Arminianism presents a love that actually doesn't save. It is a love that loves and then, if refused, turns to hatred and anger. It is not unchangeable love that endures from everlasting to everlasting. It provides atonement for all, but then withholds the means of grace that would make that salvation effectual in all lives. Are we to believe that Christ died for everyone in the deepest jungle and the darkest city, but His love doesn't provide the missionaries, preachers, or sermons that would make His death effectual?

It slanders God's *wisdom.* Would God make a plan to save everyone, then not carry it out? Would He be so foolish as to have His Son pay for the salvation of all if He knew that Christ would not be able to obtain what He paid for? Some say He didn't realize the consequences; He saw far enough to provide atonement, but couldn't see that some wouldn't take it. Does not that assertion slander the wisdom of God? Could God plan and provide atonement, but not realize that His atonement would not be accepted?

I would feel foolish if I went into a store and bought something, then walked out without it. Yet Arminianism asks us to believe that this is true of salvation—that a purchase was made, a redemption, and yet the Lord walked away without those whom He had redeemed. That view slanders the wisdom of God.

It slanders God's *power.* Arminian universalism obliges us to believe that God was able to accomplish the meriting aspect of salvation, but that the applying aspect is dependent on man and his free will. It asks us to believe that God has worked out everyone's salvation up to a point, but no further for anyone. The implication is that God has built the bridge of salvation between Him and us, and we have only to walk over it by accepting His terms of salvation through a free act of the will. "God does His part," Arminians say, "and now we must do our part."

Calvinists respond that this makes salvation dependent on the will of humanity, thereby reducing God and His power. Instead of our coming to God with our withered hands and saying, "If Thou wilt, Thou canst make us whole," this view has God coming to us with a withered hand, a hand that is not strong enough to save anyone, and saying, "If thou wilt, thou canst complete this salvation; thou canst make Me whole." In essence, modern evangelistic sermons often take such an approach: "God has done much, but He needs you to complete the job." Does that way of thinking not slander the all-sufficient power of God? It makes God dependent on the will of man.

It slanders God's *justice.* Did Christ satisfy God's justice for everyone? Did Christ take the punishment due to everybody? If He did, how can God punish anyone? Is it justice to punish one person for the sins of another and later to punish the initial offender again? As Augustus Toplady said,

> *God cannot payment twice demand;*
> *Once at my bleeding Surety's hand,*
> *And then again at mine.*[28]

God can't and won't demand payment twice. Double punishment is injustice.

• *It disables the deity of Christ.* A defeated Savior is not God. This error teaches that Christ tried to save everyone but didn't succeed. It denies the power and efficacy of Christ's blood, since not all for whom He died are saved. Hence, Christ's blood was wasted on Judas and Esau. Much of His labor, tears, and blood was poured out in vain. In other words, He will not see of the travail of His soul and be satisfied (Isa. 53:11) on behalf of many for whom He died. There will be many miscarriages—those with whom He travailed in soul yet who will not ultimately be saved. Does such defeat not make Christ less than God? No wonder Charles H. Spurgeon called this a monstrous doctrine.

• *It undermines the unity of the Trinity.* Just as parents must work together to run a family effectively, so the triune God co-labors in each of His persons with identical purposes and goals. One person cannot possibly have in mind to save some that another person has not determined to save, but Arminian universalism implicitly teaches just that. It denies the Father's sovereign election, since Christ would have died for more than God decreed to save, thereby making Christ seem to have a different agenda than that of the Father. That would have been *anathema* to Jesus, who asserted that His entire redemptive ministry was consciously designed to carry out a divinely arranged plan (John 6:38–39).

T. J. Crawford writes: "The atonement originated in the love of God. It is the consequence and not the cause of God's willingness to save sinners. In this light the Savior Himself is careful to present it. Instead of ascribing to His Father all the sternness and severity, and claiming as His own all the tenderness and compassion, He takes special pains to impress us with the assurance that the purpose of His mission was to proclaim the loving message and to execute the loving will of His Father who is in heaven."[29] In the atonement, we are not running from the Father, who as a stern Judge is ready to condemn us, to the Son, who is more gracious than the Father. Rather, in the atonement we have a way to run to the Father and rest in Him, for Christ's sake, the way a child runs to and rests in the lap of his or her father.

Then, too, Arminian redemption divides Christ from Christ, as it were. Calvinism insists that Christ's entire priestly work must be viewed as a harmonious whole. His expiation by atoning death and His priestly intercession are co-extensive. What an oxymoron it is to maintain that Christ died for everyone but intercedes only for some (cf. John 17:2, 4, 6, 9, 12, 20, 24).

Finally, Arminian redemption disavows the saving ministry of the Holy Spirit, since it claims that Christ's blood has a wider application than does the Spirit's saving work. Any presentation of salvation that makes the Father or the Spirit's work in salvation lag behind Christ's work contradicts the inherent unity of the Trinity. The Father and the Son are one. The Spirit and the Son are one. Christ cannot possibly have died for those whom the Father did not decree to save and in whom the Spirit does not savingly work. God cannot be at odds with Himself. Arminianism is inconsistent universalism.

• *It rejects all of the other points of Calvinism.* The Arminian view of the atonement rejects the doctrine of man's total depravity, teaching that man has the ability within himself to receive and accept Christ. It rejects unconditional election, teaching that God elects on the basis of foreseen faith. It rejects irresistible grace, teaching that man's will is stronger than God's. It rejects the perseverance of the saints, teaching that man can apostatize from the faith. J. I. Packer says, "It cannot be over-emphasized that we have not seen the full meaning of the cross till we have seen it as the centre of the gospel, flanked on the one hand by total inability and unconditional election and on the other by irresistible grace and final preservation."[30]

• *It detracts from the glory of God.* If God does everything in salvation, He gets all the glory. But if God can do only so much and not everything, then the person who completes the bridge gets at least some glory. That is why there is so much emphasis in mass evangelism on the free will of man. The glory of God is not exalted, and neither is the glory of Christ lifted up for providing a perfect and complete salvation. We are told of the free will of man, without which salvation cannot be put into effect. We are told to exercise our free will without being told that this will is in bondage due to our depraved nature. We cannot freely choose God and salvation on our own. We cannot complete the bridge. God completes the bridge, as we are told in 1 Corinthians 1:18–31, so that "no flesh should glory in his presence." Universal atonement exalts the will of man and debases the glory of God.

• *It undermines thankfulness and assurance.* Why should I thank God for something that *I* achieved? If the Lord Jesus did no more for me than He did for Judas and the inhabitants of Sodom, why should I thank Him rather than myself? And if there are some for whom Christ died who are in hell today, how can I be sure the atonement will atone for me?

• *It perverts evangelism.* We repeatedly hear today in evangelistic messages: "Christ died for you. What will you do for Him?" But do we ever find in the Bible that someone is told personally, "Christ died for you"? Rather, we find the work of Christ explained, followed by a call to everyone: "Repent and believe the gospel." The message is not "Believe that Christ died for you" or "Believe that you are one of the elect." It is "Believe on the Lord Jesus Christ and you will be saved."

• *It disparages the intrinsic efficacy of the atonement itself.* Arminians teach that Christ's work induces the Father to accept graciously what Jesus accomplished in place of a full satisfaction of His justice. It is as if Jesus persuaded His Father to accept something less than justice demanded. That is why Arminius claimed that when God saved sinners, He moved from His throne of justice to His throne of grace. But God does not have two thrones; His throne of justice *is* His throne of grace (Ps. 85:10). Arminianism forgets that the atonement does not win God's love but is the provision of His love. In that provision, Christ paid the full price of justice. He did not make a down payment on the debt owed; He paid the full price of sin so that the Father as Judge could justly cancel the debt (Heb. 10:14–18).

Arminianism, then, is ultimately inconsistent universalism, as Owen showed powerfully in his *A Display of Arminianism.* Owen explains the fallacy of the Arminian view of the divine design of the atonement as follows:

> God imposed his wrath due unto, and Christ underwent the pains of hell, for, either all the sins of all men, or all the sins of some men, or some sins of all men. If the last, some sins of all men, then have all men some sins to answer for, and so shall no man be saved. If the second, that is it which we affirm, that Christ in their stead and room suffered for all the sins of all the elect in the world. If the first, why, then, are not all freed from the punishment of all their sins? You will say, "Because of their unbelief; they will not believe." But this unbelief, is it a sin, or not? If not, why should they be punished for it? If it be, then Christ underwent the punishment due to it, or not. If so, then why must that hinder them more than their other sins for which he died from partaking of the fruit of his death? If he did not, then did he not die for all their sins.[31]

DISCUSSION QUESTIONS

1. Why is the atonement central to Christianity?

2. What are the four views of the extent of the atonement?

3. What was Calvin's view of the extent of the atonement?

4. List the problems with the Arminian view of the extent of the atonement.

5. What does the statement "Double punishment is injustice" mean?

NOTES

[1] Quoted in J. I. Packer, introduction to John Owen, *The Death of Death in the Death of Christ* (Edinburgh: Banner of Truth Trust, 1983), note 12. I am grateful for help received from sermons preached by Al Martin and David P. Murray in writing these chapters on the atonement.

[2] For an excellent treatment of those debates, see W. Robert Godfrey, "Tensions within International Calvinism: The Debate on the Atonement at the Synod of Dordt, 1618–1619" (Ph.D. dissertation, Stanford University, 1974).

[3] The traditional term is *extent* of the atonement. *Intent* may be more accurate, since *extent* usually refers to a physical area or geographical space, which when applied to atonement means: *How many* did Christ die for? Is it of limited or unlimited value?

[4] John Murray, *Redemption Accomplished and Applied* (Grand Rapids: Eerdmans, 1955), 62.

[5] "The Winchester Profession of Faith" (General Convention of Universalists, 1803), Christian Universalist Web site, http://www.auburn.edu/~allenkc/univart.html

[6] For Arminius' writings, see *The Works of James Arminius*, 3 vols. (Grand Rapids: Baker, 1999). For a standard work on Arminius, see Carl Bangs, *Arminius: A Study in the Dutch Reformation*, 2nd ed. (Grand Rapids: Zondervan, 1985). For a survey of Arminius' scholarship, see Richard A. Muller, *God, Creation, and Providence in the Thought of Jacob Arminius: Sources and Directions of Scholastic Protestantism in the Era of Early Orthodoxy* (Grand Rapids: Baker, 1991), 3–14.

[7] Raymond A. Blacketer, "Definite Atonement in Historical Perspective," in *The Glory of the Atonement: Biblical, Historical, and Practical Perspectives*, ed. Charles E. Hill and Frank A. James III (Downers Grove, Ill.: InterVarsity, 2004), 319.

[8] Philip Schaff, *Creeds of Christendom* (Grand Rapids: Baker, 1993), 3:546.

9 For an excellent summary of Amyraldianism, see Roger Nicole, *The Encyclopedia of Christianity*, ed. Edwin H. Palmer (Wilmington, Del.: National Foundation for Christian Education, 1964), 184–193. Further, see Roger Nicole, *Moïse Amyraut: A Bibliography* (New York: Garland Publishing, 1981), and Curt Daniel, "The History and Theology of Calvinism" (Dallas: Scholarly Reprints, 1993), 73–78. For the fullest treatment of Amyraldianism, see Brian G. Armstrong, *Calvinism and the Amyraut Heresy: Protestant Scholasticism and Humanism in Seventeenth-Century France* (Madison: University of Wisconsin Press, 1969).

10 George Smeaton, *The Apostles' Doctrine of the Atonement* (Edinburgh: Banner of Truth Trust, 1991), 541. See also Smeaton, *Christ's Doctrine of the Atonement* (Edinburgh: Banner of Truth Trust, 1991), 468–472.

11 Robert Letham, *The Work of Christ* (Downers Grove, Ill.: InterVarsity, 1993), 229.

12 Iain Murray, "Calvin and the Atonement: Notes on a Continuing Discussion," *Banner of Truth*, no. 398 (Nov. 1996): 17.

13 Blacketer, "Definite Atonement in Historical Perspective," 305.

14 Peter Lombard: "Sufficient for all, efficient for the elect" (*Libri Quatuor Sententiarum*, 3:20, in *MPL*, 192, 799). Quoted in Letham, *The Work of Christ*, 265n.

15 See Pieter Rouwendal, "Calvin's Forgotten Classical Position on the Extent of the Atonement: About Sufficiency, Efficiency, and Anachronism," *Westminster Theological Journal*, forthcoming.

16 James William Anderson, "The Grace of God and the Non-elect in Calvin's Commentaries and Sermons" (Th.D. dissertation, New Orleans Baptist Theological Seminary, 1976), 112–117, 127–141; R. T. Kendall, *Calvin and English Calvinism to 1649* (Oxford: Oxford University Press, 1979), 13–32, 210; James B. Torrance, "The Incarnation and 'Limited Atonement,'" *Evangelical Quarterly*, 55, no. 2 (April 1983): 82–94; Curt Daniel, "Hyper Calvinism and John Gill" (Ph.D. dissertation, University of Edinburgh, 1983); and M. Charles Bell, "Calvin and the Extent of the Atonement," 115–123, and *Calvin and Scottish Theology: The Doctrine of Assurance* (Edinburgh: Handsel, 1985), 13–40.

17 Alan Clifford, *Calvinus: Authentic Calvinism, A Clarification* (Norwich, England: Charenton Reformed Publishing, 1996). For a rebuttal of Clifford's view, see Murray, "Calvin and the Atonement: Notes on a Continuing Discussion," 17–20.

18 A. A. Hodge, *The Atonement* (Grand Rapids: Eerdmans, 1953), 388–391; Paul Helm, *Calvin and the Calvinists* (Edinburgh: Banner of Truth Trust, 1982), 11, 14, 30, and "Calvin and the Covenant: Unity and Continuity," *Evangelical Quarterly*, 55, no. 2 (April 1983): 65–81; W. Robert Godfrey, "Reformed Thought on the Extent of the Atonement to 1618," *Westminster Theological Journal*, 37 (1975): 137–138; Roger Nicole, "John Calvin's View of the Extent of the Atonement," *Westminster Theological Journal*, 47 (1985): 197–225; and Richard Muller, *Christ and the Decree: Christology and Predestination in Reformed Theology from Calvin to Perkins* (Grand Rapids: Baker, 1988), 34.

19 Tony Lane, "The Quest for the Historical Calvin," *Evangelical Quarterly*, 55, no. 2 (April 1983): 95–113, and Robert Letham, "Saving Faith and Assurance in Reformed Theology: Zwingli to the Synod of Dort" (Ph.D. dissertation, University of Aberdeen, 1979), 1:122–126, 2:65–67, and *The Work of Christ*, 225–247, 265–266n. I am indebted to the last citation of Letham for most of this summary.

20 Hans Boersma, "Calvin and the Extent of the Atonement," *Evangelical Quarterly*, 64, no. 4 (1992): 333–355, and G. Michael Thomas, *The Extent of the Atonement: A Dilemma for Reformed Theology from Calvin to the Consensus* (Carlisle, U.K.: Paternoster, 1997), 12–40. See Pieter Rouwendal, "Calvin's Forgotten Classical Position," forthcoming.

21 Robert A. Peterson, *Calvin's Doctrine of the Atonement* (Phillipsburg, N.J.: P&R, 1983), 90–91, and Rouwendal, "Calvin's Forgotten Classical Position," forthcoming.

22 Rouwendal sees enough distinction between this position, which he calls *the particular position*, and the classical position to merit calling this a fifth view of the atonement. The difference between the particular and the classical position is that in the former Christ did not die in any sense for all men, whereas in the latter Christ died sufficiently for all men (ibid.).

23 *Commentary* on 1 John 2:2.

24 I am indebted for assistance here to correspondence with Pieter Rouwendal.

25 John Owen, *The Works of John Owen* (Edinburgh: Banner of Truth Trust, 1965), 10:295–296.

26 Alan Clifford, *Atonement and Justification* (Oxford: Clarendon Press, 1990), 74.

27 It should be noted that a fifth (or sixth; see note 22 above) view of the extent of the atonement might be given to a minority of the Hyper-Calvinists, such as William Rushton, who denied every aspect of Christ's death being sufficient for all. Rushton said that if Christ's death was sufficient for all, all would be saved. Since all are not saved, His death cannot be sufficient for all (William Rushton, *A Defence of Particular Redemption* [Luray, Va.: Zion's Advocate Print, 1831], http://users.aol.com/libcfl2/fuller.htm). Other Hyper-Calvinists, however, did not deny every aspect of "sufficiency for all" in Christ's atonement.

28 From the hymn "Faith Reviving" by Augustus Toplady.

29 T. J. Crawford, *The Doctrine of Holy Scripture Respecting the Atonement* (Grand Rapids: Baker, 1954), 192.

30 Quoted in John Blanchard, *The Complete Gathered Gold* (Darlington, England: Evangelical Press, 2006), 35; cf. Ronald Cammenga and Ronald Hanko, *Saved by Grace: A Study of the Five Points of Calvinism*, 2nd ed. (Grandville, Mich.: Reformed Free Publishing Association, 2002), 122–123.

31 Owen, *The Works of John Owen*, 10:174.

CHAPTER 7

DEFINITE ATONEMENT

The things we have to choose between are an atonement of high value, or an atonement of wide extension. The two cannot go together.[1]

—B. B. WARFIELD

*O*n *The Other Side of Calvinism,* Laurence Vance says that Calvinists defend limited atonement with a vengeance, which simply adds insult to the injury of unconditional election. He goes on to say: "In the Calvinistic system, it makes absolutely no difference whatsoever whether Christ died for the 'non-elect'—they could not be saved if Christ died a thousand deaths for them. Calvinists do not hesitate to insist that the reason Christ's blood was shed only for the 'elect' is because God did not want any others to be saved."[2] Vance then concludes that "the precarious doctrine of limited atonement renders the salvation of any man doubtful and uncertain."[3]

Such caricatures abound in the Arminian camp. Therefore, I want to use this chapter to look at how the Calvinist view of atonement is biblical and more positive than many think. Then I will seek to answer some common objections to the Calvinist view.

BIBLICAL SUPPORT FOR DEFINITE ATONEMENT

Biblical terms, tenses, and testimonies make a sure case for definite atonement. Consider the following:

• *Biblical terms.* The Bible vividly describes what Christ did on the cross: He made a sacrifice; He made propitiation; He reconciled His people to God; He guaranteed the redemption of His own; He gave His life a ransom for many (but not all); He bore the curse of those for whom He died.

But do the biblical concepts of sacrifice, propitiation, reconciliation, redemption, ransom, and curse-bearing support Calvinism's assertion that Christ secured salvation, or do they support the Arminian notion that Christ made salvation *possible* through His death?

Arminianism does injustice to the basic biblical concept of redemption, which has its roots in the deliverance of the people of God out of Egypt. Redemption did not merely make their release from Egyptian bondage possible; it brought them out of bondage into the place of God's appointment. Likewise, with propitiation, God's wrath is satisfied by the offering up of a sacrifice, and once His wrath is satisfied, it turns away. A ransom releases the one for whom it is paid. Therefore, the onus is on anyone who says that Christ's death did not actually secure the salvation of a defined group of people to show that his view does justice to these biblical terms. Arminianism does not do that.[4]

• *Biblical tenses.* The very nature of Christ's work is reconciliation. Hebrews 9 tells us that He has obtained redemption for us. Romans 8:29–30 speaks of Christ's work with such certainty that Paul can use the aorist tense for all of his main verbs, speaking as if even glorification is already accomplished. Ephesians 5:25–27 tells us that Christ so loved the church that He gave Himself for it, not that He might make it a redeemable or perfectible church, but that He might redeem her in order to present her as His bride to Himself. Clearly, the intent of His death was nothing less than the completed salvation of every one of those for whom He died. Titus 2:14 says He "gave himself for us, that he might redeem us from all iniquity, and purify unto himself a peculiar people, zealous of good works."

• *Biblical testimonies.* The definiteness of the atonement of Christ can be affirmed irrevocably from biblical testimonies. The Bible speaks clearly of Jesus laying down His life for His sheep (John 10:11–13). In that context, He says of certain people, "Ye are not of my sheep" (v. 26). Scripture also speaks of Christ laying down His life for the children of God (John 11:51–52); dying for His church (Eph. 5:25–27; Acts 20:28); saving His people (Matt. 1:21); giving His life a ransom for many (Matt. 20:28); seeing His seed (Isa. 53:10; Ps. 22); and redeeming His own from iniquity (Titus 2:14)—all as having already happened (Rev. 5:9).

In sum, Christ died to satisfy the justice of God for His people's sins. He saved a definite number of people whom Scripture refers to as His people, His sheep, and His elect (Matt. 1:21; John 10:11–15; Rom. 8:28–39). As with God's election and the Spirit's calling, Christ's atonement is efficacious. His sacrifice of His life saves the lives of His sheep. This precious life is not laid down in vain for just any sheep (John 10:10). Jesus did not die to make salvation possible for all; He died to make the salvation of His sheep certain. He is the Good Shepherd who knows His sheep and gives "his life for the sheep" (John 10:11). This little word *for* indicates a direct exchange, a definite one for a definite many. Not one part of the sacrifice was in vain. Here, surely, is the glorious truth of a certain, though limited, atonement, for Jesus also bluntly declares to some unbelieving Israelites, "Ye believe not, because ye are not of my sheep" (John 10:26).

The doctrine of limited atonement does not mean that Christ's death is limited in power. A. W. Pink said, "The only limitation in the atonement arises from pure sovereignty; it is a limitation not of value and virtue, but of design and application."[5] Christ died for the people whom God the Father elected and for whom Christ Himself intercedes. John 17:9 says Christ intercedes specifically and exclusively for those people: "I pray for them: I pray not for the world, but for them which thou hast given me; for they are thine."

Christ died to save only His elect. That does not mean there is any insufficiency in His atoning blood. Because Christ is infinite God, His blood provides infinite satisfaction for the justice of God. If God had determined to save myriads more than He did, no more of Christ's blood would have been required. Then, too, if He had died only for one, He would have had to suffer no less, since all sin is against an infinite God and demands infinite payment from the Mediator. But though Christ's blood is sufficient for all, it is efficient only for the elect.[6] It accomplishes its purpose; whomever Christ died to save will be saved. "He shall see of the travail of his soul, and shall be satisfied" (Isa. 53:11).

The good news of Christ's definite atonement is that it means He is a *complete* Mediator. He both *merits* and *applies* salvation. Both are necessary because we are unable to do either. Christ must be a full Savior because sinners are spiritually dead and cannot independently receive a Christ presented to them. Though Christ has merited everything, God's people know that they have no legs to run to Him, no arms to embrace Him, no lips to kiss Him. He must do everything—both the meriting and the applying. Thus, He receives all honor and glory as the Alpha and Omega for His own.

OBJECTIONS ANSWERED

The major objections to limited atonement are based on textual and practical considerations. The textual objections include the following:

1. Texts in which the word *world* is used to describe the objects of Christ's death, as in John 3:16 and 1 John 2:2: "And he is the propitiation for our sins: and not for ours only, but also for the sins of the whole world."

2. Texts in which the word *all* is used to describe the objects of Christ's death, such as 2 Corinthians 5:15: "He died for all, that they which live should not henceforth live unto themselves, but unto him which died for them, and rose again"; Romans 8:32a: "He . . . spared not his own Son, but delivered him up for us all"; and 1 Timothy 2:4–6, which speaks of Christ giving Himself as "a ransom for all."

3. Texts that seem to state that some for whom Christ died may perish. One such text is Romans 14:15: "But if thy brother be grieved with thy meat, now walkest thou not charitably. Destroy not him with thy meat, for whom Christ died." Another is 2 Peter 2:1, in which the apostle speaks of false teachers who deny the Lord "that bought them."

When these texts are handled carefully and honestly, considering their context and the intent of the author, and measuring Scripture against Scripture, apparent problems are nearly always readily resolved.[7] For example, the Greek word for world (*kosmos*) has several meanings in Scripture. Sometimes it refers to the entire elect world, meaning both the Jews and Gentiles; sometimes it refers to the public who surrounded Christ, especially the Jews; sometimes it refers to all kinds of people, such as kings and subjects; sometimes it refers to humankind under the righteous judgment of God or to the kingdom of evil forces, both angelic and human, as related to the earth; sometimes it refers to creation, or to the earth itself, or in the classical sense, to an orderly universe; and sometimes it simply refers to a great number of people.[8]

As for specific texts, John 3:16 does not reflect on the atonement's extent; rather, the key to John 3:16 is in the purpose clause of verse 17: *in order that* "the world through him might be saved." *World* is referring not to everyone but to the world under judgment and condemnation. B. B. Warfield says *kosmos* is used in John 3 not to suggest that the world is so *big* that it takes a great *deal* of love to embrace it all, but that the world is so *bad* that it takes a great *kind* of love to love it at all, and much more to love it as God loved it when He gave His Son for sinners in it.[9]

In 1 John 2:1–2, the apostle is saying that Christ's defense before God is so complete that it is sufficient for the sins of the world. He is also saying that the sacrifice Christ made was not only for the Jews or for a small group of first-century believers, but for people of every tribe, tongue, and nation through all time. John Murray speaks about the ethnic universalism of the gospel, meaning that those for whom Christ died are spread among all nations. Abraham Kuyper shows that the Greek word translated "for" (*peri*, not *hyper*) means "fitting for" or "with respect to." Hence, the meaning of the Greek can be that Jesus is a propitiation just like we and the entire world need—or, just as Jesus is our propitiation, so the entire world needs that same propitiation.[10]

As for the texts that use the word *all*, 2 Corinthians 5:14–15 uses *all* in the context of the unity of death and resurrection. Christ rises for those in union with Him; therefore, His death must be thought of in those same terms.[11] The phrase "delivered him up for us all" in Romans 8:32 is in the context of God's foreordination of His people (vv. 28–30) and of Christ's intercession for the elect (vv. 33–39). The words "ransom for all" in 1 Timothy 2:4–6 are clearly set in the context of prayers being offered for all kinds of people (vv. 1–2). Since the word *all* does not always mean all individuals in either Greek or English usage, there is no compelling reason to conclude that the *all* in verses 4 and 6 refers to every single person.

What of texts that seem to speak of believers falling away from faith? The context of Romans 14:15 shows that the apostle is not talking about a brother for whom Christ died apostatizing from the faith altogether, but about one who would feel crushed if a fellow Christian became such a stumbling block in his life of faith that he would begin to traverse the road that leads to destruction. And 2 Peter 2:1 probably refers to false teachers who had been nominal members of the church but who, in their actions, were denying the Savior they once professed but never knew in truth. They may have had historical, even temporary and miraculous, faith, but they never possessed true saving faith,[12] for they rejected the Savior and did "stumble at the word, being disobedient: whereunto also they were appointed" (1 Peter 2:8b). Certainly, Christ did not redeem those who were ordained to be disobedient.

Most major practical objections to limited atonement can be summarized in two questions:

• *How can the atonement be glorious if it is limited to some?* This question really has two aspects. The first is the false idea that Christ died for a tiny remnant of people. Both the Canons of Dort and the Second Helvetic Confession reject that conclusion on the basis of Scripture passages that say heaven will house a great multitude of redeemed people that no man can number, from every kindred, tribe, tongue, and nation (Rev. 7:9–17).[13]

The second aspect is a false idea about who does the limiting in atonement. As Charles H. Spurgeon showed in the quote cited at the opening of the previous chapter, it is the Arminian, not the Calvinist, who limits Christ's redemption. The Calvinist teaches that salvation is sure for every man, woman, teenager, boy, or girl who comes to the Lord Jesus Christ. None shall be turned away (John 6:37). The Calvinist says, "In His atonement, Jesus built a bridge from the depths of my depravity to God and heaven, and, by sending His Spirit, will bring every sinner for whom the bridge was laid all the way to glory." That statement is the essence of the gospel. God will not fail to gather in every single one of His elect. There will be no empty seats in heaven.

Arminians say atonement only makes salvation possible. In doing so, they greatly limit the efficacy of the bloodletting of the Son of God. One Arminian put it this way: "The atonement would be just as efficacious and glorifying to God if not one sinner ever appropriated it." In the Arminian view, the atonement created the possibility of salvation, but men must complete the bridge by exercising their own free will.[14]

• *How can you preach the gospel to all men without distinction if Christ did not die to save all?* In other words, if you cannot come to a sinner and say, "Christ died for you," how can you ask him to believe on the Lord Jesus Christ? Doesn't Calvinism dampen evangelistic zeal? Let me offer three responses.

First, the content of the gospel is not telling people that Christ died for this or that specific person. There is not one instance in the preaching of the book of Acts, private or public, where the apostolic gospel says Christ died for any individual. The gospel says that God has sent His Son, who lived, died, and rose again. That is adequate for the vilest of sinners, for the promise is: "Believe on the Lord Jesus Christ and thou shalt be saved."

Second, the Calvinist view of the atonement guarantees the success of evangelism. The elect will be saved infallibly through the preaching of the gospel, for God determined that it would be so through the eternal covenant of redemption established among the persons of the Trinity. In His sovereign, gracious, distinguishing love, the Father has chosen certain people (Rom. 9:11–13; Eph. 1:4) whom He gave to His Son (John 6:37, 39; 17:6, 24), who, in turn, committed Himself to accomplish their redemption by obeying the precepts of God's moral law perfectly on their behalf (His active obedience) and paying the penalty due them for their disobedience to the law (His passive obedience). Thus, God can be just and the justifier of those who believe in Jesus (Rom. 3:26). Under the Trinitarian covenant, the Spirit is sent into the world by the Father and the Son (John 15:26; 16:5–15) to apply Christ's saving work to the elect.

We need to remember that the decretive and covenantal will of God is effectual. What God purposes, He performs. Christ's atonement is the work to which He committed Himself from eternity. Definite atonement flows out of the electing purpose of God and adheres fully with other doctrines of Christology that are grounded in eternity, such as the doctrines of Christ as the second Adam, of His high-priestly work, and of His covenant role.

Knowing that the elect will be gathered by the second Adam (John 17:12; Rom. 5:12–19) makes Calvinists bold in evangelism. They also are patient in it, knowing that God will save sinners in His time and way through the priestly work of Christ (Isa. 55:10–11). They are zealous, knowing that God's glory will come to be (1 Cor. 1:27–31), and prayerful, knowing that He alone will and can accomplish salvation as an ever-faithful, covenant-keeping Lord (Eph. 2:1–10).[15] Nearly all the great and zealous evangelists of the church from the sixteenth-century Reformation to the early nineteenth century, before Charles Finney (1792–1875), were committed to definite atonement rooted in this God-centered covenant theology. Would anyone dare say that George Whitefield lacked evangelistic zeal in preaching the gospel? Would anyone say the same of Spurgeon, William Carey, David Brainerd, Jonathan Edwards, or Asahel Nettleton? Each of these great evangelists professed a definite design in the atoning work of Christ and boldly heralded Him as a freely offered and willing Savior to all who repent and believe.[16]

Third, while we cannot fully grasp with our finite minds how to reconcile a definite, limited atonement with Christ's all-sufficient blood and a universal invitation to believe, such is the pattern of Scripture and the way of God (John 6:37–40). Moreover, since the atonement is not limited in itself, though it is in its design, and since the promise is that all who by faith truly come to Christ for salvation will certainly be saved (Rom. 10:13), limited atonement is not inconsistent with a universal call to faith.

This is also the position of the Canons of Dort. Affirming that Christ's blood is shed effectually only for those "who were from eternity chosen to salvation and given to Him by the Father" (Head II, Art. 8), the Canons read: "The promise of the gospel is, that whosoever believeth in Christ crucified, shall not perish, but have everlasting life. This promise, together with the command to repent and believe, ought to be declared and published to all nations, and to all persons promiscuously and without distinction, to whom God out of His good pleasure sends the gospel" (Head II, Art. 5).

Roger Nicole says our major problem in understanding definite atonement is that we think that a coextensive provision is necessary for a sincere offer of any kind; that is, Christ has to have died for every person in order for every person to be offered salvation in Him. Nicole says this premise is false even in mundane human affairs:

> For instance, advertisers who offer some objects on the pages of a newspaper do not feel that honesty in any way demands of them to have a stock coextensive with the circulation figures of the newspaper. Really, the only requisite for a sincere invitation is this—that if the conditions be fulfilled, that which is offered will actually be granted.[17]

Jesus says, "Him that cometh to me I will in no wise cast out" (John 6:37). Unlike stores with limited inventory, Jesus' stock is never exhausted.

William Symington argues likewise:

> We hold that the sacrifice of the Lord Jesus possessed an *intrinsic value sufficient for the salvation of the whole world.* In this sense it was adequate to the redemption of every human being. . . . The worth of Christ's atonement we hold to be, in the strictest sense of the term, *infinite, absolute, all-sufficient.*

*. . . This all-sufficiency is what lays the foundation for the unrestricted univer-
sality of the gospel call. . . .* Such is my impression of the sufficiency of the
atonement, that were all the guilt of all mankind concentrated in my own
person, I should see no reason, relying on that blood which cleanseth from
all sin, to indulge despair.[18]

Symington concludes: "Let sinners everywhere know that if they perish it is
not because there is not merit in Christ sufficient to meet all the demands of law
and justice against them. Let them all turn and embrace the kind, the sincere, the
urgent call to life and salvation by mere gratuity on the part of God: 'Whosoever
will, let him take the water of life freely.'"[19]

If, by grace, you take this water of life, you will be saved. No one has ever
perished who has believed in the Lord Jesus Christ. The message of the gospel is:
"The bridge is finished. Christ will enable you to put your weight on it, and He
will carry you all the way across. He welcomes all who come. Trust Him."

Without faith, Christ's atonement does us no good. We experience the benefits of Christ's accomplishment only when we, with our empty hands, embrace
Christ. The good news is that the atonement has been achieved before we exercise
faith (Rom. 5:5–11). The reconciliation is there to be received, and by grace we
receive it when Christ, by the Holy Spirit, draws us to Himself.

REDEEMED BY PRECIOUS BLOOD

Arminianism and Calvinism are based on different premises. Calvinists believe in
a definite atonement, one that holds that Jesus Christ actually redeemed everyone
He intended to redeem through His substitutionary death. As Tom Ascol says,
"Just as the high priest under the old covenant wore the names of the twelve tribes
of Israel on his breastplate when he performed his sacrificial service, so our great
High Priest under the new covenant had the names of His people inscribed on
His heart as He offered up Himself as a sacrifice for their sins."[20] Not one who
belongs to Christ will be lost.

Nicole has often said that when Calvinists declare they believe in a *limited*
atonement, Arminians can proclaim an *unlimited* atonement, but when Calvinists
proclaim a *definite* atonement, no Arminian wants to claim an *indefinite* atonement.[21] Though *definite atonement* or *particular redemption* are better expressions

than *limited atonement*, let us not forget that every Calvinist and Arminian, in actuality, believes in a limited atonement. As Ascol points out, "The Arminian view, claiming that the atonement is unlimited in its extent, is forced to conclude that it is limited in its efficacy. It failed to accomplish its universal purpose."[22] Spurgeon describes this failure well:

> Many divines . . . believe in an atonement made for everybody; but then, their atonement is just this. They believe that Judas was atoned for just as much as Peter; they believe that the damned in hell were as much an object of Jesus Christ's satisfaction as the saved in heaven; and though they do not say it in proper words, yet they must mean it, for it is a fair inference, that in the case of multitudes, Christ died in vain, for he died for them all, they say; and yet so ineffectual was his dying for them, that though he died for them they are damned afterwards.[23]

Speaking with Spurgeon, we Calvinists may say to our Arminian friends: "You are welcome to your atonement; you may keep it. We will never renounce ours for the sake of it."[24] For we need a Savior who truly saves (Matt. 1:21) with a redemption that truly redeems by "the precious blood of Christ, as of a lamb without blemish and without spot: who verily was foreordained before the foundation of the world, but was manifest in these last times for you, who by him do believe in God, that raised him up from the dead, and gave him glory; that your faith and hope might be in God" (1 Peter 1:19–21).

> *Bearing shame and scoffing rude,*
> *In my place condemned He stood;*
> *Sealed my pardon with His blood:*
> *Hallelujah! What a Savior!*[25]

Christ's atonement did not partly fail; it totally succeeded. Jesus never fails.

DISCUSSION QUESTIONS

1. What biblical proof is there for the concept of a definite atonement?

2. Does the statement "Christ died to save only His elect" mean that there is insufficiency in Jesus' atoning blood? Why or why not?

3. Why is the concept of a definite atonement good news?

4. What objections, on the basis of biblical texts, have been raised against the idea of a definite atonement?

5. How can these objections be answered biblically?

6. What are the two practical objections to the doctrine of definite atonement? How can these be answered?

7. How does the statement "Jesus never fails" apply to the atonement?

NOTES

1.   Quoted in John Blanchard, *More Gathered Gold* (Welwyn: England: Evangelical Press, 1986), 18.

2.   Laurence M. Vance, *The Other Side of Calvinism* (Pensacola, Fla.: Vance Publications, 1991), 470.

3.   Ibid., 472.

4.   See A. W. Pink, *The Satisfaction of Christ: Studies in the Atonement* (Grand Rapids: Sovereign Grace Publishers, 2001), 158–226; W. G. T. Shedd, *Dogmatic Theology* (New York: Scribner, 1888), 2:378–409; and John Owen, *The Works of John Owen* (Edinburgh: Banner of Truth Trust, 1965), 10:87–108.

5.   A. W. Pink, *The Sovereignty of God* (Edinburgh: Banner of Truth Trust, 2004), 67.

6.   See Belgic Confession of Faith, Art. 21; Heidelberg Catechism, Q. 37; and Canons of Dort, Head II, Art. 3.

7.   John Gill, *Body of Divinity* (Grand Rapids: Sovereign Grace Publishers, 1971), 467–475; Owen, *The Works of John Owen*, 10:316–421; John Murray, *Redemption Accomplished and Applied* (Grand Rapids: Eerdmans, 1955), 71–75; Pink, *The Satisfaction of Christ*, 253–266.

8.   *Vine's Expository Dictionary of New Testament Words* (Nashville: Thomas Nelson, 1985), 233–234, and Duane Edward Spencer, *TULIP: The Five Points of Calvinism in the Light of Scripture* (Grand Rapids: Baker, 1979), 36–37.

9.   B. B. Warfield, *Biblical and Theological Studies*, ed. Samuel G. Craig (Philadelphia: Presbyterian & Reformed, 1952), 516.

10.   Abraham Kuyper, *Particular Grace: A Defense of God's Sovereignty in Salvation* (Grandville, Mich.: Reformed Free Publishing, 2001), 23–33.

11.   Cf. Herman Ridderbos, *Paul: An Outline of His Theology* (Grand Rapids: Eerdmans, 1975).

12.   For helpful exegetical considerations, see Robert Letham, *The Work of Christ* (Downers Grove, Ill.: InterVarsity, 1993), 240–245.

13.   See the Conclusion of the Canons and the Second Helvetic Confession, chap. 10.

14.   Cf. Pink, *The Satisfaction of Christ*, 244.

15.   See Letham, *The Work of Christ*, 234–237.

16.   Shedd, *Dogmatic Theology*, 2:482–489, and J. I. Packer, *Evangelism and the Sovereignty of God* (Downers Grove, Ill.: InterVarsity, 1961), 92–126.

17.   Roger Nicole, "The Case for Definite Atonement," *Evangelical Theological Society Bulletin* (Fall 1967): 207.

18.   William Symington, *The Atonement and Intercession of Christ* (Grand Rapids: Reformation Heritage Books, 2006), 185–186.

19.   Ibid.

20.   Thomas K. Ascol, "For God So Loved the World," *Tabletalk*, 29, no. 9 (Sept. 2005): 16.

21.   Roger Nicole, "The 'Five Points' and God's Sovereignty," in *Our Sovereign God*, ed. James M. Boice (Birmingham, Ala.: Solid Ground Christian Books, 2008), 32–33.

22.   Ascol, "For God So Loved the World," 17.

23.   Charles Spurgeon, *New Park Street Pulpit* (Pasadena, Tex.: Pilgrim Publications, 1975), 4:70.

24.   Quoted in J. I. Packer, introduction to John Owen, *The Death of Death in the Death of Christ* (Edinburgh: Banner of Truth Trust, 1983), note 12.

25.   From the hymn "Man of Sorrows! What a Name" by Philip P. Bliss, 1875.

CHAPTER 8

IRRESISTIBLE GRACE AND EFFECTUAL CALLING

I once attended a service where the text happened to be, "He shall choose our inheritance for us"; and the good man who occupied the pulpit was more than a little of an Arminian. Therefore, when he commenced, he said, "This passage refers entirely to our temporal inheritance, it has nothing whatever to do with our everlasting destiny, for," said he, "we do not want Christ to choose for us in the matter of heaven or hell. It is so plain and easy, that every man who has a grain of common sense will choose heaven, and any person would know better than to choose hell. We have no need of any superior intelligence, or any greater Being, to choose heaven or hell for us. It is left to our own free will, and we have enough wisdom given us, sufficiently correct means to judge for ourselves," and therefore, as he very logically inferred, there was no necessity for Jesus Christ, or ourselves, to make a choice for us. We could choose the inheritance for ourselves without any assistance. "Ah!" I thought, "but my good brother, it may be very true that we could, but I think we should want something more than common sense before we should choose aright." [1]

—CHARLES H. SPURGEON

We have considered three of the five points of Calvinism suggested in the acrostic TULIP. We examined the doctrine of *total depravity*, the Calvinistic teaching that fallen man lacks all ability to save himself, even to believe in the gospel freely offered to him. Then we looked at *unconditional election*, which holds that people are saved by God's free, sovereign, and unconditional choice of

101

sinners to be redeemed by Christ and brought to faith and eventual glory. We also studied *limited* (or *definite*) *atonement*, the doctrine that states that the redeeming work of Christ is for the salvation of the elect—in other words, that Christ actually saves those for whom He died.

The fourth point of Calvinism is the doctrine of *irresistible grace*, which says that the Holy Spirit never fails in His objective to bring His own to faith. This point is an inevitable product of the first three. Our total depravity necessitates it; unconditional election is its mooring; and limited atonement is its corresponding truth, for if saving grace were resistible, Christ would have died in vain for many.[2]

A clear grasp of the doctrine of irresistible grace is sorely needed today. The contemporary church is in the midst of a crisis of confidence concerning biblical preaching and the diligent use of the means of grace by which the Holy Spirit works irresistibly in the lives of sinners. The church needs to reaffirm her faith in the invincible power of the Spirit-applied Word of truth.

In this chapter, after defining irresistible grace, I will look at how God makes sinners willing to receive His salvation by calling them and regenerating them. I also will examine the monergistic character of the effectual call, and the means and fruits of being called by God to salvation.

DEFINITION AND AGENT

In defining irresistible grace, let us first look at the term *grace*, then focus on the adjective. The Old Testament Hebrew term for *grace* and its derivatives suggests kindness, favor, and graciousness. The New Testament Greek term suggests goodwill, lovingkindness, and favor. When applied to sinful men in a redemptive context, *grace* means unmerited favor in the place of merited wrath. Too often, grace is defined only as God's unmerited favor to sinners. The word *unmerited*, however, is too weak. As sinners, we have de-merited God's favor. Not only do we *not* deserve grace, we *do* deserve hell. Grace is God's blessing freely bestowed on ill-deserving sinners. It is a blessing bestowed at the cost of Christ's sufferings and death. Grace is God's love in Christ put into action. Grace is mightier than all our sins, our adverse circumstances, and our human impossibilities. Grace is the heart of the Bible and our salvation.

Grace teaches us that the salvation of ill-deserving, hell-worthy sinners (total depravity) is the work of the triune God alone. Each of the persons of the Trinity participates in and contributes to that work. Before the foundation of the world, the Father marked those who would be saved. He then gave His own to the Son to be His people (unconditional election). In the fullness of time, the Son came into the world and redeemed them with His blood (definite atonement). But the two great acts of election and redemption do not complete the work of salvation. Included in God's plan for saving lost sinners is the renewing work of the Holy Spirit, by which redemption is applied to the elect. It is this aspect of salvation that can be said to be irresistible or efficacious. When Calvinists say that grace is irresistible, they mean that the Holy Spirit never fails to call, regenerate, and save those whom the Father has elected and Christ has redeemed. Irresistible grace is absolutely infallible; it will fulfill its intent. The objects of saving grace will be saved infallibly.

The efficaciousness of this grace is defined in the Canons of Dort in Head III–IV, Article 11, which presents both the external means that God uses to give us His grace as well as the sovereign way in which He works within us:

> When God accomplishes His good pleasure in the elect or works in them true conversion, He not only causes the gospel to be externally preached to them and powerfully illuminates their mind by His Holy Spirit, that they may rightly understand and discern the things of the Spirit of God; but by the efficacy of the same regenerating Spirit, pervades the inmost recesses of the man; He opens the closed, and softens the hardened heart, and circumcises that which was uncircumcised, infuses new qualities into the will, which though heretofore dead, He quickens; from being evil, disobedient, and refractory, He renders it good, obedient, and pliable; actuates and strengthens it, that like a good tree, it may bring forth the fruits of good actions.

The Westminster Confession (10.1) also provides a definition of irresistible grace:

> All those whom God hath predestinated unto life, and those only, he is pleased in his appointed and accepted time effectually to call, by his Word and Spirit, out of that state of sin and death in which they are by nature, to grace and salvation by Jesus Christ; enlightening their minds spiritually

and savingly to understand the things of God; taking away their heart of
stone, and giving unto them an heart of flesh; renewing their wills, and, by
his almighty power determining them to that which is good; and effectually
drawing them to Jesus Christ; yet so as they come most freely, being made
willing by his grace.

Both of these historic Reformed statements make plain that God's grace is
invincible; it will accomplish His purpose (Eph. 1:11). The elect are passive in
their internal calling and regeneration; then, by the irresistible work of the Spirit,
they are made willing in the day of His power (Ps. 110:3). The result of the
Spirit's effectual calling is that the elect "come most freely, being made willing by
His grace" (10.1).

MADE WILLING

Unfortunately, the term *irresistible* can suggest capricious force or violence to a
sinner's will. To some, it conveys the picture of a mother sitting her child down
at the kitchen table with spinach and liver and saying, "Eat!" But that is not the
meaning, as the Reformed confessional statements show. Though the irresistible
grace of God in calling sinners is forceful and compelling, it works in such a way
that the sinner's will is so renewed that he comes to Christ gladly and willingly.
If you are a believer, you know that when grace took hold of you, it brought you
willingly and lovingly to what God had predetermined for you. No one in history
has ever done anything more willingly and more lovingly than those who receive
Jesus as Lord and Savior. Think of Lydia (Acts 16:14–15) and the Philippian
jailor (Acts 16:30–34); they were not saved *against* their wills.

On the other hand, God must work within the sinner to make him willing
to come to Christ. John 6:44 says that unless the Father "draws" him, a sinner
will not believe the gospel. The original word for *draw* implies a certain compelling force. It is used in John 21:6–11 of fishermen dragging a net. Elsewhere, it is
used of Paul and Silas's being "dragged" by a mob (Acts 16:19) and of the "dragging" of poor men into court by rich men (James 2:6). The idea is that a superior
force is so exerted upon an object or person that the one doing the dragging is
successful.[3]

Some sinners are won over more easily to the gospel than others. John Bunyan said that he had to be dragged all the way to Christ. But in the end, he was willing and desirous to believe. That is irresistible grace: the Spirit breaks down our opposition until we find ourselves longing for Christ and the gospel. We may kick against the gospel *before* we are made willing to receive it, but not *after* our wills are so changed. When the Spirit works in us, He renews our wills, enables them, and restores them to true freedom. The Spirit does not ensnare the will but frees it so that it may obey God's summons joyfully. So Zacchaeus received Jesus joyfully, as we read in Luke 19:6.

R. C. Sproul writes: "The Spirit changes the recalcitrant heart of the sinner, making the unwilling willing to come to Christ. He makes the indisposed disposed to Him, the disinclined fully inclined. Our salvation is entirely of God—God the Father, God the Son, and God the Holy Spirit."[4]

In saving sinners, the Spirit does not supersede the normal processes of thought and choice. He does not overcome the sinner, but transforms him. The Spirit irresistibly draws the elect to Himself with lovingkindness and omnipotence (Jer. 31:3; Hos. 11:4; Luke 14:23). This, then, is the amazing truth of God's grace: God makes the will willing to will God in response to His call. That amounts to what theologians call *effectual calling*.

EFFECTUAL CALLING

As the Canons of Dort and the Westminster Confession imply, another term for the doctrine of irresistible grace is *effectual calling*. Simply put, the doctrine states that though grace can be, and often is, resisted, the calling of a sinner to saving faith in Jesus Christ is irresistible. However, two calls need to be distinguished: an outward or general call that everyone hears, which can be rejected (John 7:41b–42; 10:20; Heb. 12:25), and an inward call that God extends to the elect, which always results in conversion (Matt. 22:9; Acts 2:39; Rom. 9:11; 1 Tim. 6:12).

With the outward call, the gospel is preached and a call to salvation is extended to everyone who hears the message (Isa. 45:22). God is serious about offering Christ to all hearers (Matt. 11:28; 2 Cor. 5:19–21). The Canons of Dort show us that this call from God is earnest and sincere (Head III–IV, Art. 8). All men without distinction are invited to come and drink freely of the water of life in Christ Jesus (Isa. 55:1–7; John 4:14). Forgiveness and salvation are promised to all who repent and believe (2 Thess. 2:14; Rom. 10:15).

But this outward call, extended to all people, will be resisted (Acts 7:51). It will not bring sinners to Christ because men by nature are dead in sin and enslaved by the Devil (Eph. 2:1–5). Intellectually, they do not understand the gospel (Rom. 3:11a); behaviorally, they refuse to do good (Rom. 3:12); volitionally, they will not submit to God (Rom. 8:7); and affectionately, they are alienated from Him (Eph. 4:18–19). They are, of themselves, unable and unwilling to turn from their state of condemnation, depravity, and wickedness to Christ (Matt. 22:1–14). John Benton says, "Within every sinner there is a strong antipathy to the holiness of God, and the powerful attraction of sin holds him or her back from becoming a disciple of Christ."[5] Consequently, the unregenerate sinner will not respond to the gospel call (Heb. 4:6–7); he will screw down the lid on it, "holding the truth in unrighteousness" (Rom. 1:18–32). No matter how persuasive the preacher—even though it be Christ Himself (Luke 13:34)—or how serious his message (Acts 7:51), blind, deaf, and rebellious sinners will not bow before Christ as Lord and look to Him alone for salvation (Isa. 65:1–7; cf. Rom. 10:21). B. B. Warfield writes, "If the gospel is to be committed to the dead wills of sinful men and there is nothing above and beyond, who can be saved? If I am to be changed, something must lay hold of me and change me."[6]

For that change, another call is necessary. To bring sinners to salvation, the triune God must extend to them a special, inward, irresistible call in addition to the outward call contained in the gospel message. For, as Arthur Custance remarks, "If a man by nature always resists the grace of God, then in order for that grace to be effectual it must in some sense be irresistible; for if the grace of God were ineffectual none would be saved, and this we know is not the case."[7]

The inward call, John Murray writes, is "an act of God whereby sinners are translated from darkness to light and ushered into the fellowship of Christ."[8] As 1 Peter 2:9 says, "But ye are a chosen generation, a royal priesthood, an holy nation, a peculiar people; that ye should shew forth the praises of him *who hath called you out of darkness into his marvellous light*" (emphasis mine).

The electing Father is the great Inviter who does this calling. Romans 8:30 tells us, "Whom he did predestinate, them he also called." First Corinthians 1:9 says, "God is faithful, by whom ye were called unto the fellowship of his Son, Jesus Christ our Lord" (cf. 2 Tim. 1:9; John 6:44; Rom. 4:17). But the effectual call is also God's living voice in Jesus Christ. Jesus says in John 10:27, "My sheep hear my voice, and I know them, and they follow me." And the Spirit is involved in drawing men to Christ through the Word (John 16:13–14). When the Word is proclaimed, the Spirit moves it from the ear to the soul so that the gospel enlightens the mind, enabling the sinner to understand, believe, and surrender to spiritual truth. The Spirit irresistibly calls and regenerates the sinner, creating in him a new heart or nature so that he exercises faith in Christ, repents of sin, and embraces the gospel. This inward call is always effectual. The grace in it is irresistible.

Scripture describes this Spirit-wrought change as a new birth (John 3:5), a passing from death to life (John 5:24), a drawing of the Father (John 6:44), a bringing into the fold (John 10:16), an opening of the heart (Acts 16:14), a calling according to God's purpose (Rom. 8:28), an enlightening of the eyes (Eph. 1:18), a spiritual resurrection (Eph. 1:19–20), a quickening from the dead (Col. 2:13), a regeneration (Titus 3:5), a heavenly calling (Heb. 3:1), and a calling from darkness to God's marvelous light (1 Peter 2:9).[9]

Christians receive this inward call by grace. God's grace, which manifests His power, is determined to save them (Rom. 8:28–30). His work of redemption is just as sovereign in application as it is in determination and provision. Grace alone can do what nothing else can do; good advice, moral living, and the law are not sufficient. Dead men need not lectures but life. They need the kind of power that was present when Jesus said, "Lazarus, come forth" (John 11:43).

Thus, when joined with the internal or effectual call of God, the outward call is always irresistible. When the inward call comes with the power that accompanies the truth, the sinner is given the ability and the power to respond (Heb. 3:1). That response happens only in the elect (Rom. 9:11); those whom the Father has chosen and for whom the Son has died will be saved by the work of the Holy Spirit (Titus 3:5). Saving grace is not a gift that can be returned. Grace is divine favor, the attitude of God's own heart. He alone determines who will be favored and who will not. His favor cannot be stopped by sinners, even though they are by nature enemies of the Spirit's saving work.

MONERGISTIC GRACE

Two implications follow from irresistible grace and effectual calling. First, God's gracious calling is monergistic, or one-sided. It is not synergistic, or two-sided, involving God and us (Gal. 1:15). Sproul explains these technical terms well: "Monergism is something that operates by itself or works alone as the sole active party. . . . Synergism is a cooperative venture, a working together of two or more parties."[10]

The Canons of Dort support monergism by rejecting the teaching that "God in the regeneration of man does not use such powers of His omnipotence as potently and infallibly bend man's will to faith and conversion; but that all the works of grace having been accomplished, which God employs to convert man, man may yet so resist God and the Holy Spirit when God intends man's regeneration and wills to regenerate him, and indeed that man often does so resist that he prevents entirely his regeneration, and that it therefore remains in man's power to be regenerated or not" (contrary to Eph. 1:19; 2 Thess. 1:11; 2 Peter 1:3; Head III–IV, Rejection 8). The Canons also reject the synergistic teaching "that grace and free will are partial causes, which together work the beginning of conversion, and that grace, in order of working, does not precede the working of the will; that is, that God does not efficiently help the will of man unto conversion until the will of man moves and determines to do this" (contrary to Rom. 9:16; 1 Cor. 4:7; Phil. 2:13; Head III–IV, Rejection 9).

Rather, the Canons clearly teach that salvation is initiated by God calling us, not our calling on Him. The Pelagians and liberals err when they teach that we have natural ability to answer God's universal call. Lutherans err in teaching that we are provided a special ability to resist the gospel. Arminians err in teaching that all hearers of the gospel now possess a restored ability to obey God's gospel call.[11]

Here is a summary of the differences on this point between the Arminians and the Calvinists at the Synod of Dort:

Arminianism (Resistible Grace)

1. The Holy Spirit does all He can to influence each person to turn to God.

2. The Holy Spirit cannot produce repentance and faith in the soul without the soul exercising its free will to choose repentance and faith; these are, at least in part, man's personal actions and contributions.

3. The Holy Spirit's call is only outward and is always resistible.

4. The Holy Spirit's regenerating work is accomplished only when man responds and cooperates.

5. The Holy Spirit grants regeneration in response to faith; regeneration follows faith.

Calvinism (Irresistible Grace)

1. The Holy Spirit applies salvation to the elect by His calling and regenerating work.

2. The Holy Spirit grants repentance and faith as God-given gifts in the souls of the elect.

3. In addition to His outward call, the Holy Spirit works His inward, irresistible call in the hearts of the elect.

4. The Holy Spirit's saving application is accomplished by His divine, almighty power.

5. The Holy Spirit grants regeneration unto faith; regeneration precedes faith.

To deny the irresistibility of God's saving grace is to say that God can be resisted, against His will, by mere man. The Scriptures teach us that no one can thwart God's will (Eph. 1:11) or stop His hand (Dan. 4:35), and the electing God is the calling God (Rom. 8:29–30). Thus, salvation is monergistic grace (Eph. 2:1–10); it is not a work that we accomplish in whole or even in part (2 Tim. 1:9). It is not a joint venture between the Holy Spirit and us; we do not even cooperate in bringing about our salvation. The elect are not born again because they believe; rather, they believe because they are born again by the Spirit of God (1 John 5:1). That is why the believer confesses:

> I sought the Lord, and afterward I knew
> He moved my soul to seek Him, seeking me;
> It was not I that found, O Savior true,
> No, I was found of Thee.[12]

A rather legalistic Christian once criticized another Christian's testimony, saying: "I appreciated all you said about what God did for you. But you didn't mention anything about your part in it."

"Oh yes," the other Christian said. "I apologize for that. I really should have said that my part was running away, and His part was running after me until He caught me."[13]

The second implication that follows from irresistible grace and effectual calling is that monergistic grace comes to us at enormous cost. The good news of the gospel is that the cost of our sin was paid by the Father, Son, and Holy Spirit, not by us. Pardon and forgiveness did not come to us at a moment of God's weakness; they came when He was being most mighty. His righteousness, justice, and truth are maintained when He adopts believing sinners into His family. The law came by Moses, but grace comes in Jesus Christ (John 1:17). God condones no sin, not even when He shows mercy to us.

Geoff Thomas tells the story of a boy who behaved so badly that he had to stay indoors for a week. He badgered his mother to be let out, but she refused. Then one day, when the mother was under loads of pressure, the boy pleaded and argued with her so much that she finally gave in. She agreed to let him go out and even gave him a few dollars to buy some chocolate.[14]

Because of the horrible way he had been behaving, the boy did not deserve to be let out of the house or to receive money. But in letting him go out, his mother did not show grace to him. Her actions were motivated by despair, frustration, and a longing for peace. They were done at the expense of righteousness. In the long run, what she did was hurtful to her son.

God's grace to sinners is different, for it is grounded in the total satisfaction of God's righteousness. It is not given at the expense of true love and divine holiness; it is given at the expense of the Son of God's incarnation in the womb of Mary and His obedience in suffering the law's just condemnation in Gethsemane, at Gabbatha, and on Golgotha. When God shows us grace, He is faithful and just to do so because of the saving work of Jesus Christ alone.

MEANS AND FRUITS

The means by which the effectual call comes is the gospel of God's salvation in Christ applied by the Spirit. Paul told the Thessalonians that they were called "by our gospel, to the obtaining of the glory of our Lord Jesus Christ" (2 Thess. 2:14). John Calvin was fond of saying that there are two ministers preaching in every sermon: the external minister, the ordained servant of God, who brings the Word of God to the ear; and the internal minister, the Holy Spirit, who moves the Word of God to the soul, convicting it, raising it to new life, and granting it to embrace Christ by faith. John Flavel writes of the external and internal voice of Christ, concluding, "The external voice [of the ordained minister] is evermore ineffectual and successless when it is not animated by that internal spiritual voice" of the Spirit to the heart.[15]

God's gracious calling reaps many fruits. Some of them, which are expounded very ably by Bruce Demarest, include a new identity and authentic self-image in Christ (Rom. 1:6–7; 1 John 3:1–2), union and fellowship with Jesus Christ (Eph. 2:12–13), freedom to serve God and one another in love (Gal. 5:13–14), the peace of Christ (Col. 3:15), a life of proclamation and praise (1 Peter 2:9), perseverance in suffering (John 15:20; 1 Peter 2:21), a holy life (2 Tim. 1:9), and a heavenly prize and kingdom and glory (Phil. 3:13–14; 1 Thess. 2:12; 1 Peter 5:10).[16]

Knowing that God's saving grace is always irresistible and effectual is a great boon to evangelism. Evangelizing our friends can be tough work, and we fail easily. D. Clair Davis says: "No presentation is plain enough to get through to a sin-clouded mind. No amount of conviction can open glazed eyes wide enough to see Jesus. No amount of love can break down a defiant heart."[17] But when we evangelize in faith, looking to the Spirit of God irresistibly to call and regenerate our friends and bring them to faith in Christ, we have hope. Because God made it known that He had many elect in Corinth, Paul had the courage to minister there, despite his fears (Acts 18:9–10). Likewise, evangelists such as George Whitefield, David Brainerd, William Carey, and Charles H. Spurgeon all were encouraged to press on by God's irresistible grace, knowing that God's Word would not return to Him void (Isa. 55:11; cf. Acts 13:44–49). Irresistible grace was also a powerful deterrent to discouragement for Jesus (Matt. 11:25). How humbling it is for us to realize that he who plants and waters the seed of the gospel is nothing while Jesus Christ, who gives the increase through His irresistible grace, is everything (1 Cor. 3:7).

GOD'S CALL AND REGENERATION

Finally, the Canons of Dort make plain that regeneration is coterminous with God's irresistible call. After defining the internal call, the canons provide a complete confessional statement on regeneration, showing the power of the work of regeneration and how delightful and enlivening it is to those who are recipients of irresistible grace:

> And this is the regeneration so highly celebrated in Scripture and denominated a new creation: a resurrection from the dead, a making alive, which God works in us without our aid. But this is in no wise effected merely by the

external preaching of the gospel, by moral suasion, or such a mode of operation, that after God has performed His part, it still remains in the power of
man to be regenerated or not, to be converted or to continue unconverted;
but it is evidently a supernatural work, most powerful, and at the same time
most delightful, astonishing, mysterious, and ineffable; not inferior in efficacy to creation or the resurrection from the dead, as the Scripture inspired
by the author of this work declares; so that all in whose heart God works in
this marvelous manner are certainly, infallibly, and effectually regenerated,
and do actually believe. Whereupon the will thus renewed is not only actu-
ated and influenced by God, but in consequence of this influence, becomes
itself active. Wherefore also, man is himself rightly said to believe and repent,
by virtue of that grace received. (Head III–IV, Art. 12)

Like the effectual call, regeneration is done *to* us and *within* us, not *by* us. As
Iain Murray says, "We are as helpless to co-operate in our regeneration as we are
to co-operate in the work of Calvary."[18] And, like the effectual call, regeneration
is supernatural, personal, powerful, and convicting, yet drawing and delightful.
It is a surprising and mysterious work, an ineffable and fruitful work. It is the
initial breathing of life by the Spirit into the soul, which then serves as the "basis
and the springhead" of all the other parts of the order of salvation, such as faith,
repentance, justification, adoption, sanctification, and perseverance.[19] So Maurice Roberts writes, "The act of God in our regeneration is so momentous that
no single category of thought is sufficient to describe the changes it brings about
in and for us."[20]

EXTRAVAGANT LOVE

Salvation is due to the spontaneous, extravagant love of God. It is due to undeserved grace, or clemency on the part of the holy, just God to sinners under
condemnation by the law and threatened with eternal destruction. "By grace are
ye saved through faith; and that not of yourselves: it is the gift of God: not of
works, lest any man should boast" (Eph. 2:8–9).

If you are to be saved, it must be by the operation of God's irresistible grace
in your life. So you must pray that His Word might be applied to your heart to
create in you a sense of need. Tell Him of your hopeless, helpless condition. Tell

Him you see no way out of this predicament unless He is sovereignly pleased to rescue you. Pray that He would regenerate you, that He would cause a spark of divine life in your soul.

Then, as He answers your prayer and you believe as He has commanded (Acts 16:31), you will recognize that your believing was because of His working in you both to will and to do of His good pleasure (Phil. 2:13). Be encouraged, for "salvation is of the LORD" (Jonah 2:9).

DISCUSSION QUESTIONS

1. What does the Bible mean by the term *grace*?

2. How would you explain the term *irresistible grace* to a person who has never heard it?

3. Does the doctrine of irresistible grace mean that God treats us like robots? If not, how does the irresistible grace of God relate to our wills?

4. What does the term *effectual call* mean?

5. Does the idea of effectual calling have biblical support? If so, what Scripture passages support this idea?

6. What is monergism? Are Pelagians or Arminians monergistic?

7. How does Arminianism conceive of the work of the Holy Spirit in saving sinners? Where in the Bible is this view shown to be wrong?

8. What is regeneration?

9. How does regeneration take place?

NOTES

1   Charles H. Spurgeon, *A Defence of Calvinism* (Edinburgh: Banner of Truth Trust, 2008), 9.

2   Ronald Cammenga and Ronald Hanko, *Saved by Grace: A Study of the Five Points of Calvinism* (Grandville, Mich.: Reformed Free Publishing, 2002), 144.

3   Curt Daniel, "The History and Theology of Calvinism" (Dallas: Scholarly Reprints, 1993), 379–380.

4   R. C. Sproul, "'Can These Bones Live?' The Effectual Calling of the Holy Spirit," *Tabletalk*, 28, no. 7 (July 2004): 7.

5   John Benton, *Evangelistic Calvinism* (Edinburgh: Banner of Truth Trust, 2006), 22.

6   B. B. Warfield, *The Plan of Salvation* (Grand Rapids: Eerdmans, 1977), 49.

7   Quoted in Daniel, "The History and Theology of Calvinism," 378.

8   John Murray, *Redemption Accomplished and Applied* (Grand Rapids: Eerdmans, 1955), 86.

9   David N. Steele, Curtis C. Thomas, and S. Lance Quinn, *The Five Points of Calvinism: Defined, Defended, and Documented*, 2nd Ed. (Phillipsburg, N.J.: P&R, 2004), 61.

10 R. C. Sproul, *Grace Unknown: The Heart of Reformed Theology* (Grand Rapids: Baker, 1997), 183–184.

11 Bruce Demarest, *The Cross and Salvation* (Wheaton, Ill.: Crossway, 1997), 204–210.

12 From the hymn "I Sought the Lord, and Afterward I Knew," anonymous, 1878.

13 Abbreviated from James M. Boice and Philip Graham Ryken, *The Doctrines of Grace* (Wheaton, Ill.: Crossway, 2002), 153–154.

14 Geoffrey Thomas, "Praising God's Glorious Grace," sermon on Eph. 1:6, Alfred Place Baptist Church, Aberystwyth, Wales, http://www.alfredplacechurch.org.uk/sermons/eph8.htm

15 John Flavel, *The Works of John Flavel* (Edinburgh: Banner of Truth Trust, 1968), 4:170.

16 Demarest, *The Cross and Salvation*, 230–231.

17 D. Clair Davis, "Irresistible Salvation," in *The Practical Calvinist*, ed. Peter A. Lillback (Ross-shire, U.K.: Christian Focus, 2002), 40.

18 Quoted in John Blanchard, *The Complete Gathered Gold* (Darlington, England: Evangelical Press, 2006), 522.

19 Octavius Winslow, *The Work of the Holy Spirit* (Edinburgh: Banner of Truth Trust, 1972), 56–86.

20 Quoted in Blanchard, *The Complete Gathered Gold*, 523.

CHAPTER 9

PERSEVERANCE
AND ASSURANCE

All our progress and perseverance are from God.[1]

—JOHN CALVIN

$\mathcal{T}$he fifth point of Calvinism is the perseverance of the saints. The Fifth Head of the Canons of Dort, however, links two doctrines of soteriology: perseverance and assurance. While Arminianism cannot be sure of either because it bases salvation partly on man, both perseverance and assurance have always figured prominently in Calvinism. Both doctrines need to be addressed today because the lives of Christians reveal that both are sorely lacking. The fruits of perseverance and assurance—such as the diligent use of the means of grace, continuance in heartfelt obedience to God's will, desire for fellowship with God, yearning for God's glory and heaven, love for the church, and intercession for revival—clearly appear to be waning.

The need for a biblically based doctrine of perseverance and assurance is compounded by today's emphasis on feeling. How we feel often takes precedence over what we think, know, or believe. This attitude has infiltrated the church, particularly the growing charismatic movement. The movement offers emotion and excitement to fill the void created by the lack of a true understanding. Today more than ever, we desperately need rich, Calvinist thinking about perseverance and assurance coupled with vibrant, sanctified living.

So what are perseverance of the saints and assurance of faith? How do these doctrines work together in the Christian's life?[2]

PERSEVERANCE OF THE SAINTS

We first must ask, who are the saints? Many would say they are people who have been baptized or have made decisions for Christ at evangelistic meetings. However, Scripture and the Reformed confessions define *saints* as those "whom God calls, according to His purpose, to the communion of His Son, our Lord Jesus Christ, and regenerates by the Holy Spirit" (Canons of Dort, Head V, Art. 1) and as "they whom God hath accepted in his Beloved, effectually called and sanctified by his Spirit" (Westminster Confession of Faith, 17.1).

The doctrine of the perseverance of the saints teaches that all who partake of the grace and power of saving union with Christ by faith continue in that union with its benefits and fruits. By the preserving work of the triune God (1 Cor. 1:8–9), they persevere in true faith and in the works that proceed from faith so long as they continue in the world (John 6:37–40; 2 Tim. 4:7). Thus, if by the Spirit of God you are regenerate, justified,[3] adopted into God's family, and sanctified, you cannot lose that salvation (1 Peter 1:5). God will keep you forever (Jude 24–25), for your perseverance is the fruit of His preservation (Phil. 1:6). If you have confessed Christ from the heart, sin will not have dominion over you (Rom. 6:14); you "can neither totally nor finally fall away from the state of grace" (Westminster Confession of Faith, 17.1).[4]

This doctrine does *not* mean that believers are immune to sin or that they can never fail to exercise saving faith. Though their faith won't die, there are times when, sadly, it will not be active. Apart from a continuous influx of Christ into their souls, believers cannot continue or flourish. God alone gives the increase, for He never forsakes the work of His hands. When we speak of the perseverance of the saints, we *do* mean that having brought the elect into vital union with Himself, Jesus Christ continually supplies them with His grace. He is the life of their life and the strength of their strength. Furthermore, the Holy Spirit, having selected the hearts of the elect as His dwelling place, never leaves them; He promotes their sanctification until He has made their souls ripe for entrance into heaven. The faithful, covenant-keeping God keeps alive in the hearts of His elect the spark of holy love, which He Himself has kindled, despite their waywardness, slothfulness, and disobedience. He even uses His very imperfect children in promoting their own spiritual well-being through faith, prayer, confession, and the proper use of the means of grace. God, and God alone, sees to it that His

PERSEVERANCE AND ASSURANCE

children never tear themselves loose from His grip and fall prey to Satan (John 10:27–30).[5]

The great Scottish preacher Ebenezer Erskine (1680–1754) once visited a woman on her deathbed and lovingly tested her readiness for heaven. When she assured him that she was ready to depart to be with Christ because she was in that hand from which no one could pluck her, Erskine asked, "But are you not afraid that you will slip through His fingers in the end?"

"That is impossible because of what you have always told us," she said.

"And what is that?" he asked.

"That we are united to Him, and so we are part of His body. I cannot slip through His fingers because I am one of His fingers. Besides, Christ has paid too high of a price for my redemption to leave me in Satan's hand. If I were to be lost, He would lose more than I; I would lose my salvation, but He would lose His glory, because one of His sheep would be lost."

That dear saint was right. Christ's glory is bound up in the perseverance of His elect (Rom. 8:28–30). Christopher Love writes, "If the elect should perish, then Jesus Christ should be very unfaithful to his Father, because God the Father hath given this charge to Christ, that whomsoever he elected Christ should preserve them safe, to bring them to heaven."[6]

Because of God's central role in perseverance, some theologians prefer to speak of the *preservation* of the saints rather than the *perseverance* of the saints. These two notions are closely related, but they are not synonymous. The unchanging nature of God's saving design for His people and His preserving hand undergirds their perseverance. In other words, God keeps believers in the faith, preserves them from straying, and ultimately perfects them (1 Peter 1:5; Jude 24). He who promises to keep them will keep His promise. When believers sin, God may withdraw from them temporarily, but He will not disinherit them. We may be confident that God will finish the work of grace He has begun in His own (Ps. 138:8; Phil. 1:6), since Christ is both "the author and finisher of our faith" (Heb. 12:2). Believers are preserved through Christ's purchase and intercession (Luke 22:32; John 17:15), the abiding ministry of the Holy Spirit (John 14:16; 1 John 2:27), God's immutable nature and eternal grace toward His elect (Rom. 11:29), His promises of perseverance (John 10:27–30; 2 Tim. 1:12), His covenantal love (Rom. 8:29–39), and His provisions for perseverance (1 Cor. 10:13). As Charles H. Spurgeon once said, "If God lights the candle, none can blow it out."[7]

If the elect could lose their salvation, the Father's election would be ineffectual, Christ's intercession would be irrelevant, and the Spirit's sanctification would be impotent. Salvation would be destructible, contrary to what 1 Peter 1:3–5 says. The perseverance of the saints is part of the unbreakable chain of salvation granted to the elect (Rom. 8:29–30); election requires God's effectual call, which, in turn, compels God's preservation and the believer's perseverance (1 John 3:9).

However, perseverance is the believer's work as well as God's.[8] Assured of victory in Christ who keeps them, the saints strive to keep themselves in His favor by persevering. Perseverance is their life-long activity. It includes confessing Christ as Savior (Rom. 10:9), bringing forth the fruits of grace (John 15:16), and persevering to the end (Matt. 10:22; Heb. 10:28–29). True believers persevere in union with Christ (John 15) and in the "things that accompany salvation" (Heb. 6:9). God does not deal with believers "as unaccountable automatons, but as moral agents,"[9] says A. W. Pink, for believers actively persevere in the struggle against sin for sanctification (Phil. 2:12).

Perseverance is not mechanical or automatic obedience.[10] The use of "holy exercises of piety" is critical to perseverance (Canons of Dort, Head V, Art. 2). The use of the means of grace, such as reading, hearing, searching, meditating on, praying over, and practicing the Scriptures, is necessary to flee sin and promote holiness (John 5:39; 8:31–32; Heb. 10:25–26; 12:14). Examining ourselves and diligently partaking of the sacraments are also essential (1 Cor. 11:28; Canons of Dort, Head V, Art. 14). Believers persevere by giving themselves wholeheartedly to the spiritual battle and by keeping themselves from sin (1 John 5:18), remembering that the church of Christ is never glorious except when baptized in holiness. They persevere in keeping the law of God (James 1:22–25) and keeping themselves in the love of God (Jude 21). They persevere in maintaining a good conscience before God and men (Acts 24:16). They persevere in communing in love with one another as the people of Christ, a body that moves, lives, worships, and grows together (1 John 3:14; Ps. 133). They persevere in watching and praying that they might not enter into temptation (Matt. 26:41; Eph. 6:18). They persevere in making their calling and election sure (2 Peter 1:10). They run with patience the race that is set before them, looking to Jesus as the pioneer and perfecter of their faith (Heb. 12:1–2). As John Murray says, "The perseverance of the saints reminds us very forcefully that only those who persevere to the end are truly saints."[11]

So divine preservation and human perseverance are complementary. Saints persevere only because of the preserving activity of God at work in them (Phil. 2:13). God meets them in their doubts, fears, and afflictions, providing them grace and strength to "keep on keeping on." The God who commands believers to persevere provides them with the ability to do so.[12] John Owen writes, "Grace does not annul our responsibility but fits us to discharge it; it relieves from no duties, but equips for the performance of them."[13] Perseverance, therefore, extends beyond preservation to stress the believer's responsibility.

It is true that those who are kept in Christ will believe in Christ. But also true is this: those who believe in Christ will be kept in Christ.[14] Grasping this dual nature of the perseverance of the saints avoids both the error of hyper-Calvinism ("If it is certain that I will be preserved, why must I persevere?") and of Arminianism ("Since my perseverance is all-important, why should I believe in God's preservation?").

ASSURANCE OF FAITH

Assurance of faith is the believer's conviction that, by God's grace, he belongs to Christ, has received full pardon for all sins, and will inherit eternal life. Someone who has true assurance not only believes in Christ for salvation but also knows that he believes and is graciously loved by God. Such assurance includes freedom from guilt, joy in God, and a sense of belonging to the family of God.

Assurance is dynamic; it varies according to conditions and is capable of growing in force and fruitfulness. As James W. Alexander says, assurance "carries with it the idea of fullness, such as of a tree laden with fruit, or of a vessel's sails when stretched by a favouring gale."[15]

Assurance reveals itself in close fellowship with God, childlike obedience, and an intense longing to glorify Christ in all things. Assured believers view heaven as their home and long for Christ's return and their translation to glory (2 Tim. 4:6–8).

ASSURANCE, THEN PERSEVERANCE

The fruits of assurance promote perseverance. As the Canons of Dort remind us: "Of the preservation of the elect to salvation and of their perseverance in the faith, true believers for themselves may and do obtain assurance, according to the measure of their faith, whereby they arrive at the certain persuasion that they ever will continue true and living members of the church; and that they experience forgiveness of sins, and will at last inherit eternal life" (Head V, Art. 9).

The canons affirm that believers may be assured of their perseverance. That assurance, however, is grounded in "the preservation of the elect to salvation." Take away God's preservation, and every conscientious believer would despair; our failures would overwhelm whatever fruits we discover and destroy all assurance. By speaking first of God's election and preservation, the canons show us that assurance is rooted in God's sovereign grace and promises—yes, in God Himself.

Assurance helps the believer persevere, first, by encouraging him to rest on God's grace in Christ and His promises in the gospel; and second, by presenting these as a powerful motive for Christian living. As the Puritan Thomas Goodwin says, assurance "makes a man work for God ten times more than before. . . . [It] causes the heart to be more thankful, and more fruitfully and cheerfully obedient; it perfects love, opens and gives vent to a new stream of godly sorrow, adds new motives, enlarges and encourages the heart in prayer, winds up all graces to a new and higher key and strain, causing a spring tide of all."[16]

Assurance further serves perseverance through sanctification. The Canons of Dort affirm this in Head V, Article 10, saying that assurance is fostered not only by faith in God's promises and the witnessing testimony of the Holy Spirit, but also "from a serious and holy desire to preserve a good conscience and to perform good works."

PERSEVERANCE, THEN ASSURANCE

The Westminster Confession also affirms the close relationship between assurance and perseverance. However, the confession begins with perseverance of the saints (chap. 17) and then proceeds to assurance of grace and salvation (chap. 18). This order implies three things:

First, perseverance opens the way for assurance. Rooted in God's grace, objective perseverance makes possible subjective assurance, which is rooted in the believer's conscience. If a Christian does not believe in the perseverance of the saints, he cannot be sure he is going to heaven. He may know he is in a state of grace, but he has no way of knowing whether he will continue in that state. Assurance is wedded to the doctrine of perseverance. As the Dutch theologian Frans Burmann (1628–1679) writes: "Upon certainty of perseverance follows certainty of salvation; the latter does not exist without the former. Unless he perseveres, no one is saved. Some wickedly tear them apart and, while upholding the certainty of salvation, deny that of perseverance. This is a claim to assert subjective certainty without objective certainty."[17]

Second, perseverance increases assurance. Those who persist in works that spring from faith will usually attain high levels of assurance (cf. Westminster Confession of Faith, 17.2 with 18.2; 17.3 with 18.4); that is why believers must persevere to the end in faith, holiness, and obedience. To deny the necessity of perseverance is to deny abundant scriptural teaching to the contrary (Matt. 7:13–14; Luke 18:15; John 8:31–32; 15:6; Rom. 6:22; 8:22–23; 1 Cor. 15:1–2; Col. 1:21–23; 2 Tim. 2:11; Heb. 2:1, 3; 3:13–14; 12:14).[18] Such denial will weaken the resolve of the believer to run the Christian race, which, in turn, will open him to the chastening hand of his Father (Heb. 12:1–13).

Third, perseverance encourages the believer to live in hope. As believers persevere, they become increasingly confident of victory in Christ and their future with Him in glory (Rom. 5:1–11). G. C. Berkouwer says, "The perseverance of the saints is unbreakably connected with the assurance of faith, in which the believer faces the future with confidence—not with the idea that all dangers and threats have been removed, but rather with the assurance that they shall be conquered indeed."[19]

The poet Augustus Toplady says this well:

My name from the palms of His hands,
Eternity will not erase;
Impressed on His heart it remains,
In marks of indelible grace;
Yes, I to the end shall endure,
As sure as the earnest is given;
More happy, but not more secure,
The glorified spirits in heaven.[20]

PROBLEMS WITH PERSEVERANCE

How do we explain those who seem to be Christians but fall away from the faith? In the parable of the sower, Jesus describes such people, warning that not every joyful response to the gospel is a saving response. Stony-ground hearers initially receive the gospel and flourish, but wither when troubles arise. The Bible also describes people who seemed to follow the Lord for a time but fell away, such as Saul, Ahithophel, Judas Iscariot, Hymenaeus, and Alexander (1 Tim. 1:19–20). None of those men was truly a child of God (1 John 2:19). They may have possessed various degrees of convictions or impressions in God's common grace, but they lacked saving faith, and hence were never elect believers.[21] Owen offered the following syllogism that applies to such cases:

1. The elect cannot fall away (John 10:27–29).
2. Some professors of faith do fall away.
3. Hence, those professors of faith are not elect believers.[22]

Let us make sure of our own trust in Christ, lest we only seem to believe but, in the end, prove we do not.

A preacher so often warned his congregation about the dangers of a false profession that some began to think he believed a true Christian could fall from grace and be lost. A church member asked him, "Are you against the perseverance of the saints?"

"Not at all," the preacher said. "It is the perseverance of sinners that I oppose."

The man was not happy with that answer. "Do you think that a child of God can fall very low and yet be restored?" he asked.

The minister responded wisely: "I think it would be very dangerous to make that experiment."

Let no one presume on the perseverance of the saints and continue in sin. Let us pursue holiness every day, without which no one will see the Lord (Heb. 12:14).[23]

There is a grave danger here. We cannot claim assurance without manifesting the fruits of perseverance, glibly citing "once saved, always saved" while living in sin. Like Paul, we must recognize the danger of making shipwreck of our faith and becoming castaways in the end (1 Cor. 9:26–27; 10:12).[24] The Baptist theologian John Dagg rightly declares, "It is a wretched and fatal perversion if men conclude that, having been once converted, they will be saved, whatever may be their course of life."[25] Perseverance does not mean that we can live as we please once we profess Christ. It is antinomianism (*anti* means "against" and *nomos* means "the law") that says that once you are saved, you are always saved, regardless of how sinfully you live. John Murray warns, "It is utterly wrong to say that a believer is secure quite irrespective of his subsequent life of sin and unfaithfulness."[26]

Calvinists always have been reluctant to speak of the security of believers without simultaneously insisting that security lies ultimately in the preservation of God. The believer is not *inherently* indestructible, but when God has begun a work in him, He will continue to provide His Spirit for the believer's preservation until He finishes His redemption (Phil. 1:6). Thus, the "once saved, always saved" notion is incomplete, as if the justification of the sinner were the whole salvation of God, to the exclusion of the "things that accompany salvation," such as repentance unto life, faith, and holiness.

Advocates of this view deny that an important aspect of assurance is the ability to say, "Yes, I do belong to Christ because I find in myself changes which He alone can work and changes which only His unbought love prompted Him to work."[27] Ultimately, this view teaches that faith can exist in a vacuum and that the believer does not need the law as a rule of life—the essence of antinomianism.

Doctrinal antinomianism is unbiblical, but practical antinomianism, or living lawlessly while claiming grace, is even worse (Rom. 6:1–2). Practical antinomians may profess to believe, but their evil fruits disprove it. "By their fruits ye shall know them" (Matt. 7:20).

Perseverance of the saints, therefore, does not mean that everyone who claims to have received Christ as his Savior, participates in Christian work, and manifests various gifts is "eternally secure" (Matt. 7:21–23). The church includes hypocrites who manifest the external signs of persevering saints but lack the marks of true Christians. Those marks, according to the Belgic Confession, are: (1) receiving Christ by faith as the only Savior, (2) avoiding sin, (3) following after righteousness, (4) loving the true God and one's neighbor, (5) not turning aside to the right or left, (6) crucifying the flesh with the works thereof, (7) fighting against infirmities, and (8) continually taking refuge in the passion and obedience of Christ (Art. 29). The church also includes people like Demas, who seem to be godly but whose departure from the truth and the church reveal that they never really were in saving union with Christ (2 Tim. 4:10; Heb. 6:4–6).

The Westminster Confession teaches three important truths about assurance: the possibility of false assurance and self-deception (18.1); the perseverance of genuine believers, who can "neither totally nor finally fall away from the state of grace" (17.1); and the serious consequences of sin (15.4; 17.3; 18.4). Even for true believers, sin and arrested growth are displeasing to God, grieve the Holy Spirit, diminish comfort and assurance, harden the heart, wound the conscience, hurt others, and bring temporal judgments (17.3). Though sin will not keep the believer's soul out of heaven, it will keep heaven out of his soul. Spurgeon says, "It is a glorious truth that God will keep His people, but it is an abominable falsehood that sin will do them no harm."[28]

A Christian cannot enjoy assurance while living in disobedience to God. John Gill asks, "Can a man believe he shall persevere to the end and yet indulge in sin, as if he was resolved not to persevere?"[29] Despite our inevitable falling short of God's standards and our continual need to flee to Calvary for pardon, how we live matters. Anthony Burgess, one of the Westminster divines, says, "Nothing will darken thy soul more than dull, lazy, and negligent walking."[30] If assurance remained firm while obedience faltered, the believer would take for granted the great privilege of salvation through Christ and grow spiritually lazy.

Backsliding destroys assurance, and rightly so. Doubts and fears then prompt a fresh desire for renewed assurance. They urge self-examination, repentance, and acts of faith that motivate us to run anew the race that is set before us (Heb. 12). Thomas Schreiner and Ardel Caneday write: "Those who desire assurance while they are turning away from the Lord are like runners who quit running in the middle of the race but inquire of the official if they will still receive a prize for running. Our assurance in the faith is strengthened as we continue to run the race, persevering until the end to receive the prize."[31]

Finally, let us remember that scriptural passages that warn us not to fall away (such as those in Hebrews, particularly 6:4–6) do not affirm the apostasy of saints; rather, they urge us to persevere in faithfulness to God and to His revelation of the new covenant in Jesus Christ. God uses serious admonitions to keep us from backsliding and away from a host of dangers.

When our children were young, we often warned them that they would be killed if they went into the busy street in front of our home. We showed them a line that they should not cross, which was still quite far from the road. If they crossed the line and headed for the road, my wife would catch them and pull them back long before they reached the road. Similarly, God warns us about backsliding and falling away in Hebrews to keep us far from the highways of sin and to motivate us to remain committed to Him. When we cross the line and fall into sin, however, His paternal eye and chastening hand bring us to repentance and forgiveness long before we self-destruct on the highway of apostasy.

And behind the dim unknown,
Standeth God within the shadow,
Keeping watch above His own.[32]

Curt Daniel concludes: "The Reformed doctrine of perseverance is that a regenerate soul will certainly persevere through the trials of life and continue to believe and repent. He will slip and fall, develop bad habits, wrestle with doubts, but through it all he will keep on going even as he began. . . . All believers slip and fall into sin, but no true believer stays down. Just as God gave him faith and repentance unto initial conversion, so He supplies him with faith and repentance all along the way to heaven" (Canons of Dort, Head V, Art. 7).[33]

ALL BY GOD'S AMAZING GRACE

Believers who have come to Christ by grace remain wedded to Christ, knowing they are in Him by grace. Perseverance and assurance are the two sides of grace. You cannot persevere in grace without growing in assurance, and you cannot grow in assurance of faith without perseverance.[34]

This growth is not easily attained, but it is attainable through God's grace. As the Canons of Dort tell us: "The Scripture moreover testifies that believers in this life have to struggle with various carnal doubts and that under grievous temptations they are not always sensible of this full assurance of faith and certainty of persevering. But God, who is the Father of all consolation, does not suffer them to be tempted above that they are able, but will with the temptation also make a way to escape that they may be able to bear it (1 Cor. 10:13), and by the Holy Spirit again inspires them with the comfortable assurance of persevering" (Head V, Art. 11).

With this "comfortable assurance of persevering," we, with John Newton, can sing of God's "amazing grace":

Through many dangers, toils and snares,
I have already come:
'Tis grace that brought me safe thus far,
and grace will lead me home.[35]

Likewise, we can say with the singer of Psalm 73, who came through a long, dark night of struggle to a place of full assurance, both of God's preservation of him and of his own perseverance in faith:

In sweet communion, Lord, with Thee I constantly abide;
My hand Thou holdest in Thy own to keep me near Thy side.
Thy counsel through my earthly way shall guide me and control,
And then to glory afterward Thou wilt receive my soul.[36]

The doctrine of perseverance is not just a pretty ribbon that completes the package of Calvinist soteriology. It involves intense Christian watchfulness and discipleship. It requires pilgrim warfare in a world that aims to distract the mind and rip open the heart. It embraces major issues of life and death, including our eternal security in glory. Frances Roberts says, "Perseverance is the rope that ties the soul to the doorpost of heaven."[37] John Blanchard concludes: "Glory for the Christian is more certain than the grave. God has never torn up a Christian's birth certificate. It is possible to fall in grace, but not to fall from grace. The Christian can be as certain of arriving in heaven as he is that Christ has already ascended there."[38]

Because the believer's perseverance depends on the One who does the work of salvation, namely, the triune God, every believer is a jewel of Christ and can never be lost. Malachi 3:17 says, "And they shall be mine, saith the LORD of hosts, in that day when I make up my jewels; and I will spare them, as a man spareth his own son that serveth him." Thomas Brooks adds, "Earthly jewels sometimes get separated from their owner, Christ's jewels, never. . . . Earthly jewels are sometimes lost, Christ's jewels never. . . . Earthly jewels are sometimes stolen, Christ's jewels, never!"[39]

Newton, once a sea captain, told of a remarkable dream he had. In his dream, he was in Naples Harbor when a most glorious person came aboard the ship and gave Newton a beautiful jewel. Newton was thrilled. But soon another person came on deck and began to mock Newton, saying the jewel was no good and urging him to throw it away. Eventually, Newton came to believe him and flung the jewel into the sea. Immediately, he was filled with horror. "Oh, what have I done?" he cried.

Soon, the glorious person came to him again and asked him about the jewel. With shame, Newton confessed he had thrown it away. What would happen? Newton saw the glorious person go over the side of the ship and return with the jewel. As he came back on the deck, Newton held out his hand for the jewel, but the glorious one refused, saying: "No. The jewel is yours; it always will be yours; but I will keep it for you."[40]

"In the final analysis, the hope of true believers resides not in our feeble hold of God but in his powerful grasp of us," Bruce Demarest writes. "The stability and constancy of our spiritual lives rests not in our human powers but in God's eternal purpose and infinite resources."[41] God's purposes, God's promises, God's powers, God's provisions, God's protection—what comfort that gives.[42]

The Canons of Dort conclude their teaching on perseverance with these triumphant words:

> The carnal mind is unable to comprehend this doctrine of the perseverance of the saints and the certainty thereof, which God hath most abundantly revealed in His Word, for the glory of His Name, and the consolation of pious souls, and which He impresses upon the hearts of the faithful. Satan abhors it; the world ridicules it; the ignorant and hypocrite abuse it, and heretics oppose it; but the spouse of Christ hath always most tenderly loved and constantly defended it as an inestimable treasure; and God, against whom neither counsel nor strength can prevail, will dispose her to continue this conduct to the end. Now, to this one God, Father, Son, and Holy Spirit, be honor and glory forever. Amen. (Head V, Art. 15)

ARMINIANISM AND CALVINISM

Arminianism is like a bridge in Lancaster County, Pa., that is wide but goes only halfway across the river. It fails to lead a hiker safely to the other side of the river. Arminianism is wide and easy to travel, but it does not lead a person to the harbor of God's bosom. In the end, Arminianism is cruel in failing to deliver what it promises. It weakens the essence of God, exalts man, and opens the door to liberalism.

The way of Calvinism seems narrow; in some sense it is, for it expects self-denial and teaches that man cannot meet God halfway. But in the end, Calvinism brings a believer across the river into the arms of Jehovah. Believed in the mind and experienced in the soul, Calvinism's truths lead a sinner to salvation.

Calvinism gives both God and man their due. It glorifies God, humbles the sinner, and encourages the saint. It invigorates the believer who knows that if a sovereign God is for him, no one can be successful against him (Rom. 8:31). As J. C. Ryle writes: "No soldiers of Christ are ever lost, missing or left dead on the battlefield."[43]

Erroll Hulse provides a helpful illustration of how salvation is worked by our sovereign God:

> In the town of Otley in Yorkshire a group of anxious onlookers surrounded a man who was lying down flat with his hand down a rainwater drain. Among the onlookers was a mother duck expressing deep alarm. She had been leading her ducklings along the gutter and hopped over the drain, but one by one her ducklings had fallen in. One by one the man lying flat retrieved them. All ten of them were brought up unscathed and happily followed mummy duck down to the Wharfe River. There is no way that they could have come out of that drain on their own. Power of a greater kind than duck-power was needed. In the case of our salvation we must affirm that it comes entirely from an omnipotent, gracious God.[44]

Some suggest that Calvinism and Arminianism should reconcile because the Bible affirms both divine sovereignty and human responsibility. We must be Calvinists on our knees and Arminians on our feet, they say. But such a proposal is naive. Calvinism asserts the role of human responsibility every bit as much as Arminianism does. Calvinism and Arminianism cannot be joined together because of the following irreconcilable differences:

- The initiative in salvation is either with God or with man.
- Depravity is either total or partial.
- Election is either unconditional or conditional.
- Atonement is either particular or universal.
- Saving grace is either irresistible or resistible.
- The saints either must persevere in faith or they may fall away.

These differences are not just matters of emphasis; they represent different systems of thought. The five points of Calvinism are biblical and need to be proclaimed with boldness and vigor.

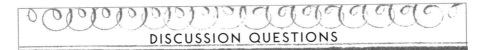

DISCUSSION QUESTIONS

1. Is there a relationship between the doctrine of the perseverance of the saints and assurance of salvation? If so, what is it?

2. How would you show a person who believes he can lose his salvation that his view misreads the Holy Scriptures? Give the Bible passages that support perseverance.

3. Why is the phrase "the perseverance of the saints" better than the expression "eternal security"?

NOTES

1 Quoted in John Blanchard, *The Complete Gathered Gold* (Darlington, England: Evangelical Press, 2006), 446.

2 Parts of this chapter are an expansion of Joel R. Beeke, "Almost Home," *Tabletalk*, 28, no. 12 (Dec. 2004): 16–18.

3 For a helpful article on the relation between justification and perseverance, see Derek W. H. Thomas, "Justification and Perseverance," *Banner of Truth*, no. 524 (May 2007): 1–7.

4 The emphasis in the doctrine of perseverance is on the regenerate for good reason. As Maurice Roberts points out: "The point of disagreement between Reformed and Arminian writers is not whether the *elect* may be lost (which neither side believes) but whether the *regenerate* may be lost" ("Final Perseverance," *Banner of Truth*, no. 265 [Oct., 1985]: 7; cf. A. A. Hodge, *Outlines of Theology* [Edinburgh: Banner of Truth Trust, 1972], 543).

5 This paragraph is abridged from Herman Kuiper, *By Grace Alone: A Study in Soteriology* (Grand Rapids: Eerdmans, 1955), 139–140.

6 Quoted in Blanchard, *The Complete Gathered Gold*, 170.

7 Ibid., 171.

8 R. C. Sproul, *Grace Unknown: The Heart of Reformed Theology* (Grand Rapids: Baker, 1997), 212.

9 A. W. Pink, *Eternal Security* (Grand Rapids: Guardian Press, 1974), 15.

10 W. Robert Godfrey, "The Means of Persevering Grace," *Tabletalk*, 28, no. 12 (Dec. 2004): 13.

11 John Murray, *Redemption Accomplished and Applied* (Grand Rapids: Eerdmans, 1955), 155.

12 John Owen, *The Works of John Owen* (Edinburgh: Banner of Truth Trust, 1965), 6:165.

13 Ibid., 11:280.

14 John Benton, *Evangelistic Calvinism* (Edinburgh: Banner of Truth Trust, 2006), 27.

15 James W. Alexander, *Consolation to the Suffering People of God* (Ligonier, Pa.: Soli Deo Gloria, 1992), 138.

16 Thomas Goodwin, *The Works of Thomas Goodwin* (Grand Rapids: Reformation Heritage Books, 2006), 1:251; 8:347.

17 Quoted in Heinrich Heppe, *Reformed Dogmatics* (London: George Allen & Unwin, 1950), 585.

18 Cf. Al Martin, "Perseverance," taped message.

19 G. C. Berkouwer, *Faith and Perseverance* (Grand Rapids: Eerdmans, 1958), 11.

20 From the hymn "A Debtor to Mercy Alone," by Augustus M. Toplady.

21 This is also a classic and common interpretation of Hebrews 6:4–6 (e.g., John Owen, *An Exposition of Hebrews*, ed. W. H. Goold [Edinburgh: Banner of Truth Trust, 1991], 5:70–91; Henry Knapp, "John Owen's Interpretation of Hebrews 6:4–6: Eternal Perseverance of the Saints in Puritan Exegesis," *Sixteenth Century Journal*, 34, 1 [2003]: 29–52; John R. De Witt, "Perseverance of the Saints," *Tabletalk*, 28, no. 1 [Jan. 2004]: 54–55; Douglas Kelly, "Perseverance of the Saints?" *Tabletalk*, 28, no. 4 [Apr. 2004]: 37–38).

22 Owen, *Works of John Owen*, 11:113ff. For a summary of Owen's arguments for perseverance against the Arminian John Goodwin, see Joel R. Beeke, *The Quest for Full Assurance: The Legacy of Calvin and His Successors* (Edinburgh: Banner of Truth Trust, 1999), 168–171.

23 I am indebted to Geoff Thomas for this illustration.

24 Maurice Roberts, "Final Perseverance, "*Banner of Truth*, no. 265 (Oct. 1985): 10–11.

[25] John Dagg, *Manual of Theology and Church Order* (Harrisonburg, Pa.: Gano Books, 1982), 296.

[26] Murray, *Redemption Accomplished and Applied*, 154.

[27] Robert L. Dabney, *Discussions: Evangelical and Theological* (London: Banner of Truth Trust, 1967), 1:173ff; cf. WCF, 18.2, and Canons of Dort, V:10.

[28] Blanchard, *The Complete Gathered Gold*, 171.

[29] John Gill, *A Body of Divinity* (London: Turner Leasseter, 1957), 578.

[30] Anthony Burgess, *Spiritual Refining* (Ames, Iowa: International Outreach, 1990), 672–673.

[31] Thomas Schreiner and Ardel Caneday, *The Race Set Before Us: A Biblical Theology of Perseverance & Assurance* (Downers Grove, Ill.: InterVarsity, 2001), 311.

[32] From the hymn "Once to Every Man and Nation," by James Russell Lowell.

[33] Curt Daniel, "The History and Theology of Calvinism" (Dallas: Scholarly Reprints, 1993), 415.

[34] Cf. R. C. Sproul, "More Than Conquerors," *Tabletalk*, 28, no. 12 (Dec. 2004): 5–6.

[35] From the hymn "Amazing Grace!" by John Newton, 1779.

[36] *The Psalter*, ed. Joel R. Beeke (Grand Rapids, Reformation Heritage Books, 2006), no. 203, stanza 1.

[37] Quoted in Blanchard, *The Complete Gathered Gold*, 170.

[38] Blanchard, *The Complete Gathered Gold*, 169.

[39] Quoted in Blanchard, *The Complete Gathered Gold*, 170.

[40] I am indebted to Geoff Thomas for this illustration.

[41] Bruce Demarest, *The Cross and Salvation* (Wheaton, Ill.: Crossway, 1997), 460.

[42] Anthony Hoekema, *Saved by Grace* (Grand Rapids: Eerdmans, 1989), 255.

[43] Blanchard, *The Complete Gathered Gold*, 171.

[44] Erroll Hulse, *Salvation: God's Work or Ours? The Five Points* (Darlington, England: Evangelical Press, 2008), forthcoming.

SCRIPTURE, GRACE, FAITH, CHRIST, AND GLORY

The Reformation was a call for authentic Christianity, an attempt to escape the medieval corruption of the faith through renewal and reform. Its teaching, which swirled around a fivefold repetition of the word sola *("alone"), was a radical message for that day (and should be for ours) because it called for a commitment to an entirely God-centered view of faith and life.*[1]

—JOHN D. HANNAH

*I*n the opening chapter, I noted that in response to the abuses of the Roman Catholic Church, the Protestants coined five slogans or battle cries: Scripture alone (*sola Scriptura*), grace alone (*sola gratia*), faith alone (*sola fide*), Christ alone (*solus Christus*), and the glory of God alone (*soli Deo gloria*). The foundations of Calvinistic doctrine can be summarized in these five watchwords of the Reformation. Let us consider the meaning and implications of each of these slogans.

SCRIPTURE ALONE (*SOLA SCRIPTURA*)

As far back as the late medieval period, men such as John Wycliffe and John Hus called people to return to Scripture. When challenged by hostile church officials, Hus repeatedly answered his opponents, "Show me from Scripture and I will repent and recant!" Hus's devotion to Scripture alone cost him his life, for this principle compelled him to attack both curialism (the principle on which papal authority stands) and conciliarism (the principle on which supreme authority rests in church tradition and in gatherings of prelates).

The Reformers developed Hus's emphasis on Scripture in a number of significant ways:

• *Authority.* The Reformers contended that all things must be tested "by Scripture alone" (sola Scriptura). This explains why the Reformers accepted some parts of Roman Catholic teaching and not others. They believed Scripture is to rule in the church, for it is the Word of God and the voice of God (*verbum Dei*). Therefore, its authority is absolute, not derivative, they said. John Calvin said that Scripture is as authoritative as if God Himself "had been giving utterance."[2] A Christian should rely on and be governed by its promises,[3] and the church should be wholly subject to its authority.[4] In fact, all other kinds of authority—papal, creedal, and civil—must be subordinate to Scripture.

The Calvinist believes that all of Scripture is the Word of God, and, therefore, he strives to submit to it. The Calvinist understands that we cannot pass judgment on Scripture; rather, Scripture passes judgment on us.

• *Infallibility and inerrancy.* The Reformers taught that the Bible's infallibility is exhaustive, for every word of every sentence is the breath of the living God. They honored 2 Timothy 3:16–17, which says, "All scripture is given by inspiration of God, and is profitable for doctrine, for reproof, for correction, for instruction in righteousness: that the man of God may be perfect, thoroughly furnished unto all good works." Also, Scripture alone is inerrant. "I have learned to hold only the Holy Scripture inerrant," Martin Luther said, quoting Augustine's letter to Jerome.[5]

According to Fred Klooster, this view of Scripture as "alone and entire" (*sola* and *tota Scriptura*) is uniquely Reformed.[6] That has led Calvinists to stress that Scripture alone can bind the consciences of believers (Westminster Confession 1.10, 20.2, 31.4).

• *Self-interpretation and self-authentication.* Reformed theologians also stressed the harmony between Scripture and the Holy Spirit (*Spiritus cum verbo*). The Holy Spirit is the true expositor of the Bible, Ulrich Zwingli said, which enables the church to recognize that Scripture interprets Scripture (Westminster Confession 1.6). The key of interpretation, therefore, belongs to the entire community of Christians, not just to Peter and his reputed successors in Rome. While tradition may aid interpretation, the true, spiritual meaning of

Scripture is its natural, literal sense, not an allegorical one, unless the particular Scripture passage being studied is clearly allegorical in nature. Equally important, as Calvin emphasized, was the self-authenticating character of the Bible. This teaching holds that the Bible's witness is confirmed by the internal testimony of the Spirit in the believer's heart (Inst., 1.7.2–4; cf. Westminster Confession 1.5). Calvin concludes: "Let this then stand as a fixed point, that those whom the Spirit has inwardly taught rest firmly upon Scripture, and that Scripture is self-authenticated, and that it is not right for it to be made to depend upon demonstration of reasoning, for it is by the Spirit's witness that it gains in our minds the certainty that it merits."[7]

• *Liberation.* The Reformers liberated the Bible from the Roman Catholic hierarchy in at least three ways: by vernacular translation, such as Luther's German Bible; by expository preaching, as recommended by Zwingli; and by straightforward grammatical-historical exegesis, best exemplified by Calvin's commentaries. They taught that the Bible is the rule of faith that guides our intellect and the rule of practice that guides our daily duty. Scripture is God speaking to us as a father speaks to his children, Calvin said.

• *Power.* The Reformers taught that God gave us Scripture as His Word of truth and of power. As His Word of truth, we can trust Scripture for time and eternity. As the Word of power, we can look to Scripture to transform and renew our minds through the Spirit of God. That power must be manifested in our lives, our homes, our churches, and our communities. While other books may inform or even reform us, only one book can transform us and conform us to the image of Christ. Only then will we become true sons and daughters of God and of the Reformation.

How well do we understand the principle of *sola Scriptura*? Do we search, love, live, and pray over the Holy Scriptures? Is the Bible the compass that leads us through the storms and over the waves that we encounter in life? Is Scripture the mirror by which we dress ourselves (James 1:22–27), the rule by which we work (Gal. 6:16), the water with which we wash (Ps. 119:9), the fire that warms us (Luke 24:32), the food that nourishes us (Job 23:12), the sword with which we fight (Eph. 6:17), the counselor who resolves our doubts and fears (Ps. 119:24), and the heritage that enriches us (Ps. 119:111–112)? Are we learning from Scripture, as John Flavel said, "The best way of living, the noblest way of suffering, and the most profitable way of dying"?[8] Has *sola Scriptura* become our personal watchword, causing us, like Luther and Calvin, to become captive in our consciences to the very words of God?

GRACE ALONE (*SOLA GRATIA*)

Does man initiate and participate in his forgiveness and salvation, or does God initiate and complete the salvation of sinners so that the whole work is attributed to sovereign grace alone (*sola gratia*)? In response to Desiderius Erasmus' *Diatribe*, Luther's *The Bondage of the Will* unequivocally sides with sovereign grace.

Luther insisted that a sinner is unable to provide or even take hold of a saving remedy. In saying this, Luther attacked the Roman Catholic system of indulgences, pilgrimages, penances, fastings, purgatory, and Mariolatry. He saw that the only way to defeat Rome's works-based system was to strike at the root of the controversy: free grace versus free will.

The English term *grace* appears 169 times in the King James Version; 204 times, if we include its derivatives. Grace is most commonly defined as the unmerited favor of God, but as we saw in chapter 8, that definition doesn't go far enough. The nineteenth-century Calvinistic Baptist William Newman once put it like this: grace is "the free favour of God . . . conferred . . . upon the *unworthy*."[9] Those who receive grace are not merely helpless sinners who are undeserving, but are hostile rebels against God with bad hearts and bad records. God is not obligated to be kind or gracious to them. They are sinners, deserving only hell. But in accord with His nature, God showers an entirely undeserved love upon them—and as He does so, their lives are changed forever. As Ephesians 2:4–5 puts it, it is out of a heart full of rich mercy and great love that God saves—rescues, frees, liberates—sinners by grace. Though they are unlovely and loathsome to Him because of their sin, God shows love toward them. He pardons their sins, gives them knowledge of Himself, and moves them to respond with sincerity to His grace. By free, sovereign grace, therefore, we mean that the supreme God of heaven and earth—the sovereign, triune God of salvation—freely wills and applies saving grace to guilty, contemptible sinners, transforming their lives so that they enjoy Him and live for His service.

Reformed theology teaches that if we experience such sovereign grace, we will understand what it really means. We will realize that if it is not free and it is not sovereign, it cannot be grace. God saves us not because of anything possible or actual, foreseen or foreordained in us, but wholly according to His sovereign, loving good pleasure.

One New Testament book that especially emphasizes God's astounding sovereign grace is Paul's letter to the Romans. According to Paul, this grace makes both Jew and Gentile co-heirs of God's kingdom with faithful Abraham (Rom. 4:16). It establishes peace between God and sinners who are His enemies (Rom. 5:2). Since only this grace is stronger than the forces of sin, it brings genuine and lasting freedom from sin's dominion (Rom. 5:20–21; 6:14). Divine grace equips Christian men and women with varied gifts to serve in the church of God (Rom. 12:6). This grace ultimately will conquer death and is the sure harbinger of eternal life for all who receive it (Rom. 5:20–21), for it is a grace that reaches back into the aeons before the creation of time and, without respect to human merit, chooses men and women for salvation (Rom. 11:5–6).

This idea that salvation owes everything to God's grace is the overarching theme not just in Romans but in all of Paul's epistles. For example, Paul begins his letter to the Philippians with a prayer for the church in which he says, "He which hath begun a good work in you will perform it until the day of Jesus Christ" (1:6). "God's seed will come to God's harvest,"[10] Samuel Rutherford writes. Salvation is neither our earning nor our doing. That is why Paul prayed with joy and thanksgiving every time he remembered the Philippians. If man had begun the work of salvation, was continuing it, and had to complete it, Paul's praise would be silenced. But because salvation flows from a divine work that persists day by day despite man's struggles and setbacks, a work that most certainly will be perfected in the great day, everything is to the praise of the glory of the triune God. This is why Paul thanks God for all the doctrines of grace and is moved to joy whenever he thinks of believers drawn to Christ. By clinging to God's grace, we, like Paul, can be joyful Christians who victoriously confess, "If God be for us, who can be against us?" (Rom. 8:31).

Grace calls us (Gal. 1:15), regenerates us (Titus 3:5), justifies us (Rom. 3:24), sanctifies us (Heb. 13:20–21), and preserves us (1 Peter 1:3–5). We need grace to forgive us, to return us to God, to heal our broken hearts, and to strengthen us in times of trouble and spiritual warfare. Only by God's free, sovereign grace can we have a saving relationship with Him. Only through grace can we be called to conversion (Eph. 2:8–10), holiness (2 Peter 3:18), service (Phil. 2:12–13), or suffering (2 Cor. 1:12).

Sovereign grace crushes our pride. It shames us and humbles us. We want to be the subjects, not the objects, of salvation. We want to be active, not passive, in the process. We resist the truth that God alone is the author and finisher of our faith. By nature, we rebel against sovereign grace, but God knows how to break our rebellion and make us friends of this grand doctrine. When God teaches sinners that their very core is depraved, sovereign grace becomes the most encouraging doctrine possible.

From election to glorification, grace reigns in splendid isolation. John 1:16 says we receive "grace for grace," which literally means "grace facing or laminated to grace." Grace follows grace in our lives as waves follow one another to the shore. Grace is the divine principle on which God saves us; it is the divine provision in the person and work of Jesus Christ; it is the divine prerogative manifesting itself in election, calling, and regeneration; and it is the divine power enabling us freely to embrace Christ so that we might live, suffer, and even die for His sake and be preserved in Him for eternity.

Calvinists understand that, without sovereign grace, everyone would be eternally lost. Salvation is all of grace and all of God. Life must come from God before the sinner can arise from the grave.

Free grace cries out for expression in the church today. Human decisions, crowd manipulations, and altar calls will not produce genuine converts. Only the old-fashioned gospel of sovereign grace will capture and transform sinners by the power of the Word and Spirit of God.

How well do we understand and live according to *sola gratia*? Have we learned experientially that grace does everything for us? When visiting an elderly friend in a nursing home some time ago, I noticed that she had nothing on her walls except a small index card, upon which she had typed:

God's
Riches
At
Christ's
Expense

"That means everything to me because I live only by grace," she said.

Is that true of us as well? Are we sons and daughters of the Reformation who sing "Amazing Grace!" from the heart? Many pay lip service to sovereign grace, but it scarcely touches their lives. How much richer are they who truly experience the words of the hymn:

> Oh! to grace how great a debtor
> Daily I'm constrained to be;
> Let that grace now, like a fetter,
> Bind my wandering heart to Thee!
> Prone to wander, Lord, I feel it;
> Prone to leave the God I love—
> Take my heart, oh, take and seal it,
> Seal it for Thy courts above![11]

FAITH ALONE (SOLA FIDE)

The Reformation's emphasis on faith alone was the result of Luther's tortured struggles to resolve the issue of how a fallen sinner may be saved. "My situation was that, although an impeccable monk, I stood before God as a sinner troubled in conscience, and had no confidence that my character would satisfy Him. Night and day I pondered," Luther said. The breakthrough came when Luther was given insight into Romans 1:17: "For therein is the righteousness of God revealed from faith to faith: as it is written, The just shall live by faith." Luther later wrote: "Then I grasped that the justice of God is the righteousness by which, through grace and sheer mercy, He justifies us through faith. Immediately I felt myself to have gone through open doors into paradise."[12]

Luther finally understood that faith is the means by which justification comes to the sinner. The gospel makes faith the only way by which a sinner receives God's grace. In the medieval scholastic tradition, theologians spoke of acquiring faith through instruction and preaching (*fides acquisita*). This faith was distinguished from infused faith (*fides infusa*), which is a gift of grace and implies adherence to all revealed truth.

The Protestants repudiated that distinction, teaching that neither of these kinds of faith justifies us. Saving faith that comes by preaching is also faith that justifies, they said. Justification by faith is a gift of God and is absolutely essential for salvation. Luther went so far as to say: "This doctrine is the head and the cornerstone. It alone begets, nourishes, builds, preserves, and defends the church of God; and without it the church of God cannot exist for one hour."[13]

The Reformers explained that Scripture's references to justification by faith alone are never speaking of justification on account of faith (*propter fidem*) but on account of Christ and His blood sacrifice, the righteousness of which is graciously imputed to undeserving sinners (*propter Christum*). As Calvin wrote, "Justification consists in the forgiveness of sins and the imputation of the righteousness of Christ."[14]

This justification by faith in Christ alone is the very heart of the gospel. Since we have no inherent righteousness that allows us to stand blameless before God, we need a righteousness outside of us (*extra nos*)—an "alien" righteousness, as Luther put it—a divinely approved righteousness that is earned for us. That is the righteousness that Christ provided.[15]

In regeneration, the Holy Spirit grants to sinners the hand of faith to receive Christ's righteousness unto salvation (John 1:12–13). Faith is not called a hand because it merits justification in any way, but because it receives the transfer of the righteousness of Christ. The hand of faith does not create; it only receives. As Calvin says, faith "justifies in no other way than as it introduces us into a participation of the righteousness of Christ."[16]

Faith and grace are not competitors. Salvation is through faith because only in faith is divine grace honored. *Sola gratia* is confirmed by *sola fide*. Gracious faith wholeheartedly assents to the truth of the gospel. It flees in poverty to Christ's riches, in guilt to Christ's reconciliation, and in bondage to Christ's liberation. It lays hold of Christ and His righteousness, uniting the sinner with his Savior. It embraces Christ in belief, clinging to His Word and relying on His promises. As Luther wrote, "Faith lays hold of Christ and grasps Him as a present possession, just as the ring holds the jewel."[17] Faith wraps the soul in Christ's righteousness, enabling the soul to live out of Christ. It commits the total person to the total Christ.[18]

How different this Reformed concept of faith was from that taught by the Roman Catholic Church. Rome blended justification and sanctification by teaching that justification was not achieved by God's *declaring* a sinner righteous, but by God's *making* him righteous. Christ's righteousness must thus be buttressed by the sinner's own righteousness in justification. There are degrees in justification, the Roman church taught, and the believer is dependent on implicit faith (*fides implicita*) in the church's teaching to receive God's grace through the sacraments.

Sola fide versus faith and works: to which do we adhere? Is our faith Christ-centered? Do we live only by that faith? Can we say with Luther, "Faith gives Christ to me; love flowing from faith gives me to my neighbor"? Do we understand, love, and live the truth of *sola fide*? Are we sons and daughters of the Reformation?

CHRIST ALONE (*SOLUS CHRISTUS*)

Reformed theology affirms that Scripture, grace, and faith all emphasize that salvation is "by Christ alone"—that is, Christ is the only Savior (cf. Acts 4:12). B. B. Warfield writes:

> It is from its object [Jesus Christ] that faith derives its value. . . . The saving power of faith resides thus not in itself, but in the Almighty Savior on whom it rests. . . . It is not faith [itself] that saves, but faith in Jesus Christ. . . . It is not strictly speaking, even faith in Christ that saves, but Christ that saves through faith.[19]

The centrality of Christ is the foundation of the Protestant faith. Luther said that Jesus Christ is the "center and circumference of the Bible"—meaning that who He is and what He did in His death and resurrection is the fundamental content of Scripture.[20]

The sixty-seven theses[21] that Zwingli wrote in 1523 emphasized this point more strongly than did Luther's ninety-five, written six years earlier. For example, Zwingli says in his second thesis, "The sum of the gospel is that our Lord Jesus Christ, the true Son of God, has made known to us the will of His heavenly Father and redeemed us by His innocence from eternal death, and reconciled us unto God." The third thesis continues, "Therefore, Christ is the only way to salvation to all who were, who are, and who shall be saved." And the fourth thesis says, "Whosoever seeks or shows another door errs, yea, is a murderer of souls and a robber."

Zwingli goes on to say: "Christ is the Head of all believers who are His body and without Him the body is dead" (thesis 7). "Christ is the only Mediator between God and us" (thesis 19). "Christ is our righteousness" (thesis 22). "God alone forgives sins through Jesus Christ, our Lord, alone" (thesis 50). "All spiritual superiors should repent without delay and set up the cross of Christ alone or they will perish, for the axe is laid at the root of the tree" (thesis 65).

In Zwingli's words we see that our Reformed forebears unabashedly proclaimed salvation by Christ alone (*solus Christus*). Only in Christ is life, and outside of Him is death, they said. God's justice can be satisfied only through Christ's obedience. Outside of Christ, God is an everlasting, all-consuming fire; in Christ, He is a gracious Father. Without Christ, we can do nothing; in Him, we can do all things (John 15:5; Phil. 4:13).

The righteousness of Christ cannot be exhausted. As Luther says, "We cannot grasp or exhaust Christ, the eternal Righteousness, with one sermon or thought; for to learn to appreciate Him is an everlasting lesson which we shall not be able to finish either in this or in yonder life."[22]

Christ alone is and can bring salvation. Paul makes plain in Romans 1 and 2 that though there is a self-manifestation of God outside of His saving work in Christ, no amount of natural theology can unite God and man. Union with Christ is the only way of salvation.

We urgently need to hear *solus Christus* in our day of pluralistic theology, which has such a low view of Scripture. As Carl Braaten says, "There is currently underway a strong trend in both Protestant and Roman Catholic theology to call into question the classical Christian confession that Jesus Christ is the one and only Savior of the world." Too many today, Braaten goes on to say, "are returning to a form of the old bankrupt nineteenth-century Christological approach of Protestant liberalism and calling it 'new,' when it is actually scarcely more than a shallow Jesus-ology, at best a revival of the liberal Protestant picture of Jesus as a moral example of middle-class piety."[23] The end result is that today many—as H. R. Niebuhr has famously said of old theological liberalism—proclaim and worship "a God without wrath who brought men without sin into a kingdom without judgment through the ministrations of a Christ without a cross."[24]

Today, postmodernism sees truth as wholly pluralistic and relativistic. There is no universal or absolute truth in any area of knowledge, not even in religion. Postmodernists, therefore, are skeptics who fully reject any classical concept of truth. The exclusive claims of Christ and Christianity are anathema to them. They see no beauty in Christ or in His stupendous work, that they should desire Him.

Our Reformed forebears, drawing on a perspective traceable all the way back
to the fourth-century writer Eusebius of Caesarea, found it helpful to think about
Christ as a Prophet, Priest, and King. The 1689 Baptist Confession, for instance,
puts it this way: "Christ, and Christ alone, is fitted to be mediator between God
and man. He is the prophet, priest and king of the church of God" (8.9).[25] Let us
look more closely at these three offices:

• *Christ the Prophet.* Christ is *the* Prophet whom we need to instruct us in
the things of God so as to scatter our blindness and ignorance. The Heidelberg
Catechism calls Him "our chief Prophet and Teacher, who has fully revealed to us
the secret counsel and will of God concerning our redemption" (Q. 31).

Although God provided prophets for His people under the old covenant—
men who instructed them as to the will of God—those who were truly alive
to God longed for the coming of *the* Prophet who would give them a deeper
and fuller understanding of God and His ways. Long before Christ, Moses had
instructed the people of God to wait for this Prophet. "The LORD thy God," he
declared in Deuteronomy 18:15, "will raise up unto thee a Prophet from the
midst of thee, of thy brethren, like unto me; unto him ye shall hearken."

Down through the long centuries, the pious of Israel waited for the Prophet
like Moses. Even the misguided Samaritans were waiting for this Prophet. When
Jesus spoke to the Samaritan woman at the well of the Jewish patriarch Jacob in
John 4, she told Him: "I know that Messias cometh, which is called Christ: when
he is come, he will tell us all things." Jesus' response was pithy and to the point:
"I that speak unto thee am *he*" (John 4:25–26). Jesus was the fulfillment of the
promise given through Moses.

As the Prophet, Jesus is the only One who can reveal what God has been purposing in history "since the world began" and who can teach and make manifest
the real meaning of the "scriptures of the prophets," the Old Testament (see Rom.
16:25–26). We can expect to make progress in the Christian life only as we heed
His instruction and teaching.

• *Christ the Priest.* Christ is also a Priest—a sorely needed High Priest, who,
as the Heidelberg Catechism says, "by the sacrifice of His body, has redeemed us,
and makes continual intercession with the Father for us" (Q. 31). In the words
of the 1689 Baptist Confession, "because of our estrangement from God and the
imperfection of our services at best, we need his priestly office to reconcile us to
God and render us acceptable to him" (8.10).

Reformed Christology insists on Christ's priestly mediation. Salvation is only in Jesus Christ because there are two things that, no matter how hard we try, we can never do; yet they must be done if we are to be saved. The first is to satisfy the justice of God through obedience to the law. We are all lawbreakers; we have all come short of the glory of God. Therefore, we need someone else to obey the law perfectly for us in thought, word, and deed. Jesus did that for thirty-three years in this world as our substitute. He actively and perfectly obeyed the law. He Himself asked, "Which of you convinceth me of sin?" (John 8:46).

The second thing we can never do is to pay the price of our sins. "The wages of sin is death" (Rom. 6:23): physical, spiritual, and eternal. Only Jesus could compress the eternity of sin's payment in His suffering and death on Calvary's cross. He voluntarily suffered and died on behalf of sinners such as we are (Heb. 9:12), paying the penalty of our sin, expiating our guilt, and freeing us from the dominion of sin (Titus 2:14), the power of the Devil (Heb. 2:14), and the consequences of sin and death (2 Tim. 1:10)—all this to reconcile us as ungodly sinners to the holy, offended God.

This is certainly a central theme in the early chapters of Paul's letter to the Romans. To cite but one text, Romans 5:10 says: "when we were enemies, we were reconciled to God by the death of his Son." What a costly reconciliation! To secure the efficacy of the reconciliation, the Priest had to sacrifice Himself. Though we were enemies of God, Christ gave up His life for us, freely and willingly, to bring about an eternal reconciliation between us and His Father.

Thus, by His active obedience to the law and His passive obedience in atoning for sin with His own death, Christ satisfied the justice of God for His elect. There is no other way to come into the presence of God than through Christ alone.

Jesus' sacrifice took place once only, but He still continues as our great High Priest, the One through whom all acceptable prayer and praise are made to God. In heavenly places, He remains our constant Intercessor and Advocate (Rom. 8:34; 1 John 2:1). Little wonder, then, that Paul adds to the doxology of Romans 16 that glory be given to God "through Jesus Christ for ever" (Rom. 16:27). Again, growth in Christ is rooted in our full-fledged reliance on Him as our Sacrifice, Mediator, and Intercessor.

• *Christ the King.* Finally, Christ is the King of a spiritual, eternal realm, ruling over it by means of His Holy Spirit. As such, He gives commands that

He expects to be obeyed. And the first command that He issues to all men and women is to heed God the Father's call to put our faith in Him. The first command of the gospel, the preaching about Jesus, which alone discloses the true meaning of the Old Testament Scriptures, is this: "Believe on the Lord Jesus Christ, and thou shalt be saved" (Acts 16:31).

All who exercise this "obedience of faith," as Paul calls it in Romans 16:26, are henceforth subjects of Christ and full citizens of His kingdom. Christ is then "our eternal King who governs us by His word and Spirit, and who defends and preserves us in the enjoyment of that salvation, He has purchased for us" (Heidelberg Catechism, Q. 31). As such, we can agree with Calvin when he says:

> We may patiently pass through this life with its misery, cold, contempt, reproaches, and other troubles—content with this one thing: that our King will never leave us destitute, but will provide for our needs until, our warfare ended, we are called to triumph. Such is the nature of his rule, that he shares with us all that he received from the Father. Now he arms and equips us with his power, adorns us with his beauty and magnificence, enriches us with his wealth.[26]

Once again, we can hope to grow in the Christian life only as we live obediently under the rule of Christ.

If you are a true son or daughter of the Reformation, Christ in His threefold office as Prophet-Priest-King will mean everything to you. The gospel is a gospel of *solus Christus* because, from beginning to end, it has everything to do with who Christ is and what He accomplished outside of us, for us, in our stead. Do you love and live *solus Christus*? Do you love Him in His person, offices, natures, and benefits? Is He your Prophet to teach you; your Priest to sacrifice for, intercede for, and bless you; and your King to rule and guide you?

Have you learned to know Christ personally and experientially as your Savior and Lord? Have you learned that He is more than an example whom we should emulate, more than a martyr who is heroic, more than a psychotherapist who can heal your inner psychological wounds, and more than a "Santa Christ" who gives you health and wealth?[27] Have you learned that, in terms of salvation, Jesus Christ is everything to you, a sinner?

A nineteenth-century musician once conducted Beethoven's Ninth Symphony so magnificently that the audience gave him an unusually long standing ovation. The conductor bowed, but the audience kept applauding. Finally, he turned to the orchestra, and with a raspy voice said, "Gentlemen, gentlemen!"

The orchestra members strained to understand. Had someone missed their cue? What was wrong with the conductor?

The conductor spoke. "Gentlemen, I am nothing," he said. "You are nothing. But Beethoven is everything!"

As you walk across the stage of life amid the praise of others, have you been overwhelmed with the true Composer of your life, the Lord Jesus Christ? He is both divine Composer and divine Musician, who, by His Spirit, brings to life His eternally decreed composition. Have you seen in your joys and sorrows that Christ is directing your life with such love and compassion that you have cried out with astonishment to others, "I am nothing and you are nothing, but Jesus Christ is everything"? Can you say with Paul, "For me to live is Christ, and to die is gain" (Phil. 1:21)? Have you experienced something of the depth of this confession: "your life is hid with Christ in God" (Col. 3:3)? Do you know that "all things are yours; . . . and ye are Christ's; and Christ is God's" (1 Cor. 3:21b–23)?

TO GOD ALONE BE THE GLORY (*SOLI DEO GLORIA*)

Most serious Christian thinkers acknowledge that glorifying God is one of man's callings, both in this life and in the life to come. Calvinist theology, however, goes beyond this in emphasizing the following truths:

• *God's goal is to manifest His glory.* He manifests His glory in all that He does, most remarkably in displaying His moral excellence to His creatures and evoking their praise for its beauty and for the benefit it brings them (cf. Eph. 1:3). God's glory is that which makes Him appear glorious to angels and men.

The word *glory* in Hebrew, *kabod*, derives from a root word meaning "weight." For example, the value of a gold coin was determined by its weight. To have weight, therefore, is to have value or worth. The Greek word for glory, *doxa*, originally meant "opinion." This word refers to the worth or value which we, in our opinion, assign to someone or something. The Hebrew idea speaks of what is inherent in God—His intrinsic value or worth; the Greek idea speaks of the response of intelligent and moral beings to the value or worth they see manifested by God's Word and works.

In both testaments of the Bible, the word *glory* means the display of excellence and praiseworthiness (glory *shown*), as well as the response of honor and adoration to this display (glory *given*). God's glory is the beauty of His manifold perfections, as well as the awesome radiance that breaks forth from those perfections. His moral excellence of character shines forth in greatness and worth in His acts of creation, providence, and redemption (Isa. 44:23; John 12:28; 13:31–32). Seeing this excellence, God's worshipers give Him glory by praising, thanking, and obeying Him (John 17:4; 21:19; Rom. 4:20; 15:6, 9; 1 Peter 4:12–16).

The seraphim declared in Isaiah 6:3, "The whole earth is full of [God's] glory." They affirmed that God is to receive glory in everything, even the damnation of the wicked, but the ultimate glory of God is that the earth is to be filled with the display of His saving grace. As Romans 5:21 says, "That as sin hath reigned unto death, even so might grace reign through righteousness unto eternal life by Jesus Christ our Lord." So the greatest display of God's glory in the world is shown through the person of His Son. As Acts 3:13 says, "The God of our fathers, hath glorified His Son Jesus."

• *Man's chief end is to glorify God.* In all that he does, by word and by deed, man must seek to bring glory to his Creator and Redeemer. Calvin embodied this truth in his life and writings, as well as in his death. As his life drew to an end, Calvin's body was ravaged by numerous diseases. His pain became so severe that his dearest friends begged him to stop working. Calvin replied, "What? Would my Lord find me idle?" How typical that was of the man who lived by the motto: "My heart I offer to Thee, Lord, promptly and sincerely."

Calvinists likewise devote their lives to the glory of God. They are men and women who are convinced that their chief end in life is to glorify God. As the Heidelberg Catechism states so beautifully, their only comfort in life and death is that they belong to their faithful Savior, Jesus Christ (Q. 1). When the Calvinist clings to *soli Deo gloria* in his spiritual pilgrimage, he confesses that all God does is good. Based on Scripture and for Christ's sake, he is confident that all things will work to the glory of God and for his good (Rom. 8:28).

• *Man's chief delight is to praise God.* We find supreme happiness in praising God. It is the highest, most rewarding act. The Westminster Shorter Catechism expresses this most succinctly when it says, "Man's chief end is to glorify God, and to enjoy Him forever" (Q. 1).

Glory to God alone is the heartbeat of the Reformation. The giving of glory to God, of course, is not intended to give Him something that He lacks. When God is glorified in human lives and with human words, He is not made one whit more glorious than He always has been and always will be. In the words of the seventeenth-century Puritan divine, Thomas Watson, "God's glory is such an essential part of His being, that He cannot be God without it."[28] Rather, a doxology extols God for who He is and acknowledges why He is worthy of human praise and adoration.

Do we understand this kind of glory? Do we love to glorify God and live for Him? Can we say, at times, with Jonathan Edwards: "The greatest moments of my life have not been those that have concerned my own salvation, but those when I have been carried into communion with God and beheld His beauty and desired His glory. . . . I rejoice and yearn to be emptied and annihilated of self in order that I might be filled with the glory of God and Christ alone"?[29]

The true Calvinist yearns to use every gift that God has given to glorify God. He resolves to live out Paul's command: "Ye are bought with a price: therefore glorify God in your body, and in your spirit, which are God's. . . . Whether therefore ye eat, or drink, or whatsoever ye do, do all to the glory of God" (1 Cor. 6:20; 10:31).

Paul's doxological paradigm in Romans 11:36 sets the standard for living to God's glory alone: "For of him, and through him, and to him all things: to whom be glory forever" (Rom. 11:36). These three prepositions—*of, through,* and *to*— say it all. "Of him" indicates that God is the source of all things. Everything has its origin or cause in God (John 1:3). "Through him" indicates that God is the sustainer of all He created; He alone holds it all together (Col. 1:17). "To him" indicates God is the goal; all things exist for Him. Commenting on Romans 11:36, Calvin says: "He is the source of all things in that they have proceeded from him; he is the Creator. He is the agent through whom all things subsist and are directed to their proper end. And he is the last end to whose glory all things redound."[30]

Using this paradigm, how does the Calvinist glorify God? By confessing his sins to God and fleeing to Christ for forgiveness and for having God's nature restored to him. By praising, worshiping, and delighting in the triune God as

Creator, Provider, and Redeemer. By trusting God and surrendering all things into His hands. By being fervently zealous for the triune God's glory. By walking humbly, thankfully, and cheerfully before God and becoming increasingly conformed to the image of His Son. By knowing, loving, and living the commands of God's Word. By being heavenly minded and cherishing the desire to be with God forever.

Soli Deo gloria is the Calvinist's highest ambition. No other goal or desire can measure up to living for God's glory. The true Calvinist finds purpose and joy in glorifying God. By grace, he believes, knows, loves, and lives the doxology:

Praise ye the Lord, ye saints below,
And in His courts His goodness show;
Praise ye the Lord, ye hosts above,
In heaven adore His boundless love.

Praise ye the Lord; all creatures, sing
The praises of your God and King;
Let all that breathe, His praise proclaim
And glorify His holy Name.[31]

DISCUSSION QUESTIONS

1. What are the five *solas*?

2. What does each of them mean?

3. Why are these *solas* very important for a God-glorifying life?

4. What is the biblical support for each of the *solas*?

5. Do you have problems theologically with any of the *solas*? Outline from the Bible how you can resolve your problems.

NOTES

1 John D. Hannah, *To God be the Glory* (Wheaton, Ill.: Crossway, 2000), 6.

2 Inst., 1.7.1.

3 Inst., 3.2.6–7.

4 Inst., 4.8.

5 Martin Luther, *What Luther Says: An Anthology*, ed. Ewald M. Plass (St. Louis: Concordia, 1959), 1:87.

6 Fred Klooster, "The Uniqueness of Reformed Theology: A Preliminary Attempt at Description" (Grand Rapids: The Reformed Ecumenical Synod, 1979), 1.

7 Inst., 1.7.5.

8 Quoted in John Blanchard, *Gathered Gold* (Welwyn, England: Evangelical Press, 1984), 17.

9 William Newman, "Biblical and Theological Terms Defined," *The Baptist Magazine*, 24 (1832): 388. Italics added.

10 Samuel Rutherford, "Letter to Marion Macknaught, Anworth, June 6, 1624," in *Letters of the Rev. Samuel Rutherford* (New York: Robert Carter & Brothers, 1881), 31.

11 From the hymn "Come, Thou Fount of Every Blessing," by Robert Robinson, 1758.

12 Cf. *D. Martin Luthers Werke*, ed. J. C. F. Knaake et al. (Weimar: Herman Bohlaus, 1883), 40I, 33, 7–9.

13 Luther, *What Luther Says*, 2:704.

14 Inst., 3.11.2.

15 R. C. Sproul, *Justified by Faith Alone* (Wheaton, Ill.: Crossway, 1999), 34–35.

16 Inst., 3.11.20.

17 Quoted in Blanchard, *Gathered Gold*, 98.

18 A few of these paragraphs are condensed from Joel R. Beeke, "The Relation of Faith to Justification," in *Justification by Faith Alone*, ed. Don Kistler (Morgan, Pa.: Soli Deo Gloria, 2003), 53–105.

19 B. B. Warfield, *Biblical and Theological Studies* (Philadelphia: P&R, 1968), 423–425.

20 Luther, *What Luther Says*, 1:145–148.

21 Philip Schaff, *Creeds of Christendom* (Grand Rapids: Baker, 1993), 3:197-207.

22 Luther, *What Luther Says*, 2:714–715.

23 Carl E. Braaten, "Salvation Through Christ Alone," *Lutheran Forum* (Nov. 1988): 8, 10–11.

24 H. Richard Niebuhr, *The Kingdom of God in America* (Hamden, Conn.: Shoe String Press, 1956), 193.

25 *A Faith to Confess. The Baptist Confession of 1689*, 4th ed. (Haywards Heath, Sussex: Carey Publications Ltd., 1982), 30.

26 Inst., 2.15.4.

27 Sinclair B. Ferguson, *In Christ Alone: Living the Gospel-Centered Life* (Orlando: Reformation Trust, 2007), 15–19.

28 Thomas Watson, *A Body of Divinity* (London: Banner of Truth Trust, 1958), 5.

29 Jonathan Edwards, *The Works of Jonathan Edwards*, ed. Edward Hickman (Edinburgh: Banner of Truth Trust, 1974), 1:lxv–lxxiii.

30 *Commentary* on Romans 11:36.

31 *The Psalter*, ed. Joel R. Beeke (Grand Rapids, Reformation Heritage Books, 2006), no. 410 (Psalm 150).

CHAPTER 11

PHILOSOPHICAL
CALVINISM

James Grier

> *What you leave behind is not what is engraved in stone monuments, but what
> is woven into the lives of others.* [1]

> —PERICLES

ar too many critics focus on one aspect of John Calvin's theology and use it to characterize his life and work. For example, one often hears him called the theologian of predestination or the father of the five-point theology of TULIP. But Calvin considered his primary task to be pastoral; he even wrote his *Institutes of the Christian Religion* for the instruction of believers in the way of truth rather than as a full-orbed work in theology. His commentaries and his preaching give us great insight into his passion for the people of God and their instruction in the things of God. For this reason, the best title for Calvin may be "theologian of the Word." [2]

One title that never seems to be given to Calvin is *philosopher*, or even *philosophical theologian*. However, that is not because his education did not give him a good working knowledge of this discipline. [3] Neither is it because he did not use philosophical methods in doing theology. [4] Often in the *Institutes*, Calvin used philosophical means to clarify theological points, and he used philosophic reasoning to destroy arguments and positions that he considered non-orthodox. Perhaps the best way to describe Calvin's use of philosophy is as a handmaid to theology. [5]

In his landmark Stone Lectures at Princeton Seminary in 1898, Abraham Kuyper presented Calvinism as a unified and comprehensive life system. He could make that argument because Calvin, in his writings, addressed so many major philosophical questions, and the theological system that came to be known by Calvin's name has continued to concern itself with major issues. This chapter will consider Calvin's thoughts on three of those issues: the questions of reality (metaphysics), knowledge (epistemology), and conduct (ethics).

THEORY OF REALITY (METAPHYSICS)

Metaphysics is the area of philosophy that deals with the question of what is real.[6] Some answers deny the possibility of any knowledge in metaphysics. Among those answers that have affirmed knowledge of reality, historically there have been monistic answers, dualistic answers, and pluralistic answers. Monists assert that there is only one order of reality, and that reality encompasses all that is. Greek dualism asserts that there are two realities, forms and matter. The forms are considered metaphysically complete, while matter is a lower reality that is subject to flux and impermanence. Man participates in both realities—his immortal spirit is the form of his being and his body is the deficient, lower aspect of his being. Pragmatism and some forms of realism propose more than two realities and thus are examples of metaphysical pluralism.

In his *Institutes*, his commentaries, and his sermons, Calvin provides a rich understanding of what is real. Although he did not communicate his understanding in the philosophical forms of his day, he had deep insights into the issues of metaphysics:

• *Christian theistic dualism: the Creator and His creation.* Although Calvin did not discuss the notion of creation *ex nihilo* (out of nothing), it is clear that he taught this position.[7] The category of uncreated reality has only one member, and He is the triune God of Scripture. Since there is only one God, there is no other being at His level of reality who can interdict His will or actions. This self-existing God is sovereign, has foreordained whatsoever comes to pass, and has revealed Himself in nature, in His Son, and in Scripture. And He has chosen, by wise, inter-Trinitarian counsel, to create.

That brings us to the second level of reality, created reality, which includes heaven, earth, angels, men, sea life, birds, land animals, plants, and everything else that exists. Not only did the triune God foreordain the existence of all things and create them, He sustains all things by the word of His power. Thus, created reality is metaphysically dependent on the triune God for its existence as well as its maintenance. Christian theistic metaphysics affirms this kind of dualism, not the Greek dualism of form and matter that views man as a synthesis of the eternal and the temporal, and that holds that matter is ontologically deficient.

Calvin taught that created reality, including man, was greatly affected by sin.[8] God's judgment placed the creation in the bondage of corruption (Rom. 8:19–25). As a theologian of the Word, Calvin taught that our knowledge of creation and sin is derived from the Word of God. We need the light of Scripture to understand the present condition of created reality. Thus, our understanding of reality is dependent on God's self-disclosure in Scripture.

• *Implications of redemptive history to created reality.* Since Scripture is the key to understanding the nature of created reality and its corruption, it is also the key to understanding the reconciliation of all things to God in the consummation. Whatever view is taken to explain the present condition of the created reality, one thing remains a constant: sin is not a metaphysical issue that has brought metaphysical deficiency to creation.

As the last Adam and the Mediator, Christ reconciled all things to God. The redemptive victory of Christ includes a new heaven and new earth wherein dwell righteousness. Scripture is also the key to understanding this complete renovation of the created heaven and earth as an aspect of Christ's redemptive victory.

THEORY OF KNOWLEDGE (EPISTEMOLOGY)

Calvin often refers to the epistemic gap between God's exhaustive knowledge and our finite knowledge.[9] This gap is not intended to preclude reliable knowledge at our level of existence, but rather to show the transcendence of the Sovereign whose thoughts and ways are higher than ours.[10]

Epistemology answers four basic questions: (1) What is the origin of knowledge? (2) What is the nature of knowledge? (3) What are the tests of knowledge? and (4) What are the limits of knowledge? Let us look briefly at how Calvin wrestled with each of these questions:

• *Origin of Knowledge.* Epistemological systems usually begin with man (either individually or in a social setting) or with a transcendent source of knowledge. Those who follow Calvin in developing a Christian theistic epistemology begin their reflections on the source of knowledge with the triune God who has revealed Himself in creation, His Son, and Scripture.

Creation is a reality that declares the glory of God. Every aspect of created reality exists because it has a place in the plan of God, and its meaning and significance are dependent on that plan. Creation is an anthropomorphic revelation in a form adapted to man's created cognitive capacity. God intended man to interpret reality by immersing himself ever more fully into the knowledge of God, who interprets every aspect of creation.

The incarnate Son is the full, personal revelation of God to man.[11] He is the Logos who reveals God and does the will of God without fail. Although He was incarnate on earth for a very short time, Christ gave a full revelation of the glory of God as the second Adam. The Son is the most obvious form of anthropomorphic special revelation from God.

Calvin said the revelation of God in Scripture is the primary source of our knowledge. The centrality of Scripture flows out of our understanding that the agent of knowledge (man) and the objects of knowledge (created reality) were both affected by the first Adam's sin.[12] Creation was subjected to the bondage of corruption and groans under the weight of judgment. It was subjected in hope, but its revelation of God is not as perspicuous as it was before sin. Thus, the knowledge of God found in creation is now tied to Scripture because we cannot interpret that knowledge independently. Sin, death, and corruption are present because of Adam's sin; without the light of Scripture, we would not know this and we would assume that they have always existed. We need Scripture to interpret the history and present situation of creation, but also to know the future of the created reality.

Because man naturally suppresses every aspect of God's revelation in creation and in Scripture, he needs powerful help to know himself, others, the world, and God. This aid is provided by the second Adam and His redemptive work. Through the work of Christ, and by repentance and faith in Him, man can acquire true knowledge. God's sovereign grace brings release from the kingdom of darkness and entrance into the kingdom of the Son. Efficaciously, the Spirit draws the sinner and removes his blindness so that he can see the glory of God in the face of Jesus Christ. There is powerful help for the sinner through His victory. Through the Word of God, the Holy Spirit brings life and truth to the sinner.

There is little wonder that Calvin found Scripture to be our primary source of knowledge, since all knowledge originates in God's self-disclosure and is in a form adapted to man. Scripture is the primary source of that knowledge; without it, we would not know creation, history, present reality, and the future. We would be devoid of any knowledge of our Savior and His redemption on our behalf were it not for the God-breathed Word.

• *Nature of Knowledge.* In Western epistemology, the discussion of the nature of knowledge has centered around two positions. The first is that knowledge is subjective and therefore is internal to the agent of knowledge; the second is that knowledge is objective and therefore is external.

Since Immanuel Kant, many have said that knowledge is composed of objective elements that are gained through experience and subjective elements that are known through *a priori* categories of the mind. In the empirical tradition following John Locke, others have viewed all knowledge as objective, thus coming to man through sense perception. The rationalistic subjective position in the tradition of Plato found true knowledge to be in the mind in advance of experience. Kant synthesized the positions by combining concepts (in the mind in advance of experience) and percepts (received through sense perception) into a composite answer to the issue of the nature of knowledge.

Calvinistic philosophy views the created order as an extra-mental reality that man encounters in the pursuit of knowledge. This objective referent for knowledge is revelatory in character and gets both its being and its meaning from its place in the plan of God. God created man's mind as a fit instrument to gain knowledge of the created order. Thus, the mind enables man to come into fruitful contact with God, himself, others, and the world. Man is a revelatory being who lives in a revelatory environment to learn revelatory truth.

• *Tests of Knowledge.* Every philosophy proposes some means to test truth claims. In the empirical tradition, the test is correspondence between the reality and the truth claim. This tradition works from the particular to the general in forms of induction. In the rationalistic tradition, the test is coherence between the truth claim and other known truth. This tradition works from the general to the particular in the forms of deduction. In the pragmatic/instrumental tradition, the test of truth is workability.

Calvinistic theistic philosophy redefines both correspondence and coherence, given its starting point in the triune God of Scripture and His self-disclosure.[13]

Correspondence focuses on implicating our knowledge into the knowledge of God. Simply put, our knowledge can be judged true if it corresponds with what God knows about the object of knowledge. The assertion that all men are sinners (except the second Adam) is true if our knowledge corresponds to God's knowledge about man. God has revealed this aspect of His knowledge to us in Scripture. The same is true of knowledge in every realm, since God has interpreted every aspect of creation. As Calvin affirmed, Scripture is our primary source of knowledge, so it seems obvious that we must use Scripture in every pursuit of knowledge, not just for personal devotion.

Coherence is redefined as an expression of God's creation of a cosmos and not a chaos. Since all truth coheres in the mind of God, we can test truth claims to see whether they cohere with our knowledge that corresponds with God's knowledge. Things that do not logically cohere with our correspondent knowledge of God's knowledge should be rejected. However, if a truth claim does cohere, we should tentatively accept it until it is confirmed or denied based on our growing correspondent knowledge. True knowledge implicates us ever deeper into God's knowledge and its coherence. Now the necessity of seeing all knowledge as revelatory is much clearer.[14]

• *Limits of Knowledge.* Consistent empiricism would limit knowledge to that which can be gained through sense perception. Consistent rationalism would limit knowledge to that which exists in the mind in advance of experience and which can be deduced logically from it. Kant's synthesis of these two notions limited knowledge of the external world to that which comes to man as a sense perception, to which the categories of the mind add their component. Kant held that we can have sure knowledge of the objective, extra-mental world. But when it comes to religion, freedom, and ethics, we move into the area of speculative reason. This reality is amenable to faith as opposed to facts.

In principle, everything that God has revealed is knowable. The secret things belong to Him, but what He has chosen to reveal belongs to us (Deut. 29:29). This truth simply affirms that God's knowledge is not exhausted in His self-revelation. We do not need to know all things exhaustively in order to know some things truly. Neither do we need to know exhaustively the inter-connectedness of all things to know the coherence of some things. It would seem obvious that, given the scope of God's self-disclosure, we are not in any danger of running out of areas in which to pursue knowledge. The technical limit of knowledge, that is, what God has chosen to reveal, still leaves us with the daunting task of thinking God's thoughts after Him and thus bringing all thought into captivity to Jesus Christ, the Logos of God.

THEORY OF CONDUCT (ETHICS)

Ethics answers three basic questions: (1) What should I do? (2) What is good? and (3) What should motivate me to choose the right and the good? How did Calvin answer these questions?

• *What should I do?* Every philosophical system includes a theory of obligation, or what we ought to do. For Calvin, divine command constitutes the essence of man's moral obligation.[15] John Murray expresses Calvin's understanding of obligation very well.[16] He says a distinction exists between perpetually binding commands and temporary binding commands. A perpetually binding command is obligatory in every household administration of God; a temporary binding command is usually an application of a perpetually binding command to the immediate household administration. For example, all of the commands concerning sacrifices in the old covenant have been fulfilled in Christ and are not binding on the new covenant people of God. New covenant commands such as baptism, witnessing, and prayer will come to completion in the consummation and will not be obligatory for the people of God on the new earth.

The thread of unity for the perpetually binding commands runs from the creation ordinances all through the canon of Scripture to the end of the world and the final judgment. While in a state of creaturely righteousness, Adam was given a set of commands to govern life in the garden. They were inclusive of his relation to his wife; the proper use of his sexuality; his labor of dominion; his dressing and guarding of the garden, and, by implication, keeping the Sabbath; and, finally, his abstaining from eating the fruit of the Tree of Knowledge of Good and Evil.[17] Adam needed special, verbal revelation from God to interpret and choose what was in harmony with God's perceptive will.

Additional commands were given after the flood: permission to eat animal flesh, prohibition against eating blood, and the establishment of capital punishment. When God delivered His people out of Egypt by blood and by power, He met with them at Mount Sinai. In His Ten Commandments, we have an explication of the creation ordinances for the direction of the life of His redeemed people. Much case law was added to apply these commands to the household administration. The prophets took these commands and wove them into the fabric of Israel's life in the land promised to Abraham.

Later, the Lord Jesus in the Sermon on the Mount showed how they are embodied in Him; He then passed them on to His disciples in a richer, deeper form. These same commands were taken by the apostles into the life of the church and woven into the fabric of their epistles. At the final judgment, these perpetually binding commands will be the standard for judgment, and all impenitent violators of these commands will be excluded from the new earth.

These perpetually binding commands are augmented by temporary binding commands in the church. Hermeneutical skill is needed when dealing with what may be temporary.

• *What is good?* Since we believe that the Bible is our only and sufficient rule for faith and practice, it must govern every aspect of belief and conduct. Direct commands in both their positive and negative forms do not cover every decision of life. This is the place where a biblical theory of values comes into play. God has declared what is good in His revelation. In doing so, He has given value to the things He has created. For example, we are not free to place whatever value we wish on the church, family, or government. The appropriate value is that which God assigns in His Word. Axiology (value theory) is the second component of ethics.

Value theory answers three questions: (1) Can value be defined? (2) Can values be checked by a standard? and (3) Can values be classified? Although Calvin never directly discussed values in his writing or preaching, the implications from his discussion of the Bible as our source of knowledge provide the opportunity to develop an understanding of values.[18]

Value is the worth placed on people, groups of people, objects, and events. Since everything gets its being and meaning from its place in the plan of God, it seems appropriate that value should be derived from God's plan, as well. One of the beauties of a Calvinistic philosophy is its correlation between being, fact, obligation, and value. Most contemporary philosophical systems assert values to be subjective statements of preference, either of the individual or the social group; there is no known standard by which to judge one value system inferior or superior to another. Christian theistic philosophy contends that the origin and standard for values is the self-revealing God of Scripture. An essential ingredient in using the Bible as our rule for faith and practice is to hold biblical values in an appropriate order, given the present providence of God in our lives.

Value theory also enables the classification of values into intrinsic values and extrinsic values. Historically, the concept of intrinsic value has been connoted by the phrase *summum bonum*: highest good.[19] Since Scripture asserts that in the kingdom of God, *soli Deo gloria* is our highest good, then, by definition, this is the end value of the Christian life. An intrinsic value is an end in itself; it is not sought "in order that . . ." It would be valuable if nothing else existed because it is nonderived. Every value set has at least one intrinsic value that provides the organizing principle for all of the other values in the set.

Extrinsic values include instrumental values and beneficial values. Extrinsic values are derived; they get their value or disvalue from their effective production or from what they lead to. Instrumental values can be evaluated by their effective production of something. They are a good means, a neutral means, or a poor means. What matters is not what they lead to but whether they are efficient producers of that thing. Beneficial values are always a means to the highest good. They may be efficient producers of the good and thus be both instrumentally good and beneficially good at the same time. They may be inefficient producers of the good and thus be instrumentally poor yet beneficially good. Or they may be neutral means to the good. The distinction is best summarized by saying that instrumental values are a good means, while beneficial values are a means to the good. The mindset or frame of reference includes the value set. For the believer, the mindset consists of the correspondent and coherent knowledge we have with God. We derive the value set from Scripture, which covers every facet of life.

• *What should motivate me to choose the right and the good?* The answer to this question constitutes the final ingredient of a theory of ethics. The focus is on the internal dynamic of the agent in choosing the right and the good. This rubric is discussed under the motivation for obeying God and pursuing the good. Many motives have been proposed, but the most promising are gratitude for undeserved grace, fear of God, and faith as allegiance or loyalty to Christ.

THE TASK IS NOT COMPLETE

The church owes a debt of gratitude to God for the gift of John Calvin. Even though he was not a philosopher, Calvin's preaching, his exegetical works, and his manual (*Institutes of the Christian Religion*) assist believers to walk in the way of truth and provide rich marrow for the continued development of Calvinistic philosophy. Not everyone will agree with my construction of this philosophy, but perhaps most will agree that the task of developing a Christian philosophy is not complete. To have the opportunity to build on Calvin and his heritage is a great privilege and joy.

DISCUSSION QUESTIONS

1. Calvin is rarely called a philosopher. Why, then, is philosophy important?

2. What is a Calvinistic theory of reality?

3. How does Calvinism approach the subject of epistemology (how we know what we know)?

4. Outline what is entailed in a Calvinistic theory of ethics.

NOTES

[1] Quoted in Jeffrey Thompson Parker, *Flicker to Flame: Living with Purpose, Meaning, and Happiness* (Garden City, N.Y.: Morgan James Publishing, 2006), 118.

[2] This chapter purposely does not include quotations from Calvin's writings. It is hoped that by developing the implications of his writings, a Christian philosophy can be achieved without constantly referencing his writings.

[3] Inst., 1.15.6.

[4] Paul Helm, *John Calvin's Ideas* (Oxford: Oxford University Press, 2004), 1–9.

[5] For insight into Calvin's use of philosophy, see Charles Partee, *Calvin and Classical Philosophy* (Leiden: E. J. Brill, 1977).

[6] For a discussion of Calvin's metaphysics, see Edward A. Dowey, *The Knowledge of God in Calvin's Theology* (Grand Rapids: Eerdmans, 1993).

[7] John Calvin, *Sermons on Job*, trans. Arthur Golding (Edinburgh: Banner of Truth Trust, 1993), 685.

[8] Inst., 1.15.6.

[9] Ibid., 1.13.1.

[10] John Murray, *Principles of Conduct* (Grand Rapids: Eerdmans, 1968), 50–51.

[11] Inst., 2.14.3.

[12] Inst., 1.16.6. For a discussion of this topic in the Calvinistic tradition, see Robert L. Reymond, *The Justification of Knowledge* (Philadelphia: P&R, 1976), 85–93, and John Frame, *The Doctrine of the Knowledge of God* (Nutley, N.J.: P&R, 1987).

[13] For a discussion of the tests of truth in Calvinistic thought, see Cornelius Van Til, *A Christian Theory of Knowledge* (Philadelphia: P&R, 1969). See also Alvin Plantinga, *Warranted Christian Belief* (New York: Oxford University Press, 2000).

[14] Helm argues that Reformed epistemologists like Plantinga and Wolterstorff misrepresent Calvin by asserting that he is a presuppositionalist and not a foundationalist (*John Calvin's Ideas*, 240–245).

[15] Inst., 1.2.3; 1.3.1.

[16] Murray, *Principles of Conduct*, 142.

[17] Ibid., 27–106.

[18] For an older discussion of this subject in a Calvinistic tradition, see James Olthius, *Facts, Values and Ethics* (Toronto: Wedge Publications, n.d.).

[19] For a discussion of the biblical idea of *summum bonum*, see Cornelius Van Til, *Christian Ethics: In Defense of the Faith*, vol. 3 (Philadelphia: P&R, 1970).

PART THREE

CALVINISM
IN
THE HEART

CHAPTER 12

CULTIVATING
THE SPIRIT

Michael A. G. Haykin

*A praying man can never be very miserable, whatever his condition be, for he
has the ear of God; the Spirit within to indite, a Friend in heaven to present,
and God Himself to receive his desires as a Father. It is a mercy to pray, even
though I never receive the mercy prayed for.*[1]

—WILLIAM BRIDGE

istorically, the Reformed tradition has had a passionate interest in the
Holy Spirit.[2] A key source for this pneumatological passion was John Calvin himself, who had "a constant and even distinctive concern" with the person and
work of the Spirit.[3] B. B. Warfield, the distinguished American Presbyterian theologian, even spoke of Calvin as "preeminently the theologian of the Holy Spirit."[4]

In the English-speaking world, Calvin's deep interest in the Spirit and His
work was passed on to that Reformed tradition associated with the names of the
Puritans and their successors, and the Calvinistic Dissenters and evangelicals of
the eighteenth and nineteenth centuries. In discussing the work of the Spirit,
Calvin's heirs emphasized the Spirit's sovereignty in every area of the salvation
of sinners. The early Stuart Puritan, John Preston, for instance, maintained that
spiritual fortitude comes from the sanctifying work of the Holy Spirit, who is "the
only means to strengthen the inward man."[5] But he also could argue that there
are various means of godliness that the Christian must be diligent in using to

attain this spiritual strength, such disciplines as "hearing the word, receiving the sacrament, prayer, meditation, conference, the communion of saints, particular resolutions to [do] good."[6] However, none of these means of grace or spiritual disciplines were sufficient in and of themselves to nourish the soul of the believer or sustain the inner life of a congregation—only the Spirit was sufficient for that. The late-eighteenth-century English Calvinistic Baptist John Sutcliff thus observed that the "influences" of the Holy Spirit are "the soul, the great animating soul of all religion. These withheld, divine ordinances are empty cisterns, and spiritual graces are withering flowers."[7]

Yet the best representatives of the Reformed tradition were also certain that to seek the Spirit's power apart from the appointed means was both unbiblical and foolish. Benjamin Keach, the most significant Calvinistic Baptist theologian of the late seventeenth century, wrote in 1681, in a direct allusion to the Quakers, who had dispensed with the sacraments of baptism and the Lord's Supper:

> Many are confident they have the Spirit, Light, and Power, when 'tis all mere Delusion. . . . Some Men boast of the Spirit, and conclude they have the Spirit, and none but they, and yet at the same time cry down and villify his blessed Ordinances and Institutions, which he hath left in his Word, carefully to be observed and kept, till he comes the second time without Sin unto Salvation. . . . The Spirit hath its proper Bounds, and always runs in its spiritual Channel, *viz.* The Word and Ordinances, God's public and private Worship.[8]

It was thus a given for this Spirit-driven tradition that, as the Elizabethan Puritan Richard Greenham put it, "we draw near to God by means."[9]

The above quote from Preston lists a number of such means of piety, but there were four that were especially regarded as central by this tradition: the Scriptures, prayer, the sacraments, and spiritual fellowship.

A SPIRITUALITY OF THE WORD

In strong contrast to medieval Roman Catholicism, which had majored on symbols and images as the means for cultivating spirituality, the Reformation, coming on the heels of the invention of the printing press, turned to words as the primary vehicle of spiritual cultivation. One clear illustration of this is the career of William Tyndale. A consuming passion to give the people of England the Word of God so gripped him that from the mid-1520s until his martyrdom in 1536, his life was directed to this sole end.

Like the rest of the Reformers, Tyndale was convinced beyond a shadow of a doubt that knowledge of the Scriptures was essential to Christian spirituality. Thus, Tyndale could state in his 1530 "Prologue" to his translation of Genesis: "The Scripture is a light, and sheweth us the true way, both what to do and what to hope for; and a defence from all error, and a comfort in adversity that we despair not, and feareth us in prosperity that we sin not."[10]

Standing in this word-centered spirituality that comes down from the Reformation is the eighteenth-century American theologian Jonathan Edwards. Like Tyndale, he was convinced that the Scriptures "are the light by which ministers must be enlightened, and the light they are to hold forth to their hearers; and they are the fire whence their hearts and the hearts of their hearers must be enkindled."[11] Not surprisingly, biblical meditation was central to his piety. Samuel Hopkins, one of his close friends and his first biographer, noted that Edwards was, "as far as it can be known, much on his knees in secret, and in devout reading of God's word and meditation upon it."[12] Hopkins also noted that Edwards "had an uncommon thirst for knowledge, in the pursuit of which, he spared no cost nor pains." He thus "read all the books, especially books of divinity," that he could get. But, Hopkins emphasized, "he studied the Bible more than all other books, and more than most other divines do. His uncommon acquaintance with the Bible appears in his sermons, and in most of his publications; and his great pains in studying it are manifest in his manuscript notes upon it."[13]

A good example of the fruit of his lifelong meditation on Scripture can be seen in what has been termed Edwards' "Blank Bible." This was a small printed Bible that Edwards owned in which blank sheets were placed between all of the pages. These blank sheets were divided into two columns so that Edwards could then write commentary on adjacent texts. Edwards' "Blank Bible" contains as many as ten thousand entries, written on the entire Bible between 1730 and 1758.[14]

"ALL IS NOTHING WITHOUT PRAYER"

Another means by which Reformed believers historically have drawn near to God is prayer. As the Puritan theologian Thomas Goodwin once remarked, "Our speaking to God by prayers, and his speaking to us by answers thereunto, is one great part of our walking with God."[15] And Greenham was unequivocal when he declared that in the Christian life "all is nothing without prayer."[16]

But as mature Christians also have known, to persevere in the discipline of prayer one needs the empowering of God the Holy Spirit, for prayer is, and always has been, one of the great struggles in the Christian life. Another Puritan, John Bunyan, best known for his classic book *The Pilgrim's Progress*, refers to his struggles with prayer in a tract titled *I Will Pray with the Spirit*, which he wrote around 1662.[17] Bunyan stresses that only the Spirit can enable the believer to persevere in prayer once he or she has begun:

> May I but speak my own Experience, and from that tell you the difficulty of Praying to God as I ought; it is enough to make your poor, blind, carnal men, to entertain strange thoughts of me, For, as for my heart, when I go to pray, I find it so loath to go to God, and when it is with him, so loath to stay with him, that many times I am forced in my Prayers; *first* to beg God that he would take mine heart, and set it on himself in Christ, and when it is there, that he would keep it there (Psalm 86.11). Nay, many times I know not what to pray for, I am so blind, nor how to pray I am so ignorant; only (blessed be Grace) the *Spirit helps our infirmities* [Rom. 8:26].
>
> Oh the starting-holes that the heart hath in time of Prayer! none knows how many by-ways the heart hath, and back-lanes, to slip away from the presence of God. How much pride also, if enabled with expressions? how much hypocrisy, if before others? and how little conscience is there made of Prayer between God and the Soul in secret, unless the *Spirit of Supplication* [Zech.12:10] be there to help?[18]

This passage displays a couple of the most attractive features of the Puritans: their transparent honesty and their in-depth knowledge of the human heart. From experience, Bunyan well knew the allergic reaction of the old nature to the presence of God. So were it not for the Spirit, none would be able to persevere in prayer. Little wonder that Bunyan says right after the above passage, "When the Spirit gets into the heart then there is prayer indeed, and not till then."[19]

Generations of Christians, though, also testify that for all who persevere in this discipline of prayer, there are times of exquisite delight when the duty slides over into pure joy. John Owen, one of Bunyan's good friends, once observed with regard to Ephesians 2:18 ("Through [Christ] we both have access by one Spirit unto the Father"): "No tongue can express, no mind can reach, the heavenly placidness and soul-satisfying delight which are intimated in these words. To come to God as a Father, through Christ, by the help and assistance of the Holy Spirit, revealing him as a Father unto us, and enabling us to go to him as a Father, how full of sweetness and satisfaction is it!"[20]

"THE KING IS PLEAS'D TO SIT WITH US"

Another place Calvinists have regarded as being rich in spiritual nourishment is the Lord's Table. This may come as a surprise to many evangelicals, who in recent times do not appear to have seen participation at the table as an important spiritual discipline. They have tended to write off any talk about the Lord's Supper nourishing the soul as Roman Catholic teaching. But it was not always so, as two samplings of eighteenth-century Calvinistic reflections on the Lord's Supper reveal.

Anne Dutton, a prolific Calvinistic author who corresponded with many of the leading evangelical figures of the eighteenth century, was certain that in the Lord's Supper, "the King is pleas'd to sit with us, at his Table."[21] In fact, so highly did she prize this means of grace that she could state that the celebration of the Supper "admits" believers "into the nearest approach to his [that is, Christ's] glorious self . . . on the Earth, on this side of the presence of his glory in heaven."[22] Other Reformed believers of this era might have seen this statement as erring a little on the side of exaggeration. She seems to say of the table what they would have said of preaching. Nevertheless, they would have generally endorsed her view of the table as a place where God's people have rich fellowship with their Redeemer.

Similar sentiments can be found in *Hymns In Commemoration Of the Sufferings Of Our Blessed Saviour Jesus Christ* by Joseph Stennett I, the pastor of an early-eighteenth-century Calvinistic Baptist Church that met in London. Stennett describes the church's celebration at the table as a "perpetual memorial" of Christ's death, a death that is to be commemorated. And he calls the bread and wine "proper Symbols" and "Figures." Yet, Stennett also says of these symbols:

Thy Flesh is Meat indeed,
Thy Blood the richest wine;
How blest are they who often feed
On this Repast of thine! [23]

Stennett makes it clear that the feeding involved at the table is by faith, but his language clearly indicates that for him the Lord's Supper is a place of rich spiritual nourishment:

Here may our Faith still on Thee feed
The only Food Divine;
To Faith thy Flesh is Meat indeed,
Thy Blood the Noblest wine. [24]

"ONE OF THE BEST HELPS TO KEEP UP RELIGION"

The New Testament knows nothing of solitary Christianity. One of the great sources of spiritual strength is Christian friendship and fellowship. Calvin, who has had the undeserved reputation of being cold, harsh, and unloving, knew this well and had a rich appreciation of friendship. The French Reformed historian Richard Stauffer reckoned that there were few men at the time of the Reformation "who developed as many friendships"[25] as Calvin. Two of his closest friends were his fellow Reformers Guillaume Farel and Pierre Viret. Calvin celebrated his friendship with these men in his preface to his *Commentary on Titus*, where he stated:

I do not believe that there have ever been such friends who have lived together in such a deep friendship in their everyday style of life in this world as we have in our ministry. I have served here in the office of pastor with you two. There was never any appearance of envy; it seems to me that you two and I were as one person.[26]

This brotherly friendship is well revealed in the extensive correspondence of these three men. In their letters to one another, not only are theological problems and ecclesiastical matters frankly discussed, but there is an openness in relation to the problems of their private lives.

Here is but one example: On Jan. 27, 1552, Calvin wrote to Farel and chided him for reports he had heard—true reports, one must add—about the undue length of Farel's sermons. "You have often confessed," Calvin reminds his friend, "that you know this is a fault and that you would like to correct it."[27] Calvin went on to encourage Farel to shorten his sermons lest Satan use Farel's failing in this regard to destroy the many good things being produced by his ministry.

Another example of the importance of friendship for Reformed believers can be found in the diary of Esther Burr, the third of Jonathan and Sarah Edwards' eight daughters and a Christian housewife living in Colonial New Jersey. In the mid-1750s, Esther unequivocally declared: "Nothing is more refreshing to the soul (except communication with God himself), than the company and society of a friend."[28]

The wife of Aaron Burr Sr., president of what would become Princeton University, and the mother of two small children, Esther earnestly sought to know the presence of God in the hurly-burly of her daily life. As she did so, she came to appreciate the fact that friends are a divine gift. Writing in her diary on Jan. 23, 1756, she said she was convinced that "'Tis . . . a great mercy that we have any friends—What would this world be without 'em—A person who looks upon himself to be friendless must of all creatures be miserable in this Life—'tis the Life of Life."[29] For Esther, Christian friends were one of this world's greatest sources of happiness. Why did Esther put such a value upon friendship? Surely it was because she realized that Christian friends and conversation with them are vital for spiritual growth.

Similar convictions are found in something she wrote the previous year on April 20, 1755, to her closest friend, Sarah Prince:

> I should highly value (as you my dear do) such *charming friends* as you have about *you—friends* that one might unbosom their whole soul to. . . . I esteem *religious conversation* one of the best helps to keep up religion in the soul, excepting secret devotion, I don't know but the very best—Then what a lamentable thing that 'tis so neglected by God's own children.[30]

Notice the connection between friendship and what Esther calls "religious conversation." For the Christian, true friends are those with whom one can share the deepest things of one's life. They are people with whom one can be transparent and open. In Esther's words, they are people to whom one can "unbosom [one's] whole soul." In the course of conversation about spiritual things, the believer can find strength and encouragement for living the Christian life. In referring to spiritual conversation with friends as "one of the best helps to keep up religion in the soul," Esther obviously viewed it as a means of grace, one of the ways in which God the Holy Spirit keeps Christians in fellowship with the Savior.

OTHER MEANS OF GRACE

Calvinists have always made much of the means of grace, including other means, some of which are discussed in chapter 15. The Victorian Calvinist Charles H. Spurgeon, for instance, in an 1868 article in his magazine *The Sword and the Trowel*, could advocate seasons of solitude spent in silence, fasting, and prayer. Still, much will have been accomplished if we can recommit ourselves to these four means—the Word, prayer, the Lord's Table, and spiritual friendship—so as to have a bolder profession of Christ, a more watchful life, and a more tender conscience toward God. May we be given strength to "draw near to God" through these means He has given.

DISCUSSION QUESTIONS

1. Is John Sutcliff biblically accurate when he says "influences" of the Holy Spirit are "the soul, the great animating soul of all religion"? Why or why not?

2. What does the phrase "the spirituality of the Word" mean?

3. Why has the Reformed tradition emphasized with Richard Greenham that "all is nothing without prayer"?

4. How does friendship help Christians become mature in Christ?

5. What other means of grace have been helpful in your Christian walk and why?

NOTES

[1] Quoted in I. D. E. Thomas, *The Golden Treasury of Puritan Quotations* (Chicago: Moody Press, 1975), 216.

[2] Most of this chapter originated as a paper at "Our Holy God," a conference sponsored by the Alliance of Confessing Evangelicals, Nassau Christian Center, Princeton, N.J., Oct. 27, 2007. It also serves as an abridged form of several chapters in Michael Haykin, *The God Who Draws Near: An Introduction to Biblical Spirituality* (Darlington, England: Evangelical Press, 2007).

[3] Richard B. Gaffin, "The Holy Spirit," *The Westminster Theological Journal*, 43 (1980): 61.

[4] B. B. Warfield, "Calvin's Doctrine of the Knowledge of God," in *Calvin and Augustine*, ed. Samuel G. Craig (Phillipsburg, N.J.: P&R, 1980), 107. See also his "John Calvin: The Man and His Work" and "Calvin as a Theologian," in ibid., 21ff., 487ff.

[5] Quoted in Simon K. H. Chan, "The Puritan Meditative Tradition, 1599–1691: A Study of Ascetical Piety" (D.Phil. thesis, Magdalene College, Cambridge University, 1986), 13.

[6] Ibid.

[7] John Sutcliff, *Jealousy for the Lord of Hosts Illustrated* (London: W. Button, 1791), 12.

[8] Benjamin Keach, *Tropologia: A Key to Open Scripture-Metaphors* (London: Enoch Prosser, 1681), II, 2:312, 314.

[9] Chan, "The Puritan Meditative Tradition," 11.

[10] William Tyndale, *Doctrinal Treatises and Introductions to Different Portions of the Holy Scriptures* (Cambridge: Cambridge University Press, 1848), 399.

[11] Jonathan Edwards, "The True Excellency of a Gospel Minister," in *The Works of Jonathan Edwards* (Edinburgh: Banner of Truth Trust, 1974), 2:959.

[12] Samuel Hopkins, "The Life and Character of the Late Reverend Mr. Jonathan Edwards," in *Jonathan Edwards: A Profile*, ed. David Levin (New York: Hill and Wang, 1969), 39.

[13] Ibid., 40–41.

[14] Stephen J. Stein, "The Spirit and the Word: Jonathan Edwards and Scriptural Exegesis," in *Jonathan Edwards and the American Experience*, ed. Nathan O. Hatch and Harry S. Stout (Oxford: Oxford University Press, 1988), 121.

[15] Thomas Goodwin, *The Works of Thomas Goodwin* (Edinburgh: James Nichol, 1890), 3:362.

[16] Quoted in John H. Primus, *Richard Greenham: Portrait of an Elizabethan Pastor* (Macon, Ga.: Mercer University Press, 1998), 138.

[17] For the date, see introduction to *John Bunyan: The Doctrine of the Law and Grace unfolded and I will pray with the Spirit*, ed. Richard L. Greaves (Oxford: Clarendon Press, 1976), xl–xli. Subsequent quotations are taken from this text, which is the latest critical edition.

[18] Ibid., 256–257.

[19] Ibid., 257.

[20] John Owen, *The Works of John Owen* (Edinburgh: Banner of Truth Trust, 1965), 4:82.

[21] Anne Dutton, *Thoughts on the Lord's Supper, Relating to the Nature, Subjects, and Right Partaking of This Solemn Ordinance* (London: 1748), 21.

[22] Ibid., 25.

[23] *Hymns In Commemoration Of the Sufferings Of Our Blessed Saviour Jesus Christ, Compos'd For the Celebration of his Holy Supper* (London: N. Cliff and D. Jackson, 1713), 35.

24 Ibid., 23.

25 Richard Stauffer, *The Humanness of John Calvin*, trans. George H. Shriver (Nashville: Abingdon Press, 1971), 47.

26 John Calvin, quoted in Richard Stauffer, *The Humanness of John Calvin*, trans. George H. Shriver (Nashville: Abingdon Press, 1971), 57.

27 Ibid., 57–58, n33.

28 Esther Edwards Burr, *The Journal of Esther Edwards Burr 1754–1757*, ed. Carol F. Karlsen and Laurie Crumpacker (New Haven: Yale University Press, 1984), 185.

29 Ibid.

30 Ibid., 112.

CHAPTER 13

CALVIN'S
GOD-EXALTING PIETY

*We are God's: let us therefore live for him and die for him. We are God's: let
his wisdom and will therefore rule all our actions. We are God's: let all the
parts of our life accordingly strive toward him as our only lawful goal.*[1]

—JOHN CALVIN

$\mathscr{F}$ew people enjoy being called pietistic today. Tragically, *piety* and its English
derivatives have become pejorative words and concepts. John Calvin would
be aghast. For him, piety was not only a positive trait, it was the essence of true
biblical Christianity. For Calvin, the preeminent systematician of the Protestant
Reformation, theological understanding and practical piety, truth and usefulness,
were inseparable. Theology deals first with knowledge—knowledge of God and of
ourselves—but there is no true knowledge where there is no true piety.

Calvin's concept of piety (*pietas*) was rooted in the knowledge of God and
included attitudes and actions that were directed to the adoration and service
of God.[2] Piety is one of the major themes of Calvin's theology. John T. McNeill
says that Calvin's theology is "piety described at length."[3] Indeed, Calvin was
determined to confine theology within the limits of piety.[4] In the preface to his
Institutes, which was addressed to King Francis I, Calvin says that the book's purpose is "solely to transmit certain rudiments by which those who are touched with
any zeal for religion might be shaped to true godliness [*pietas*]."[5] This comprehensive sense of piety profoundly impacted Calvin's successors (such as the English
Puritans, Dutch Further Reformation divines, and some of the German Pietists
and their descendants) down to the present day.

After an introductory look at the definition and purpose of piety in Calvin's thinking, this chapter will show how Calvin's piety impacted the theological, ecclesiological, and practical dimensions of his thought.[6]

THE DEFINITION AND IMPORTANCE OF PIETY

For Calvin, piety designates a proper attitude toward God and obedience to Him. Flowing out of the knowledge of who and what God is (theology), piety includes heartfelt worship, saving faith, filial fear, prayerful submission, and reverential love.[7]

In his first catechism, Calvin writes, "True piety consists in a sincere feeling which loves God as Father as much as it fears and reverences Him as Lord, embraces His righteousness, and dreads offending Him worse than death."[8] In the *Institutes*, Calvin writes, "I call 'piety' that reverence joined with love of God which the knowledge of his benefits induces."[9] This love and reverence for God is a necessary concomitant to true knowledge of Him.

Such piety embraces all of life. Calvin writes, "The whole life of Christians ought to be a sort of practice of godliness"[10]—or, as the subtitle of the first edition of the *Institutes* states, "Embracing almost the whole sum of piety & whatever is necessary to know of the doctrine of salvation: A work most worthy to be read by all persons zealous for piety."[11]

PIETY'S SUPREME GOAL: *SOLI DEO GLORIA*

The goal of piety is to recognize and praise the glory of God—glory that shines in God's attributes, in the structure of the world, and in the death and resurrection of Jesus Christ.[12] The desire to glorify God supersedes even the desire for personal salvation in every truly pious person.[13] We were created that God might be glorified in us, and the regenerate yearn to live out this purpose.[14] Furthermore, God redeems, adopts, and sanctifies His people that His glory would shine in them and deliver them from impious self-seeking.[15] As a result, the pious man's deepest concern is God Himself and the things of God—God's Word, God's authority, God's gospel, God's truth. He yearns to know more of God and to commune more with Him.

But how do we glorify God? Calvin writes: "God has prescribed for us a way in which he will be glorified by us, namely, piety, which consists in the obedience of his Word. He that exceeds these bounds does not go about to honor God, but rather to dishonor him."[16] Obedience to God's Word means taking refuge in Christ for forgiveness of our sins, knowing Him through the Scriptures, serving Him with a loving heart, doing good works in gratitude for His goodness, and exercising self-denial to the point of loving our enemies.[17] This response involves total surrender to God Himself, His Word, and His will (Rom. 11:33–12:2).[18]

Calvin's motto well sums up the piety with which he lived: "I offer thee my heart, Lord, promptly and sincerely." This is the desire of all who are truly pious. However, this desire can be realized only through communion with Christ and participation in Him, for outside of Christ even the most religious person lives for himself. Only in Christ can the pious live as willing servants of their Lord, faithful soldiers of their Commander, and obedient children of their Father.[19]

THEOLOGICAL DIMENSIONS

There are a number of theological dimensions to this understanding of piety. They include:

• *Piety's profound root: mystical union.* Piety is rooted in the believer's mystical union with Christ, so this union must be our starting point.[20] Such a union is possible because Christ took on our human nature, filling it with His sinless virtue. Union with Christ in His humanity is historical, ethical, and personal. However, we do not lose our identity in Him; there is no thought of a mixture of human substances between Christ and us. Nonetheless, Calvin states, "Not only does he cleave to us by an indivisible bond of fellowship, but with a wonderful communion, day by day, he grows more and more into one body with us, until he becomes completely one with us."[21] This union is one of the gospel's greatest mysteries.[22] Because of Christ's perfection in our nature, the pious may draw by faith whatever they need for their sanctification (John 6:51).[23]

If Christ had died and risen but had not applied His salvation to believers for their regeneration and sanctification, His work would have been ineffectual. Our piety shows that the Spirit of Christ is working in us what already has been accomplished in Christ. Christ administers His sanctification to the church so that the church may live piously for Him.[24]

• *Piety's double bond: the Spirit and faith.* Union and communion with Christ are realized only through Spirit-worked faith, Calvin teaches. Communion is actual, not because believers participate in the essence of Christ's nature, but because the Spirit of Christ unites believers so intimately to Christ that they become, as it were, flesh of His flesh and bone of His bone. From God's perspective, the Spirit is the bond between Christ and believers, whereas from our perspective, faith is the bond. These perspectives do not contradict each other, since one of the Spirit's principal operations is to work faith in a sinner.[25]

Only the Spirit can unite Christ in heaven with the believer on earth. Just as the Spirit united heaven and earth in the incarnation, so in regeneration He raises the elect from earth to commune with Christ in heaven and brings Christ into the hearts and lives of the elect on earth.[26] Thus, communion with Christ is always the result of the Spirit's work—a work that is astonishing and experiential rather than comprehensible.[27] The Holy Spirit is the link that binds the believer to Christ, the channel through which Christ is communicated to the believer.[28]

Faith unites the believer to Christ by means of the Word, enabling the believer to receive Christ as He is clothed in the gospel and graciously offered by the Father.[29] Consequently, Calvin says, "We ought not to separate Christ from ourselves or ourselves from him," but participate in Christ by faith, for this "revives us from death to make us a new creature."[30]

By faith, the believer possesses Christ and grows in Him. What's more, the degree of his faith exercised through the Word determines his degree of communion with Christ.[31] "Everything which faith should contemplate is exhibited to us in Christ," Calvin writes.[32] The believer who excels in piety learns to grasp Christ so firmly by faith that Christ dwells within his heart, though He remains in heaven.[33] The pious live by what they find in Christ rather than by what they find in themselves.[34]

• *Piety's double cleansing: justification and sanctification.* According to Calvin, believers receive from Christ by faith the "double grace" of justification and sanctification, which together provide a twofold cleansing.[35] Justification offers imputed purity while sanctification brings actual purity.[36]

Calvin views justification as including the remission of sins and the right to eternal life, by which "God receives us into his favor as righteous men."[37] He goes on to say that "since God justifies us by the intercession of Christ, he absolves us not by the confirmation of our own innocence but by the imputation of righteousness, so that we who are not righteous in ourselves may be reckoned as such in Christ."[38]

Calvin also regards justification as "the principal hinge by which religion is supported," the soil out of which the Christian life develops, and the substance of piety.[39] Justification not only serves God's honor by satisfying the conditions for salvation, it also gives the believer's conscience "peaceful rest and serene tranquility."[40] As Romans 5:1 says, "Therefore being justified by faith, we have peace with God through our Lord Jesus Christ." This is the heart and soul of piety. Believers do not need to worry about their status with God because they are justified by faith.

Sanctification is the process by which the believer increasingly becomes conformed to Christ in heart, conduct, and devotion to God. It is the continual remaking of the believer by the Holy Spirit, the increasing consecration of body and soul to God.[41] In sanctification, the believer offers himself to God as a sacrifice. This does not come without great struggle and slow progress; it requires cleansing from the pollution of the flesh and renouncing of the world.[42] It demands repentance, mortification, and daily conversion.

Justification and sanctification are inseparable, Calvin says. To separate one from the other is to tear Christ in pieces;[43] it is like trying to separate the sun's light from the heat that light generates.[44] Believers are justified for the purpose of worshiping God in holiness of life.[45]

ECCLESIOLOGICAL DIMENSIONS

Calvin's view of piety also contains a number of ecclesiological dimensions, including:

• *Piety through the church.* Calvin's piety is rooted in the Word and nurtured in the church. While breaking with the clericalism and absolutism of Rome, Calvin nonetheless maintains a high view of the church.[46] Believers are engrafted into Christ *and* His church because spiritual growth happens within the church. The church is mother, educator, and nourisher of every believer, for the Holy Spirit acts in her. Believers cultivate piety by the Spirit through the church's teaching ministry, progressing from spiritual infancy to adolescence to full manhood in Christ. They do not graduate from the church until they die.[47] This lifelong education is offered within an atmosphere of genuine piety in which

believers love and care for one another under the headship of Christ.[48] Such
education encourages the growth of one another's gifts and love because it is
"constrained to borrow from others."[49]

Progress in piety is impossible apart from the church, for piety is fostered by
the communion of saints. Within the church, believers "cleave to each other in
the mutual distribution of gifts."[50] Each member has his own place and gifts to
use within the body.[51] Ideally, the entire body uses these gifts in symmetry and
proportion, ever reforming and growing toward perfection.[52]

• *Piety of the Word.* The Word of God is central to the development of
Christian piety in the believer. Calvin's relational model explains how.

True religion is a dialogue between God and man. The part of the dialogue
that God initiates is revelation, wherein He comes down to meet us, address us,
and make Himself known to us in the preaching of the Word. The other part of
the dialogue is man's response to God's revelation. This response, which includes
trust, adoration, and godly fear, is what Calvin calls piety.

The preaching of the Word saves us and preserves us as the Spirit enables
us to appropriate the blood of Christ and respond to Him with reverential love.
By the Spirit-empowered preaching of men, "the renewal of the saints is accomplished and the body of Christ is edified," Calvin says.[53]

Furthermore, Calvin teaches that the preaching of the Word is our spiritual
food and our medicine for spiritual health. With the Spirit's blessing, ministers
are spiritual physicians who apply the Word to our souls as earthly physicians
apply medicine to our bodies. Using the Word, these spiritual doctors diagnose,
prescribe for, and cure spiritual disease in those plagued by sin and death. The
preached Word is used as an instrument to heal, cleanse, and make fruitful our
disease-prone souls.[54] The Spirit, or the "internal minister," promotes piety by
using the "external minister" to preach the Word. As Calvin says, the external
minister "holds forth the vocal word and it is received by the ears," but the internal minister "truly communicates the thing proclaimed . . . that is Christ."[55]

• *Piety in the sacraments.* Calvin defines the sacraments as testimonies "of
divine grace toward us, confirmed by an outward sign, with mutual attestation of
our piety toward him."[56] Thus, the sacraments are "exercises of piety." They foster
and strengthen our faith, and help us offer ourselves as living sacrifices to God.

In the sacraments, God accommodates Himself to our weakness, Calvin says.
He comes to His people in the sacraments, encourages them, enables them to

know Christ better, builds them up, and nourishes them in Him. Baptism promotes piety as a symbol of how believers are engrafted into Christ, renewed by the Spirit, and adopted into the family of the heavenly Father.[57] Likewise, the Lord's Supper shows how His adopted children are fed by their loving Father. Calvin loves to refer to the Supper as nourishment for the soul. "The signs are bread and wine which represent for us the invisible food that we receive from the flesh and blood of Christ," he writes. "Christ is the only food of our soul, and therefore our heavenly Father invites us to Christ, that refreshed by partaking of him, we may repeatedly gather strength until we shall have reached heavenly immortality."[58]

Calvin teaches that Christ gives Himself, not just His benefits, to us in the Supper. Christ also makes us part of His body as He gives us Himself. Calvin cannot precisely explain how that happens in the Supper, for it is better experienced than explained.[59] However, he does say that Christ does not leave heaven to enter the bread. Rather, by the Spirit's work within us, we are called to lift our hearts up to heaven, where Christ is, and not cling to the external bread and wine.

When we meet Christ in the sacraments, we grow in grace; that is why they are called means of grace. The sacraments therefore encourage us in our progress toward heaven. They promote confidence in God's promises through Christ's "signified and sealed" redemptive death. Since they are covenants, they contain promises by which "consciences may be roused to an assurance of salvation," Calvin says.[60]

Finally, the sacraments promote piety by prompting us to thank and praise God for His abundant grace. We offer this sacrifice of gratitude in response to Christ's sacrifice for us. We surrender our lives in light of the heavenly banquet God spreads for us in the Supper. By the Spirit's grace, the Supper enables us as a royal priesthood to offer ourselves as living sacrifices of praise and thanksgiving to God.[61] The Lord's Supper thus prompts both piety of grace received and piety of gratitude given.[62]

• *Piety in the Psalter.* Calvin views the book of Psalms as the canonical manual of piety. In the preface to his five-volume commentary on the Psalms—his largest exposition of any Bible book—Calvin writes: "There is no other book in which we are more perfectly taught the right manner of praising God, or in which we are more powerfully stirred up to the performance of this exercise of piety."[63] Calvin's preoccupation with the Psalter was motivated by his belief that the book of Psalms teaches and inspires genuine piety by (1) teaching us our need for God; (2) serving as our sung creed; (3) demonstrating God's amazing goodness; (4) fostering prayer; (5) providing a vehicle for communal worship; (6) showing the depth of communion we may enjoy with God; and (7) covering the full range of spiritual experience, including faith and unbelief, joy in God and sorrow over sin, and divine presence and divine desertion. As Calvin says, the psalms are "an anatomy of all parts of the soul."[64]

Calvin immersed himself in the book of Psalms for twenty-five years as a commentator, preacher, biblical scholar, and worship leader.[65] Early on, he began work on metrical versions of psalms to be used in public worship. Later, he recruited the talents of men such as Clement Marot, Louis Bourgeois, and Theodore Beza to produce the Genevan Psalter. Two years before his death, Calvin was delighted to see its first complete edition.[66]

The Genevan Psalter, a remarkable collection of 125 melodies, clearly expresses Calvin's convictions that piety is best promoted when priority is given to text over tune, while recognizing that psalms deserve their own music. Since music should help the reception of the Word, Calvin says, it should be "weighty, dignified, majestic, and modest"—fitting attributes for the benefit of a sinful creature in the presence of God.[67] This protects the sovereignty of God in worship and promotes proper conformity between the believer's inward disposition and his outward confession.

Psalm-singing is one of the four principal acts of church worship, Calvin believed. He saw it as an extension of prayer. Also, Calvin thought that corporate singing subdued the fallen heart and retrained wayward affections in the way of piety. Like preaching and the sacraments, psalm-singing disciplines the heart's affections in the school of faith and lifts the believer to God. It also amplifies the effect of the Word upon the heart and multiplies the spiritual energy of the church.[68] With the Spirit's direction, psalm-singing tunes the hearts of believers for glory.

The Genevan Psalter was an integral part of Calvinist worship for centuries. It set the standard for succeeding French Reformed psalm books, as well as those in English, Dutch, German, and Hungarian. As a devotional book, it warmed the hearts of thousands, but the people who sang from it understood that its power was not in the book or its words, but in the Spirit who impressed those words on their hearts.

The Genevan Psalter promoted piety by stimulating a spirituality of the Word that was corporate and liturgical, and that broke down the distinction between liturgy and life. The Calvinists freely sang psalms not only in their churches but also in homes and workplaces, on the streets, and in the fields.[69] The singing of psalms became a "means of Huguenot self-identification."[70] In fact, this pious exercise became a cultural emblem. T. Hartley Hall writes, "In scriptural or metrical versions, the Psalms, together with the stately tunes to which they were early set, are clearly the heart and soul of Reformed piety."[71]

PRACTICAL DIMENSIONS

Although Calvin views the church as the nursery of piety, he also emphasizes the need for personal piety. The Christian strives for piety because he loves righteousness, longs to live to God's glory, and delights to obey God's rule of righteousness set forth in Scripture.[72] For Calvin, such piety "is the beginning, middle, and end of Christian living."[73] Here is a summary of what Calvin says on pious Christian living in Book 3 of the *Institutes* of 1559:[74]

   • *Prayer.* Prayer is the principal and perpetual exercise of faith and the chief element of piety.[75] As the believer comes to God in prayer, he receives a sense of God's gracious character even as he offers praises to God and asks for His faithfulness. Prayer encourages piety both privately and corporately.[76]

For Calvin, prayer is the essence of the Christian life. It is a precious gift, not an academic problem.[77] For this reason, he devotes the second-longest chapter of the *Institutes* (Book 3, Chapter 20) to prayer, providing six purposes for it: (1) to fly to God with every need and gain from Him what is lacking in ourselves to live the Christian life; (2) to learn to desire wholeheartedly only what is right as we place all our petitions before God; (3) to become prepared to receive God's benefits and responses to our petitions with humble gratitude; (4) to be led to meditate on God's kindness to us as we receive what we have asked for; (5) to cultivate the proper spirit of delight for God's answers in prayer; and (6) to confirm God's faithful providence so that we may glorify Him and trust in His present help more readily as we witness Him regularly answering our prayers.[78]

Right prayer is governed by rules, Calvin says. These include praying with a heartfelt sense of reverence; a heartfelt sense of need and repentance; a heartfelt sense of humility and trust in God; and a heartfelt sense of confident hope. All four rules are repeatedly violated by even the holiest of God's people. Nevertheless, for Christ's sake, God does not desert the pious but has mercy for them.[79]

• *Repentance.* Repentance is the fruit of faith and prayer. Like Martin Luther, Calvin sees repentance as a lifelong process. He says that repentance is not merely the start of the Christian life; it *is* the Christian life. It involves confession of sin as well as growth in holiness. Repentance is the lifelong response of the believer to the gospel in outward life, mind, heart, attitude, and will.[80]

Repentance begins with turning to God from the heart because of a pure, earnest fear of Him. It involves dying to self and sin (mortification) and coming alive to righteousness (vivification) in Christ.[81] Mortification is the means to vivification, which Calvin defines as "the desire to live in a holy and devoted manner, a desire arising from rebirth; as if it were said that man dies to himself that he may begin to live to God."[82]

• *Self-denial and cross-bearing.* Self-denial is the sacrificial dimension of piety, a fruit of the believer's union with Christ. It includes (1) realizing that we belong to God rather than to ourselves, (2) desiring to orient our entire lives toward God, and (3) yielding ourselves and all that we possess to God as living sacrifices.

While self-denial focuses on inward conformity to Christ, cross-bearing centers on outward Christ-likeness. Those who are in fellowship with Christ must prepare themselves for a hard, toilsome life filled with many kinds of evil, Calvin says. This is not simply due to sin's effect on this fallen world, but also because of the believer's union with Christ. Because His life was a perpetual cross, ours also must include suffering.[83] We not only participate in the benefits of His atoning work on the cross, we also experience the Spirit's work of transforming us into the image of Christ.[84]

Cross-bearing tests piety, Calvin says. Through cross-bearing, we are roused to hope, trained in patience, instructed in obedience, and chastened in pride. Cross-bearing is our medicine and our chastisement; it reveals the feebleness of our flesh and teaches us to suffer for the sake of righteousness.[85]

• *The present and future life.* Through cross-bearing, we learn contempt for the present life when compared to the blessings of heaven. This life is nothing compared to what is to come; it is like smoke or a shadow. "If heaven is our homeland, what else is the earth but our place of exile? If departure from the world is entry into life, what else is the world but a sepulcher?" Calvin asks.[86]

"No one has made progress in the school of Christ who does not joyfully await the day of death and final resurrection," he concludes.[87]

Typically, Calvin uses the *complexio oppositorum* when explaining the Christian's relation to this world, presenting opposites to find a middle way between them. Thus, on the one hand, cross-bearing crucifies us to the world and the world to us. On the other hand, the devout Christian enjoys this present life, albeit with due restraint and moderation, for he is taught to use things in this world for the purpose that God intended for them. Calvin was no ascetic; he enjoyed good literature, good food, and the beauties of nature. But he rejected all forms of earthly excess. The believer is called to Christlike moderation, which includes modesty, prudence, avoidance of display, and contentment with our lot.[88] The hope of the life to come gives purpose to and enjoyment of our present life. This life is always straining after a better, heavenly life.[89]

• *Obedience.* For Calvin, unconditional obedience to God's will is the essence of piety. Piety links love, freedom, and discipline by subjecting all to the will and Word of God.[90] Love is the overarching principle that prevents piety from degenerating into legalism. At the same time, law provides the content for love.

Piety includes rules that govern the believer's responses. Privately, adherence to these rules takes the form of self-denial; publicly, they are expressed in the exercise of church discipline, as Calvin implemented in Geneva. In either case, the glory of God compels disciplined obedience. For Calvin, the pious Christian is neither weak nor passive but dynamically active in the pursuit of obedience—much like a distance runner, a diligent scholar, or a heroic warrior, submitting to God's will.[91]

CALVIN'S EXAMPLE

Calvin strove to live a life of genuine piety himself—theologically, ecclesiastically, and practically.[92] Calvin shows us the piety of a warm-hearted Reformed theologian who speaks from the heart. Having tasted the goodness and grace of God in Jesus Christ, he pursued piety by seeking to know and do God's will every day. He communed with Christ; practiced repentance, self-denial, and cross-bearing; and was involved in vigorous social improvements.[93] His theology worked itself out in heartfelt, Christ-centered piety.[94]

For Calvin and the Calvinists of sixteenth-century Europe, doctrine and prayer, as well as faith and worship, were integrally connected. The Reformation included a reform of piety, or spirituality, as much as a reform of theology. The spirituality that had been cloistered behind monastery walls for centuries had broken down; medieval spirituality was reduced to a celibate, ascetic, and penitential devotion in the convent or monastery. Calvin helped Christians understand piety in terms of living and acting every day according to God's will (Rom. 12:1–2) in the midst of human society. Through his influence, Calvinistic spirituality focused on how one lived the Christian life in the family, the fields, the workshop, and the marketplace.[95]

Calvin helped Protestants change the entire focus of the Christian life. His piety, and that of his followers, served as a comprehensive pattern for the Reformation. May God enable us also to live pious lives to His glory. Only then will we be genuine sons and daughters of the Calvinistic Reformation.

DISCUSSION QUESTIONS

1. How did Calvin understand the term *piety*?

2. Piety has the glory of God for its ultimate goal. How does a person glorify God?

3. What is the soil out of which piety grows?

4. What is the relationship between piety and justification? Piety and sanctification?

5. What role does the church play in fostering piety?

6. How does the Lord's Supper help us grow in piety?

7. How did Calvin set an example of true Christian piety?

NOTES

[1] Inst., 3.7.1.

[2] Serene Jones, *Calvin and the Rhetoric of Piety* (Louisville: Westminster /John Knox, 1995).

[3] Quoted in John Hesselink, "The Development and Purpose of Calvin's Institutes," in *Articles on Calvin and Calvinism, Vol. 4: Influences upon Calvin and Discussion of the 1559 Institutes*, ed. Richard C. Gamble (New York: Garland, 1992), 215–216.

[4] See Brian A. Gerrish, "Theology within the Limits of Piety Alone: Schleiermacher and Calvin's Doctrine of God" (1981), reprinted in *The Old Protestantism and the New: Essays on the Reformation Heritage* (Chicago: University of Chicago Press, 1982), chap. 12.

[5] John Calvin, *Institutes of the Christian Religion*, ed. John T. McNeill, trans. Ford Lewis Battles (Philadelphia: Westminster Press, 1960), 9.

[6] Most of this chapter is abridged from Joel R. Beeke, "Calvin on Piety," in *The Cambridge Companion to John Calvin*, ed. Donald K. McKim (Cambridge: Cambridge University Press, 2004), 125–152.

[7] Cf. Lucien Joseph Richard, *The Spirituality of John Calvin* (Atlanta: John Knox Press, 1974), 100–101; Sou-Young Lee, "Calvin's Understanding of *Pietas*," in *Calvinus Sincerioris Religionis Vindex*, ed. W. H. Neuser and B. G. Armstrong (Kirksville, Mo.: Sixteenth Century Studies, 1997), 226–233; and H. W. Simpson, "*Pietas* in the *Institutes* of Calvin," in *Reformational Tradition: A Rich Heritage and Lasting Vocation* (Potchefstroom, South Africa: Potchefstroom University for Christian Higher Education, 1984), 179–191.

[8] Ed. and trans. Ford Lewis Battles (Pittsburgh: Pittsburgh Theological Seminary), 2.

[9] Inst., 1.2.1.

[10] Inst., 3.19.2.

[11] *Institutes of the Christian Religion: 1536 Edition*, trans. Ford Lewis Battles, rev. ed. (Grand Rapids: Eerdmans, 1986). The original Latin title reads: *Christianae religionis institutio total fere pietatis summam et quidquid est in doctrina salutis cognitu necessarium complectens, omnibut pietatis studiosis lectu dignissimum opus ac recens editum* (*Joannis Calvini opera selecta*, ed. Peter Barth, Wilhelm Niesel, and Dora Scheuner, 5 vols. [Munich: Chr. Kaiser, 1926–52], 1:19). From 1539 on, the titles were simply *Institutio Christianae Religionis*, but "zeal for piety" continued to be a great goal of Calvin's work. See Richard A. Muller, *The Unaccommodated Calvin: Studies in the Foundation of a Theological Tradition* (New York: Oxford University Press, 2000), 106–107.

[12] Inst., 3.2.1; *CO* 43:428, 47:316.

[13] *CO* 26:693.

[14] *CO* 24:362.

[15] *CO* 26:225, 29:5, 51:147.

[16] *CO* 49:51.

[17] *CO* 26:166, 33:186, 47:377–378, 49:245, 51:21.

[18] *CO* 6:9–10.

[19] *CO* 26:439–440.

[20] Howard G. Hageman, "Reformed Spirituality," in *Protestant Spiritual Traditions*, ed. Frank C. Senn (New York: Paulist Press, 1986), 61.

[21] Inst., 3.2.24.

[22] Dennis Tamburello points out that "at least seven instances occur in the *Institutes* where Calvin uses the word *arcanus* or *incomprehensibilis* to describe union with Christ" (2.12.7; 3.11.5; 4.17.1, 9, 31, 33; 4.19.35; *Union with Christ: John Calvin and the Mysticism of St. Bernard* [Louisville: Westminster /John Knox, 1994], 89, 144).

[23] *Commentary* on John 6:51.

[24] Inst., 2.16.16.

[25] Inst., 3.1.4.

[26] Inst. 4.17.6; *Commentary* on Acts 15:9.

[27] *Commentary* on Ephesians 5:32.

[28] Inst., 3.1.1, 4.17.12.

[29] Inst., 3.2.30–32.

[30] Inst., 3.2.24; *Commentary* on 1 John 2:12.

[31] John Calvin, *Sermons on the Epistle to the Ephesians*, trans. Arthur Golding (1577; reprint Edinburgh: Banner of Truth Trust, 1973), 1:17–18. Hereafter, *Sermon* on Ephesians text.

[32] *Commentary* on Ephesians 3:12.

[33] *Sermon* on Ephesians 3:14–19.

[34] *Commentary* on Habakkuk 2:4.

[35] Inst., 3.11.1.

[36] John Calvin, *Sermons on Galatians*, trans. Kathy Childress (Edinburgh: Banner of Truth Trust, 1997), 2:17–18. Hereafter, *Sermon* on Galatians text.

[37] Inst., 3.11.2.

[38] Inst., 3.11.3.

[39] Inst., 3.11.1, 3.15.7.

[40] Inst., 3.13.1.

[41] Inst., 1.7.5.

[42] *Commentary* on John 17:17–19.

[43] Inst., 3.11.6.

[44] *Sermon* on Galatians 2:17–18.

[45] *Commentary* on Romans 6:2.

[46] Inst., 4.1.1, 3–4; cf. Joel R. Beeke, "Glorious Things of Thee Are Spoken: The Doctrine of the Church," in *Onward, Christian Soldiers: Protestants Affirm the Church*, ed. Don Kistler (Morgan, Pa.: Soli Deo Gloria, 1999), 23–25.

[47] Inst., 4.1.4–5.

[48] *Commentary* on Psalm 20:9.

[49] *Commentary* on Romans 12:6.

[50] *Commentary* on 1 Corinthians 12:12.

[51] *Commentary* on 1 Corinthians 4:7.

[52] *Commentary* on Ephesians 4:12.

[53] Inst., 4.3.2. Cf. Inst., 4.1.5; *Commentary* on Ephesians 4:12; 1 Corinthians 13:12.

[54] John Calvin, *Sermons of M. John Calvin, on the Epistles of S. Paule to Timothie and Titus*, trans. L. T. (1579; reprint facsimile, Edinburgh: Banner of Truth Trust, 1983), 1 Timothy 1:8–11.

[55] John Calvin, *Calvin: Theological Treatises*, ed. J. K. S. Reid (Philadelphia: Westminster Press, 1954), 173. Cf. Brian Armstrong, "The Role of the Holy Spirit in Calvin's Teaching on the Ministry," *Calvin and the Holy Spirit*, ed. P. DeKlerk (Grand Rapids: Calvin Studies Society, 1989), 99–111.

[56] Inst., 4.14.1.

[57] Inst., 4.16.9; Ronald S. Wallace, *Calvin's Doctrine of the Word and Sacrament* (London: Oliver and Boyd, 1953), 175–183. Cf. H. O. Old, *The Shaping of the Reformed Baptismal Rite in the Sixteenth Century* (Grand Rapids: Eerdmans, 1992).

[58] Inst., 4.17.8–12.

[59] Inst., 4.17.24, 33.

[60] *Commentary* on 1 Corinthians 11:25.

[61] Inst., 4.18.13.

[62] "Calvin's Eucharistic Piety," in *The Legacy of John Calvin*, ed. David Foxgrover (Grand Rapids: CRC, 2000), 53.

[63] *CO* 31:19; translation taken from Barbara Pitkin, "Imitation of David: David as a Paradigm for Faith in Calvin's Exegesis of the Psalms," *Sixteenth Century Journal*, 24, no. 4 (1993): 847.

[64] *Commentary* on the Psalms, 1:xxxix. See James A. De Jong, "An Anatomy of All Parts of the Soul: Insights into Calvin's Spirituality from His Psalms Commentary," in *Calvinus Sacrae Scripturae Professor* (Grand Rapids: Eerdmans, 1994), 1–14.

[65] John Walchenbach, "The Influence of David and the Psalms on the Life and Thought of John Calvin" (Th.M. thesis, Pittsburgh Theological Seminary, 1969).

[66] More than 30,000 copies of the first complete, 500-page Genevan Psalter were printed by more than fifty different French and Swiss publishers in the first year, and at least 27,400 copies were published in Geneva in the first few months (Jeffrey T. VanderWilt, "John Calvin's Theology of Liturgical Song," *Christian Scholar's Review* 25 [1996]: 67. Cf. John Witvliet, "The Spirituality of the Psalter: Metrical Psalms in Liturgy and Life in Calvin's Geneva," in *Calvin Study Society Papers, 1995–1997*, ed. David Foxgrover [Grand Rapids: CRC, 1998], 93–117).

[67] Preface to the Genevan Psalter (1562). Charles Garside Jr., *The Origins of Calvin's Theology of Music: 1536–1543* (Philadelphia: The American Philosophical Society, 1979), 32–33.

[68] *CO* 10:12; cited in Garside, *The Origins of Calvin's Theology of Music*, 10.

[69] Witvliet, "The Spirituality of the Psalter," 117.

[70] W. Stanford Reid, "The Battle Hymns of the Lord: Calvinist Psalmody of the Sixteenth Century," in *Sixteenth Century Essays and Studies*, ed. C. S. Meyer (St. Louis: Foundation for Reformation Research, 1971), 2:47.

[71] T. Hartley Hall, "The Shape of Reformed Piety," in Robin Maas and Gabriel O'Donnell, *Spiritual Traditions for the Contemporary Church* (Nashville: Abingdon Press, 1990), 215. Cf. Reid, "The Battle Hymns of the Lord," 2:36–54.

[72] Inst., 3.6.2.

[73] *Commentary* on 1 Timothy 4:7–8.

[74] Chapters 6–10 of Book 3 were first translated into English in 1549 as *The Life and Conversation of a Christian Man* and have been reprinted often as *The Golden Booklet of the True Christian Life*.

[75] See R. D. Loggie, "Chief Exercise of Faith: An Exposition of Calvin's Doctrine of Prayer," *Hartford Quarterly*, 5 (1965): 65–81, and H. W. Maurer, "An Examination of Form and Content in John Calvin's Prayers" (Ph.D. dissertation, University of Edinburgh, 1960).

[76] Cf. Thomas A. Lambert, "Preaching, Praying, and Policing the Reform in Sixteenth Century Geneva" (Ph.D. dissertation, University of Wisconsin-Madison, 1998), 393–480.

[77] Charles Partee, "Prayer as the Practice of Predestination," in *Calvinus Servus Christi*, ed. Wilhelm H. Neuser (Budapest: Pressabteilung des Raday-Kollegiums, 1988), 246.

[78] Inst., 3.20.3.

[79] Inst., 3.20.4–16.

[80] Inst., 3.3.1–2, 6, 18, 20.

[81] Inst., 3.3.5, 9.

[82] Inst., 3.3.3; cf. Randall C. Gleason, *John Calvin and John Owen on Mortification: A Comparative Study in Reformed Spirituality* (New York: Peter Lang, 1995), 61.

[83] Richard C. Gamble, "Calvin and Sixteenth-Century Spirituality," in *Calvin Studies Society Papers*, 34–35.

[84] Inst., 3.8.1–2.

[85] Inst., 3.8.3–9.

[86] Inst., 3.9.4.

[87] Inst., 3.9.5.

[88] Ronald S. Wallace, *Calvin's Doctrine of the Christian Life* (London: Oliver & Boyd, 1959), 170–195.

[89] Inst., 3.9.3.

[90] Lionel Greve, "John Calvin, William Perkins and John Wesley: An Examination of the Origin and Nature of Pietism" (Ph.D. dissertation, Hartford Seminary Foundation, 1975), 20.

[91] John S. Leith, *John Calvin's Doctrine of the Christian Life* (Louisville: Westminster/John Knox Press, 1989), 82–86.

[92] See *Selected Works of Calvin*, ed. and trans. Henry Beveridge (Grand Rapids: Baker, 1983), 1:c. For more on piety in Calvin's life, see Ford Lewis Battles, *The Piety of John Calvin* (Grand Rapids: Baker, 1978), 16–20.

[93] Merwyn Johnson, "Calvin's Ethical Legacy," in *The Legacy of John Calvin*, 79–83.

[94] Cf. Erroll Hulse, "The Preacher and Piety," in *The Preacher and Preaching*, ed. Samuel T. Logan, Jr. (Phillipsburg, N.J.: P&R, 1986), 71.

[95] Hughes Oliphant Old, "What is Reformed Spirituality? Played Over Again Lightly," in *Calvin Studies VII*, ed. J. H. Leith (Davidson, N.C.: n.p., 1994), 61.

CHAPTER 14

SANCTIFICATION
IN PURITAN THOUGHT

There is no imagination wherewith man is besotted, more foolish, none so pernicious, as this—that persons not purified, not sanctified, not made holy in their life, should afterwards be taken into that state of blessedness which consists in the enjoyment of God. Neither can such persons enjoy God, nor would God be a reward to them. Holiness indeed is perfected in heaven: but the beginning of it is invariably confined to this world.[1]

—JOHN OWEN

alvinism has a reputation as an ivory tower school of thought, dealing in high and lofty doctrines that have no practical benefits for ordinary people in the church or society at large. Nothing could be further from the truth. In actuality, Calvinism has practical outworkings in nearly every sphere of life. Our challenge is to limit our discussion only to major areas of practical application.

As in so many areas of the Christian life, the Puritans stand out as models for all believers when it comes to sanctification. They did not minimize their depravity or the intensity of the war involved in walking the King's highway of holiness. Rather, they thought long and hard on the process of sanctification in the Christian life, identifying many spiritual disciplines believers can follow. In their thinking and doing in this area, we see Calvinism in its most practical form.

I will use this chapter to consider the Puritan view of sanctification, and in the next I will delve into some of the spiritual disciplines that are the means of

sanctification. With the Spirit's blessing, Christians who understand and implement this teaching can grow substantially in the faith.[2]

THE IDEA OF SANCTIFICATION

The singular aspect of the Puritan doctrine of sanctification is its full development
and balanced perspective. Owen Watkins says the Puritans took up the work of
the Continental Reformers on justification (what God had done for sinners at
Calvary) and completed it with detailed studies of sanctification (what God does
within the soul and body of the believer).[3]

Holiness, the noun, stems from the adjective *holy*; *sanctify*, the verb, means "to
make holy."[4] These terms have to do with being separated and set apart for God.
This is what has been done for the Christian—he has been separated from sin and
consecrated to God. The Puritans saw no disparity between the Old Testament
and New Testament concepts of holiness, though they saw that the testaments do
vary in their emphases on what holiness involves. The Old Testament especially
stresses ritual and moral holiness, while the New Testament stresses an inward,
transforming holiness (Lev. 10:10–11; 19:2; 1 Thess. 5:23; Heb. 10:10).[5]

The classic Puritan definition of sanctification is stated in the Westminster
Shorter Catechism. Question 35 asks, "What is sanctification?" The answer runs
thus: "Sanctification is the work of God's free grace, whereby we are renewed in
the whole man after the image of God, and are enabled more and more to die
unto sin, and live unto righteousness." This definition implies that the Puritans
saw the word *sanctification* as describing the entire process of being conformed to
Christ's image. This process begins with the new birth and continues throughout
the life of the saint until his days on earth end.

The answer to Question 36 explains in more detail why the Puritans considered the theme of sanctification so important. The question asks, "What are the
benefits which in this life do accompany or flow from justification, adoption, and
sanctification?" Here is the answer: "The benefits which in this life do accompany
or flow from justification, adoption, and sanctification, are, assurance of God's
love, peace of conscience, joy in the Holy Ghost, increase of grace, and perseverance therein to the end."

Taken together, Questions 35 and 36 reveal the Puritan passion to see young
believers grow in Christ into the assurance of God's love, peace of conscience, joy

in the Holy Spirit, and increasing grace. The Puritans viewed these benefits as fruits of sanctification. They also understood sanctification as the basic disposition of a true believer. From their perspective, believers who do not seek to advance in sanctification dishonor God and impoverish their spiritual lives. Believers must seek sanctification for the glory of God and the good of their souls.

The Puritan idea of sanctification includes the following emphases:

• *Sanctification is rooted in the essence of God.* Holiness is God's essence (Isa. 57:15); it is the heart of everything the Bible declares about Him. His justice is holy justice; His wisdom is holy wisdom; His power is holy power; His grace is holy grace. Among God's attributes, only His holiness is celebrated before the throne of heaven. In the prophet Isaiah's vision of the heavenly throne room, the seraphim cry, "Holy, holy, holy, is the LORD of hosts" (Isa. 6:3). Isaiah calls God "the Holy One" twenty-six times. Stephen Charnock notes that the word *holy* precedes God's name more than any other attribute (Ps. 99).[6]

God's holiness is "a transcendental attribute that, as it were, runs through the rest, and casts lustre upon them," John Howe writes. "It is an attribute of attributes . . . and so it is the very lustre and glory of His other perfections."[7] God reveals majestic holiness in His works (Ps. 145:17), in His law (Ps. 19:8–9), and especially at the cross of Christ (Matt. 27:46). Holiness is His permanent crown, His glory, His beauty. Holiness is "more than a mere attribute of God," says Jonathan Edwards. "It is the sum of all His attributes, the outshining of all that God is."[8]

God's holiness suggests two truths about Him. First, it shows the separateness of God from all His creation and from all that is evil. God's holiness testifies of His purity, His absolute moral perfection, His separateness from everything outside of Himself, and His complete freedom from sin (Job 34:10; Isa. 5:16; 40:18; Hab. 1:13).[9]

Second, since God is holy and set apart from all sin, He cannot be approached by sinners apart from a holy sacrifice (Lev. 17:11; Heb. 9:22). He cannot be the Holy One and remain indifferent to sin (Jer. 44:4); rather, He must punish it (Ex. 34:6–7). Since all men are sinners through the tragic fall of Adam and through daily transgressions, they cannot appease God by their efforts. We creatures, made after the image of our holy Creator, voluntarily chose through Adam to become unholy and unacceptable in the sight of our Creator. Blood must be shed if we are to be granted remission of sin (Heb. 9:22). Only the perfect, atoning obedience of the God-man, Christ Jesus, can fulfill the demands of God's holiness on behalf of sinners (1 Tim. 2:5). Thanks be to God that Christ agreed to accomplish atonement for us at the initiation of His Father and with His full approbation (Ps. 40:7–8; Mark 15:37–39). As 2 Corinthians 5:21 says, "For he hath made him to be sin for us, who knew no sin; that we might be made the righteousness of God in him." Likewise, the Dutch Reformed Lord's Supper Form states, "The wrath of God against sin is so great, that (rather than it should go unpunished) He hath punished the same in His beloved Son Jesus Christ with the bitter and shameful death of the cross."[10]

- *Sanctification involves both status and condition.* We are not called to holiness so as to merit acceptance with God. That can be done only through our Savior, Jesus Christ. This is clearly biblical teaching: "We are sanctified through the offering of the body of Jesus Christ once for all" (Heb. 10:10). Christ is our sanctification (1 Cor. 1:30); therefore, the church as the bride of Christ is sanctified (Eph. 5:25–26). As the Puritan Walter Marshall explains, the believer's *status* before God is one of sanctity in Christ on account of His perfect obedience, which has fully satisfied the justice of God for all sin.[11]

However, this status does not mean that the believer is in a wholly sanctified *condition* (1 Cor. 1:2). Several attempts have been made to express the relationship between the believer's status and his condition before God, the foremost being Luther's statement *simul justus et peccator* ("at once righteous and a sinner"). He was saying that the believer is righteous in God's sight because of Christ, yet remains a sinner according to his own nature.[12] However, from the onset of Christian experience (which coincides with regeneration), the believer's status affects his condition. So Paul prays that the Thessalonians may be wholly sanctified, meaning that sanctification has begun in the believing Thessalonians but still must be completed (1 Thess. 5:23).

In terms of the believer's condition (which is what the Puritans usually mean when they speak of holiness), sanctification is never complete in this life. It progresses toward that goal, but, as Romans 7 tells us, our moral and spiritual reach exceeds our moral and spiritual grasp. Many Christians today fail to understand this because their notion of what constitutes perfect righteousness is so dreadfully low.

In the context of sanctification, the Westminster Larger Catechism offers masterful teaching on the Ten Commandments. Having laid down the principles that sanctification involves motives as well as actions and that each prohibition in God's law includes a corresponding directive, the catechism offers far-reaching expositions of the principles of the Decalogue.[13] Like Calvin, the Puritans set the Ten Commandments within the framework of sanctification established by the two great commandments to love the Lord our God with all our hearts and to love our neighbors as ourselves (Matt. 22:37–39). Once we grasp this concept, they said, we begin to see how high Scripture's standard of holiness is and how urgently we need to take refuge in Christ's perfect obedience every day.

Thus, perfect righteousness means being motivated by and exercising perfect love to God and to my neighbor. It means I am motivated to love God, which I express in worship, adoration, and devotion to Him. It means that I am motivated to love my neighbor, which I express in helpfulness, sympathy, edifying advice and speech, and acts of kindness toward others. Righteousness motivates me to surrender myself to help and encourage others, however little I may feel connected to them. Calvinism has always honored God's law thus.

The law produces spiritual conflict because of the indwelling (though no longer dominant) sin still present in the believer. Indwelling sin, combined with worldly pressures to succumb to various temptations, cannot help but produce spiritual conflict. The believer has many enemies. The world, the flesh, and the Devil continually seek to prevent our advance in holiness and to subvert our practice of righteousness. They keep us from mortifying sin and work to undermine the reality of our repentance. In the Puritan vision, we must battle for holiness every step of the way, or we will not progress (Heb. 12:14).[14]

Yet, as Thomas Boston notes, the work of sanctification will progress in us because "of the continued application of the blood of Christ to the believer by the Spirit."[15] "Sanctification is progressive," says Thomas Watson. "If it does not grow it is because it does not live."[16] The believer "does not stay at a standstill, but grows from one degree and measure of grace to another, 'until he come to a perfect man, to the measure of the stature of the fullness of Christ' (Eph. 4:13)," adds Andrew Gray. "He is like the morning sun, 'that shineth more and more unto the perfect day.'"[17]

In the mind of the Puritans, then, it was essential for the believer to recognize his conflict with sin and seek to maintain habits of righteousness. Others will see that a believer is changing from one degree of glory to another (2 Cor. 3:18), though he usually cannot see it himself. What he knows most vividly is not growth but the battle that he must continually fight against temptation. So he cries out: "Lord, I am weak; help me to be strong and to do righteousness." That is practical, biblical, Calvinist truth, the Puritans said. It is what the believer experiences.

Reading the spiritual journals of Puritans such as Thomas Shepard[18] (in many ways, spiritual journal-keeping was a quintessentially Puritan endeavor), in which preachers repeatedly accuse themselves of grievous sin, makes it clear that they were all too aware of their failures to show perfect love toward God and men. Like them, we fall far short of conforming to the spirit of the Decalogue, both in what we do (sins of commission) and in what we fail to do (sins of omission). These writers were not saying that they acted as badly as they possibly could all the time; rather, like Paul, they were confessing: "I delight in the law of God after the inward man. I have before me a vision of what real holiness involves. I wish I could fulfill it, but day by day I fall short. So help me, God. I confess that I am a miserable sinner."

The true believer holds holiness before God in Christ, and yet he must also cultivate it in the strength of Christ (Eph. 1:4). Our status in holiness is conferred, whereas our condition in holiness must be pursued. Through Christ we are both made holy in our standing before God and called to reflect that standing by being holy in daily life (Phil. 3:12); we are called to be in life what we already are in principle by grace (Rom. 6:11–12). Our faithful Savior pledges that the work of God in us will continue until glory so that, though we are yet imperfect, the work of sanctification itself will prove to be invincible (Phil. 1:6, 11).

• *Sanctification is a divine work of renewal that is comprehensive and moral.* Sanctification makes us increasingly conform to the image of Jesus (2 Cor. 5:17). It springs from a renewal of the heart (the core of the person), which is true transformation. God changes the heart, and out of that change comes new character.

This change is comprehensive, meaning that it affects all of one's life at all times. The word the Puritans used to describe this process was *universal.*[19] They often quoted 1 Timothy 4:4–5, which tells us that *everything* is to be sanctified.[20] Holiness, then, affects our privacy with God, the confidentiality of our homes, the competitiveness of our work, the pleasures of social friendship, and our Lord's Day worship. No time is exempt from the call to holiness; it must be practiced every hour of every day. In short, the call to holiness is a whole-life commitment to live God-ward (2 Cor. 3:4) and to set all things apart to the lordship of Jesus Christ.

Holiness must be inward, filling our entire heart. It also must be outward, extending to all of life so that, as 1 Thessalonians 5:23 says, our "whole spirit and soul and body may be preserved blameless unto the coming of our Lord Jesus Christ." As Boston said, "Holiness is a constellation of graces."[21]

This change is also moral, meaning that it affects the spiritual quality of our living. Drawing on Galatians 5:22–23, the Puritans said that the attributes of love, joy, peace, longsuffering, gentleness, goodness, faithfulness, kindness, and temperance together make up the moral profile of a believer who dwells in Christ. The Gospels clearly show how all of these character qualities are expressed in Christ's perfect life.[22]

Puritan sermons often focused on sanctification. Without a doubt, the Puritans were evangelistic—in fact, they were the first to create extended evangelistic tracts.[23] But when the Puritans wrote those tracts, they did so to lead people out of sin into the Christian life, in which they were to practice holiness to the glory of God. Thus, the theme of sanctification was never out of sight. When the Puritans dealt with assurance, they stressed what Question 36 of the Shorter Catechism also stresses: you cannot hope that God's Holy Spirit will give you strong, joyful assurance unless you are laboring on a daily basis to live a holy life. "Holiness to the Lord" was the Puritan motto for everyone's life at every point, just as it was their motto for community life at every point. No group of divines focused on sanctification as much as the Puritans.

• *Sanctification must be expressed in repentance and righteousness.* Repentance and righteousness represent the twofold nature of turning from sin to obedience. Repentance is turning from sin, the Puritans said. It is a daily work of faith; it would not be a good work were it otherwise (Isa. 1:16–17). However, the Puritans were clear that repentance is far more profound than remorse. While true repentance may start with remorse, the latter, in itself, will not produce a changed life. And repentance is essentially just that: a changed life. True repentance is more than being sorry; it is an actual turning from sin.

THE PRIMARY AGENT OF SANCTIFICATION

The agent of sanctification is the triune, covenant God. The Puritans taught that the covenant faithfulness of the Father, Son, and Spirit motivates the believer to covenant faithfulness. So they presented the gospel as God's extension of His covenant to the sinner and they identified the church as God's covenant people. The Puritans explained sanctification as the Christian's proving and experiencing of God's covenant faithfulness. In short, they saw it as the Christian walking in covenant with his God.

The Puritans believed that God was a covenant God. They believed that the covenant was at the very heart of the Bible and that Scripture itself teaches us to integrate all of its teaching about God's mercy within this covenantal frame of reference. In undertaking to be the God of certain people, God required them to be His people in the world. Were they alive today, the Puritans would strongly oppose any teaching that radically separates the Old Testament order of things from the New Testament order of things; rather, they would stress the promise of God as the basis for godly living under both testaments. The Puritans loved to preach on passages such as Galatians 3 and Hebrews 11, in which all these things are clearly set forth. Sanctification must be viewed as covenant blessing from a covenant God who has laid hold of us and brought us to new birth in order to bring us to glory, they said.

The Puritans also stressed sanctification as the special work of the Holy Spirit as sanctifier. The Spirit acts alone in initial sanctification, which coincides with regeneration, but He continues to work in progressive sanctification, which involves the believer's activity. So the believer "acts not but as he is acted [upon] by the Holy Spirit."[24] And the Spirit perseveres in His work of sanctification and does a complete work in the end.[25] Reflecting on this truth, John Owen says that sanctification "is the immediate work of God by his Spirit upon our whole nature, proceeding from the peace made for us by Jesus Christ, whereby, being changed into his likeness, we are kept entirely in peace with God, and are preserved unblameable or in a state of gracious acceptation with him, according to the terms of the covenant, unto the end."[26] Through His sanctifying work, the Holy Spirit produces Christlikeness in His people, who are new creatures in Christ, risen with Him out of spiritual death. In them, the Christ-nature—that is, the sum total of all that His human life is—finds new expression.

In explaining the sanctifying change that the Spirit works in believers, the Puritans stressed the importance of *habit*. This concept had been basic in explaining spiritual life at least since Thomas Aquinas (1225–1274), whose understanding of habit was not much different from ours, though we probably would opt for the word *orientation* today. Likewise, the Puritans viewed habit as a behavioral pattern. So love, peace, and other fruits of the Spirit are habits of acting and reacting to circumstances. The believer keeps rejoicing, whatever may be going on; he keeps loving, whatever may be happening; he remains at peace in himself before the Lord, whatever may be transpiring. He does not allow his conduct to be determined by what goes on around him; rather, he lives out the disposition of Jesus Christ in every circumstance, whatever that circumstance may be. He strives for what Boston calls "habitual holiness, that is, a habitual aversion of the soul to evil, and inclination to good."[27]

THE OBJECT OF SANCTIFICATION

The object of sanctification is the believer. The Puritans viewed the believer from three perspectives.

• *The believer as a human individual.* From the Puritan perspective, the human individual is best thought of in terms of three capacities: the capacity to think, the capacity to make decisions, and the capacity to feel. Thus, the Puritans talked about three faculties: the faculty of reason, the faculty of will, and the faculty of affection (or emotion). They said that in evangelizing or discipling others, it is wise to focus first on what the mind must grasp; second, on what the will must decide; and third, on the affections, or the fruits and marks of grace (such as Galatians 5:22–23 and the Beatitudes in Matthew 5). One would thus show how the qualities of love, joy, hope, and desire provide energy for the continued acts of the will that form the path of godly behavior. A wise preacher, the Puritans maintained, applies Scripture to instruct the mind, direct the will, and draw out the affections.

• *The believer as fallen and disordered.* Before grace comes, a person is fallen and disordered. He does not live rationally, for he does not live according to the truth that the mind is supposed to grasp. He does not live sensibly, because his will is led by irrational feelings rather than by known truth. His moral nature has been twisted; he is essentially egocentric.

Even after he is regenerated, the believer remains fallen and disordered due to ongoing battles with his old nature and with sin (Rom. 7:14–25). Boston summarizes this well, saying: "Although the whole man is sanctified, yet no part of the man is perfectly sanctified in this life. It is neither midnight to them as with the unregenerate, nor mid-day as with the glorified, but twilight, which is a mixture of darkness and light. Hence arises the combat betwixt the flesh and Spirit (Gal. 5:17). Every grace has a weed of the contrary corruption by the side of it, which occasions this struggle, and imperfection in the best of their works."[28]

The intent of gospel teaching is thus to restore us to God-centeredness and to help us in our battles with sin, the Puritans argued. That is the framework for teaching the gospel as it applies to the Christian life.

• *The believer as redeemed and justified.* Those who are being sanctified are those who have been redeemed by Christ's blood and justified by faith. Those whom the Spirit justifies, He sanctifies. As Robert Traill writes, "Never a man is justified but he is also sanctified; and never a man is sanctified but he is also justified; all the elect of God, all the redeemed, have both these blessings passing upon them."[29]

Because the believer is redeemed by Christ and justified in Him by grace, the Puritans could appeal to believers to resort to the same grace of God for sanctification. Since "justification is an act of God as a gracious judge," Traill wrote, believers may be comforted that "sanctification is a work of God as a merciful physician."[30]

May all praise be given to God, who as gracious Judge is ever willing to be the merciful Physician.

DISCUSSION QUESTIONS

1. What does the term *sanctification* mean?

2. How did the Puritans believe that sanctification happened?

3. Who is the primary agent of sanctification? Who is the object?

NOTES

1 Quoted in I. D. E. Thomas, *The Golden Treasury of Puritan Quotations* (Chicago: Moody Press, 1975), 141.

2 Parts of chapters 14 and 15 on sanctification have been adapted from Joel R. Beeke, *Holiness: God's Call to Sanctification* (Edinburgh: Banner of Truth Trust, 1994); "Cultivating Holiness," *Reformation & Revival*, 4, no. 2 (Spring 1995): 81–112; and "The Utter Necessity of a Godly Life," *2000–2001 Yearbook: Church and School Directory, Heritage Netherlands Reformed Congregations* (Grand Rapids: Reformation Heritage Books, 2000), 93–115. I am also indebted to a lecture by J. I. Packer I heard in the 1980s.

3 Owen Watkins, *The Puritan Experience* (London: Routledge and Kegan Paul, 1972), 5–16.

4 This relationship is apparent in the Dutch word for sanctification, *heiligmaking* (literally, "holy-making").

5 Cf. Lawrence O. Richards, *Expository Dictionary of Bible Words* (Grand Rapids: Zondervan, 1985), 339–340.

6 Stephen Charnock, *The Existence and Attributes of God* (Evansville, Ind.: Sovereign Grace, 1958), 449.

7 John Howe, *The Works of the Rev. John Howe* (Ligonier, Pa.: Soli Deo Gloria, 1990), 2:59.

8 Jonathan Edwards, *The Works of Jonathan Edwards* (Edinburgh: Banner of Truth Trust, 1974), 1:101; cf. R. C. Sproul, *The Holiness of God* (Wheaton, Ill.: Tyndale House, 1985).

9 R. A. Finlayson, *The Holiness of God* (Glasgow: Pickering and Inglis, 1955), 4.

10 *The Psalter* (Grand Rapids: Eerdmans, 1991), 136.

11 Walter Marshall, *The Gospel Mystery of Sanctification* (Grand Rapids: Reformation Heritage Books, 1999), 40ff., 228ff. In the twentieth century, John Murray developed this idea under the nomenclature of "definitive sanctification" (John Murray, *Collected Writings of John Murray* [Edinburgh: Banner of Truth Trust, 1977], 2:277–284).

12 Cf. Heidelberg Catechism, Question 1 (the believer's status) and Question 114 (the believer's condition).

13 The best study on the Puritan view of the law is Ernest Kevan, *The Grace of Law: A Study in Puritan Theology* (Morgan, Pa.: Soli Deo Gloria, 1993).

14 Thomas Boston, *The Complete Works of Thomas Boston* (Stoke-on-Trent, U.K.: Tentmaker Publications, 2002), 6:585–586.

15 Ibid., 6:591.

16 Quoted in John Blanchard, *The Complete Gathered Gold* (Darlington, England: Evangelical Press, 2006), 303; cf. John Owen, *The Works of John Owen* (Edinburgh: Banner of Truth Trust, 1965), 3:386–405.

17 Andrew Gray, *A Door Opening into Everlasting Life* (Sioux Center, Iowa: Netherlands Reformed Book and Publishing, 1989), 88.

18 Thomas Shepard, *God's Plot: Spirituality in Thomas Shepard's Cambridge*, ed. Michael McGiffert (Amherst, Mass.: University of Massachusetts Press, 1994).

19 For example, see Thomas Manton, *The Complete Works of Thomas Manton*, ed. T. Smith (1870; repr., Worthington, Pa.: Maranatha, 1980), 17:449, and Boston, *Complete Works*, 6:559.

20 Thomas Goodwin, *The Works of Thomas Goodwin* (Grand Rapids: Reformation Heritage Books, 2006), 3:389.

21 Quoted in John Blanchard, *Gathered Gold* (Welwyn, England: Evangelical Press, 1984), 144.

22 Gray, *A Door Opening into Everlasting Life*, 53–75.

23 The first extended evangelistic tract was Richard Baxter's *A Call to the Unconverted* (Grand Rapids: Zondervan, 1970). Later in Baxter's lifetime, Joseph Alleine lifted numerous points from Baxter and reproduced them as his own in his evangelistic work *Alarm to the Unconverted* (Edinburgh: Banner of

Truth Trust, 1995).

[24] Boston, *Complete Works*, 1:655–656, 659.

[25] See Robert Traill, *Works of Robert Traill* (Edinburgh: Banner of Truth Trust, 1975), 3:78–100.

[26] Owen, *Works of John Owen*, 3:369.

[27] Boston, *Complete Works*, 1:659.

[28] Ibid., 1:658.

[29] Traill, *Works of Robert Traill*, 3:72.

[30] Ibid., 3:73.

CHAPTER 15

SANCTIFICATION
IN PURITAN PRACTICE

It is no small advantage to the holy life to "begin the day with God." The saints are wont to leave their hearts with Him over night, that they may find them with Him in the morning. Before earthly things break in upon us, and we receive impressions from abroad, it is good to season the heart with thoughts of God, and to consecrate the early and virgin operations of the mind before they are prostituted to baser objects. When the world gets the start of religion in the morning, it can hardly overtake it all the day.[1]

—THOMAS CASE

*H*aving delved into Puritan thinking on sanctification, it is important for us to consider how they put their comprehensive views on sanctification into practice. The short answer is that they did it through diligent use of the means of grace. They believed that the Christian who is undergoing sanctification must strive to be more like God by cleansing himself from all filthiness of the flesh and spirit so as to come to mature holiness in the fear of God (2 Cor. 7:1). That meant several things for the Puritans in their day-to-day lives.

PURSUING TRINITARIAN GODLIKENESS

The first element of sanctification is the pursuit of trinitarian godlikeness. Specifically, that involves:

• *Imitating the character of the Father.* In his first letter, the apostle Peter quotes God's command recorded in Leviticus 11:44: "Be ye holy; for I am holy"

(1 Peter 1:16). God's holiness ought to be our primary reason for cultivating holy living. We must seek to be like our heavenly Father in righteousness and integrity; in the Spirit, we must strive to think God's thoughts after Him by means of His Word, to be of one mind with Him, and to live and act as He would have us do.[2] Stephen Charnock writes, "We do not so glorify God by elevated admirations, or eloquent expressions, or pompous services for him, as when we aspire to a conversing with him with unstained spirits, and live to him in living like him."[3]

• *Conforming to the image of Christ.* This is a favorite theme of the apostle Paul, who writes, "Let this mind be in you, which was also in Christ Jesus: who . . . made himself of no reputation, and took upon him the form of a servant . . . and . . . humbled himself, and became obedient unto death, even the death of the cross" (Phil. 2:5–8). Christ was the essence of humility; He was willing to give up all of His rights in order to obey God and serve sinners. If you would be holy, Paul says, be like Christ in His humility. Do not aim to be Christlike as a condition of salvation, but as a fruit of salvation received by faith.

You must look to Christ for growth in this area, for He is the fount and path of holiness. The Puritans recommended following the advice of Augustine, who said it is better to limp on the path than to run outside of it.[4] John Calvin taught that you should set Christ before you as the mirror of sanctification and seek grace to mirror Him.[5] Ask in each situation you encounter, "What would Christ think, say, or do?" Then trust Him for holiness. He will not disappoint you (James 1:2–7).

You have unlimited room for growth in holiness because Jesus is the bottomless well of salvation. You cannot go to Him too much for holiness, for He is holiness par excellence. He lived holiness; He merited holiness; He sends His Spirit not only to bring sinners to Himself but also to make them holy like Himself. As Colossians 3:11b says, "Christ is all, and in all." Likewise, Martin Luther states, "We in Christ equals justification; Christ in us equals sanctification."[6]

• *Submitting to the mind of the Holy Spirit.* In Romans 8:5–6, Paul divides people into two categories: those who are controlled by their sinful natures (i.e., the carnally minded who follow fleshly desires) and those who follow after the Spirit (i.e., those who *mind* "the things of the Spirit"). The Holy Spirit is sent to us to bring our minds into submission to His mind (1 Cor. 2). He makes us holy, and the holier we become, the more we are willing to bow as servants under His control. We must beg for grace to be willing servants more fully and consistently.

How does the Spirit work this holy grace of submission to His mind, thereby making us holy? According to the Puritans:

1. He shows us our need for holiness through conviction of sin, righteousness, and judgment (John 16:8).

2. He implants the desire for holiness in us. His saving work never leads to despair but always to sanctification in Christ.

3. He grants Christlikeness in holiness. He works on our whole nature, molding us after Christ's image.

4. He provides strength for us to live holy lives by indwelling and influencing our souls. If we live by the Spirit, we will not gratify the desires of our sinful natures (Gal. 5:16); rather, we will live in obedience to and dependence on Him.

5. Through humble feeding on Scripture and the exercise of prayer, He teaches us His mind and establishes an ongoing realization that holiness is essential to being worthy of God and His kingdom (1 Thess. 2:12; Eph. 4:1) and for fitness in His service (1 Cor. 9:24–25; Phil. 3:13).

EXERCISING MORTIFICATION

The second element of sanctification is mortification, which involves putting to death every form of sin. The Puritans used the word *mortification* to describe the discipline of watching and praying against sinful habits in such a way that, whenever a bad impulse arises, you immediately recognize what is happening and ask the Lord for strength to refuse it. You ask Him to drain the life of that impulse in you. John Owen pictures this process of appealing to the Spirit as what the woman with the bleeding disorder did in touching the hem of Jesus' garment (Luke 8:43–48). She knew that if she could just touch Christ, she would be healed. Likewise, Owen says, we must stretch out the hand of faith and touch the Lord, from whom we gain strength to say no to sin and thereby take a step toward breaking a bad habit.[7]

Thomas Boston compares the believer to a man whose natural passions are being put to death. "His lusts are upon the cross, nailed through and pierced to the heart, not to come down till they have breathed out their last (Gal. 5:24)," he says. "Like a dying man taking leave of friends, he is parting with his old lusts."[8]

ASPIRING TO DO GOD'S WILL

The third element of sanctification, often called *vivification*, is being quickened from the heart to do the will of God. It involves seeking God's strength to exercise good habits in obedience to the Decalogue, the Sermon on the Mount, and the ethical sections of the Epistles. Vivification makes us more responsive to God; it is as if we become more spiritually alive. Responsiveness to God is the essence of spiritual life, just as unresponsiveness to Him is the essence of spiritual death.

Boston pictures vivification as a man raised from the dead. He writes, "So the sanctified sinner lives as one of another world, not conforming himself to the sinful courses of this world, but being transformed into the likeness to those of the better world."[9]

USING THE MEANS OF GRACE

The fourth element of sanctification is using the means of grace that God provides. The best way to do that, according to John Flavel, is to pursue "a diligent and constant use and improvement of all holy means and duties, to preserve the soul from sin, and maintain its sweet and free communion with God."[10] Likewise, Jeremy Taylor advises, "If thou meanest to enlarge thy religion do it rather by enlarging thy ordinary devotions than thy extraordinary."[11]

The Puritans suggested a variety of spiritual disciplines to help cultivate Christlikeness and holiness. We can classify these divisions into four groups—private, family, corporate, and neighborly disciplines. Since family worship is covered in chapter 24, I will discuss only the other three kinds of disciplines here. Some disciplines, such as Bible study, could be listed in two or more groups, but for brevity's sake, each discipline will be discussed only once in this chapter. Each of the disciplines is biblical and can be used uniquely by the Holy Spirit to advance holiness in believers.

• *Private disciplines.* The private disciplines focus on the Bible and prayer. First, we should read and search the Scriptures. Absorbing God's Word is the primary road to holiness and to spiritual growth, for the Spirit blesses the reading and searching of God's Word. Jesus prayed, "Sanctify them through thy truth: thy word is truth" (John 17:17). Peter advised, "Desire the sincere milk of the word, that ye may grow thereby" (1 Peter 2:2).

Richard Greenham asserts that we should read our Bibles with more diligence than men dig for treasure. He says diligence makes rough places plain, the difficult easy, and the unsavory tasty.[12]

If you would grow in sanctification, read through the Bible diligently at least once a year. Also, take time to study the Word. Absorb it into your soul by comparing Scripture with Scripture (John 5:39). Proverbs 2:1–5 offers principles of serious personal Bible study: teachability (receiving God's words), obedience (storing God's commandments), discipline (applying the heart), dependence (crying for knowledge), and perseverance (searching for hidden treasure).[13]

Don't forget to sing the Scriptures, too. Psalm-singing has been a great boon for private devotions for believers who have engaged in it.[14]

Do not expect to grow in holiness if you spend little time alone with God and do not take His Word seriously. When you are tempted to pursuits off the road of holiness, let Scripture teach you how to live a holy life in an unholy world. Follow the advice of Henry Smith: "We should set the Word of God always before us like a rule, and believe nothing but that which it teacheth, love nothing but that which it prescribeth, hate nothing but that which it forbiddeth, do nothing but that which it commandeth."[15] If we do these things, we will concur with Flavel, who attested that "the Scriptures teach us the best way of living, the noblest way of suffering, and the most comfortable way of dying."[16]

Second, we should meditate on the Bible. After reading Scripture, we must meditate on it (Ps. 1:2). Reading offers knowledge, but meditation and study add depth to that knowledge. The difference between reading and meditation is like the difference between drifting in a boat and rowing toward a destination.

The Puritans spoke often of meditating on God's Word. Thomas Hooker defines the art of meditation as "a serious intention of the mind, whereby we come to search out the truth and settle it effectually upon the heart."[17] He and other Puritans suggest the following ways to meditate on Scripture:

1. Pray for the power to harness your mind—to focus by faith on the task of meditation.

2. Read the Scriptures, then select a verse or two or a doctrine upon which to meditate.[18]

3. Memorize verse(s) to stimulate meditation, to strengthen faith, to help you witness and counsel others, and to serve as a means of divine guidance.

4. Meditate on what you know about your verse(s) or subject, probing the book of Scripture, the book of conscience, and the book of nature.[19] As you meditate, think of applications to your own life. "Take every word as spoken to yourselves," Thomas Watson writes.[20]

5. Stir up affections, such as love, desire, hope, zeal, and joy, to glorify God.[21]

6. Arouse your mind to some duty and holy resolution.[22]

7. Conclude with prayer, thanksgiving, and psalm-singing.[23]

Third, we should pray and work (*ora et labora*). Prayer and work belong together. They are like two oars that, when used together, keep a rowboat moving forward. If you use only one oar—praying without working or working without praying—you will row in circles.

Holiness takes well-planned, hard, and sweating prayer and work, the Puritans said. Careful planning as to how you are going to live for the Lord is necessary if you want to achieve much of abiding value for Him. Yet the Puritans were not self-reliant. They understood that daily living for a Christian must go something like this:

1. Look ahead and see what you have to do.

2. Go to the Lord in prayer and say, "Lord, I do not have what it takes to do this; I need divine help."

3. Rely on the Lord to answer the prayer you have offered, then proceed expectantly to the task that lies before you.

4. After completing the task, return to the Lord to thank Him for the help He gave.

5. Ask His forgiveness for all your failures and sins in the process, and ask for grace to fulfill your task more faithfully the next time.

The Puritan method of daily sanctification includes earnest prayer and hard work without self-reliance; all the exertion of energy is done in faith. By grace, sanctification is both faithful effort and fruitful effort.

Holiness and prayer are closely related because prayer is the primary means of maintaining communion with God. Michael Haykin has addressed the role of prayer in Calvinistic spirituality (see chapter 12), but it is worth noting here that the Puritans were prone to give five methods for fighting our natural tendency to lapse into half-hearted prayer:

1. Give priority to prayer. Prayer is the first and most important thing you are called to do. "You can do more than pray after you have prayed, but you cannot do more than pray until you have prayed," John Bunyan writes. "Pray often, for prayer is a shield to the soul, a sacrifice to God, and a scourge to Satan."[24]

2. Give yourself—not just your time—to prayer. Remember that prayer is not an appendix to your life and your work, it is your life—your real, spiritual life—and your work. Prayer is the thermometer of your soul.

3. Give room to prayer. The Puritans did this in three ways. First, they had real prayer closets—rooms or small spaces where they habitually met with God. When one of Thomas Shepard's parishioners showed him a floor plan of the new house he hoped to build, Shepard noticed that there was no prayer room and lamented that homes without prayer rooms would be the downfall of the church and society. Second, block out stated times for prayer in your daily life. The Puritans did this every morning and evening. Third, between those stated times of prayer, commit yourself to pray in response to the least impulse to do so. That will help you develop the "habit" of praying, so that you will pray your way through the day without ceasing. Remember that conversing with God through Christ is our most effective way of bringing glory to God and of having a ready antidote to ward off all kinds of spiritual diseases.

4. Give the Word to prayer. The way to pray, said the Puritans, is to bring God His own Word. That can be done in two ways. First, pray *with* Scripture. God is tender of His own handwriting. Take His promises and turn them inside out, and send them back up to God, by prayer, pleading with Him to do as He has said. Second, pray *through* Scripture. Pray over each thought in a specific Scripture verse.

5. Give theocentricity to prayer. Pour out your heart to your heavenly Father. Plead on the basis of Christ's intercessions. Plead to God with the groanings of the Holy Spirit (Rom. 8:26). Recognize that true prayer is a gift of the Father, who gives it through the Son and works it within you by the Spirit, who, in turn, enables it to ascend back to the Son, who sanctifies it and presents it acceptable to the Father. Prayer is thus a theocentric chain, if you will—moving from the Father through the Son by the Spirit back to the Son and the Father.

Holiness and work are closely related because of the need to persevere in personal discipline, and discipline takes time and effort. As Paul advises Timothy, "Exercise thyself rather unto godliness" (1 Tim. 4:7). Holiness is not achieved sloppily or instantaneously;[25] it calls for continual commitment, diligence, practice, and repentance.[26] "If we sometimes through weakness fall into sin, we must not despair of God's mercy, or continue in sin, since . . . we have an eternal covenant of grace with God."[27] You and I must resolve, as did Jonathan Edwards, "never to give over, nor in the least to slacken, my fight with my corruptions, however unsuccessful I may be."[28]

How critical it is that we live each day in total commitment to God, forming habits of holiness, rooting out every inconsistency, and refusing to fall prey to the one-more-time syndrome. Remember, postponed obedience is disobedience. Tomorrow's holiness is impurity *now*. Tomorrow's faith is unbelief *now*. Aim not to sin at all (1 John 2:1) and ask for divine strength to bring every thought into captivity to Christ (2 Cor. 10:5), for Scripture indicates that our thought lives ultimately determine our character: "For as he thinketh in his heart, so is he" (Prov. 23:7).

Fourth, we should keep a journal. Journaling or diary-keeping is an optional means of grace that has greatly benefited many believers in cultivating holiness. Journaling can help us express thoughts to God and to ourselves that otherwise remain buried. It can assist us in meditating and praying, in remembering the Lord's works and faithfulness, in understanding and evaluating ourselves, in monitoring our goals and priorities, and in maintaining other spiritual disciplines.[29]

• *Corporate disciplines.* The corporate disciplines revolve around the worship and life of the church.

First, we should make diligent use of the preached Word. Cultivate the habit of listening seriously and fervently to the sermons of your pastor on the Lord's Day. And listen throughout the week to sermons of other good preachers who encourage you to grow in sanctification.

The Puritans relished good sermons. They attended church faithfully, took careful notes, and often talked and prayed their way through the sermon afterward with their children. These practices were the fruit of Puritan pastors teaching their people how to listen to sermons. Here is a digest of Watson's advice:

1. Prepare to hear the Word by bathing your soul in prayer.
2. Come to the Word with a holy appetite and a tender, teachable heart.

3. Be attentive to the preached Word.

4. Receive with meekness the engrafted Word (James 1:21).

5. Mingle the preached Word with faith.

6. Strive to retain what has been preached and pray about the Word proclaimed.

7. Put the Word into practice; be doers of it.

8. Beg the Spirit to accompany the Word with effectual blessing.

9. Familiarize yourself with the Word by sharing it with others.[30]

Point No. 7 is key. Merely listening to and not practicing the Word will contribute to our condemnation. Watson solemnly warns that "the word will be effectual one way or the other; if it does not make your hearts better, it will make your chains heavier. . . . Dreadful is their case who go loaded with sermons to hell."[31]

Puritan ministers frequently published their sermons in books. More than 90 percent of the seven hundred Puritan books reprinted since the beginning of the resurgence of Puritan literature in the late 1950s consist of revised sermons.[32] According to Alan F. Herr: "The printing of sermons constituted a rather large business in Elizabethan England. It has been estimated that more than forty per cent of all publications issued at that time were religious or philosophical in nature and it is evident that sermons account for a large part of those religious publications."[33] In the last three decades of the sixteenth century alone, more than three hundred volumes of Puritan sermons were published in England.[34]

Second, we should make diligent use of the sacraments. God's sacraments enrich His Word by pointing us away from ourselves. Each sign—the water, the bread, and the wine—directs us to Christ and His sacrifice on the cross. The sacraments are visible means through which Christ invisibly communes with us and we with Him. They spur us to Christlikeness and therefore to holiness.

Grace received through the sacraments is similar to that received through the Word. Both convey Christ. But Robert Bruce writes, "While we do not get a better Christ in the sacraments than we do in the Word, there are times when we get Christ better."[35]

Flee often to Christ in the sacraments. Faith in Him is a powerful motivator for holiness, since faith and the love of sin do not mix. Be careful, however, not to seek holiness in your experiences of Christ, but rather in Christ Himself. William Gurnall admonishes: "When thou trustest in Christ *within* thee, instead of Christ *without* thee, thou settest Christ against Christ. The bride does well to esteem her husband's picture, but it were ridiculous if she should love it better than himself, much more if she should go to it *rather than to him to supply her wants.* Yet thou actest thus when thou art more fond of Christ's image in thy soul than of him who painted it there."[36]

Third, we should seek fellowship in the church. Spend time with mentors in holiness (Eph. 4:12–13; 1 Cor. 11:1).[37] The church ought to be a fellowship of mutual caring and a community of prayer (1 Cor. 12:7; Acts 2:42). Talk to and pray with fellow believers whose godly walk you admire (Col. 3:16). Heed Proverbs 13:20, which says, "He that walketh with wise men shall be wise." Watson said that association promotes assimilation. A Christian life lived in isolation from other believers will be defective and spiritually immature. We cannot have a *heavenly* fellowship if we promote a *hindering* fellowship.

Such conversation should include the corporate and private reading of godly treatises of believers of times past, for these, too, can promote holiness. Luther said some of his best friends were dead men. Read classics that speak out against sin, exalt the grandeur of Christ, and promote holiness. Let Watson be your mentor in *The Mischief of Sin*, Owen in *Temptation and Sin*, Jeremiah Burroughs in *The Evil of Evils*, and Ralph Venning in *The Plague of Plagues*.[38] But also read J. C. Ryle's *Holiness*, Octavius Winslow's *Personal Declension and Revival of Religion in the Soul*, and Flavel's *Keeping the Heart*.[39] Let these writers of old become your spiritual mentors and friends.

Fourth, we should sanctify the Lord's Day. Sabbath observance can greatly improve personal spirituality. We ought to view this day as a joyful privilege, not a tedious burden, in which our private worship of God, our use of spiritual disciplines, our visiting of the widows and the poor, and other godly practices can be sustained without interruption. As J. I. Packer says, "We are to rest from the business of our earthly calling in order to prosecute the business of our heavenly calling."[40]

• *Neighborly disciplines.* The neighborly disciplines govern our lives in relation to the world outside the church.

First, we should evangelize and serve others. Christ expects us to witness to others and to serve them (Matt. 28:19–20; Heb. 9:14). We are motivated to do this by a sense of duty to obey (Deut. 13:4), gratitude (1 Sam. 12:24), gladness (Ps. 100:2), humility (John 13:15–16), and love (Gal. 5:13). Serving others is often hard work, but we are called to use every spiritual gift that God has granted us (cf. Rom. 12:4–8; 1 Cor. 12:6–11; Eph. 4:7–13).[41] This kind of service is actually one of our greatest rewards in life. To see people drawn closer to Christ through the Spirit's blessing on God's Word and the use of our gifts is a profoundly humbling experience. It draws us closer to God. Thus, evangelism and service can be important means of grace and spiritual disciplines for our own profit.

Second, we should flee worldliness. Our neighbors and work associates are watching how we Christians live. For their sake and for our own, we must strike out against the pride of life, the lusts of the flesh and eye, and all forms of sinful worldliness the minute they knock on the doors of our hearts and minds. If we allow these temptations to roam about in our minds and gain a foothold in our lives, we are already their prey. We must follow Daniel's example: "Daniel purposed *in his heart* that he would not defile himself with the portion of the king's meat, nor with the wine which he drank: *therefore* he requested of the prince of the eunuchs that he might not defile himself" (Dan. 1:8; emphasis added).

The books we read, the recreation and entertainment we engage in, the music we listen to, the friendships we form, and the conversations we have all affect our minds. Everything we do should be judged against the standard of Philippians 4:8: whatever is true, honest, just, pure, lovely, and of good report should be uppermost in our thoughts. We must live *above* the world and not be *of* the world while yet *in* the world (Rom. 12:1–2). If we stand *on* the Word, we will not stand *with* the world.

Third, we should exercise stewardship of time and money. Time is short and must be used wisely for the good of others, for the days are evil (Eph. 5:15–16). Even as you should take time to reach out to other people in Christian ways, you should take time to prepare yourself and your family for a useful and fruitful life, and, above all, for eternity.

The disciplined use of money for the good of others is rooted in the principle that God owns everything (1 Cor. 10:26). Giving reflects faith in God's provision and is an act of worship (Mark 12:41–44; Phil. 4:18). It should be sacrificial, generous, and motivated by love, thankfulness, and cheerfulness (2 Cor. 8:1–5; 9:7). Giving reaps bountiful blessing (Luke 6:38), for the godly man experiences that "it is more blessed to give than to receive" (Acts 20:35).

Fourth, we should develop a scriptural formula for holy living before God and man. When hesitating over a course of action, ask yourself the following questions, based on 1 Corinthians:

1. Does this glorify God? (1 Cor. 10:31)
2. Is this consistent with the lordship of Christ? (1 Cor. 7:23)
3. Is this consistent with biblical examples? (1 Cor. 11:1)
4. Is this lawful and beneficial for me—spiritually, mentally, and physically? (1 Cor. 6:9–12)
5. Does this help others positively and not hurt others unnecessarily? (1 Cor. 10:33; 8:13)
6. Does this bring me under any enslaving power? (1 Cor. 6:12)

KEEPING FOCUSED ON THE BENEFITS OF SANCTIFICATION

Though pursuing holiness is hard work, the Puritans taught that God provides us with several motives to be holy. To encourage us in the pursuit of holiness, they say we should focus on the following biblical truths:

• *God has called us to holiness for our good and His glory.* "For God hath not called us unto uncleanness, but unto holiness," 1 Thessalonians 4:7 says. Whatever God calls us to do is necessary. His call, as well as the benefits we experience from holy living, should persuade us to seek and practice holiness.

Holiness fortifies our spiritual well-being, for God assures us that "no good thing will he withhold from them that walk uprightly" (Ps. 84:11b). Flavel says, "What health is to the heart, that holiness is to the soul."[42] Thomas Goodwin quips that "a sanctified heart is better than a silver tongue."[43] In Richard Baxter's work on holiness, the very chapter titles are enlightening: "Holiness is the only way of safety"; "Holiness is the only honest way"; "Holiness is the most gainful way"; "Holiness is the most honourable way"; and "Holiness is the most pleasant way."[44]

But most important, holiness glorifies the God we love (Isa. 43:21). "Holiness makes most for God's honour,"[45] Thomas Brooks says. Flavel observes that "so in love is Christ with holiness that He will buy it with His blood for us."[46] The Puritan Peter Vinke devoted a full sermon to the question, "How is Gospel-Grace the Best Motive to Holiness?"[47]

• *Holiness makes us resemble God and preserves our integrity.* Watson writes: "We must endeavour to be like God in sanctity. It is a clear glass in which we can see a face; it is a holy heart in which something of God can be seen."[48] Christ is a pattern of holiness for us in His holy humility (Phil. 2:5–13), holy compassion (Mark 1:41), holy forgiveness (Col. 3:13), holy unselfishness (Rom. 15:3), holy indignation against sin (Matt. 23), and holy prayer (Heb. 5:7). Holiness that resembles God and is patterned after Christ saves us from hypocrisy and resorting to a "Sunday only" Christianity. It gives vitality, purpose, meaning, direction, and contentment to daily living. "The holy person is the only contented man in the world," Gurnall writes.[49]

Flavel says the standard of our conduct largely depends on the condition of our hearts. If we sanctify the inner life, we will grow in integrity and in all the graces of God, a condition that will provide more stability in times of temptation and trial.[50]

• *Holiness gives evidence of justification and election, and it fosters assurance.* Sanctification is the inevitable fruit of justification (1 Cor. 6:11). The two are different but never separate; God Himself has joined them. Justification is organically linked to sanctification because new birth infallibly issues in new life. The justified walk in "the King's highway of holiness," Owen says.[51] Richard Sibbes adds, "By grace we are what we are in justification, and work what we work in sanctification."[52] Through Christ, justification gives God's child the *title* for heaven and the boldness to enter, while sanctification gives him the *fitness* for heaven and the preparation necessary to enjoy it. Sanctification is the personal appropriation of the fruits of justification.[53]

Election is also inseparable from holiness. As 2 Thessalonians 2:13b says, "God hath from the beginning chosen you to salvation through sanctification of the Spirit." Election is a comforting doctrine for the believer because it is the sure foundation of the grace of God working within him. No wonder our Reformed forebears considered election to be one of the believer's greatest comforts, for sanctification demonstrates election.[54]

Holiness also fosters assurance (1 John 2:3; 3:19). As the Heidelberg Catechism teaches, "Everyone may be assured in himself of his faith by the fruits thereof" (Question 86). Reformed divines agreed that most of the forms and degrees of assurance experienced by true believers, especially daily assurance, are gradually acquired in the path of sanctification through careful cultivation of God's Word, the other means of grace, and corresponding obedience.[55] Increasing hatred of sin by means of mortification and a growing desire to obey God by means of vivification accompany the progress of faith as it grows into assurance.

• *Holiness undergirds effective service to God.* Paul joins sanctification and usefulness, saying that "if a man therefore purge himself . . . , he shall be a vessel unto honor, sanctified, and meet for the master's use, and prepared unto every good work" (2 Tim. 2:21). God uses holiness to assist the preaching of the gospel and to build up the credit of the Christian faith. That holiness is dishonored by the carelessness of Christians and hypocrites, who often serve as Satan's best allies.[56] In our daily living, we are always doing good or harm; our conduct is an open epistle for all to read (2 Cor. 3:2). Holy living impresses as nothing else can; no argument can match it. It displays the beauty of genuine religion. As Matthew Henry says, "The beauty of holiness needs no paint [make-up]."[57] Holiness gives credibility to witness and to evangelism (Phil. 2:15).[58]

• *Holiness fits us for heaven (Rev. 21:27).* Life is a brief shadow. Ultimately, it is meant to prepare us to meet God in righteousness and peace. That kind of meeting is impossible for someone who does not bear fruits of holiness, for as Hebrews 12:14 says, we are to "follow [literally, pursue] . . . holiness, without which no man shall see the Lord." Brooks writes, "The way of holiness that leads to happiness is a narrow way; there is but just room enough for a holy God and a holy soul to walk together."[59]

Edwards notes: "The heaven I desired was a heaven of holiness."[60] That is the desire of every true believer, for unholy people would not feel at home in a holy heaven. Watson puts it this way: "If God should justify a people and not sanctify them, He would justify a people whom He could not glorify."[61]

THE JOY OF SANCTIFICATION

A holy life should emanate joy in the Lord, not negative drudgery (Neh. 8:10). The idea that holiness requires a gloomy disposition is a tragic distortion of Scripture, for Scripture asserts that those who cultivate holiness experience true joy. Jesus said, "If ye keep my commandments, ye shall abide in my love; even as I have kept my Father's commandments, and abide in his love. These things have

I spoken unto you, that my joy might remain in you, and that your joy might be full" (John 15:10–11). Those who obediently pursue holiness as a way of life will know the joy that flows from communion with God. That joy includes the following:

- *The supreme joy: fellowship with God.* There is no greater joy than communion with God. "In thy presence is fullness of joy," says Psalm 16:11b. True joy springs from God as we walk in fellowship with Him. When we break fellowship with God by sinning, we can only return, like David, with penitential prayer, begging, "Restore unto me the joy of thy salvation" (Ps. 51:12a). The words Jesus spoke to the thief on the cross represent the chief delight of every child of God: "Today shalt thou be with me in paradise" (Luke 23:43b).

- *The ongoing joy: abiding assurance.* True holiness obeys God and trusts Him. It says with assurance, "We know that all things work together for good to them that love God" (Rom. 8:28a), even when the end cannot be seen. Like faithful workers on a Persian carpet who blindly hand up colors to the one working out the pattern above them, God's saints hand Him even the black strands He calls for, knowing that His pattern is perfect, even though it cannot be seen. Do you know this profound, childlike trust of believing the words of Jesus: "What I do thou knowest not now; but thou shalt know hereafter" (John 13:7b)? Such ongoing, stabilizing joy surpasses understanding. Holiness reaps joyous contentment, for "godliness with contentment is great gain" (1 Tim. 6:6).

- *The anticipated joy: eternal, gracious reward.* Jesus endured His sufferings by anticipating the joy of His reward (Heb. 12:1–2). Believers, too, may look forward to entering into the joy of their Lord as they pursue holiness throughout their lives. By grace, they may joyously anticipate the eternal reward of hearing, "Well done, thou good and faithful servant. . . . Enter thou into the joy of thy Lord" (Matt. 25:21). John Whitlock notes, "Here is the Christian's way and his end—his way is holiness, his end, happiness."[62]

Holiness is its own reward, for everlasting glory is holiness perfected. "The souls of believers are at their death made perfect in holiness," says the Westminster Shorter Catechism, Question 37. The bodies of believers will be raised immortal and incorruptible, perfect in holiness, complete in glorification (1 Cor. 15:49, 53). Finally, the believer will be what he has desired to become ever since his regeneration: perfectly holy. He will enter into the eternal glory of Jesus Christ as a child of God and fellow-heir with Him (Phil. 3:20–21; Rom. 8:17). He will

finally be like Christ, holy and without blemish (Eph. 5:25–27), eternally mag-
nifying and exalting the unfathomable bounties of God's sovereign grace. Truly,
as Calvin states, "The thought of the great nobility God has conferred upon us
ought to whet our desire for holiness."[63]

THE WAY OF SANCTIFICATION

To be truly sanctified, our hearts need continual mortification. As Owen warns
us:

> We must be exercising [mortification] every day, and in every duty. Sin
> will not die, unless it be constantly weakened. Spare it, and it will heal its
> wounds, and recover its strength. We must continually watch against the
> operations of this principle of sin: in our duties, in our calling, in conversa-
> tion, in retirement, in our straits, in our enjoyments, and in all that we do. If
> we are negligent on any occasion, we shall suffer by it; every mistake, every
> neglect is perilous.[64]

Let us press on, then, in uprooting sin and cultivating holiness. Let us fight
the good fight of faith under the best of generals, Jesus Christ; with the best internal advocate, the Holy Spirit; by the best of assurances, the promises of God; for
the best of results, everlasting glory.

Are you convinced that cultivating holiness is worth the price of denying
sin and following God? Do you know genuine, Spirit-worked, Christ-centered,
Father-glorifying holiness? Do you know the joy of experiencing Jesus' easy yoke,
the joy of not belonging to yourself, but to your "faithful Savior Jesus Christ,"
who makes you "willing and ready, henceforth, to live unto Him" (Heidelberg
Catechism, Question 1)?

"Would you be holy? Then you must *begin with Christ*. Would you continue
to be holy? Then *abide in Christ*," Ryle says.[65] Spurgeon puts it this way: "Holiness is not the way to Christ; Christ is the way of holiness."[66] Outside of Him,
there is no holiness. Holiness is not a mere list of dos and don'ts; it is a life in Jesus
Christ. Christ is the way of sanctification (1 Cor. 1:30).

DISCUSSION QUESTIONS

1. What is Trinitarian godlikeness? How is it to be sought?

2. What is mortification? Is this a biblical concept? Why or why not?

3. What resources has God given us to help us grow in holiness?

4. What are the benefits of sanctification?

5. Why is joy an essential part of the Christian life? Are you a joyful Christian? Why or why not? If not, what can you do to remedy the situation?

NOTES

[1] Quoted in I. D. E. Thomas, *The Golden Treasury of Puritan Quotations* (Chicago: Moody Press, 1975), 141.

[2] A. W. Pink, *The Doctrine of Sanctification* (Swengel, Pa.: Bible Truth Depot, 1955), 25.

[3] Stephen Charnock, *The Existence and Attributes of God* (Evansville, Ind.: Sovereign Grace, 1958), 453.

[4] Aurelius Augustine, *Against Two Letters of the Pelagians*, 3.5.14, in *A Select Library of the Nicene and Post-Nicene Fathers*, first series, ed. P. Schaff (Grand Rapids: Eerdmans, 1982), 5:404.

[5] Inst., 3.14.4ff.; cf. Thomas Goodwin, *The Works of Thomas Goodwin* (Grand Rapids, Reformation Heritage Books, 2006), 6:220.

[6] Quoted in John Blanchard, *More Gathered Gold* (Welwyn, England: Evangelical Press, 1986), 147.

[7] John Owen, *Overcoming Sin and Temptation*, ed. Kelly M. Kapic and Justin Taylor (Wheaton, Ill.: Crossway, 2006), 73–78.

[8] Thomas Boston, *The Complete Works of Thomas Boston* (Stoke-on-Trent, U.K.: Tentmaker Publications, 2002), 1:657.

[9] Ibid.

[10] John Flavel, *The Works of John Flavel* (Edinburgh: Banner of Truth Trust, 1968), 5:423.

[11] Quoted in Robert M. McCheyne, *Memoirs and Remains of Robert Murray M'Cheyne* (Edinburgh: Banner of Truth Trust, 2002), 54.

[12] Richard Greenham, *The Works of the Reverend and Faithfull Servant of Iesus Christ, M. Richard Greenham*, ed. H[enry] H[olland] (London: Felix Kingston for Robert Dexter, 1599), 390.

[13] Jerry Bridges, *The Practice of Godliness* (Colorado Springs: NavPress, 1983), 52.

[14] See Joel R. Beeke and Ray B. Lanning, "The Transforming Power of Scripture," in *Sola Scriptura! The Protestant Position on the Bible*, ed. Don Kistler (Morgan, Pa.: Soli Deo Gloria, 1995), 257–260.

[15] Henry Smith, *The Works of Henry Smith* (Edinburgh: James Nichol, 1860), 1:494.

[16] John Flavel, *Keeping the Heart* (Morgan, Pa.: Soli Deo Gloria, 1998), http://www.iclnet.org/pub/resources/text/ipb-e/epl-10/web/flavel-keeping.html

[17] Thomas Hooker, *The Application of Redemption by the Effectual Work of the Word and Spirit of Christ, for the Bringing Home of Lost Sinners to God* (London: Peter Cole, 1659), 2:210.

[18] For a list of profitable subjects for meditation, see *The Works of Stephen Charnock* (Edinburgh: James Nichol, 1865), 3:307.

[19] George Swinnock, *The Works of George Swinnock* (Edinburgh: Banner of Truth Trust, 1998), 2:417.

[20] Thomas Watson, "How We May Read the Scriptures with Most Spiritual Profit," in *Heaven Taken by Storm*, ed. Joel R. Beeke (Morgan, Pa.: Soli Deo Gloria, 1992), 113–129.

[21] Richard Baxter, *The Saints' Everlasting Rest* (Ross-shire, U.K.: Christian Focus, 1998), 579–590, and Jonathan Edwards, *The Religious Affections* (London: Banner of Truth Trust, 1959), 24.

[22] William Bates, *The Works of the Rev. W. Bates D.D.* (Harrisonburg, Va.: Sprinkle, 1990), 3:145, and Thomas White, *A Method and Instructions for the Art of Divine Meditation* (London: for Tho. Parkhurst, 1672), 53.

[23] See Nathanael Ranew, *Solitude Improved by Divine Meditation, or A Treatise Proving the Duty, and Demonstrating the Necessity, Excellency, Usefulness, Natures, Kinds, and Requisites of Divine Meditation* (Morgan, Pa.: Soli Deo Gloria, 1995). For a fuller treatment of Puritan meditation, see Simon Chan, "The Puritan Meditative Tradition, 1599–1691: A Study in Asceticality" (Ph.D. dissertation, Cambridge University, 1986), or Joel R. Beeke, *Puritan Reformed Spirituality* (Darlington, England: Evangelical Press, 2006), 73–100.

24 John Bunyan, *Prayer* (Edinburgh: Banner of Truth Trust, 1999), 23ff.

25 Cf. Jay Adams, *Godliness Through Discipline* (Grand Rapids: Baker, 1973), 3.

26 Bridges, *The Practice of Godliness*, 41–56.

27 *The Psalter*, ed. Joel R. Beeke (Grand Rapids, Reformation Heritage Books, 2006), 126.

28 For Edwards' seventy resolutions to promote holiness made at 19 years of age, see Jonathan Edwards, *The Works of Jonathan Edwards*, ed. Edward Hickman (Edinburgh: Banner of Truth Trust, 1974), 1:xx–xxii.

29 Donald S. Whitney, *Spiritual Disciplines for the Christian Life* (Colorado Springs: NavPress, 1991), 196–210.

30 Watson, *Heaven Taken by Storm*, 16–18, and *A Body of Divinity* (London: Banner of Truth Trust, 1971), 377–379.

31 Ibid., 379.

32 For a listing and brief reviews of all of these titles, see Joel R. Beeke and Randall Pederson, *Meet the Puritans* (Grand Rapids: Reformation Heritage Books, 2006).

33 Alan F. Herr, *The Elizabethan Sermon* (New York: Octagon Books, 1969), 67.

34 Ibid., 27.

35 Robert Bruce, *The Mystery of the Lord's Supper*, trans. and ed. Thomas F. Torrance (Richmond: John Knox Press, 1958), 82.

36 Quoted in Joel R. Beeke, *Holiness: God's Call to Sanctification* (Edinburgh: Banner of Truth Trust, 1994), 18–19.

37 See *Belgic Confession of Faith*, Article 28.

38 Thomas Watson, *The Mischief of Sin* (Pittsburgh: Soli Deo Gloria, 1994); John Owen, "Temptation and Sin," in *The Works of John Owen*, vol. 6; Jeremiah Burroughs, *The Evil of Evils; or The Exceeding Sinfulness of Sin* (Pittsburgh: Soli Deo Gloria, 1992); and Ralph Venning, *The Plague of Plagues* (London: Banner of Truth Trust, 1965).

39 John Charles Ryle, *Holiness: Its Nature, Hindrances, Difficulties, and Roots* (Greensboro, N.C.: Homiletic Press, 1956); Octavius Winslow, *Personal Declension and Revival of Religion in the Soul* (London: Banner of Truth Trust, 1960); and Flavel, "Keeping the Heart," in *The Works of John Flavel*, 5:417–507.

40 J. I. Packer, *A Quest for Godliness: The Puritan Vision of the Christian Life* (Wheaton, Ill: Crossway, 1990), 239. Cf. Erroll Hulse, "Sanctifying the Lord's Day: Reformed and Puritan Attitudes," in *Aspects of Sanctification*, 1981 Westminster Conference Papers (Hertfordshire: Evangelical Press, 1982), 78–102. For a helpful monograph on the Puritan Sabbath, see James Dennison, *The Market Day of the Soul* (Grand Rapids: Reformation Heritage Books, 2008).

41 Whitney, *Spiritual Disciplines for the Christian Life*, 93ff.

42 Quoted in John Blanchard, *The Complete Gathered Gold* (Darlington, England: Evangelical Press, 2006), 302.

43 Ibid., 306.

44 Richard Baxter, "The Spiritual and Carnal Man Compared and Contrasted; or, The Absolute Necessity and Excellency of Holiness," in *The Select Practical Works of Richard Baxter* (Glasgow: Blackie & Son, 1840), 115–291.

45 Quoted in Blanchard, *The Complete Gathered Gold*, 305.

46 Flavel, *The Works of John Flavel*, 1:538–549.

47 Peter Vinke, in *Puritan Sermons, 1659–1689* (Wheaton, Ill.: Richard Owen Roberts, 1981), 4:264–284.

48 Watson, *A Body of Divinity*, 172.

49 Quoted in Blanchard, *The Complete Gathered Gold*, 311.

50 Flavel, *Keeping the Heart*, 37–45; cf. Daniel Webber, "Sanctifying the Inner Life," in *Aspects of Sanctification*, 54–56, and Boston, *The Complete Works of Thomas Boston*, 6:602–604.

51 Owen, *The Works of John Owen*, 11:254ff.

52 Quoted in Blanchard, *The Complete Gathered Gold*, 308.

53 Cf. Robert Traill, *Works of Robert Traill* (Edinburgh: Banner of Truth Trust, 1975), 3:72–77, and Joel R. Beeke, *Jehovah Shepherding His Sheep* (Grand Rapids: Reformation Heritage Books, 1997), 186–188.

54 Cf. Walter Marshall, *The Gospel Mystery of Sanctification* (Grand Rapids: Reformation Heritage Books, 2000), 220–221.

55 Joel R. Beeke, *Assurance of Faith: Calvin, English Puritanism, and the Dutch Second Reformation* (New York: Peter Lang, 1991), 160ff.; cf. Westminster Confession, Chapter 18, and the Canons of Dort, Head V, for an appreciation of the intertwining of holiness and assurance. Also, see John J. Murray, "Good Works in the Scheme of God's Grace," *Banner of Truth*, no. 524 (May 2007): 11, and William K. B. Stoever, "Nature, Grace and John Cotton: The Theological Dimension in the New England Antinomian Controversy," *Church History*, 44, no. 1 (March 1975): 27–31.

56 Ryle, *Holiness*, 62.

57 Quoted in Blanchard, *The Complete Gathered Gold*, 306.

58 Leonard J. Coppes, *Are Five Points Enough? Ten Points of Calvinism* (Manassas, Va.: Reformation Educational Foundation, 1980), 94–96.

59 Quoted in Blanchard, *The Complete Gathered Gold*, 309, 311.

60 Ibid.

61 Ibid., 309.

62 Thomas, *The Golden Treasury of Puritan Quotations*, 140.

63 Quoted in Blanchard, *More Gathered Gold*, 153.

64 Owen, *The Works of John Owen*, 3:310.

65 Ryle, *Holiness*, 71–72.

66 Quoted in John Blanchard, *Gathered Gold* (Welwyn, England: Evangelical Press, 1984), 146.

PART FOUR

CALVINISM
IN
THE CHURCH

CHAPTER 16

REFORMING
THE CHURCH

Derek W. H. Thomas

The model for church polity which Calvin devised for use in Geneva was characterized by strong organization and a scrupulous supervision of morals and customs.[1]

—BENGT HÄGGLUND

*C*hurch names, in many cases, are based on their particular ecclesiastical tradition and polity. For instance, Baptists were known for their insistence on believer's baptism. Methodists were so named because of their methodical approach to holiness. Lutherans were distinguished by their adherence to tenets of Martin Luther's theology. Episcopalians were so labeled because of their view of the office of bishop (Greek, *episkopos*) as distinct from pastor or elder. Presbyterians owe their name to their insistence that a bishop or elder is a presbyter, and that Scripture teaches a representative form of church government under which elders are elected by the people of God.

Presbyterianism was developed during the seventeenth century and found classical expression in the Form of Presbyterial Church-Government,[2] the document produced by the Westminster Assembly in 1645. However, Presbyterianism is firmly rooted in the Calvinistic churches of Europe, particularly the church in Geneva that was led by the Reformer John Calvin. As such, it embodies the unique Calvinistic vision for the structure of the church.

The two critical questions of the sixteenth-century Reformation were, in the words of the Philippian jailor, "What must I do to be saved?" (Acts 16:30), and, to cite Cyprian, "Where can I find a true church?" Cyprian insisted, "You cannot have God for your Father unless you have the church for your mother,"[3] a metaphor that Calvin took up and explored unapologetically, reintroducing this emphasis with considerable zeal. Thus, we find Calvin describing the visible church in Book IV of his *Institutes of the Christian Religion* in language drawn from Cyprian's maternal metaphor: "For there is no other way to enter into life unless this mother conceive us in her womb, give us birth, nourish us at her breast, and lastly, unless she keep us under her care and guidance until, putting off mortal flesh, we become like the angels."[4]

For Calvin, the church was crucial to a full understanding of the nature of God's redemptive purposes in this fallen world. He believed the salvation of sinners does not happen in a vacuum, but in the crucible of the visible church. "I am duly clear in my own conscience, and have God and the angels to witness, that since I undertook the office of a teacher in the church, *I have had no other purpose than to benefit the church*,"[5] Calvin writes in the preface of the *Institutes*. John T. McNeill notes that "Calvin saw the Reformation as the restoration of the true Catholic Church that had been almost completely suppressed and undiscoverable in the previous era."[6] And Henry Meeter, in a summation of the main tenets of Calvinism, includes the "outstanding doctrine" of the church.[7]

Beset on one hand by a resurgent Catholicism and on the other by a persistent sectarianism, Calvin (as had Luther to some extent before him) wrestled with the precise relationship of the church—which consisted, as Luther had said, of "the whole number of the predestined"[8]—to that which is "visible." As those before and after him concluded, certain "marks" (*notae*) indicate ecclesiastical validity. Calvin writes, "In order that the title 'church' may not deceive us, every congregation that claims the name 'church' must be tested by this standard as by a touchstone."[9]

Scholars of Luther's theology have insisted that these marks function more as a description of the "ideal church" than as prerequisites for a body to be considered a church. But for Calvin, the marks were more than descriptive; they were constitutive of a true church, apart from which no church existed. He says, "Wherever we see the Word of God purely preached and heard, and the sacraments administered according to Christ's institution, there, it is not to be doubted, a church of God exists [cf. Eph. 2:20]."[10]

Thus, the marks of the church played a different role in ecclesiastical Calvinism, drawn as they were from the more descriptive attributes in the Nicene Creed—"one, holy, catholic and apostolic church."[11] By testing the visibility of the church's unity, holiness, catholicity, and apostolicity, Calvin said, "the face of the church emerges into visibility before our eyes."[12]

Calvin did not follow Martin Bucer in elevating discipline to the status of the *notae*. However, he did not disparage the importance of the right administration of discipline for the well-being of the church. Discipline was the sinew (*pro nervis*) by which the members of the body were held together, each in its own place.[13] He did go so far as to say, in the first edition of the *Institutes* in 1536, that "example of life" was among the "certain sure notes"[14] of the visible church.

Concerned as Calvin was about the visible state of the church, it is also important to remember his conviction that "from the light of eternity" (*sub specie aeternitatis*), God's church cannot be extinguished altogether, no matter how feeble it may appear here on earth. This truth alone prevented Calvin from refusing to give the title "church" to particular congregations that were still technically Roman Catholic, saying, "To the extent that some marks of the church remain, we do not impugn the existence of churches among them."[15]

EMERGING CALVINISTIC ECCLESIASTICAL POLITY

Calvin returned to Geneva in 1541 after his three-and-a-half year exile in Strasbourg upon the condition that the city accept his vision of the church's fourfold office: pastor, teacher, elder, and deacon. Calvin had presented this concept firmly in an ecclesiastical manifesto published in 1541 under the title *Les Ordonnances Ecclessiastique*. According to Alexandre Ganoczy, Calvin owed this fourfold view of ecclesiastical office to Bucer.[16]

The Ecclesiastical Ordinances drafted by Calvin were approved by the Genevan councils within two months of his return. As David F. Wright notes, "It is hard to exaggerate the significance of this formulation of the new church order to be implemented in Geneva. . . . Though revision at the hands of the councils weakened some of its provisions and left others ambiguous, it very largely represented what through Calvin in particular became a distinctive feature of the Reformed tradition, namely, a clearly defined ordering of congregational life."[17] And Bengt Hägglund writes that the "model for church polity which Calvin devised for use in Geneva was characterized by strong organization and a scrupulous supervision of morals and customs."[18]

For Calvin, this meant that while there was only one church in Geneva, there were three parishes—the seed of what would become a "connectional" rather than a strictly "congregational" or "independent" church polity. This model, extended to become a national church, would exist first in France, then in Scotland and the Netherlands.

The Ordinances dealt with the "four orders of office instituted by our Lord for the government of his church," namely, pastors, doctors (i.e., teachers or lecturers), elders, and deacons. Virtually everything in the Ordinances was presented under these four heads. The doctors were, in reality, a subset of pastors or ministers and subject to precisely the same code of discipline.[19] The eldership, Calvin insisted, was an order of apostolic ministry, even though in Geneva the elders also served as representatives of the city council. The word *elder* was used to define the New Testament concepts of both *presbyter* and *bishop*. In a comment on 1 Timothy 5:17, which says that some elders are worthy of "double honour," Calvin wrote:

> The plain meaning of the words is that there were some who ruled well and honourably, but who did not hold a teaching office. The people elected earnest and well-tried men, who, along with the pastors in a common council and with the authority of the Church, would administer discipline and act as censors for the correction of morals.[20]

In other words, Calvin saw in Scripture the basis of a "consistory" or "session," and he sought to implement that structure in Geneva.

Among the elders were pastors whom Calvin considered more responsible for the spiritual growth of the church by maintaining purity of doctrine. The role of the pastor, according to Calvin, is "to represent God's Son." He adds in a comment on 1 Timothy 3:1:

> For it is no light matter to represent God's Son (*sustinere personam Filii Dei*) in such a great task as erecting and extending God's Kingdom, in caring for the salvation of souls whom the Lord Himself has deigned to purchase with His own blood, and in ruling the Church which is God's inheritance.[21]

Calvin describes how pastors are to be chosen. They are not to thrust themselves forward; rather, they must be called according to the order prescribed by the church. In Geneva, that consisted of a selection and trial by the company of pastors, presentation to the city council, and approval by the congregation. The process involved ordination, which he described as a "legitimate act of consecration before God, something that could be done only by the power of the Holy Spirit."[22]

Calvin held the office of deacon in high esteem, and the church in Geneva demonstrated an advanced understanding of the role deacons played in ministries of mercy and compassion.[23] Deacons demonstrated skills in social work as well as pastoral care; they dispensed relief to the poor and visited those who were in the hospital. Calvinistic polity today commonly sees the diaconate as a "nursery" from which the presbyter/elder/bishop is chosen, but Calvin viewed this as an undermining of the offices.[24]

Calvin's ecclesiastical polity varied from Roman Catholic or Anglican episcopacy—that is, government by monarchical bishops who were regarded as elders' overseers or superintendents. Calvin's ecclesiastical thought also distanced itself from Independency, which insisted on the autonomy of the local congregation. Some Independents also came to disagree with the view that the church's ruling elders should be distinct from teaching elders (or pastors).

ECCLESIASTICAL CALVINISM

Three fundamental principles emerged in ecclesiastical Calvinism, the chief being the parity of elders and bishops. It is noteworthy that even the Anglican bishop of Durham, J. B. Lightfoot, taught that the New Testament bishops and elders were equal and synonymous.[25] Equally important is the issue of the plurality of elders. Presbyterians, "insisting on the sufficiency of Scripture, maintain that by precept and example the New Testament presents a church order in which a plurality of elders join in governing the church."[26] Third is the matter of connectionalism. Local churches are organized into a presbytery or, among Continental Reformed churches, a classis, a body that technically has all the powers of Episcopal bishops, such as the authority to direct a minister to leave a congregation and undertake outreach elsewhere.[27]

Ecclesiastical Calvinism, then, ensures the government of the church by scriptural church officers, church courts, and confessional standards. As Kevin Reed

insists, wherever these three are present, there is "Presbyterian government."[28]
There have been, of course, subtle differences in this form of government as it
developed in places such as Scotland and North America as opposed to Holland and other parts of Europe. Differences emerged on the relative powers of
"higher courts" over local congregations. In some cases, debates continue to be
heard as to whether it is "government from the top down" or "government from
the bottom up," suggesting nervousness over what may appear to be a form of
bureaucratic tyranny as to the former and an insipient congregationalism as to
the latter. Nevertheless, such government continues to be the essence of Presbyterian or Reformed ecclesiastical polity, its roots firmly planted in the soil of
sixteenth-century Geneva. Thus, the influence of Calvinistic ecclesiastical polity
is still hugely visible as it spreads to the various continents of the globe in the
twenty-first century.

DISCUSSION QUESTIONS

1. Where does the term *Presbyterianism* come from?

2. What was Calvin's view of the church?

3. How was Calvin's view different from both the episcopacy of the
    Anglican Church and the church polity of the Independents?

4. What roles did Calvin see for elders in the life of the local
    church?

NOTES

1 Bengt Hägglund, *History of Theology*, 4th ed., trans. Gene J. Lund (St. Louis: Concordia, 2007), 264.

2 The full title of the document is "The Form of Presbyterial Church-Government ASSEMBLY AT EDINBURGH, February 10, 1645, Sess. 16. ACT *of the* GENERAL ASSEMBLY *of the* KIRK *of* SCOTLAND, *approving the Propositions concerning Kirk-government, and Ordination of Ministers.*"

3 Cyprian, *On the Unity of the Catholic Church* 6 (*Corpus Christianorum, Series Latina*, 3.1.214).

4 Inst., 4.1.4.

5 Inst., 1.4 (emphasis added).

6 John T. McNeill, *The History and Character of Calvinism* (Oxford: Oxford University Press, 1954), 216. McNeill adds: "The doctrine of the Church was one to which Calvin gave high importance and which he labored to clarify" (ibid., 214).

7 Henry Meeter, *The Basic Ideas of Calvinism*, 6th ed., rev. Paul A. Marshall (Grand Rapids: Baker, 1990), 46.

8 Martin Luther, *D. Martin Luthers Werke: Kritische Gesamtausgabe*, ed. J. K. F. Knaake et al (Weimar, 1883), 2:287. Luther is dependent on the work of Augustine at this point; see Augustine, *City of God*, passim, and *On Baptism* III.xix.26 (*Patrologiae Cursus Completus; Series Latinae*, 221 vols. [Paris, 1844–1855], 43.152). Luther complained that he did not want "to build the church as Plato wants to build the state, which would be nowhere" (WA 7, 683). Cited by Paul D. L. Avis, *The Church in the Theology of the Reformers* (Atlanta: John Knox Press, 1981), 4.

9 Inst., 4.1.11.

10 Inst., 4.1.9. The First Scots Confession (1560), ch. 18, and the Belgic Confession (1561), Art. 29, added a third mark, discipline.

11 Cf. G. C. Berkouwer, *The Church* (Grand Rapids: Eerdmans, 1976), 13–14.

12 Inst., 4.1.9. Harro Höpfl has argued that Calvin's interest in the invisible aspect of the church's identity increasingly receded into the background until his early emphasis on the church as a communion of saints was entirely eclipsed (*The Christian Polity of John Calvin* [Cambridge: Cambridge University Press, 1982], 34). This claim, however, is an exaggeration based on the observation of the amount of material given in the expanded final edition of the *Institutes* to the visible aspect of the church from that given in the 1536 edition.

13 Inst., 4.12.1.

14 *CO* 1:89; cf. Alister McGrath, *Reformation Thought: An Introduction*, 3rd ed. (Oxford: Blackwell, 1999), 209.

15 Inst., 4.2.12.

16 Alexandre Ganoczy, *Calvin: Théologien de l'Eglise et du Ministère* (Paris, 1964), 298–299.

17 David F. Wright, "Calvin's Role in Church History," in *The Cambridge Companion to John Calvin*, ed. Donald K. McKim (Cambridge: Cambridge University Press, 2004), 284.

18 Hägglund, *History of Theology*, 264.

19 Calvin doubled as a lecturer throughout his time in Geneva, though the formal establishment of the Academy did not materialize until 1559, five years before Calvin's death.

20 John Calvin, *The Second Epistle of Paul to the Corinthians*, and *The Epistles to Timothy, Titus, and Philemon*, trans. T. A. Smail, ed. David W. Torrance and Thomas F. Torrance (Grand Rapids: Eerdmans, 1991), 262. There is no hint here, of course, of what would later become a "divine-right" Presbyterianism (see

John Richard de Witt, *Jus Divinum: The Westminster Assembly and the Divine Right of Church Government* [Kampen: J. H. Kok, 1969]).

21 Calvin, *The Epistles to Timothy, Titus, and Philemon*, 226.

22 Ibid., 293. *Commentary* on 2 Timothy 1:6 (*CO* 52:349–350).

23 For a sampling of social concern in Geneva, see William Monter, *Calvin's Geneva* (New York: John Wiley and Sons, 1967); *Studies in Genevan Government (1536–1605)* (Geneva: Librarie Droz, 1964); and William C. Innes, *Social Concern in Calvin's Geneva* (Allisan Park, Pa.: Pickwick Publications, 1983).

24 See the remarks Calvin makes in his commentary on 1 Timothy 3:13, *The Epistles to Timothy, Titus, and Philemon*, 229 (*CO* 52:286–287).

25 See his essay, "The Christian Ministry," in his *St. Paul's Epistle to the Philippians* (London: Macmillan, 1873), 179–267.

26 Edmund Clowney, *The Church* (Downers Grove, Ill.: InterVarsity Press, 1995), 205.

27 Donald MacLeod, *A Faith to Live By* (Ross-shire, U.K.: Mentor Publications, 1998), 264.

28 Kevin Reed, *Biblical Church Government* (Dallas: Presbyterian Heritage Publications, 1983), 4. For a brief summary of the development of Presbyterianism in Britain and America, see Roy Taylor's chapter, "Presbyterianism," in *Who Runs the Church: Four Views on Church Government* (Grand Rapids: Zondervan, 2004), 73–79.

CHAPTER 17

FOUNDATIONS
OF REFORMED WORSHIP

Ray Lanning

The acceptable way of worshipping the true God is instituted by Himself, and so limited by His own revealed will, that He may not be worshipped according to the imaginations and devices of men, or the suggestions of Satan, under any visible representation, or any other way not prescribed in the Holy Scripture.[1]

—WESTMINSTER CONFESSION OF FAITH

Of the many changes enacted by the Reformers, none was more dramatic than the change in public worship. The Latin Mass was cast out along with all of its accessories: altars, priests, and acolytes; vestments and paraments; crucifixes, candles, communion wafers, tabernacles, and monstrances; images and relics of deceased saints; rosaries, rood screens, and altar rails; and choirs and pipe organs. The issue of public worship assumed great urgency, because the Mass was central to the faith and life of the pre-Reformation church. Something substantial was needed to replace it in the faith and devotion of the people.

Martin Luther led the way with his German Mass, which recast the Roman Mass in the language of the people and purged it of perceived corruptions. John Calvin felt compelled to go further. He proposed a return to the simpler form and manner of the ancient or pre-papal church. Calvin has been vindicated, surely, over the past hundred years by the liturgical change in the churches of Europe and North America. In Lutheran and Anglican churches, many Roman practices

have been reintroduced, and "doing as Rome does" has tended to obscure any
sense of theological difference with Catholicism. In other Protestant churches,
liturgical chaos has erupted in the absence of any controlling regard for Scripture,
the witness of the ancient church, or the Reformation.

It is not possible here to present a comprehensive history of Reformed worship. I begin with Calvin because his influence is all-pervasive, no matter what
branch of the Reformed family of churches is in view. I then follow Calvin's influence as it extended to England and Scotland through the work of John Knox,
the Puritans, and the Westminster Assembly of Divines. Finally, I briefly discuss
subsequent developments in North America.

CALVIN'S LITURGY

Calvin introduced a true liturgy of the Word. The exposition of the Holy Scriptures was the central act of worship, the great catalytic agent that evoked and
illuminated all other acts of worship. The sacraments, reduced to baptism and the
Lord's Supper, were made subordinate to the preaching of the Word and shorn of
unbiblical embellishment. And the congregation once again found its voice lifted
in song as metrical versions of psalms were introduced.

Calvin's liturgy is included in his *Treatises on the Sacraments*[2] under the heading "Forms of Prayer for the Church." There was no better guide to Reformed
liturgical practice in the days of Calvin. The same volume presents Calvin's commentary on his liturgical and sacramental practice in the latter part of the section
titled "Catechism of the Church of Geneva."[3]

Calvin's service for the Lord's Day is a liturgy of the Word in at least three
senses. First, the central act of the liturgy is the sermon, the faithful expounding
of God's Word for the edification of His church. The sermon is preceded by the
invocation of God's name, the confession of sins with absolution, the singing of a
psalm, and the minister's prayer for the help of the Holy Spirit in preaching—all
of which prepare for profitable hearing of the Word. The sermon is followed by
intercessory prayer, incorporating an expanded paraphrase of the Lord's Prayer;
repetition of the Apostles' Creed; administration of the sacraments; and finally, a
benediction. All are acts of faith in response to God's Word.

Second, the service includes only those elements that have a warrant in the
Word of God; later generations called this directive the "regulative principle of

worship." No scope is given to the mind or imagination of man. Calvin said that following one's own notions, other men's inventions, or man-made traditions in worship is an act of apostasy and idolatry, a falling away from the truth of God's Word, and the worship of something false in the place of what God has instituted. Commenting on Christ's word to the Samaritan woman in John 4:22, "Ye worship ye know not what," Calvin observes, "However much in their obstinacy those who worship God from their own notions or men's traditions flatter and praise themselves, this one Word thundering from heaven overthrows every divine and holy thing they think they possess: *Ye worship that which ye know not.*"[4]

Third, the content of each part of the liturgy is drawn from Scripture, from Psalm 124:8, used as an invocation at the commencement of the service, to the Aaronic benediction (Num. 6:24–26) at the close. The prayers abound with Scripture citations and allusions, each paragraph invoking some particular promise, precept, or precedent, followed by the application of it to the needs of the congregation or the wider church. When Scripture is not being read, preached, or appropriated in prayer, it is being sung as praise to God in the form of a metrical version of a psalm. First to last, Calvin's liturgy is an encounter with the truth of Holy Scripture.

In regard to the sacraments, great attention has been paid to Calvin's notion of how Christ is present in the sacrament of the Lord's Supper. A careful examination of Calvin's "Manner of Celebrating the Lord's Supper" shows that he denied any local presence of Christ in the Communion elements. Rather, the sacrament is a means by which communicants, exercising faith in the promise of Christ, are to "raise our hearts and minds on high, where Jesus Christ is, in the glory of his Father, and from whence we look for him at our redemption." Calvin goes on to say: "Let us not amuse ourselves with these earthly and corruptible elements which we see with the eye, and touch with the hand, in order to seek him there, as if he were enclosed in the bread or wine."[5]

This part of the liturgy has been called Calvin's *Sursum Corda* (lift up your hearts).[6] More than a bare kind of memorialism, this whole-souled act of faith brings the believer into the courts of heaven, there to be fed with the life-giving flesh and blood of the crucified, risen, and ascended Christ.

Equally clear is the way in which Calvin subordinated the sacraments to the ministry of the Word. On any given Lord's Day, there might be a sacrament, but there would certainly be a sermon. Calvin taught his catechumens that the sacraments were added to the preaching of the Word as another means by which God communicates Himself to us.[7]

Calvin placed the celebration of the Lord's Supper within the framework of the liturgy of the Word. He says, "On the day of communion, the minister adverts to it at the end of his sermon, or indeed, if he sees cause, makes it the sole subject of [the] sermon, in order to expound to the people what our Lord means to teach and signify by this ordinance, and in what way it behooves us to receive it."[8] It is fitting that the sacrament be administered only by ministers of the Word, "for the two things, viz., to feed the Church with the doctrine of piety, and administer the sacrament, are united by an indissoluble tie."[9]

Calvin's form for the Lord's Supper is richly didactic. He took pains to emphasize the Master-disciple relationship between Christ and the believer, making the sacrament a means of disciple formation. Its value is in what it teaches and signifies, not in any spiritual power inherent in its actions or elements.

The administration of the sacrament is reduced to simplest terms and includes only those things that Christ did in Scripture. In a note appended to the "Manner of Celebrating the Lord's Supper," Calvin defends this biblical conformity and simplicity. To remedy the corruptions, adulterations, and abuses of the Mass, Calvin asserts that "we have found no means better or more proper than to return to the pure institution of Jesus Christ, which we follow simply, as is apparent."[10]

On the question of frequency, though Calvin apparently favored a weekly celebration, his liturgy makes no mention of this. There seems to be no idea of any stated schedule of the sacrament; the rubric simply requires "that the Sunday before the Supper is dispensed it is intimated [announced] to the people."[11] There are three reasons for this: first, so that each person may prepare himself to receive the sacrament worthily; second, to exclude young persons who have not been instructed or have not made public profession of their faith; and third, to encourage "strangers" (unbelievers or unconverted persons; further in the form, the term is used for "those who are not of the company of the faithful") to "come and present themselves for instruction in private."[12]

One aspect of Reformed worship only touched on in Calvin's liturgy is its emphasis on congregational song. Nothing was more distinctive of public worship in the church of Geneva than the congregational singing of metrical versions of psalms.

Metrical psalmody translates the poetry of the Hebrew Psalms into the poetic forms or measures ("meter") of another language. These metrical versions may then be set to existing tunes or tunes cast in the mold of the music of a given culture. The result is psalmody in a form accessible to the common man, textually and musically.

Calvin's metrical psalmody went a step further by adapting psalms for use in public worship. His versions, and later those of his colleagues Clement Marot and Theodore Beza, included elements of exposition and application. The result was a liturgical translation that enabled the people of Geneva to embrace the ancient psalms of David as their own songs of praise. All sense of distance—linguistic, temporal, cultural, intellectual, or spiritual—was transcended.

Calvin believed in the uniqueness of psalms and their innate suitability for singing in worship since they are part of the written Word of God. In his commentary on the book of Psalms, Calvin writes, "I have been accustomed to call this book . . . 'An Anatomy of all the Parts of the Soul;' for there is not an emotion of which any one can be conscious that is not here represented as in a mirror." Calvin further argues that "a better and more unerring rule for guiding us in this exercise [prayer] cannot be found elsewhere than in the Psalms."[13]

Calvin's liturgy reveals that he drew a straight line between the biblical content of the Reformed faith and the biblical way in which that content should be proclaimed, expounded, embraced, and acted on in public worship. What Calvin says about his "Form of Administering Baptism" may be said of his liturgy as a whole: "We have a form of baptism such as Jesus Christ instituted, the Apostles kept, and the Church put in practice; and there is nothing for which we can be blamed, unless it be for not being wiser than God himself."[14]

Calvin achieved a balance between form and freedom that was lost in the generations that followed. On the one hand, Calvin was not averse to written forms of prayer and instruction, much less the stated use of such acts of devotion as reading the Ten Commandments, praying the Lord's Prayer, or repeating the Apostles' Creed. On the other hand, Calvin left room for extemporaneous discourse and prayer.

As for the daily services or "ordinary meetings" in the churches, Calvin was content to leave these in the hands of the minister who conducted them, saying, "The minister leads the devotions of the people in whatever words seem to him suitable, adapting his address to the time and subject of the discourse which he is to deliver."[15] The service for the morning of the Lord's Day also leaves some parts to the discretion of the minister in charge. Regarding the prayer before a sermon, the rubric states that "the form of prayer suitable for this the minister selects for himself at pleasure."[16] The prayer of thanksgiving after the administration of the Lord's Supper is to be offered in the form provided, "or one similar to it."[17]

Why have any formularies? Calvin and his colleagues were reforming public worship. They wished to bar the door against both the return of old corruptions, adulterations, and abuses, and the introduction of new ones. The best way seemed to be a careful formulation of the general manner of conducting the principal service of public devotion and of administering the sacraments. The freedom of the ministers was limited to secure purity and uniformity of practice where it mattered most.

JOHN KNOX

Scotland's John Knox may be considered the most important early Reformed liturgist after Calvin.[18] Arriving on the Continent in 1554 as a refugee from the wave of persecution instituted under Queen Mary, Knox made his way first to Frankfurt, Germany, and then to Geneva.

In Frankfurt, Knox was called to be minister of a band of English exiles that had formed a church "to worship according to their own conscience and in their own tongue."[19] The exiles soon disagreed about how to administer the sacrament of the Lord's Supper. One party wished to retain the order for Holy Communion found in Thomas Cranmer's *Book of Common Prayer*; the other favored an English version of Calvin's liturgy.

Knox was not willing to use the order from the *Book of Common Prayer*, but he was not ready to adopt Calvin's form without the advice of the congregations of exiles in other places. A new liturgy was drafted but failed to win approval. A second committee went to work, producing an order that was more generally accepted. This order was followed for a brief period, until the arrival of more English exiles resulted in the banishment of Knox from Frankfurt at the end of March 1555.

Knox took refuge in Geneva. He was joined by other like-minded brethren from Frankfurt, who formed a new congregation of English exiles. William D. Maxwell writes, "Thus originated the English Church at Geneva, the cradle of Puritanism, and a paramount influence upon the Reformation in Scotland."[20]

The founders of the Genevan church took up the liturgy spurned in Frankfurt and added to it a collection of fifty English versions of psalms in meter. This was soon published as *The Forme of Prayers and Ministration of the Sacraments, etc., used in the English Congregation at Geneva: and approved, by the famous and godly learned man, John Calvyn.*[21]

This Genevan service book of 1556 followed the outlines of Calvin's liturgy. It differed from Calvin's only by way of omission. There was no stated reading of the law, for example, but the use of the Lord's Prayer and the Apostles' Creed was retained. The chief characteristics of Calvin's liturgy were present: the centrality of preaching, subordination of the sacraments to the Word, restoration of congregational praise, and a balance between form and freedom in the matter of prayer and other parts of the service.

When the exiles returned home, Knox's Genevan service book went with them. For the Puritans of England, it provided an alternative to the *Book of Common Prayer*, down to the time of the Westminster Assembly of Divines. Knox carried the service book home to Scotland, where it became the first service book of the newly reformed Church of Scotland. Charles W. Baird devotes an entire chapter to recalling "the First Sacrament in Scotland," administered by Knox by means of his Genevan liturgy.[22]

THE WESTMINSTER DIVINES

The sixteenth-century controversy at Frankfurt was a prelude to a more prolonged conflict over the form of public worship that raged in Britain for most of the seventeenth century.[23] At the heart of the conflict was Cranmer's *Book of Common Prayer* in the form that it assumed after Elizabeth I took her place on the English throne. For some, use of the Prayer Book was the mark of true English churchmanship and proof of loyalty to the crown. For others, including nearly all of the Puritans, the Prayer Book was an offense to conscience, the more so as time passed.

Things went from bad to worse when Elizabeth died in 1603 and the English crown passed to Scotland's King James VI. His Scottish Presbyterian upbringing notwithstanding, James flatly refused Puritan demands for liturgical reform and the abolition of the Anglican episcopate.

The conflict extended into Scotland when James's son, Charles I, attempted to restore Episcopal church government and impose a new liturgy on the Church of Scotland in 1637. Scotland's Presbyterians, binding themselves to a national covenant, rose in defense of the Reformed faith, worship, and order of their national church. When Charles sought to impose his will by force, the result was war between England and Scotland. Meanwhile, the archbishop of Canterbury, William Laud, not content with the inherited status quo, set about the task of vigorously enforcing conformity to the Prayer Book and enhancing the ceremonial usages connected with it, thereby stoking fires of rebellion in England itself.

More broadly, political strife increased as the powers of the king were pitted against the rights of Parliament. Charles determined to prevail by force of arms. Royalist forces rallied to the king and Parliament put its own army in the field under the Earl of Essex and, later, Oliver Cromwell. Civil war broke out within the realm of England.

The English Parliament appealed to the Scottish Covenanters for help. The result was the Solemn League and Covenant of 1643.[24] In return for Scottish help in defending Parliament's rights and powers against the monarch, the English agreed to further reformation of the churches of England and Ireland to bring them into conformity with the faith, worship, and order of the Church of Scotland. The first step was the calling of a national assembly of England's divines, or theologians, to be held in the city of Westminster, seat of the national government in central London.

The Assembly of Divines at Westminster (1643–1648) produced a number of important documents known as the Westminster Standards, including the well-known Confession of Faith and the Larger and Shorter Catechisms. Less known today are the Form of Presbyterial Church-Government, a church-order document; a new metrical version of the Psalms, known as Rous's Version, after the member of Parliament chiefly responsible for it, Francis Rous; and the Directory for Public Worship.[25]

The Form of Presbyterial Church-Government provided the model for all subsequent Presbyterian church-order documents. Rous's Version, after considerable revision, was adopted as the authorized book of praise of the Church of Scotland in 1650. It remains in use in Scotland and many other parts of the world. The Scottish Psalter of 1650 and the Genevan Psalter are the two most important metrical versions of the Psalms used by Reformed Christians.[26]

However, the Directory for Public Worship was the most radical document produced by the divines. Long years of strife had hardened positions, forcing each side to delineate and defend its views in the clearest and stoutest terms.

At the Westminster Assembly, the English Puritans, with the help of Presbyterians from Scotland, set out to achieve a great reformation of public worship in the Church of England. Note the use of the word *directory* rather than *liturgy*. The preface states that "long and sad experience hath made it manifest, that the Liturgy used in the Church of England, (notwithstanding all the pains of religious intentions of the Compilers of it,) hath proved an offence, not only to many of the godly at home, but also to the reformed Churches abroad."[27] "The reading of all the prayers" was deemed a burden now to be dispensed with, because, among other evils, it tended "to make and increase an idle and unedifying ministry, which contented itself with set forms made to their hands by others."[28]

At the same time, the divines were mindful of their mandate to provide for "uniformity in divine worship" among the churches, according to the design of the Solemn League and Covenant. The simplest way would have been to adopt another liturgy, whether Calvin's or Knox's, or the liturgy of the Reformed Churches in the Netherlands, with which the divines seem to have been well-acquainted.[29]

Instead, the divines said it was enough to set forth "the general heads, the sense and scope of the prayers, and other parts of public worship" and to secure "consent of all the churches in those things that contain the substance of the service and worship of God."[30] The actual content of public worship was left to ministers, with the charge that "each one, by meditation, by taking heed to himself, and the flock of God committed to him, and by wise observing the ways of Divine Providence, may be careful to furnish his heart and tongue with further or other materials of prayer and exhortation, as shall be needful upon all occasions."[31]

The contents of the directory make fascinating reading for students of Reformed liturgy and preaching.[32] The order for worship is basically Calvin's, simplified in the manner of Knox. The directions for stated prayers and the sacraments provide a helpful exposition of relevant passages in the Westminster Confession and Catechisms. A careful study of the directory would go far toward improving the conduct of public worship in many Reformed and Presbyterian churches today.

Even so, the directory introduced a negative factor into Presbyterian worship, a process of liturgical attrition that would intensify in later generations. Presbyterian worship was reduced over time to a long prayer, a longer sermon, the singing of a psalm or two, and a benediction. A number of things provided for in the directory passed out of use, including the recitation of the Lord's Prayer and the Apostles' Creed. Since everything depended on the ability and inclinations of the ministers, and ministers stayed in their charges for decades, congregations were captive to the habits of their pastors, for better or worse.

The importance attached to preaching in Presbyterian worship led over time to a relative devaluing of the other parts of the service. In 1849, Princeton's Samuel Miller called attention to this swing of the pendulum in reaction to Rome's emphasis on liturgy at the expense of preaching. In his *Thoughts on Public Prayer*, Miller wrote:

> Yet, while we censure Romanists and others, for undervaluing preaching, we must not excuse Presbyterians if they sometimes appear to undervalue public prayer; and to be less concerned than they ought to be, to secure its rightful and edifying performance. Nothing is more certain than there is sometimes an appearance of this. It would be difficult to estimate the amount that has been written . . . concerning the composition of sermons. . . . But how much less of the nature of counsel seems to have been given to candidates for the holy ministry, to aid them in the acceptable performance of public prayer! And how much less attention seems to be bestowed on the part of those candidates on this whole subject! . . . Whether this has arisen from an impression that public prayer was a matter of comparatively small importance; or from a notion that it may safely be left, by its nature to take care of itself; or from a morbid desire to recede as far as possible from giving any countenance to prescribed forms, it is not necessary to decide. Whatever may have been the reason, it is doubtless an erroneous one.[33]

The same could be said of congregational singing. Few tunes were in use; for a long time in Scotland, there were only twelve tunes, and rare was the congregation that made use of all of these. Bad habits of singing and emergency measures such as "lining" the psalms[34] became fixed as the usages of orthodox piety. Presbyterians seemed to cultivate a negative aesthetic of liturgical indifference, to distinguish their worship from the despised elegance of the Roman or Anglican rites. The editors of the *Bay Psalm Book* famously remarked, "If therefore the verses are not always so smooth or elegant as some may desire or expect, let them consider that God's Altar needs not our polishings."[35]

WINDS OF CHANGE

The influence of the Westminster Directory extended to North America as British Colonies were planted there. Anglicans brought their Prayer Book, but New England's Puritans and the Presbyterians in other Colonies would have nothing to do with it. They adhered steadfastly to the way of worship they had followed in the mother country, as English Nonconformists or Scottish Presbyterians, until winds of change began to blow.

The first great challenge to the Directory came from eighteenth-century Methodism and the Great Awakening. A piety of emotion and sudden conversion collided with a piety of doctrine, nurture, and order. The worship of Presbyterian churches suddenly seemed cold and confining. The familiar words of the Scottish Psalter seemed antique and remote compared with the hymns of Isaac Watts and Charles Wesley. The revival fueled a growing dissatisfaction with inherited forms and customs. But what should take their place?

In the nineteenth century, Presbyterians were drawn in two directions. First, there was a move toward greater freedom and innovation, driven by the influence of revivalism. Metrical psalmody gave way to "imitations" of psalms and the hymns of Watts. Choirs and musical instruments were introduced, not without significant opposition, in the middle decades of the 1800s. In the wake of D. L. Moody's campaigns, the gospel hymns of Ira Sankey, Fanny Crosby, and others found their way into Presbyterian worship.

Second, near the end of the nineteenth century, some Presbyterians began to promote a greater degree of ceremonialism in worship, inspired in part by the Romantic or Victorian hunger for medievalism of all kinds, monumentalized in Gothic church architecture. A. A. Hodge published a new service book, *Manual of Forms*, in 1877,[36] the first to appear since the Directory. An era of experimentation and eclecticism set in, which only intensified in the twentieth century. Bits of Anglican liturgy were borrowed to dress up Presbyterian worship with chants and responsive readings. Numerous feast days and holy seasons reappeared on the church's calendar, as well as such secular or civic observances as Mother's Day and the Fourth of July. At the same time, Presbyterians embraced the latest styles and methods of American evangelicalism. On any given Sabbath, a Presbyterian church could be as formal as the Episcopalians in the morning and as free as the Baptists at night.

Change seemed to run amok in the mid- to late twentieth century when Pentecostal worship penetrated the mainline churches in the wake of the charismatic renewal. Hymnody and organ music gave way to the singing of choruses, lifting of hands, shaking of tambourines, strumming of guitars, and beating of drums. Preaching steadily declined in biblical fidelity, doctrinal content, the amount of time devoted to it, and occasions for hearing it. In the 1960s, many questioned whether there was any place left for preaching in the modern context. An age of worship wars commenced and continues today.

Presbyterianism thus finds itself alienated from much of its Reformation heritage of worship. So-called traditionalists contend for the innovations of the nineteenth and early twentieth centuries, with ever-diminishing success against the advocates of contemporary worship. Many theologically conservative Presbyterian churches are content to worship in a manner at variance with their own doctrinal standards, whether it be traditional, contemporary, or blended.

Is there a way out of this chaos? We can be thankful that the Reformers and their heirs left us substantial help in the form of their stated principles, their writings, and their liturgical forms and directories. Those who are taking a renewed interest in the beliefs and writings of Calvin, Knox, and the Westminster divines may likewise profit from the rediscovery of how these fathers in the faith worshiped, and why.

DISCUSSION QUESTIONS

1. How did Calvin order the worship service in Geneva?

2. What role did the sacraments of baptism and the Lord's Supper play in worship in Geneva?

3. Why did Calvin promote the singing of psalms in corporate worship?

4. What did John Knox contribute to the Calvinistic understanding of worship?

5. What is the importance of the Westminster Standards in the development of the Reformed understanding of worship?

6. How should we respond to current views on worship? Why?

NOTES

1 *Westminster Confession of Faith* (Glasgow: Free Presbyterian Publications, 1994), 90 (ch. 21, sec. 1).

2 John Calvin, *Treatises on the Sacraments*, in *Tracts by John Calvin*, trans. Henry Beveridge (Grand Rapids: Reformation Heritage Books, 2002), 2:100–122.

3 Ibid., 2:81–94.

4 John Calvin, "The Gospel according to St. John, 1–10," *Calvin's New Testament Commentaries*, trans. T. H. L. Parker (Grand Rapids: Eerdmans, 1959), 99.

5 Calvin, *Treatises on the Sacraments*, in *Tracts by John Calvin*, 2:121–122.

6 A part of the Roman Mass in which the priest says, "Lift up your hearts," and the people respond, "We lift them up to the Lord."

7 Calvin, *Treatises on the Sacraments*, in *Tracts by John Calvin*, 2:83.

8 Ibid., 2:119.

9 Ibid., 2:93.

10 Ibid., 2:122.

11 Ibid., 2:119.

12 Ibid., 2:120.

13 John Calvin, "The Author's Preface," *Commentary on the Book of Psalms*, trans. James Anderson (Edinburgh: Calvin Translation Society, 1845; repr. Grand Rapids: Baker, 2003), 1:xxxvi–xxxvii.

14 John Calvin, *Treatises on the Sacraments*, in *Tracts by John Calvin*, 2:118.

15 Ibid., 2:100.

16 Ibid., 2:101.

17 Ibid., 2:106.

18 As a theologian, England's Thomas Cranmer was certainly a Calvinist. Liturgically, however, he chose to follow Luther rather than Calvin, and was content to revise the Roman Mass into something more amenable to the Protestant faith.

19 William D. Maxwell, *John Knox's Genevan Service Book, 1556, The Liturgical Portions of the Genevan Service Book used by John Knox while a Minister of the English Congregation of Marian Exiles at Geneva, 1556–1559* (Edinburgh: Oliver and Boyd, 1931), 3.

20 Ibid., 7.

21 See facsimile of the title page, ibid., 81.

22 Charles W. Baird, *The Presbyterian Liturgies: Historical Sketches* (Grand Rapids: Baker, 1957), 116–128.

23 The writer apologizes to learned colleagues for the grossly oversimplified account of seventeenth-century British history inserted here. It is impossible in a few paragraphs to do justice to that long and eventful period, the ebb and flow of the respective fortunes of Parliament and the Stuart kings, and the contending and sufferings of Scotland's Covenanters and England's Puritans.

24 The text of the Solemn League and Covenant appears in full, *inter alia*, in *Westminster Confession of Faith* (Glasgow: Free Presbyterian Publications, 1958), 355–360.

25 With the exception of Rous's version of the Psalms, all these documents appear in their original form in *Westminster Confession of Faith* (Glasgow: Free Presbyterian Publications, 1958). Regarding the Directory for the Public Worship of God, readers should be aware that many Presbyterian denominational constitutions include liturgical directories with the same title or a similar one, but with great alteration in the contents.

26 The Genevan Psalter was reproduced in many of the languages of Europe, wherever Calvinism took root, Britain excepted; the Scottish Psalter was carried to every part of the English-speaking world and was the common version for Presbyterians in North America until the 1870s.

27 Preface to the Directory for the Public Worship of God, in *Westminster Confession of Faith*, 373.

28 Ibid., 374.

29 Compare, for example, the "Form for the Administration of Baptism" from the Liturgy of the Reformed Churches in The Netherlands with the section in the Directory titled "Of the Administration of the Sacraments, and First, of Baptism."

30 Preface to the Directory for the Public Worship of God, in *Westminster Confession of Faith*, 374.

31 Ibid.

32 "[The Directory] contains perhaps the finest brief description of expository preaching to be found in the English language," according to Sinclair B. Ferguson (*Dictionary of Scottish Church History and Theology* [Downers Grove, Ill.: InterVarsity, 1993], 864).

33 Samuel Miller, *Thoughts on Public Prayer* (Philadelphia: Presbyterian Board of Publications, 1849), 15–16.

34 "Lining" the psalms was a concession to illiterate people in the congregation. The precentor would read the text of the psalm one line at a time, then the people would repeat it in song.

35 "The Preface," *The Whole Booke of Psalmes Faithfully Translated into English Metre* (1640; repr. Salem, Mass.: New England & Virginia Company, n.d.).

36 Archibald A. Hodge, *Manual of Forms for Baptism, Admission to the Communion, Administration of the Lord's Supper, Marriage and Funerals, Ordination of Elders and Deacons, etc., Conformed to the Doctrine and Discipline of the Presbyterian Church* (Philadelphia: Presbyterian Board of Publication, 1882).

CHAPTER 18

ROOTS OF
REFORMED PREACHING

Robert Oliver

Calvin preached from the Bible every day, and under the power of that preaching the city began to be transformed. As the people of Geneva acquired knowledge of God's Word and were changed by it, the city became, as John Knox called it later, a New Jerusalem from which the gospel spread to the rest of Europe, England, and the New World.[1]

—JAMES MONTGOMERY BOICE

*P*rotestantism was dominant in England when Queen Elizabeth I died in 1603. The great shift from Roman Catholicism to Reformed Protestantism had not come primarily because of the legislation of Elizabeth's Parliaments, although that may have prepared the way. The change had been brought about by a new knowledge of and love for Scripture among the people, which prompted a resolve to implement the gospel in the home, at work, and in the church. And that knowledge and love for Scripture among the people had been born out of similar feelings among the clergy, who gave the Word of God to the people in the form of preaching.

Elizabeth was nervous about these tendencies. A skillful politician, she prevented alterations to the structure and discipline of the Church of England, but she could not legislate the thinking of a growing number of her subjects. Religious changes in Tudor times had always depended on the initiative of the sovereign, but now there was a new understanding. This understanding would not come to full expression until the following century, but the seeds were sown under Elizabeth. According to the nineteenth-century English historian John Richard Green, between the middle of Elizabeth's reign and the 1640s, "England became the people of the book and that book was the Bible."[2]

It was the Puritans in the pulpits who drove this change. Elizabeth did not favor much preaching, but at the parish level, a number of able men were opening up the riches of Scripture to people who had never been so privileged. Professor A. G. Dickens writes:

> Throughout Elizabethan England Puritan preachers dominated the pulpits, even though many of them were intermittently engaged in disputes with their bishops. As their sermons show, their preaching ability and their numbers had no equivalent in pre-Reformation or mid-Tudor England. In England were Edward Dering and Henry Smith, at Norwich John More, in Suffolk John Knewstub, in Essex Richard Rogers, in Kent Dudley Fenner, in Sussex Thomas Underdown, in Leicestershire Anthony Gilby and Arthur Hildersham, in North Oxfordshire, John Dod, in Yorkshire Giles Wigginton, Edmund Bunney, John Favour and several others. And in Cambridge itself the young men could model their styles on the great master, William Perkins. These are merely a small selection from the more obvious names.[3]

Describing the ministry of Henry Smith in London, William Haller says, "The grocers, locksmiths and other virile illiterates, also the persons of quality, who flocked to St. Clement's to hear Smith, were, we must remember, the very men for whose attention Marlowe and Shakespeare were competing."[4]

This phenomenon was not confined to the capital. A few years later, George Walker (1581–1651) said that in his native Lancashire, where Roman Catholicism still had many adherents, many people "were ready and willing to run many miles to hear sermons when they have them not at home, and lay aside all care of profit, leaving their labour and work on weekdays to frequent public meetings for prophecy and expounding God's word."[5]

To trace the origins of this zeal for preaching, let us turn our attention to John Calvin in Geneva.

"THE MOST PERFECT SCHOOL OF CHRIST"

Against the claims of the Roman Catholic Church, the Reformers cited Scripture as their final authority. But Rome, which also claimed Scripture, declared that it had the *magisterium*, or sole right to interpret the Bible. To support that claim, she pointed to the multiplicity of interpretations that had arisen among Protestant groups. It was therefore critical for Reformed teachers to show that their explanations of the Word of God were supported by the text. The Bible demanded the highest standards of exposition, and its teaching had to be made plain to the people.

Calvin excelled in this practice. In his last address to the Senate of the Republic of Geneva, Calvin acknowledged his weaknesses and failures as a preacher, but "in regard to the doctrine which I have delivered in your hearing, I declare that the Word of God entrusted to me, I have taught, not rashly nor uncertainly, but purely and sincerely."[6]

Working from Scripture in the original languages, Calvin used his studies to fortify his lectures, which then became the basis of his commentaries. He treated Scripture with reverence, saying, "The truths of revelation are so high as to exceed our comprehension, but, at the same time, the Holy Spirit has accommodated them so far to our capacity, as to render all Scripture profitable for instruction."[7]

Calvin's objective was to present a clear, understandable explanation of the truth. "I do not love strained expositions,"[8] he wrote. His commentaries were models of brevity and lucidity. Other men, such as Philip Melanchthon, were called to produce works of great detail. Calvin did not criticize such approaches, but that was not his objective. He said of the work of an expositor: "It is almost his only task to unfold the mind of the writer whom he has undertaken to expound; he misses his mark or at least strays outside his limits, by the extent to which he leads his readers away from the meaning of the author."[9] For this reason, Calvin was impatient with those who sought hidden meanings in their exposition of Scripture: "Let us know, then, that the true meaning of Scripture is the natural and simple one . . . and let us embrace and hold it resolutely," he wrote. "Let us not merely neglect as doubtful, but boldly set aside as deadly corruptions, those pretended expositions which lead us away from the literal sense."[10]

T. H. L. Parker summarized Calvin's method of rigorous scholarship:

For Calvin, the historical document is of prime importance; it cannot be dispensed with; it cannot be left aside in favour of the substance that is extracted from it; in brief, it must never cease to be a historical document. But then this document is seen as addressed to all men of every age, to be for every age God's message, meaning life or death for every man. Nothing, therefore, could be of more concern than this document. It is not right to treat it as history unrelated to every generation.[11]

Calvin wrote his commentaries in Latin so that his work would be available to scholars across Europe. The earlier expositions were dictated to secretaries, but later ones are transcripts of lectures to students who were educated in Latin. His teaching quickly spread across the Continent.

Calvin was not just a scholar; he was also a preacher, and he took this calling seriously. For many years, he preached almost every day in French to the citizens of Geneva. He was systematic in this endeavor, too, working through books of the Old and New Testaments. Yet he was also convinced that sermons should not be lectures or running commentaries. So he kept close to his text, while allowing himself freedom in elaboration, explanation, and continuous application. He preached without notes to ensure lively contact with his audience. He believed that preaching must penetrate the conscience.

In 1548, Calvin wrote to Protector Somerset, regent for the young King Edward VI of England:

What I have thus suggested as to the manner of instruction, is only that the people be so taught as to be touched to the quick, and that they may feel that what the Apostle says is true (Heb. 4), that "the word of God is a two-edged sword, piercing even through the thoughts and affections to the very marrow of the bones". I speak thus, Monseigneur, because it appears to me that there is very little preaching of a lively kind in the kingdom, but that the greater part deliver it from a written discourse. I see very well the necessity which constrains you to that; for in the first place you have not as I believe, such well approved and competent pastors as you desire. Wherefore, you need forthwith to supply this want. Secondly, there may very likely be among them many flighty persons who would go beyond all bounds, sowing their own silly fancies, as so often happens on occasions of a change. But all these considerations ought not to hinder the ordinance of Jesus Christ from having free course in the preaching of the gospel. Now this preaching ought not to be lifeless, but lively, to teach, to exhort, to reprove, as Saint Paul says, speaking thereof to Timothy.[12]

The warmth and unction that pervade Calvin's printed sermons make them valuable even for today. One of the most encouraging trends of recent years has been the recovery and publication of Calvin's sermons. Introducing his translation of Calvin's sermons on 2 Samuel, Douglas Kelly wrote:

> Painstakingly careful and fair as he is to the historical context of the reigns of the judges and early kings of Israel, Calvin can never keep you long in the presence of Saul and Abner, Samuel and Jonathan, David and Bathsheba, Nathan and Solomon without introducing you to Another. If you will read these sermons prayerfully, Calvin will take your hand and place it in the hands of One whose Word and Spirit were already preparing his Old Testament saints to reach forward to him who held them and who holds us.[13]

By the mid-1550s, Geneva was becoming known as a center of Reformed biblical scholarship. It was a refuge for persecuted Protestants from across Europe, as well as a magnet for young men who wished to study under Calvin's supervision.

Meanwhile, in England, the Protestant King Edward VI died in 1553 and was succeeded by his Roman Catholic half sister, Mary. She came to the throne determined to wipe out Protestantism and to restore Roman Catholicism. Within two years, Parliament was persuaded to change the laws and bring back the old machinery for punishing the "heresy" of Protestantism. Foreseeing what would prove to be the most bitter persecution in English history, a number of prominent Protestants and students left England and took refuge in Protestant centers abroad, such as Geneva. There they experienced an orderly church life that aimed to reflect the teaching of the New Testament and the faithful and regular exposition of the Word of God. Among these refugees was John Knox, the Scottish Reformer who had been ministering for some years in England. Knox wrote of Geneva: "It is the most perfect school of Christ that ever was in the earth since the days of the apostles. In other places I confess Christ to be truly preached;

but manners and religion so sincerely reformed, I have not yet seen in any other place."[14]

An English congregation began meeting in Geneva in October 1554. Inspired to take the Reformation of the English church beyond the point it had reached in the reign of Edward VI, they produced a new service book that drew heavily from Calvin's Genevan liturgy. This group then produced a new translation of the New Testament, a confession of faith, and a metrical Psalter. Then came the greatest project of all, a new translation of the Scriptures: the Geneva Bible. Work began on this translation during the persecution of Protestants in England, but the Bible was not published until 1560, after Queen Mary was dead and Elizabeth was on the throne. William Whittingham, one of the exiles, stayed in Geneva to shepherd the translation through the press to publication.

The Geneva Bible was a breakthrough in Bible production. It was printed in Roman type instead of the old black-letter type. It was a portable quarto, not a folio. It was the first English Bible to be printed in verses for easy reference, and it included a concordance. Each book of the Bible was preceded by a summary and included detailed marginal notes. In short, it was a study Bible. It would remain the most popular version of the Scriptures for almost a century.

PURITAN EXPOSITION

Frustrated in their efforts to reform the Church of England, the Protestant exiles who returned to England after Queen Mary died soon turned their energies to preaching and teaching the Word. By the middle of Elizabeth's reign, they were influencing her subjects at every level of society. Through them, God blessed Calvin's methodology to change Protestantism across the Continent.

For example, the preacher Henry Smith, mentioned above, whose oratory gained him the nickname "silver-tongued Smith," graduated from Oxford, then studied under Richard Greenham of Dry Drayton in Cambridgeshire. From 1587 to 1590, Smith lectured at St. Clement Danes Church in London. His preaching was much like Calvin's in its flowing style. He did not work systematically through books of the Bible as Calvin had, but his sermons reveal careful exegesis. A sermon titled "The Banquet of Job's Children" does not assume knowledge of the book of Job but sketches the background in a few deft sentences. Like Calvin, Smith used running exegesis to explain how the feast of Job's children leads to a joyful appreciation of God's mercies. "To a good man, riches are good, honours are good, health is good, liberty is good because he doeth good with them; but to an evil man they are evil, because they make him worse, and he doeth evil with them,"[15] he says. Well aware that feasting and mirth can lead to spiritual carelessness, Smith commended Job's prayers and sacrifices for his children.

The year that Smith preached this sermon was not one for feasting, but for prayer and humiliation before God because the kingdom was in danger. Smith observes, "We see the Romans coming in again," which may refer to the threat of the Spanish Armada or, more likely, a warning against the increased activities of Roman Catholic seminary priests who became a growing menace in the 1580s. He goes on to say, "We see the papists carving of images and people kneeling before them." The whole sermon pulsates with the vitality of sixteenth-century London. One can hear the sounds of the citizens, and there in their midst is this eloquent Puritan preacher faithfully expounding and applying the Word of God.[16]

Puritan preaching later developed a more formal style, but it did not lose its emphasis on application to urgent matters of the day. Some ministers preached through entire books of the Bible, although their expositions were generally more detailed than Calvin's. These preachers were later Puritans, and they ministered to congregations that expected detailed exposition of the Word of God. Thomas Manton excelled as such a preacher. Thomas Goodwin opened up the epistle to the Ephesians in magnificent detail. The greatest work of this period surely was John Owen's *Commentary on the Epistle to the Hebrews*, published when Owen no longer had freedom to preach to a large congregation. Other preachers of this period, such as John Flavel, preached extended series on such themes as the person and work of Christ.

Later, the form of Puritan expositional preaching was to introduce a text with careful exegesis, identify its main doctrine, and then prove this doctrine with a series of subordinate propositions, each demanding careful exegesis. Puritan preachers took the authorship of the Holy Spirit seriously and believed that Scripture spoke with one voice. The immediate context thus had to harmonize with the wider context of Scripture, which was called "the analogy of faith" (*analogia fidei*). Finally, the text was applied to listeners in a series of "uses," which addressed various situations.

The form of preaching changed some over time, but the objective remained essentially the same. Owen titled a short treatise on the exposition of Scripture "Causes, Ways and Means of Understanding the Mind of God." Calvin would not have faulted that title. In handling his theme, Owen insisted that the expositor depends on the help of the Holy Spirit to enlighten his mind and to strengthen him for his responsibility. Likewise, Calvin, in commenting on Psalm 119:18, had written, "Having admitted that power to keep the law is imparted to men by God, he at the same time adds, that every man is blind until he also enlightens the eyes of his understanding."[17]

THE GENEVA BIBLE

The Bible translated by the exiles in Geneva played an important role in passing along Calvinist methods of exposition and laid a foundation for English and Scottish Puritanism. Scholars could read Calvin's Latin commentaries, but it was not until the 1570s that Arthur Golding's translations of Calvin's sermons began to appear. Several years before that time, the literate layperson was helped by the Geneva Bible, which made England "the land of the book."

William Tyndale had recognized that Bible readers needed help, so he had added prologues and notes to his translations. The authorities did not like this innovation; Henry VIII, who sanctioned the publication of the Bible in English, strictly forbade the inclusion of explanatory notes. Any explanation must be in the hands of the professionals, he decreed.

By contrast, the notes or aids that the exiles in Geneva offered with their Bible included maps and illustrations of the tabernacle and high priest's vesture, tables of chronology, meanings of words and alternative translations, the structure and contents of books and chapters, and statements of Reformed doctrine. The language was English but the expositor was Calvin. The Geneva Bible was an extraordinary version, described by Professor David Daniell as "a masterpiece of Renaissance scholarship and printing and Reformation Bible thoroughness."[18] Its reputation was unjustly blackened by the supporters of Archbishop Laud and their successors, but it was much loved by a growing body of Englishmen. Between 1560 and 1644, the Geneva Bible was published in some 140 editions, outdistancing any other version in that period, including the Authorized Version of 1611.

The Geneva Bible flourished in an age of growing literacy. Many farmers and merchants as well as members of the gentry could now carry God's Word to church. The parson had to develop a sermon well grounded in Scripture or he could be challenged by biblically literate hearers. The householder who responded to the preaching of the Puritans could gather his family and servants in order to read God's Word and explain it to them.

Hostility to the Geneva Bible was fueled by a growing body of ecclesiastics who were the sworn enemies of Puritanism. They found a ready ally in James I, upholder of the supposed divine right of kings, who was nervous about informed discussion of his policies. The Authorized Version of 1611 (commonly called the King James Bible) was the product of James's reign. The translators of the King James Bible retained a great deal of the Geneva text in their work, but the rules he approved for the translators stated, "No Marginal Notes at all to be affixed, but only for the Explanation of the *Hebrew* or *Greek* words, which cannot without some circumlocution so briefly and fitly be express'd in the text."[19]

The King James Version did not immediately end the dominance of the Geneva Bible. Puritans continued to prefer the Geneva Bible for a half-century longer; even Authorized Version translators such as Lancelot Andrewes continued to use and preach from the Geneva Bible. The Geneva Bible taught several generations of Englishmen not only to read the Bible but to exegete it and to listen to preaching with the noble spirit of the Bereans, who "received the word with all readiness of mind, and searched the scriptures daily, whether these things were so" (Acts 17:11). A succession of able ministers and alert listeners thus produced one of the most remarkable periods of Bible literacy and preaching in English history.

DISCUSSION QUESTIONS

1. How did Calvin regard preaching? Why?

2. Were the Puritans in agreement with Calvin about the importance of preaching? Why or why not?

3. What is the importance of the Geneva Bible?

NOTES

1   James Montgomery Boice, *Whatever Happened to the Gospel of Grace? Rediscovering the Doctrines that Shook the World* (Wheaton, Ill.: Crossway, 2001), 83–84.

2   John Richard Green, *A Short History of the English People* (London: Macmillan, 1909), 460.

3   A. G. Dickens, *The English Reformation* (London: Fontana, 1972), 428.

4   William Haller, *The Rise of Puritanism* (Philadelphia: University of Pennsylvania Press, 1984), 32.

5   Quoted in Leland Ryken, *Worldly Saints: The Puritans As They Really Were* (Grand Rapids: Zondervan, 1990), 94.

6   John Calvin, *Selected Works*, trans. Henry Beveridge (Grand Rapids: Baker, 1983), 1:xc.

7   Quoted in Graham Miller, *Calvin's Wisdom* (Edinburgh: Banner of Truth Trust, 1992), 19.

8   *Commentary* on Joel 2:23.

9   John Calvin, *The Epistles of Paul the Apostle to the Romans and to the Thessalonians*, trans. Ross Mackenzie (Edinburgh: Oliver and Boyd, 1961), 1.

10 John Calvin, *The Epistles of Paul the Apostle to the Galatians, Ephesians, Philippians and Colossians*, trans. T. H. L Parker (Edinburgh: Oliver and Boyd, 1965), 85.

11 T. H. L. Parker, *Calvin's New Testament Commentaries* (London: S. C. M. Press, 1971), 91.

12 Calvin, *Selected Works*, 5:190.

13 John Calvin, *Sermons on 2 Samuel, Chapters 1–13*, trans. Douglas Kelly (Edinburgh: Banner of Truth Trust, 1992), xv.

14 Quoted in W. Stanford Reid, *Trumpeter of God: A Biography of John Knox* (New York: Charles Scribner's Sons, 1974), 132.

15 Henry Smith, *The Sermons of Mr. Henry Smith* (London: William Tegg, 1866), 2:19.

16 Henry Smith, *The Works of Henry Smith* (Edinburgh: James Nichol, 1867), 2:3–13.

17 *Commentary* on Psalm 119:18.

18 David Daniell, *The Bible in English: Its History and Influence* (New Haven: Yale University Press, 2003), 291.

19 Ibid., 439.

CHAPTER 19

APPLYING THE WORD

From the manner in which our ministers entered upon the work, it is evident that it must have been the prominent object of their lives to convert men to God. They were remarkable for what was called experimental preaching. They told much of the exercises of the human soul under the influence of the truth of the gospel. The feeling of a sinner while under the convicting power of the truth; the various subterfuges to which he resorted when aware of his danger; the successive applications of truth by which he was driven out of all of them; the despair of the soul when it found itself wholly without a refuge; its final submission to God, and simple reliance on Christ; the joys of the new birth and the earnestness of the soul to introduce others to the happiness which it has now for the first time experienced; the trials of the soul when it found itself an object of reproach and persecution among those whom it loved best; the process of sanctification; the devices of Satan to lead us into sin; the mode in which the attacks of the adversary may be resisted; the danger of backsliding, with its evidences, and the means of recovery from it. . . . These remarks show the tendency of the class of preachers which seem now to be passing away.[1]

—FRANCIS WAYLAND

ntil the mid-nineteenth century, John Calvin and the Calvinists were often labeled "experimental" or "experiential." In particular, many Calvinistic ministers of the Word were called "experimental preachers." Such preaching lay at the heart of Calvinism, but this vital emphasis is now lost in many quarters; even modern-day Calvinists frequently ask what is meant by these terms.[2]

In this chapter, I will outline the definition of experiential Calvinistic preaching. There are two questions to be considered. First, what is Calvinistic

experiential preaching? Second, what are its essential characteristics? Throughout, I will emphasize how Calvinist preachers aim to apply the Word to their
hearers' hearts.

A DEFINITION OF EXPERIENTIAL PREACHING

The term *experimental* comes from the Latin *experimentum*, meaning "trial." It is
derived from the verb *experior*, meaning "to try, prove, or put to the test." That
verb also can mean "to find or know by experience," thus leading to the word
experientia, meaning "knowledge gained by experiment." Calvin used *experiential*
and *experimental* interchangeably, since both words in biblical preaching indicate the need for measuring experienced knowledge against the touchstone of
Scripture. Experiential preaching addresses the vital matter of how a Christian
experiences the truth of biblical, Calvinistic doctrine in his life.

Therefore, a working definition of experiential preaching might be: preaching that seeks to explain in terms of biblical, Calvinistic truth how matters ought
to go, how they do go, and the end goal of the Christian life. It aims to apply
divine truth to the whole range of the believer's personal experience, including
his relationships with his family, the church, and the world around him.[3] In other
words, it addresses the entire range of Christian living, focusing heavily on a
believer's spiritual well-being and maturity. With the Spirit's blessing, the mission
of such preaching is to transform the believer in all that he is and does to become
more and more like the Savior.

How different experiential preaching is from what we often hear today. The
Word of God too often is preached in a way that will not transform listeners
because it fails to discriminate and fails to apply. Such preaching is reduced to a
lecture, a demonstration, a catering to what people want to hear, or the kind of
subjectivism that is divorced from the foundation of Scripture. It fails to explain
biblically what the Reformers called vital religion: how a sinner must be stripped
of his self-righteousness, driven to Christ alone for salvation, and led to the joy
of simple reliance on Christ. It fails to show how a redeemed sinner encounters
the plague of indwelling sin, battles against backsliding, and gains victory by
faith in Christ.

But when God's Word is preached experientially, it is "the power of God
unto salvation" (Rom. 1:16) that transforms men and nations. Such preaching is

transforming because it accurately reflects the vital experience of the children of God (cf. Rom. 5:1–11), clearly explains the marks and fruits of the saving grace necessary for a believer (Matt. 5:3–12; Gal. 5:22–23), and sets before believer and unbeliever alike their eternal futures (Rev. 21:1–9).

CHARACTERISTICS OF EXPERIENTIAL CALVINISTIC PREACHING

There are ten marks that are typical of such experiential Calvinistic preaching:

1. *Experiential Calvinistic preaching is Word- and Christ-centered.* That is, it focuses on God's written Word, the Bible, and His living Word, Jesus Christ.

Biblical preaching flows out of the scriptural passage as it is expounded in accord with sound exegetical and hermeneutical principles. Jeremiah 3:15 says that God has given preachers to His people to "feed [them] with knowledge and understanding." Proper preaching does not add an experiential part to the text being preached. Rather, with the Spirit's light, it draws the true experience of believers from the text. The minister must bring the sincere milk of the Word in order that, by the Spirit's blessing, experiential preaching will foster true conviction of sin and true growth (John 16:7–8; 1 Peter 2:2; Rom. 10:14).

According to Isaiah 8:20, all of our beliefs, including our experiences, must be tested against Holy Scripture. That is really what the word *experimental* intends to convey. Just as a scientific experiment tests a hypothesis against a body of evidence, so experimental preaching examines experience in the light of the teaching of the Word of God.

While Calvinistic preaching is rooted in grammatical and historical exegesis, it also involves spiritual, practical, and experimental application. In 1 Corinthians 2:10–16, Paul says that good exegesis is spiritual. Since the Spirit always testifies of Jesus Christ, sound exegesis finds Christ not only in the new covenant, but also in the old. It was said in the ancient world that all roads led to Rome; so the preaching of all texts today must lead ultimately to Christ. Jesus Himself said, "Search the scriptures; for in them ye think ye have eternal life: and they are they which testify of me" (John 5:39). Likewise, when He spoke with His disciples following the resurrection, Jesus said, "These are the words which I spake unto you, while I was yet with you, that all things must be fulfilled, which were written in the law of Moses, and in the prophets, and in the psalms, concerning me" (Luke 24:44–45).

The great theme and controlling contour of experiential preaching is Jesus Christ, for He is the supreme focus, prism, and goal of God's revelation. Therefore, a true Calvinistic preacher must be "determined not to know any thing . . . save Jesus Christ, and him crucified" (1 Cor. 2:2). William Perkins, one of the fathers of Calvinistic Puritanism, says that the heart of all preaching is "to preach one Christ, by Christ, to the praise of Christ."[4] The New England divine Cotton Mather puts it this way: "Exhibit as much as you can of a glorious Christ. Yea, let the motto upon your whole ministry be: *Christ is all.* Let others develop the pulpit fads that come and go. Let us specialize in preaching our Lord Jesus Christ."[5]

Consequently, Christ must be the beginning, middle, and end of every sermon (Luke 24:27; 1 John 1:1–4). Preaching must exalt Christ for awakening, justifying, sanctifying, and comforting sinners (Eph. 5:14; 1 Cor. 1:30; Isa. 61:2). As John says, "In him was life; and the life was the light of men. . . . The Word was made flesh, and dwelt among us, (and we beheld his glory, the glory as of the only begotten of the Father), full of grace and truth" (John 1:4, 14; cf. Ps. 36:9; 119:130).

Exegesis offers sound analysis of the words, grammar, syntax, and historical setting of Scripture. Experiential preaching does not minimize these aspects of interpretation, but neither is it content with them. A minister who presents only the grammatical and historical meaning of God's Word may be lecturing or discoursing, but he is not preaching. The Word must be applied spiritually. Spiritual exegesis is thus christological, and, through Christ, it will be theological, bringing all glory to the triune God.

Experiential Calvinistic preaching, then, teaches that the Christian faith must be experienced, tasted, and lived through the saving power of the Holy Spirit. It stresses the knowledge of scriptural truth, which is able to make us wise unto salvation through faith in Christ (2 Tim. 3:15). Specifically, such preaching teaches that Christ, the living Word (John 1:1) and the very embodiment of the truth, must be experientially known and embraced. It proclaims the need for sinners to experience who God is in His Son. As John 17:3 says, "And this is life eternal, that they might know thee the only true God, and Jesus Christ, whom thou hast sent." The word *know* in this text, as well as in other biblical usages, does not indicate casual acquaintance, but a deep, abiding relationship. For example, Genesis 4:1 uses the word *know* to suggest marital intimacy: "And Adam knew Eve his wife;

and she conceived, and bare Cain." Experiential preaching stresses the intimate, personal knowledge of God in Christ.

Centering on the written Word and the living Word preserves experiential preaching from unbiblical mysticism. Mysticism separates experience from the Word of God, whereas historic Reformed conviction demands Word-centered, God-glorifying, Christ-exalting, Spirit-worked, experiential Christianity. That kind of preaching is essential to the health and prosperity of the church.

Such preaching is liberating—not only for the congregation but also for the preacher. How freeing and reassuring it is for ministers to know that what God blesses in the ministry is not their ingenuity, intellect, insight, or persuasiveness— though all of these gifts must be used in dependence on the Holy Spirit. Rather, God blesses the proclamation of His Son in His own Word to His glory and the salvation of sinners. Calvinistic ministers believe that they are but ambassadors of Christ, called to declare what God has given them to declare. That is where they cast their anchors as they bring their congregations the Word of the living God week after week, in season and out of season (2 Tim. 4:2).

2. *Experiential Calvinistic preaching is applicatory.* The English word *application* comes from two Latin words, *ap* meaning "to" and *plico* meaning "fold." Application thus involves joining something to something else. Applicatory preaching is the process of riveting truth so powerfully in people that they cannot help but see how they must change and how they can be empowered to do so.

Applicatory preaching matches the text to every aspect of a listener's life, promoting, by the grace of the Spirit, a religion that is power and not mere form (2 Tim. 3:5). Robert Burns defines such religion as "Christianity brought home to men's business and bosoms." He goes on to say that the principle on which it rests is that "Christianity should not only be known, and understood, and believed, but also felt, and enjoyed, and practically applied."[6]

Such searching and particular application is the secret of powerful experiential preaching. Paul was never content merely to declare the truth, but he could write the Thessalonians that his "gospel came not unto you in word only, but also in power, and in the Holy Ghost, and in much assurance" (1 Thess. 1:4–5). To use Richard Baxter's language, Paul wanted to screw the truth into the hearts and minds of men and women. Baxter writes, "It would grieve one to the heart to hear what excellent doctrine some ministers have in hand, while yet they let it die in their hands for want of close [searching] and lively [living] application."[7]

If only it could be said of more ministers' preaching today what has been said of Jonathan Edwards' preaching: all his doctrine was application and all his application was doctrine.

Applicatory preaching must target the spiritual maturity and condition of the preacher's audience. Archibald Alexander writes: "The word of God should be so handled, that it may be adapted to Christians in different states and stages of the divine life; for while some Christians are like 'strong men,' others are but 'babes in Christ, who must be fed with milk, and not with strong meat.'"[8] Alexander goes on to explain how the Calvinistic preacher also should rightly divide the Word by making specific applications to the backsliding, the worldly minded, the afflicted, and the dying believer.[9]

Even a cursory look at Jesus' Sermon on the Mount, apostolic preaching in the Acts of the Apostles, and the great preaching of ages past by men such as Calvin or Edwards shows that good preaching is rich with application. A sermon that lacks application may be good teaching, but it is not preaching. Charles H. Spurgeon exaggerates only slightly when he says, "Where the application begins, there the sermon begins."

The best preachers in the Bible and from church history included application *throughout* their sermons, not only when concluding. Charles Bridges writes:

> The method of perpetual application, where the subject will admit of it, is probably best calculated for effect—applying each head distinctly; and addressing separate classes [or groups] at the close with suitable exhortation, warning, or encouragement. The Epistle to the Hebrews [itself a series of sermons] is a complete model of this scheme. Argumentative throughout, connected in its train of reasoning, and logical in its deductions—each successive link is interrupted by some personal and forcible conviction; while the continuity of the chain is preserved entire to the end.[10]

The Puritan preachers, who learned from the Reformers, were masters of the art of application. This art is beautifully summarized in a short chapter titled "Of the Preaching of the Word" in the Directory for the Public Worship of God, composed by the Calvinistic and Puritan Westminster divines:

He [the preacher] is not to rest in general doctrine, although never so much cleared and confirmed, but to bring it home to special use, by application to his hearers: which albeit it prove a work of great difficulty to himself, requiring much prudence, zeal, and meditation, and to the natural and corrupt man will be very unpleasant; yet he is to endeavour to perform it in such a manner, that his auditors may feel the word of God to be quick and powerful, and a discerner of the thoughts and intents of the heart; and that, if any unbeliever or ignorant person be present, he may have the secrets of his heart made manifest, and give glory to God.[11]

The Westminster divines identified six kinds of application:
- *Instruction*: doctrinal application.
- *Confutation*: refuting contemporary error.
- *Exhortation*: pressing and admonishing the sheep to obey the imperatives and duties set forth in the text being preached, as well as expounding "the means that help to the performance of them."
- *Dehortation*: rebuking sin, stirring up conviction of its heinousness and hatred for it, as well as declaring its dread consequences and showing how to avoid it.
- *Comfort*: encouraging believers to press on in the good fight of faith, despite various troubles and afflictions.
- *Trial*: preaching standards and marks of grace for purposes of self-examination and correction so as to stir up believers to do their duty, to be humbled by their sin, and to be strengthened with comfort, according to their spiritual condition.[12]

To this list we might add *doxological application*, or preaching and applying those truths of Scripture that bring people to sense the beauty and glory of God and His truth, and move them to praise Him as He has revealed Himself in Scripture. This kind of preaching lifts up our hearts and affections to end in the beauty, glory, and love of the triune God in and through Jesus Christ our Lord.[13]

Finally, it needs to be said that applicatory preaching is often costly preaching. As has often been said, when John the Baptist preached *generally*, Herod heard him gladly. But when John applied his preaching *particularly*, he lost his head. Both internally in a preacher's own conscience, as well as in the consciences of his people, a fearless application of God's truth will cost a price. And yet, how needful such preaching is. One day, every preacher will stand before God's judgment seat to give an account of how he handled God's Word among the flock of sheep entrusted to him. Woe be to that preacher who has not striven to bring home the Word of God to the souls and consciences of his hearers.

Preachers, I urge you to remember that we are not to speak *before* people but *to* people. Application is not only critical; it is the main thing to be done. And those who fear God will want God's Word personally administered to them. Daniel Webster said, "When I attend upon the teachings of the gospel, I wish to have it made a personal matter—*a personal matter—a personal matter.*"[14]

3. *Experiential Calvinistic preaching is discriminatory.* It clearly defines the difference between a Christian and non-Christian, opening the kingdom of heaven to one and shutting it against the other.

The Heidelberg Catechism calls preaching and Christian discipline the keys of the kingdom of heaven. Referencing Matthew 16:19, it says that "by these two, the kingdom of heaven is opened to believers and shut against unbelievers." If preaching does not discriminate, it is not the kingdom work for which Christ commissioned His apostles and servants.

Discriminatory preaching, then, opens the kingdom of heaven by offering the forgiveness of sins and eternal life to all who embrace Christ as Savior and Lord by true faith, but it also shuts the kingdom of heaven by proclaiming the wrath of God and His eternal condemnation upon those who are unbelieving, unrepentant, and unconverted. Such preaching teaches that our religion must result in a personal, experienced relationship with Jesus Christ. If our religion is not experiential, we will perish—not because experience itself saves, but because the Christ who saves sinners must be experienced personally as the foundation upon which the house of our eternal hope is built (Matt. 7:22–27; 1 Cor. 1:30; 2:2).

Jesus shows us how to preach discriminatorily in the Sermon on the Mount. He begins the sermon by describing the true citizens of the kingdom of heaven through the Beatitudes, which also are a beautiful summary of Christian experience. The first three beatitudes (blessings on those who are poor in spirit, those who mourn, and the meek) focus on the inward disposition of the believer; the fourth (those who hunger and thirst after righteousness) reveals the heartbeat of experiential faith; and the last four (those who are merciful, pure in heart, peacemakers, and persecuted) show faith in the midst of the world. The Beatitudes thus reveal the marks of genuine piety. The remainder of Jesus' sermon shows the fruits of grace in a believer's life.

Bridges presents three aspects of discriminatory preaching. First, preaching must distinctly "trace the line of demarcation *between the Church and the world*," he says. Ministers must bear in mind that there are fundamentally two kinds of hearers before them—the saved and the unsaved. Bridges stresses the biblical support for this division:

> They are described by *their state before God*, as righteous or wicked (Prov. 14:32; Mal. 3:18)—by *their knowledge or ignorance of the Gospel*, as spiritual or natural men (1 Cor. 2:14–15)—by *their special regard to Christ*, as believers or unbelievers (Mark 16:16; John 3:18, 36)—by *their interest in the Spirit of God*, "being in the Spirit, or having not the Spirit of Christ" (Rom. 8:9)—by *their habits of life*, "walking after and minding, the things of the Spirit, or the things of the flesh" (Rom. 8:1, 5)—by their respective *rules of conduct*, the word of God, or "the course of this world" (Ps. 119:105; Eph. 2:2)—by *the Masters whom they respectively obey*, the servants of God, or the servants of Satan (Rom. 6:16)—by *the road in which they travel*, the narrow way or the broad road (Matt. 7:13–14)—by *the ends to which their roads are carrying them*, life or death—heaven or hell (Rom. 8:13; Matt. 25:46).[15]

Second, preachers must identify the line that separates the false professor or hypocrite from the true believer. Jesus Himself draws that line sharply when He speaks of those who claim to belong to His professing church and cry, "Lord, Lord, have we not prophesied in thy name? . . . and in thy name done many wonderful works?" only to hear His response: "I never knew you: depart from me, ye that work iniquity" (Matt. 7:22–23).

Of this second line of discrimination, Bridges writes: "Every part of the Christian character has its counterfeit. How easily are the delusions of fancy or feeling mistaken for the impressions of grace. The genuineness of the work of God must be estimated, not by the extent, but by the influence, of Scriptural knowledge—not by a fluency of gifts, but by their exercise in connexion with holiness and love."[16] David Brainerd puts it this way: "*Labour to distinguish clearly*, upon experiences and affections in religion, that you may make a difference between the gold and the shining dross. I say, labour here, if ever *you would be an useful Minister of Christ.*"[17]

Ministers need to help their hearers rightly examine themselves. Second Corinthians 13:5a says, "Examine yourselves, whether ye be in the faith; prove your own selves." Pastors must not assume or presume that all churchgoers, including children, are saved; and they are to avoid presumed church "unregeneration," as if only a few who have professed faith in Christ are truly saved. Rather, preachers are to present repeatedly before their people the biblical marks of those who have been born again and have come to Christ by way of saving faith and genuine repentance.

Third, Bridges says, preachers "must also regard *the different individualities of profession within the Church.*"[18] Like Jesus, preachers must distinguish between the blade, the ear, and the full corn in the ear (Mark 4:28). Like Paul, they must differentiate between babes and adults in grace (1 Cor. 3:1). Like John, they must preach to various believers as little children, young men, and fathers in grace (1 John 2:12–14).

Alexander makes the case for discriminatory preaching. He writes: "The promises and threatenings contained in the Scriptures [must] be applied to the characters to which they properly belong. How often do we hear a preacher expatiating on the rich consolations of the exceeding great and precious promises of God, when no mortal can tell, from anything which he says, to whom they are applicable. In much of preaching, there is a vague and indiscriminate application of the special promises of the covenant of grace, as though all who heard them were true Christians, and had a claim to the comfort which they offer." After concluding that, in true preaching, "the saint and the sinner are clearly distinguished by decisive scripture marks, so that every one may have a fair opportunity of ascertaining to which class he belongs, and what prospects lies before him," Alexander goes on to lament:

> It is much to be regretted that this accurate discrimination in preaching has gone so much out of use in our times. It is but seldom that we hear a discourse from the pulpit which is calculated to afford much aid to Christians in ascertaining their own true character; of which will serve to detect the hypocrite and formalist, and drive them from all their false refuges. In the best days of the reformed churches, such discriminating delineation of char-

acter, by the light of Scripture, formed an important part of almost every sermon. But we are now more attentive to the rules of rhetoric than to the marks of true religion. How do Owen, Flavel, Boston, and Erskine abound in marks of distinction between the true and false professor? And the most distinguished preachers of our own country,—the Mathers, Shepards, Stoddards, Edwardses, as also the Blairs, Tennents, Davies, and Dickinsons, were wise in so dividing the word of truth, that all might receive their portion in due season.[19]

In short, discriminatory preaching must remain faithful to God's Word. Grace is to be offered indiscriminately to all (Matt. 13:24–30); however, the divine acts, marks, and fruits of grace that God works in His people must be explained to encourage the elect to know themselves aright and to uncover the false hopes of the hypocrite. As Bishop Joseph Hall says, "The minister must discern between his sheep and wolves; in his sheep, between the sound and unsound; in the unsound, between the weak and the tainted; in the tainted, between the nature, qualities, and degrees of the disease and infection; and to all these he must know to administer a word in season. He hath antidotes for all temptations, counsels for all doubts, evictions for all errors; for all languishings, encouragements."[20]

Hall concludes that it is difficult to decide "which we should guard most against, the infusion of a false peace, or the inflaming of the wounds which we ought to heal."[21] Little wonder, then, that Baxter warns preachers that when, as spiritual physicians, they apply the wrong spiritual medication to their parishioners, they can become murderers of souls, which has grave ramifications for eternity.[22] Preachers must be honest with every soul and strive to bring them and the touchstone of Holy Scripture together.

4. *Experiential Calvinistic preaching is both realistic and idealistic.* It is realistic because it explains how matters *actually* go in the lives of God's people (e.g., Rom. 7:14–25) and it is idealistic because it explains how matters *ought* to go in their lives (e.g., Rom. 8). Both are essential. Telling how matters go without indicating how they should go lulls the believer to cease from pressing forward to grow in the grace and knowledge of Christ (2 Peter 3:18). Only telling how matters should be rather than how they really are discourages the believer from being assured that the Lord has worked in his heart. He may fear that the marks and fruits of grace are too high for him to claim. The true believer thus needs to hear both. He must

be encouraged in spite of all his infirmities not to despair for Christ's sake (Heb. 4:15). He also must be warned against assuming that he has reached the end of his spiritual pilgrimage and be urged to "press toward the mark for the prize of the high calling of God in Christ Jesus" (Phil. 3:14).

Every Christian is a soldier. To win the war against evil, a believer must put on the whole armor of God (Eph. 6:10–18). Experiential preaching brings the believer to the battlefield, shows him how to fight, tells him how to win skirmishes, and reminds him of the victory that awaits him, for which God will receive the glory. "For of him, and through him, and to him, are all things: to whom be glory for ever. Amen" (Rom. 11:36).

5. *Experiential Calvinistic preaching stresses inward knowledge.* The old Calvinistic preachers were fond of stressing the difference between head knowledge and heart knowledge in Christian faith. Head knowledge is not enough for true religion; it also demands heart knowledge. Proverbs 4:23 says, "Keep thy heart with all diligence; for out of it are the issues of life." Romans 10:10a adds, "For with the heart man believeth unto righteousness."

Heart knowledge of God results from an experiential encounter with Christ through the wondrous work of the Spirit. Such knowledge transforms the heart and bears heavenly fruit. It causes the believer to savor the Lord and delight in Him (Job 34:9; Isa. 58:14). It drives him to taste and see that God in Christ loves lost, depraved, hell-worthy sinners (Ps. 34:8). It includes an appetite for God's truth. As Jeremiah says, "Thy words were found, and I did eat them; and thy word was unto me the joy and rejoicing of mine heart" (Jer. 15:16a). Heart knowledge feasts on God, His Word, His truth, and His Son (Ps. 144:15; 146:5).

Heart knowledge does not lack head knowledge, but head knowledge may lack heart knowledge (Rom. 10:8–21). Some people pursue religion as an objective study or to appease their consciences without ever allowing it to penetrate their hearts. They have never felt guilty and condemned before the holy justice of God. They have not experienced deliverance in Christ, so they are unaware of the kind of gratitude for such deliverance that masters a believer's soul, mind, and strength. By contrast, those who experience saving heart knowledge find sin such an unbearable burden that Christ is altogether necessary. The grace of deliverance through the Savior is then so overwhelming that their lives shine forth with gratitude.

6. *Experiential Calvinistic preaching is centered not on self but on the triune God and on other people.* Some people have accused the Puritans of being self-centered

in their passion for godly experience. But as J. I. Packer argues, the Puritans were not interested in tracing the experience of the Spirit's work in their souls to promote their own experience, but to be driven out of themselves into Christ, in whom they could then enter into fellowship with the triune God.[23] Thus, experiential preaching, being grounded in the Word of God, is first of all theocentric rather than anthropocentric.

However, experiential Calvinistic preaching also addresses the believer's relationship with others in the church and the world. If experiential preaching led me to examine only my experiences and my relationship with God, it would fall short of affecting my interactions with my family, church members, and society. It would be self-centered. Instead, true experiential preaching brings a believer into the realm of vital Christian experience, prompting a love for God and His glory, as well as a burning passion to declare that love to others around him. A believer so instructed cannot help but be evangelistic, since vital experience and a heart for missions are inseparable. He views every unconverted person as a mission field.

7. *Experiential Calvinistic preaching aims for balanced thinking.* It seeks biblical balance in every area, striving to proclaim the whole counsel of God. Balance is especially needed:

• *Between the objective and subjective dimensions of Christianity.* The objective is the food for the subjective; thus, the subjective is always rooted in the objective. For example, the Puritans stated that the primary ground of assurance is the promises of God, but those promises must become increasingly real to the believer through the subjective evidences of grace and the internal witness of the Holy Spirit. Without the Spirit's experiential application, the promises of God lead to self-deceit and carnal presumption. On the other hand, without the promises of God and the illumination of the Spirit, self-examination tends to introspection, bondage, and legalism. Objective and subjective Christianity must not be separated.

We must seek to live in a way that reveals Christ's internal presence based on His objective work of active and passive obedience. The gospel of Christ must be proclaimed as objective truth, but it also must be applied by the Holy Spirit and inwardly appropriated by faith. We therefore reject two kinds of religion: one that separates subjective experience from the objective Word, thereby leading to mysticism, and one that presumes salvation on the false grounds of historical or temporary faith.[24]

• *Between the sovereignty of God and the responsibility of man.* Nearly all of our Reformed forefathers stressed the twin biblical truths that God is fully sovereign and man is fully responsible. But how these truths can be resolved logically is beyond our finite minds.

When Spurgeon was asked how these grand biblical doctrines could be reconciled, he responded that he didn't know that friends needed reconciliation. However, he went on to compare these doctrines to the rails of a track upon which Christianity runs. Just as normal rails, which run parallel to each other, appear to merge in the distance, so the doctrines of God's sovereignty and man's responsibility, which seem separate in this life, will merge in eternity. Our task is not to force their merging in this life, but to keep them in balance and live accordingly. We must strive for experiential Christianity that does justice both to God's sovereignty and to our responsibility.

• *Between doctrinal, experiential, and practical Christianity.* Just as Reformed preachers taught that experiential preaching must offer a balance of doctrine and application, Christian living also involves more than experience. Biblical Christian living is grounded in sound doctrine (head), sound experience (heart), and sound practice (hands).

8. *Experiential Calvinistic preaching is sincerely earnest.* Such preaching strives to emulate Paul: "Therefore seeing we have this ministry, as we have received mercy, we faint not; but have renounced the hidden things of dishonesty, not walking in craftiness, nor handling the word of God deceitfully; but by manifestation of the truth commending ourselves to every man's conscience in the sight of God" (2 Cor. 4:1–2).

Earnest experiential preaching avoids all levity. Baxter writes: "Of all the preaching in the world, I hate that preaching which tends to make the hearers laugh, or to move their minds with tickling levity and affect them as stage plays used to, instead of affecting them with a holy reverence for the name of God."[25]

Rather, such earnest preaching aims to please God rather than men. God is its witness. All masks are stripped away; all flattery is abhorred. Here is Baxter again: "Oh sirs, how plainly, how closely, how earnestly should we deliver a message of such moment as ours. . . . In the name of God, brethren, labor to awaken your own hearts before you go into the pulpit that you may be fit to awaken the hearts of sinners. Remember, they must be awakened or damned. And a sleepy preacher will hardly awaken drowsy sinners. . . . Speak to your people as to men that must be awakened either here or in hell."[26]

9. *Experiential Calvinistic preaching coincides with holy living.* It is impossible to separate godly experiential living from true experiential ministry. The holiness of a minister's heart is not merely an ideal; it is absolutely necessary, both personally and for his calling as a minister of the gospel, if his experiential Calvinism is to be effective. Holiness of life must be his consuming passion.

The unique channels of experiential preaching are experiential preachers. An experiential Calvinistic preacher experiences keenly the solemnity of what Paul writes in 1 Thessalonians 2:4a: "But as we were allowed of God to be put in trust with the gospel, even so we speak." True ministers of the gospel speak as men approved by God to be entrusted with the gospel. God has tested their hearts and has found them to be fit vessels, sanctified by His grace to declare the riches of His grace.

How critical, then, is this question: what kind of men are approved by God and entrusted with the gospel as holy men of God? I will mention three characteristics:

First, they are men whose lives pulsate with the awakening power of the gospel, such that they are single-minded men who fear God rather than swivel-headed men who fear other people (1 Thess. 2:6). Fearing God, they esteem His smiles and frowns to be of greater weight and value than the smiles and frowns of men.

Second, they are men who manifestly love the people among whom they minister. Paul could say of himself to the Thessalonians, "So being affectionately desirous of you, we were willing to have imparted unto you, not the gospel of God only, but also our own souls, because ye were dear unto us" (1 Thess. 2:8). There is no aloofness in the experimental preacher, no ministerial distance from the people. Baxter writes: "The whole of our ministry must be carried on in a tender love to our people. . . . They should see that we care for no outward thing, neither wealth nor liberty nor honor nor life in comparison with their salvation."[27]

Third, they are men whose lives are manifesting growing experience. James Stalker writes: "A ministry of growing power must be one of growing experience. . . . Power for work like ours is only to be acquired in secret. . . . The hearers may not know why their minister with all his gifts does not make a religious impression on them. But it is because he is not himself a spiritual power."[28]

Scripture says there should be no disparity between the heart, character, and life of a man who is called to proclaim God's Word and the content of his message. Jesus condemned the Pharisees and scribes for not doing what they proclaimed. He faulted them for the difference between their words and deeds, between what they professionally declared and how they acted in their daily life. Professional clerics, more than anyone else, should consider the scathing words of Christ: "The scribes and the Pharisees sit in Moses' seat. All therefore whatsoever they bid you observe, that observe and do; but do not ye after their works: for they say, and do not" (Matt. 23:2–3). Ministers are called to be as experientially holy in their private relationships with God, in their role as husbands and fathers at home, and in their calling as shepherds among their people as they appear to be in the pulpit. There must be no disjunction between their calling and living, their confession and practice.

Scripture says there is a cause-and-effect relationship between the character of a man's life as a Christian and his fruitfulness as a minister (Matt. 7:17–20). A minister's work is usually blessed in proportion to the sanctification of his heart before God. Ministers therefore must seek grace to build the house of God with sound experiential preaching and doctrine, as well as with a sanctified life. Their preaching must shape their lives, and their lives must adorn their preaching. E. M. Bounds writes: "The preacher is more than the sermon. . . . All the preacher says is tinctured, impregnated by what the preacher is. . . . The sermon is forceful because the man is forceful. The sermon is holy because the man is holy. The sermon is full of divine unction because the man is full of divine unction. . . . The sermon cannot rise in its life-giving forces above the man."[29] John Boys summarizes all of this well when he quips, "He doth preach most who doth live best."[30]

Ministers must be what they preach, not only applying themselves to their texts but applying their texts to themselves. Their hearts must be transcripts of their sermons.[31] Otherwise, as John Owen warns, "If a man teach uprightly and walk crookedly, more will fall down in the night of his life than he built in the day of his doctrine."[32]

10. *Experiential Calvinistic preaching is marked by a prayerful dependence on the Holy Spirit.* Such preachers keenly feel their inability to preach rightly, to bring anyone to Christ, and to mature Christ's saints. They know they are totally dependent on the work of the Spirit to effect regeneration and conversion when, how, and in whom He will. They believe that the Spirit alone persuades sinners to

seek salvation, renews corrupt wills, and makes scriptural truths take root in stony hearts. As Thomas Watson writes, "Ministers knock at the door of men's hearts, the Spirit comes with a key and opens the door."[33]

Packer writes of man-made soul-winning: "All devices for exerting psychological pressure in order to precipitate 'decisions' must be eschewed, as being in truth presumptuous attempts to intrude into the province of the Holy Ghost." Such pressures may even be harmful, he goes on to say, for while they "may produce the outward form of 'decision,' they cannot bring about regeneration and a change of heart, and when the 'decisions' wear off those who registered them will be found 'gospel-hardened' and antagonistic." Packer concludes: "Evangelism must rather be conceived as a long-term enterprise of patient teaching and instruction, in which God's servants seek simply to be faithful in delivering the gospel message and applying it to human lives, and leave it to God's Spirit to draw men to faith through this message in his own way and at his own speed."[34]

This sense of dependency prompts experiential Calvinistic preachers to strive, albeit with many shortcomings, to bathe all their preaching in prayer. They aim to be "men of the closet" first of all. Baxter says: "Prayer must carry on our work as well as preaching; he preacheth not heartily to his people, that prayeth not earnestly for them. If we prevail not with God to give them faith and repentance, we shall never prevail with them to believe and repent."[35] And Robert Traill writes, "Many good sermons are lost for lack of much prayer in study."[36]

The well-known story of Puritan-minded Robert Murray M'Cheyne illustrates best what Traill means. An old sexton in M'Cheyne's church noticed the awe on the face of a visitor and invited him into the minister's study. "Tell me," said the visitor, "having sat under this godly man's ministry, what is the secret of his success?" The sexton told the visitor to sit at M'Cheyne's desk. Then he asked the man to put his hands on the desk. Then to put his face in his hands and weep. Next the two men walked into the church sanctuary and ascended to the pulpit. "Lean over the pulpit," the sexton said. "Now stretch out your hands and weep. Now you know the secret of M'Cheyne's ministry."

The church today desperately needs preachers whose private prayers season their pulpit messages, and who continually remind themselves that awakening, heart-engaging, life-transforming preaching does not lie in ministerial eloquence, passion, or powers of persuasion, but in the sovereign good pleasure of

---

God through the ministry of the Holy Spirit. Above all, let us pray unceasingly that God might provide seminaries and seminary teachers that model experiential religion and preaching, and that He will send forth into His white and ready fields thousands of such Spirit-dependent preachers to proclaim the unsearchable riches of Jesus Christ to needy sinners and to hungry saints all over the globe.

DISCUSSION QUESTIONS

1. What does the term *experiential* mean as it is used in this chapter?

2. What is the great theme of "experiential Calvinistic preaching"?

3. Why is the application of God's Word costly?

4. What does the term *discriminatory* mean?

5. How is genuine experiential Calvinistic preaching realistic and idealistic at the same time?

6. Why is balance so necessary in the life of the Christian?

7. How does experiential Calvinistic preaching encourage holiness?

8. Why is experiential Calvinistic preaching needed today?

Notes

1 Quoted in Iain Murray, *Revival and Revivalism* (Edinburgh: Banner of Truth Trust, 1994), 321–322.

2 For several thoughts in this chapter, I am indebted to an address by Ian Hamilton on "Experimental Preaching" at the 2004 Banner of Truth Conference in Grantham, Pa. Some parts are also revised from my "Reformed Experiential Preaching" in *Feed My Sheep: A Passionate Plea for Preaching* (Morgan, Pa.: Soli Deo Gloria, 2002), 94–128, and *Puritan Evangelism: A Biblical Approach* (Grand Rapids: Reformation Heritage Books, 2007).

3 Cf. Paul Helm, "Christian Experience," *Banner of Truth*, no. 139 (April 1975): 6.

4 William Perkins, *Works of William Perkins* (London: John Legatt, 1613), 2:762.

5 Cotton Mather, *Manuductio ad ministerium: Directions for a Candidate to the Ministry* (New York: AMS Press, 1978), 16.

6 Robert Burns, introduction to *Works of Thomas Halyburton* (London: Thomas Tegg, 1835), xiv–xv.

7 Richard Baxter, *The Reformed Pastor* (Edinburgh: Banner of Truth Trust, 1974), 147.

8 Archibald Alexander, in *The Princeton Pulpit*, ed. John T. Duffield (New York: Charles Scribner, 1852), 42.

9 Ibid., 42–45.

10 Charles Bridges, *The Christian Ministry* (London: Banner of Truth Trust, 2006), 275.

11 *Westminster Confession of Faith* (Glasgow: Free Presbyterian Publications, 1994), 380.

12 Ibid.

13 For this suggestion, I am indebted to a conversation with Dr. Joseph Pipa, president of Greenville Presbyterian Theological Seminary.

14 "Funeral of Mr. Webster," *The New York Daily Times*, Oct. 30, 1852.

15 Bridges, *The Christian Ministry*, 277.

16 Ibid., 278.

17 Quoted in Bridges, *The Christian Ministry*, 279–280.

18 Ibid., 279.

19 Alexander, in *The Princeton Pulpit*, 40–42.

20 Quoted in Bridges, *The Christian Ministry*, 279–280.

21 Ibid., 280.

22 Ibid.

23 Cf. J. I. Packer, *A Quest for Godliness: The Puritan Vision of the Christian Life* (Wheaton, Ill.: Crossway, 1990), 117–118, and "The Puritan Idea of Communion with God," in *Press Toward the Mark*, Puritan and Reformed Studies Conference, 1961 (London: n.p., 1962), 7.

24 Joel R. Beeke, *The Quest for Full Assurance: The Legacy of Calvin and His Successors* (Edinburgh: Banner of Truth Trust, 1999), 125, 130, 146.

25 Baxter, *The Reformed Pastor*, 119–120.

26 Ibid., 147, 148.

27 Ibid., 117.

28 James Stalker, *The Preacher and His Models* (New York: A. C. Armstrong & Son, 1891), 53, 55.

29 Edward M. Bounds, *Preacher and Prayer* (Chicago: Christian Witness Co., 1907), 8, 9.

30 John Boys, *The Works of John Boys: An Exposition of the Several Offices* (Morgan, Pa.: Soli Deo Gloria, 1997).

[31] Gardiner Spring, *The Power of the Pulpit* (Edinburgh: Banner of Truth Trust, 1986), 154.

[32] John Owen, *The Works of John Owen* (Edinburgh: Banner of Truth Trust, 1976), 13:21ff.

[33] Thomas Watson, *A Body of Divinity* (London: Banner of Truth Trust, 1967), 154.

[34] Packer, *A Quest for Godliness*, 163–164.

[35] Baxter, *The Reformed Pastor*, 122.

[36] Robert Traill, *Works of Robert Traill* (Edinburgh: Banner of Truth Trust, 1975), 1:246.

CHAPTER 20

CALVIN'S EVANGELISM

It ought to be the great object of our daily wishes, that God would collect churches for Himself from all the countries of the earth, that He would enlarge their numbers, enrich them with gifts, and establish a legitimate order among them.[1]

—JOHN CALVIN

One of the most common charges raised against Calvinism as a theological perspective is that it is not conducive to fueling a long-term passion for missions and evangelism. Views of John Calvin's attitude toward outreach have ranged from hearty to moderate support on the positive side[2] and from indifference to active opposition on the negative side.[3]

Some have argued that the very Roman Catholicism the Reformers opposed kept the evangelistic torch of Christianity burning via the powerful forces of the papacy, the monasteries, and the monarchs, while Calvin, the Reformers, and the Puritans who followed them tried to extinguish it.[4] But others assert that Calvin was largely responsible for relighting the torch of biblical evangelism during the Reformation,[5] claiming him as a theological father of the Reformed missionary movement.[6]

To assess Calvin's view of evangelism correctly, we first must understand what he himself had to say on the subject. We find scores of references to evangelism in Calvin's *Institutes of the Christian Religion*, commentaries, sermons, and letters. Second, we must look at the entire scope of Calvin's evangelism, in both his teaching and his practice. This includes Calvin's evangelistic work in his own flock, in Geneva, in greater Europe, and in mission opportunities overseas. As we shall see, Calvin was more of an evangelist than is commonly recognized.

CALVIN: TEACHER OF EVANGELISM

How was Calvin's teaching evangelistic? In what way did his instruction oblige believers to seek the conversion of all people, both within the church as well as outside it?

Along with other Reformers, Calvin taught evangelism in a general way by earnestly proclaiming the gospel and by reforming the church according to biblical requirements. More specifically, Calvin taught evangelism by focusing on the universality of Christ's kingdom and the responsibility of Christians to help extend that realm.

The universality of Christ's kingdom is an oft-repeated theme in Calvin's teaching.[7] Calvin says all three persons of the Trinity are involved in the spreading of the kingdom. The Father will show "not only in one corner, what true religion is . . . but he will send forth his voice to the extreme limits of the earth."[8] Jesus came "to extend his grace over all the world."[9] And the Holy Spirit descended to "reach all the ends and extremities of the world."[10] In short, innumerable offspring "who shall be spread over the whole earth" will be born to Christ.[11]

How will the triune God extend His kingdom throughout the world? Calvin's answer involves both God's sovereignty and our responsibility. The work of evangelism is God's work, not ours, but He uses us as His instruments, Calvin says. Citing the parable of the sower, Calvin explains that Christ sows the seed of life everywhere (Matt. 13:24–30), gathering His church not by human means but by heavenly power.[12] The gospel "does not fall from the clouds like rain," however; rather, it is "brought by the hands of men to where God has sent it."[13] Jesus teaches us that God "uses our work and summons us to be his instruments in cultivating his field."[14] The power to save rests with God, but He reveals His salvation through the preaching of the gospel.[15] God's evangelism causes our evangelism.[16] We are His co-workers, and He allows us to participate in "the honor of constituting his own Son governor over the whole world."[17]

Calvin taught that the ordinary method of "collecting a church" is by the outward voice of men, "for though God might bring each person to himself by a secret influence, yet he employs the agency of men, that he may awaken in them an anxiety about the salvation of each other."[18] He goes so far as to say, "Nothing retards so much the progress of Christ's kingdom as the paucity of ministers."[19] Still, no human effort has the final word. It is the Lord, says Calvin, who "causes the voice of the gospel to resound not only in one place, but far and wide through the whole world."[20]

This union of divine sovereignty and human responsibility in evangelism offers several lessons. First, as Reformed evangelists, we must pray daily for the extension of Christ's kingdom. As Calvin says, "We must daily desire that God gather churches unto himself from all parts of the earth."[21] Since it pleases God to use our prayers to accomplish His purposes, we must pray for the conversion of the heathen.[22] Second, we must not become discouraged at a lack of visible success in evangelistic effort, but pray on. "Our Lord exercises the faith of his children, in that he doth not out of hand perform the things which he has promised them. And this thing ought specially to be applied to the reign of our Lord Jesus Christ," Calvin writes. "If God pass over a day or a year [without giving fruit], it is not for us to give over, but we must in the meanwhile pray and not doubt but that he heareth our voice."[23] Third, we must work diligently for the extension of Christ's kingdom, knowing that our work will not be in vain. Our salvation obligates us to work for the salvation of others.[24] Moreover, it is not enough for every man to be busy with other ways of serving God. Calvin notes, "Our zeal must extend yet further to the drawing of other men." We must do everything we are capable of to draw all men on earth to God.[25]

There are many reasons why we must evangelize. Calvin offers the following:

• *God commands us to do so.* "We should remember that the gospel is preached not only by the command of Christ but at his urging and leading."[26]

• *We want to glorify God.* True Christians yearn to extend God's truth everywhere so that "God may be glorified."[27]

• *We want to please God.* Calvin writes, "It is a sacrifice well-pleasing to God to advance the spread of the gospel."[28]

• *We have a duty to God.* "It is very just that we should labor . . . to further the progress of the gospel," Calvin says.[29] He adds, "It is our duty to proclaim the goodness of God to every nation."[30]

• *We have a duty to our fellow sinners.* Our compassion should be intensified by knowing that "God cannot be sincerely called upon by others than those to whom, through the preaching of the gospel, his kindness and gentle dealings have become known."[31]

• *We are grateful to God.* We owe it to God to strive for the salvation of others; if we do not, we are behaving in a contradictory manner. Calvin says,

"Nothing could be more inconsistent concerning the nature of faith than that deadness which would lead a man to disregard his brethren, and to keep the light of knowledge . . . in his own breast."[32]

Calvin never assumed that the missionary task was completed by the apostles. His conviction that the Great Commission (Matt. 28:18–20) referred only to the apostolic ministry was motivated by his opposition to the Roman Catholic doctrine of apostolic succession. He wanted to show that the apostolate was a temporary, extraordinary office that terminated with the twelve apostles.[33] However, Calvin taught that the apostles only began to fulfill the church's call to spread the gospel.[34] He taught that every minister should be willing "to go a distance, in order to spread the doctrine of salvation in every part of the world."[35] Indeed, he said, every Christian should testify of God's grace by word and deed to those whom he or she meets.[36]

CALVIN: PRACTITIONER OF EVANGELISM

Calvin believed we must make full use of the opportunities God gives to evangelize. "When an opportunity for edification presents itself, we should realize that a door has been opened for us by the hand of God in order that we may introduce Christ into that place and we should not refuse to accept the generous invitation that God thus gives us," he writes.[37]

On the other hand, when opportunities are restricted and doors are closed to our witness, we should not persist in trying to do what cannot be done. Rather, we should pray and seek for other opportunities. "The door is shut when there is no hope of success. [Then] we have to go a different way rather than wear ourselves out in vain efforts to get through it," Calvin writes.[38] Difficulties in witnessing are not an excuse to stop trying, however. To those suffering severe restrictions and persecutions in France, Calvin wrote, "Let every one strive to attract and win over to Jesus Christ those whom he can."[39]

Calvin practiced evangelism in his own congregation, in his home city of Geneva, in Europe (particularly France), and overseas (particularly Brazil):

• *In the congregation.* For Calvin, evangelism involved presenting Christ so that people, by the power of the Spirit, might come to God in Christ, but it also involved presenting Christ so that the believer might serve Him as Lord in the fellowship of His church and in the world. Thus, evangelism centered on a continual, authoritative call to every gospel-hearer to exercise faith in the crucified and risen Christ. This summons was to a whole-life commitment. Calvin was an outstanding practitioner of this kind of evangelism within his own congregation.

His evangelism began with preaching. His intent in preaching was to evangelize as well as edify. William Bouwsma writes: "He preached regularly and often: on the Old Testament on weekdays at six in the morning (seven in winter), every other week; on the New Testament on Sunday mornings; and on the Psalms on Sunday afternoons. During his lifetime he preached, on this schedule, some 4,000 sermons after his return to Geneva: more than 170 sermons a year." Preaching was so important to Calvin that when he was reviewing the accomplishments of his lifetime on his deathbed, he mentioned his sermons ahead of his writings.[40] On average, he would preach on four or five verses in the Old Testament and two or three verses in the New Testament. He would consider a small portion of the text at a time, first explaining the text, then applying it to the lives of those in his congregation. Calvin's sermons were never short on application; rather, the application was often longer than the exposition in his sermons.

He was also succinct. Calvin's successor, Theodore Beza, said of the Reformer's preaching, "Every word weighed a pound."[41]

Calvin frequently instructed his congregation on how to listen to a sermon. He told them what to look for in preaching, in what spirit they should listen, and how they should listen. His goal was to help people participate in the sermon as much as they could so that it would feed their souls. Coming to a sermon, Calvin said, should include "willingness to obey God completely and with no reserve."[42] "We have not come to the preaching merely to hear what we do not know," Calvin added, "but to be incited to do our duty."[43]

Calvin also reached out to unsaved people through his preaching, impressing on them the necessity of faith in Christ and what that meant. Calvin made it clear that he did not believe everyone in his flock was saved. Though charitable toward church members who maintained a commendable, outward lifestyle, he also referred more than thirty times in his commentaries and repeatedly in his *Institutes* (nine times within 3.21 to 3.24) to the small numbers of those who received the preached Word with saving faith.[44] He writes, "For though all, without exception, to whom God's Word is preached, are taught, yet scarce one in ten so much as tastes it; yea, scarce one in a hundred profits to the extent of being enabled, thereby, to proceed in a right course to the end."[45]

For Calvin, the most important tasks of evangelism were building up the children of God in the faith, convicting unbelievers of the heinousness of sin, and directing them to Christ Jesus as the only Redeemer.

• *In Geneva.* Calvin did not confine preaching to his own congregation. He also used it as a tool to spread the Reformation throughout the city of Geneva. On Sundays, the Genevan Ordinances required sermons in each of the three churches at daybreak and 9 a.m. At noon, children went to catechism classes. At 3 p.m., sermons were preached again in each church.

Weekday sermons were scheduled at various times in the three churches on Mondays, Wednesdays, and Fridays. By the time Calvin died, a sermon was preached in every church each day of the week.

Even that wasn't enough. Calvin wanted to reform Genevans in all spheres of life, so that both the Genevan church and the city could become a model for Christ's reign throughout the world. These goals were, in large measure, realized.

• *Throughout Europe.* Inspired by Calvin's truly ecumenical vision, Geneva became a nucleus from which evangelism spread throughout the world. According to the Register of the Company of Pastors, eighty-eight men were sent out between 1555 and 1562 from Geneva to different places in the world. These figures are woefully incomplete. In 1561, which appears to have been the peak year for missionary activity, the dispatch of only twelve men is recorded, whereas other sources indicate that nearly twelve times that number—no fewer than 142—went forth on respective missions.[46]

That is an amazing accomplishment for an effort that began with a small church struggling within a tiny city-republic. Yet Calvin himself recognized the strategic value of the effort. He wrote to Heinrich Bullinger, "When I consider how very important this corner [of the world, i.e., Geneva] is for the propagation of the kingdom of Christ, I have good reason to be anxious that it should be carefully watched over."[47]

In a sermon on 1 Timothy 3:14, Calvin preached, "May we attend to what God has enjoined upon us, that he would be pleased to show his grace, not only to one city or a little handful of people, but that he would reign over all the world; that everyone may serve and worship him in truth."

During Calvin's second Genevan ministry, the city became a refuge center for those suffering religious persecution. Between 1542 and 1555, Geneva's population doubled, largely due to refugees coming from all over Europe. The reputation and influence of the Genevan community spread to neighboring France, then to Scotland, England, the Netherlands, parts of western Germany, and sections of Poland, Czechoslovakia, and Hungary.

Geneva did not merely *receive* refugees, however. The Geneva Academy, established in 1559, assumed a critically important role in *sending* missionaries all over Europe for the proclamation of the gospel and the organization of Reformed churches. Philip Hughes writes:

> Calvin's Geneva was something very much more than a haven and a school. It was not a theological ivory tower that lived to itself and for itself, oblivious to its responsibility in the gospel to the needs of others. Human vessels were equipped and refitted in this haven . . . that they might launch out into the surrounding ocean of the world's need, bravely facing every storm and peril that awaited them in order to bring the light of Christ's gospel to those who were in the ignorance and darkness from which they themselves had originally come. They were taught in this school in order that they in turn might teach others the truth that had set them free.[48]

Influenced by the Academy, John Knox took the evangelical doctrine back to his native Scotland. Englishmen were equipped to lead the cause in England; Italians received what they needed to teach in Italy; and Frenchmen (who formed the great bulk of refugees) were taught how to spread Calvinism to France.

France, Calvin's homeland, was a country of special focus for him. It was only partly open to Reformed evangelism. Religious and political hostilities, which also threatened Geneva, were a constant danger in France. Nonetheless, Calvin and his colleagues made the most of the opening they had. The minutes of the Company of Pastors in Geneva address supervision over the missionary efforts in France more than in any other country.[49]

Here's how it worked. Reformed believers from France took refuge in Geneva. While there, many began to study theology. They then felt compelled to return to their own people as Reformed evangelists and pastors. After passing a rigorous theological examination, each was given an assignment by the Company of Pastors, usually in response to a formal request from a French church needing a pastor. In most cases, the receiving church was fighting for its life under persecution.

A good number of the refugees who returned to France as pastors eventually were killed, but their zeal encouraged their parishioners. Their mission, which, according to the pastors, sought "to advance the knowledge of the gospel in France, as our Lord commands," was successful; Reformed evangelistic preaching led to the conversions of tens of thousands. In 1555, there were five Reformed churches in France. Seven years later, there were more than two thousand.[50] This was one of the most astonishing revivals in church history.[51]

Some of the French Reformed congregations became very large. For example, Pierre Viret pastored a church of eight thousand communicants in Nimes. More than ten percent of the French population in the 1560s—two million to three million of a population of twenty million—belonged to these churches.[52]

Such rapid growth encountered considerable persecution. After the massacre at Vassy and the peace of Amboise in 1563, Calvin wrote, "I would always counsel that arms be laid aside and that we all perish rather than enter again on the confusions that have been witnessed."[53]

During the St. Bartholomew's Day Massacre of 1572, some seventy thousand Protestants were killed. Nevertheless, the church continued. Persecution eventually drove out many of the French Protestants, known as the Huguenots. They left France for many different nations, enriching the church wherever they went.

• *In Brazil.* Calvin knew there were nations and people who had not yet heard the gospel, and he felt that burden keenly. Though there is no record that he ever came into contact with the newly discovered worlds of Asian and African paganism, Calvin was involved with the Indians of South America through the Genevan mission to Brazil.

With the help of a Huguenot sympathizer, Gaspard de Coligny, admiral of France, and the support of Henry II, then king of France, Nicolas Durand (also called Villegagnon) led an expedition to Brazil in 1555 to establish a colony. The colonists included former prisoners, some of whom were Huguenots.

When trouble erupted in the new colony near Rio de Janeiro, Villegagnon turned to the Huguenots in France, asking for better settlers. He also appealed to Coligny, as well as to Calvin and the church in Geneva. That letter has not been preserved, and there is only a brief summary of what happened in the account of the Company of Pastors. Nonetheless, we have some insight into those events through the personal journal of Jean de Léry, a shoemaker and student of theology in Geneva who was soon to join the Brazilian colony. He wrote, "The letter asked that the church of Geneva send Villegagnon immediately ministers of the Word of God and with them numerous other persons 'well instructed in the Christian religion' in order better to reform him and his people and 'to bring the savages to the knowledge of their salvation.'"[54] Responsibility for evangelism to the heathen was thus laid squarely at the feet of the church of Geneva.

Calvin "saw a wonderful door opening here," writes G. Baez-Camargo, "and so he took steps at once to organize a missionary force."[55] The Geneva church's reaction, according to de Léry, was this: "Upon receiving these letters and hearing this news, the church of Geneva at once gave thanks to God for the extension of the reign of Jesus Christ in a country so distant and likewise so foreign and among a nation entirely without knowledge of the true God."[56]

The Company of Pastors chose two ministers to send to Brazil. The Register succinctly notes: "On Tuesday 25 August [1556], in consequence of the receipt of a letter requesting this church to send ministers to the new islands [Brazil], which the French had conquered, M. Pierre Richier and M. Guillaume Charretier were elected. These two were subsequently commended to the care of the Lord and sent off with a letter from this church."[57] Eleven laymen were also recruited for the colony, including de Léry.

The pastors and laymen set sail from Europe in September 1556 and landed in Fort Coligny (in Rio de Janeiro) the following March. However, the work with the Indians in Brazil did not go well. Shortly after their arrival, Pastor Richier wrote to Calvin that the savages were incredibly barbaric. "The result is we are frustrated in our hope of revealing Christ to them."[58] Richier did not want to abandon the mission, however. He told Calvin that the missionaries would advance the work in stages and wait patiently for six young boys who were placed with the Indians (the Tupinambas) to learn their language. "Since the Most High has given us this task, we expect this Edom to become a future possession for Christ," he added confidently.[59] Meanwhile, he trusted that the witness of pious and industrious members of the Reformed church in the colony would influence the Indians.

Richier was a striking witness of Calvin's missionary emphasis in four ways: (1) obedience to God in doing what is possible in a difficult situation, (2) trust in God to create opportunities for further witness, (3) insistence on the importance of the lives and actions of Christians as a means of witness, and (4) confidence that God will advance His kingdom.

The rest of the story is tragic.[60] Villegagnon became disenchanted with Calvin and the Reformers. On Feb. 9, 1558, just outside Rio de Janeiro, he strangled three of the Genevan Calvinists and threw them into the sea. Others fled for their lives. Later, the Portuguese attacked and destroyed the remainder of the settlement.

Thus ended the mission to the Indians. There is no record of any Indian converts. But was that the true end of the story? When an account of the martyrs of Rio de Janeiro was published six years later, it began with these words: "A barbarous land, utterly astonished at seeing the martyrs of our Lord Jesus Christ die, will some day produce the fruits that such precious blood has been at all times wont to produce."[61] That assessment echoed Tertullian's famous statement, "The blood of the martyrs is the seed of the church." Today, the Reformed faith is growing in Brazil among conservative Presbyterians through Reformed preaching, the Puritan Project, and various ministries that reprint Reformed and Puritan titles in Portuguese.

RESTRAINTS ON EVANGELISM DURING THE REFORMATION

It is clear that Calvin was interested in spreading the gospel overseas, but that interest was limited by the following realities of the sixteenth century:

• *Time constraints.* The Reformation was still so new in Calvin's time that he was obliged to concentrate on building up the truth in the churches. A mission church not built on foundational truth is not equipped to carry its message to foreign lands.

• *Work at home.* Those who critique Calvin for failing to extend his evangelistic efforts to the foreign mission field are quite unfair. After all, did not Christ command His disciples to begin spreading the gospel in Jerusalem and Judea (home missions), and then move on to Samaria and the uttermost parts of the earth (foreign missions)? Obviously, the established church should be involved in both home and foreign missions, but we err when we esteem one more important than the other.

• *Government restrictions.* Nearly every door to the heathen world was closed for Calvin and his fellow Reformers. The world of Islam to the south and east was guarded by Turkish armies. Likewise, overseas mission work for the Reformers was virtually impossible because most of the governments in Europe were controlled by Roman Catholic princes, kings, and emperors. In 1493, Pope Alexander VI had divided the New World between the Spanish and the Portuguese, who controlled the sea lanes.[62] While the French ignored the pope and sent their own ships to the New World,[63] all of these countries were Roman Catholic, meaning that Protestant ministers were forbidden to sail overseas for mission work. Gordon Laman notes that a "religious imperialism" had joined "with the commercial and political imperialism" of Spain and Portugal.[64] Then, too, persecution of Protestants was widespread. Calvin wrote: "Today, when God wishes his gospel to be preached in the whole world, so that the world may be restored from death to life, he seems to ask for the impossible. We see how greatly we are resisted everywhere and with how many and what potent machinations Satan works against us, so that all roads are blocked by the princes themselves."[65]

For Calvin and other Reformers, going out into the world didn't necessarily mean leaving Europe. The mission field of unbelief was right within the realm of Christendom. France and Europe were open to the Genevan church. Strengthened by Calvin's evangelistic theology, believers zealously responded to the mission call.

OUTREACH TO GOD'S GLORY

This historical survey should dispel the myth that Calvin and his followers promoted inactivity and lack of interest in evangelism. Rather, the truths of sovereign grace taught by Calvin, such as election, are precisely the doctrines that encourage missionary activity. Where biblical, Reformed truth is loved, appreciated, and rightly taught, evangelism and mission activity abound.

The glory of God was Calvin's motivating factor for evangelizing and engaging in missions. When the gospel is proclaimed throughout the nations, God will bless it and build His church everywhere. Charles Chaney writes, "The fact that the glory of God was the prime motive in early Protestant missions and that it has played such a vital part in later missionary thought and activity can be traced directly to Calvin's theology."[66]

Divine glory is what Calvin's Reformed evangelism was all about, and that is what our evangelism must be about. May God help us speak and live evangelistically for His glory, to obey His Word, to look for open evangelistic doors, and to pray with Calvin: "May we daily solicit thee in our prayers, and never doubt, but that under the government of thy Christ, thou canst again gather together the whole world . . . when Christ shall exercise the power given to him for our salvation and for that of the whole world."[67]

DISCUSSION QUESTIONS

1. How would you respond to the charge that Calvin's teaching was not evangelistic?

2. Outline the way in which Calvin actually did evangelism in Geneva, in France, and in Brazil.

3. What hindered evangelism during the time of the Reformation? Are there hindrances to evangelism today? If so, what are they?

4. How does the sovereignty of God encourage evangelism?

NOTES

[1] Inst., 3.20.42.

[2] Johannes van den Berg, "Calvin's Missionary Message," *The Evangelical Quarterly*, 22 (1950): 174–187; Walter Holsten, "Reformation und Mission," *Archiv für Reformationsgeschichte*, 44, no. 1 (1953): 1–32; Charles E. Edwards, "Calvin and Missions," *The Evangelical Quarterly*, 39 (1967): 47–51; and Charles Chaney, "The Missionary Dynamic in the Theology of John Calvin," *Reformed Review* 17, no. 3 (March 1964): 24–38. Parts of this chapter have been abridged from Joel R. Beeke, "John Calvin: Teacher and Practitioner of Evangelism," *Reformation and Revival*, 10, no. 4 (Fall 2001): 107–132.

[3] Gustav Warneck writes, "We miss in the Reformers not only missionary action, but even the idea of missions . . . [in part] because fundamental theological views hindered them from giving their activity, and even their thoughts a missionary direction" (*Outline of a History of Protestant Missions* [Edinburgh: Oliphant Anderson & Ferrier, 1906], 9). Warneck goes on to state that Calvin thought the church is not obliged to send out any missionaries (ibid., 19–20)! Ralph D. Winter even says that the Reformers "did not even talk of mission outreach" ("The Kingdom Strikes Back," in *Perspectives on the World Christian*

Movement [Pasadena: William Carey Library, 1992], B–18, quoted in Scott J. Simmons, "John Calvin and Missions: A Historical Study," http://www.aplacefortruth.org/calvin.missions1.htm.

4 William Richey Hogg, "The Rise of Protestant Missionary Concern, 1517–1914," in *Theology of Christian Mission*, ed. G. Anderson (New York: McGraw-Hill, 1961), 96–97.

5 David B. Calhoun, "John Calvin: Missionary Hero or Missionary Failure?" *Presbuterion*, 5, no. 1 (Spring 1979): 16–33 (I am greatly indebted to this article for the first part of this chapter), and W. Stanford Reid, "Calvin's Geneva: A Missionary Centre," *Reformed Theological Review*, 42, no. 3 (1983): 65–74.

6 Samuel M. Zwemer, "Calvinism and the Missionary Enterprise," *Theology Today*, 7, no. 2 (July 1950): 206–216, and J. Douglas MacMillan, "Calvin, Geneva, and Christian Mission," *Reformed Theological Journal*, 5 (Nov. 1989): 5–17.

7 *Commentary* on Psalm 2:8; 110:2; Matthew 6:10; 12:31; John 13:31.

8 *Commentary* on Micah 4:3.

9 John Calvin, *Sermons of M. John Calvin on the Epistles of S. Paule to Timothie and Titus*, trans. L. T. (repr. Edinburgh: Banner of Truth Trust, 1983), 161–172.

10 *Commentary* on Acts 2:1–4.

11 *Commentary* on Psalm 110:3.

12 *Commentary* on Matthew 24:30.

13 *Commentary* on Romans 10:15.

14 *Commentary* on Matthew 13:24–30.

15 Inst., 4.1.5.

16 *Commentary* on Romans 10:14–17.

17 *Commentary* on Psalm 2:8.

18 *Commentary* on Isaiah 2:3.

19 John Calvin, *Letters of Calvin*, ed. Jules Bonnet, trans. David Constable and Marcus Robert Gilchrist (Eugene, Ore.: Wipf & Stock, 2007), 4:263.

20 *Commentary* on Isaiah 49:2.

21 Inst., 3.20.42.

22 John Calvin, *Sermons of Master John Calvin upon the Fifthe Book of Moses called Deuteronomie*, trans. Arthur Golding (Edinburgh: Banner of Truth Trust, 1987), sermon on Deuteronomy 33:18–19. (Hereafter *Sermon* on text.)

23 *Sermon* on Deuteronomy 33:7–8.

24 *Commentary* on Hebrews 10:24.

25 *Sermon* on Deuteronomy 33:18–19.

26 *Commentary on* Matthew 13:24–20.

27 Calvin, *Letters of Calvin*, 4:169.

28 Ibid., 2:453.

29 Ibid.

30 *Commentary* on Isaiah 12:5.

31 Inst., 3.20.11.

32 *Commentary* on Isaiah 2:3.

33 Van den Berg, "Calvin's Missionary Message," 178–179.

34 *Commentary* on Psalm 22:27.

35 *Commentary* on Matthew 28:19. See also *Commentary* on Isaiah 12:5; Matthew 24:14; and 2 Corinthians 2:12.

[36] Inst., 4.20.4.

[37] *Commentary* on 2 Corinthians 2:12.

[38] Ibid.

[39] Calvin, *Letters of Calvin*, 3:134.

[40] William J. Bouwsma, *John Calvin: A Sixteenth-Century Portrait* (New York: Oxford University Press, 1988), 29.

[41] Quoted in David L. Larsen, *The Company of the Preachers* (Grand Rapids: Kregel, 1998), 165.

[42] Quoted in Leroy Nixon, *John Calvin, Expository Preacher* (Grand Rapids: Eerdmans, 1950), 65.

[43] *CO* 79:783.

[44] See Inst., 3.24.12.

[45] *Commentary* on Psalm 119:101.

[46] Ibid., 45–46; cf. Simmons, "John Calvin and Missions," 9–15.

[47] Calvin, *Letters of Calvin*, 2:227.

[48] Philip Hughes, "John Calvin: Director of Missions," in *The Heritage of John Calvin*, ed. John H. Bratt (Grand Rapids: Eerdmans, 1973), 44.

[49] Robert M. Kingdon, *Geneva and the Consolidation of the French Protestant Movement* (Madison: University of Wisconsin Press, 1967), 31.

[50] Gordon D. Laman, "The Origin of Protestant Missions," *Reformed Review*, 43 (Autumn 1989): 59.

[51] Fred. H. Klooster, "Missions—The Heidelberg Catechism and Calvin," *Calvin Theological Journal*, 7 (Nov. 1972): 192.

[52] Simmons, "John Calvin and Missions," 7.

[53] Quoted in Williston Walker, *John Calvin: The Organizer of Reformed Protestantism* (New York: Knickerbocker, 1906), 385.

[54] R. Pierce Beaver, "The Genevan Mission to Brazil," in *The Heritage of John Calvin*, 61.

[55] G. Baez-Camargo, "The Earliest Protestant Missionary Venture in Latin America," *Church History*, 21, no. 2 (June 1952): 135.

[56] Beaver, "The Genevan Mission to Brazil," 61.

[57] Philip E. Hughes, ed. and trans., *The Register of the Company of Pastors of Geneva in the Time of Calvin* (Grand Rapids: Eerdmans, 1966), 317.

[58] Beaver, "The Genevan Mission to Brazil," 62.

[59] Ibid., 64.

[60] Simmons, "John Calvin and Missions," 17.

[61] Baez-Camargo, "The Earliest Protestant Missionary Venture in Latin America," 144.

[62] Edwards, "Calvin and Missions," 47.

[63] Beaver, "The Genevan Mission to Brazil," *The Reformed Journal*, 17 (1967): 15.

[64] Laman, "The Origin of Protestant Missions," 53.

[65] *Commentary* on Genesis 17:23.

[66] Charles Chaney, "The Missionary Dynamic in the Theology of John Calvin," *Reformed Review*, 17 (March 1964): 36–37.

[67] Quoted in J. Graham Miller, *Calvin's Wisdom* (Edinburgh: Banner of Truth Trust, 1992), 221.

CHAPTER 21

PURITAN
EVANGELISM

*The importance of [Puritan preaching] is that it challenges our modern idea
that preaching "gospel sermons" means just harping on a few great truths—
guilt, and atonement, and forgiveness—set virtually in a theological vacuum.
The Puritan view was that preaching "gospel sermons" meant teaching the
whole Christian system—the character of God, the Trinity, the plan of salvation, the entire work of grace. To preach Christ, they held, involved preaching all this. . . . In this way, they would say, preaching the gospel involves
preaching the whole counsel of God. Nor should the preaching of the gospel
be thought of as something confined to set evangelistic occasions, as if at other
times we should preach something else. If one preaches the Bible biblically,
one cannot help preaching the gospel all the time, and every sermon will be at
least by implication evangelistic.*[1]

—J. I. PACKER

*I*t is clear that John Calvin did not lack evangelistic zeal, despite what
his critics say. Likewise, Calvin's Reformed heirs, the Puritans, spread
the gospel in a thoroughly scriptural manner and were equally passionate about
evangelism.[2]

In this chapter, I will define Puritan evangelism, then outline the scriptural
basis for Puritan preaching—doctrinally, practically, experimentally, and symmet-
rically. Finally, I will examine the primary methods they used to communicate the
gospel—a plain style of preaching and the practice of catechetical evangelism.

PURITAN EVANGELISM DEFINED

The word *Puritan* refers specifically to those people who were ejected from the Church of England by the Act of Uniformity in 1662. The term also applies, however, to those in Britain and North America who, for several generations after the Reformation, worked to reform and purify the church and to lead people toward biblical, godly living consistent with the Reformed doctrines of grace.[3] Doctrinally, Puritanism was a kind of broad and vigorous Calvinism; experientially, it was a warm and contagious kind of Christianity; evangelistically, it was tender as well as aggressive.

Evangelism was not a word the Puritans commonly used, but they were evangelists nonetheless. Richard Baxter's *Call to the Unconverted* and Joseph Alleine's *Alarm to the Unconverted* were pioneer works in evangelistic literature. For these and other Puritans, evangelism was a Word-centered task of the church, particularly of her ministers. They were truly "fishers of men," seeking to awaken the unconverted to their need of Christ, to lead them to faith and repentance, and to establish them in a lifestyle of sanctification.

The expression "Puritan evangelism," then, refers to the Puritans' proclamation of the truth of God's Word regarding the salvation of lost men from sin and its consequences. This salvation is granted by grace, received by faith, grounded in Christ, and reflective of the glory of God. For the Puritans, evangelism not only involved presenting Christ so that people would come to God through Him by the power of the Spirit; it equally involved presenting Christ so that believers might grow in Him and serve Him as Lord in the fellowship of His church and in the extension of His kingdom in the world. In short, Puritan evangelism involved declaring the entire economy of redemption by focusing on the saving work of all three persons of the Trinity, while simultaneously calling sinners to a life of faith and commitment, and warning that the gospel will condemn forever those who persist in unbelief and impenitence.[4]

CHARACTERISTICS OF PURITAN
EVANGELISTIC PREACHING

We can identify several characteristics of the Puritans' pulpit-based evangelism, characteristics that have marked Calvinistic evangelism down to the present day:

• *Puritan preaching was thoroughly biblical.* Puritanism was a Scripture-based movement, and the Puritans themselves were people of the living Book. They loved, lived, and breathed Scripture, relishing the power of the Spirit that accompanied the Word. They regarded the sixty-six books of Scripture as the library of the Holy Spirit, graciously bequeathed to them. "The faithfull Minister, like unto Christ, [is] one that preacheth nothing but the word of God," said Puritan Edward Dering.[5] John Owen agreed: "The first and principal duty of a pastor is to feed the flock by diligent preaching of the word."[6]

Calvinistic evangelism is always grounded in the Bible. As Calvinists, we must search the Scriptures more frequently and love the Word of God more fervently. As we learn to think, speak, and act more biblically, our messages will become more authoritative and our witness more effective and fruitful.

• *Puritan preaching was holistically evangelistic.* The Puritans used all of Scripture to confront the whole man. They did not merely pressure the human will to respond on the basis of a few dozen texts that emphasize the volitional aspect of evangelism.

Much modern evangelism, convinced that the first aim of preaching is to call upon men to believe, stresses a decisional act of faith on the part of the sinner. It does not believe the regenerating work of the Holy Spirit is necessary prior to faith. It holds that we believe in order to be born again—that faith precedes and effects regeneration. Faith, of course, is essential to salvation from beginning to end (e.g., Rom. 1:17; Heb. 11:6), and there is no time lapse between regeneration and the Spirit's implanting of saving faith in the heart of a sinner. Puritan evangelism, however, had a deeper and wider message to the unconverted.

Certainly, the duty to respond to the gospel in faith is important, but so are other duties. There is the duty to repent—not just as a temporary feeling of sorrow, but as a full amendment of life. The Puritans preached that sinners are to "cease to do evil" (Isa. 1:16b) and to be holy as God is holy (1 Peter 1:16b). They are to love God and His holy law with heart, mind, and strength, and to let nothing stand in the way of obedience. They are to "strive to enter in at the strait gate" (Luke 13:24).

Some church leaders would argue that such preaching leads to legalism. Nevertheless, it is justified on this ground: in the work of conversion, God does not normally begin with a conscious decision of faith, but with conviction of sin and a sense of total helplessness to obey God's commands. Thus, the Puritan evangelists preached about the legal obligations and liabilities under which sinners toil before showing them the way of deliverance through faith in Christ's blood. They preached the law before the gospel in much the same way Paul wrote the first three chapters of Romans. The apostle first explains the holiness of God and His law so that the mouths of sinners are stopped and the whole world may be found guilty before God. Likewise, the Puritans believed that, through a confrontation with the demands of the law, the Holy Spirit would bring sinners to know their helplessness before God and their need for salvation. The gospel is meaningful only to sinners who recognize their sinfulness. The Puritans, then, were not afraid to use the law of God as an instrument of evangelism.

This type of evangelism is clearly rooted in Scripture. John the Baptist preached repentance (Matt. 3:1–2) before he preached, "Behold the Lamb of God, which taketh away the sin of the world" (John 1:29). Jesus began His ministry with the same message. Matthew 4:17 says, "From that time Jesus began to preach, and to say, Repent: for the kingdom of heaven is at hand." He continued that theme with Nicodemus, saying, "Ye must be born again" (John 3:7b), and with the rich young ruler, confronting him first of all with the commandments (Mark 10:19).

Far too many modern evangelists also do not believe that the necessity of holiness is a suitable subject for the unconverted, so they do not present the gospel as a divine remedy for corrupt and impotent sinners. The Puritans, by contrast, believed that the best news for sinners who are truly convicted of sin is that deliverance from the power of sin is possible through faith in Christ. Such sinners need more than forgiveness or pardon; they want sin to be put to death in themselves forever. They want to live for the glory of God. They want to be holy as God is holy. They want to be conformed to the character of the Father, the image of the Son, and the mind of the Spirit.

All of this leads us to conclude that the teaching of modern evangelism on the nature of faith and its relationship to regeneration fails the test of the Word of God. The Puritans taught that a "regeneration" that leaves men without the indwelling power of the Holy Spirit and without the practice of holy living is not what is promised in Scripture.[7] According to the Bible, a regenerate person is not simply changed in his religious opinions; a regenerate person has been given a new nature by the Holy Spirit. He is born of the Spirit to become spiritual (John

3:6). He has been re-created, so all things are new. Such a person ceases to be self-centered and becomes God-centered. "They that are after the flesh do mind the things of the flesh; but they that are after the Spirit the things of the Spirit" (Rom. 8:5). The regenerate man loves God, loves holiness, loves the Bible, loves the godly, and loves the thought of going to heaven to commune with God, leaving sin behind forever.

The discrepancies between Puritan and modern evangelism should prompt us to revert to the older message that addressed the whole of Scripture to the whole man.

• *Puritan preaching was unashamedly doctrinal.* The Puritan evangelist saw theology as an essentially practical discipline. William Perkins called it "the science of living blessedly for ever,"[8] and William Ames characterized it as "the doctrine or teaching of living to God."[9] Sinclair Ferguson writes: "To them, systematic theology was to the pastor what a knowledge of anatomy is to the physician. Only in the light of the whole body of divinity (as they liked to call it) could a minister provide a diagnosis of, prescribe for, and ultimately cure spiritual disease in those who were plagued by the body of sin and death."[10]

The Puritans thus preached the doctrine of God without equivocation. They proclaimed God's majestic being, His trinitarian personality, and His glorious attributes.[11] All of their evangelism was rooted in a robust, biblical theism, quite unlike modern evangelism, which too often approaches God as if He were a next-door neighbor who can adjust His attributes to our needs and desires.

Puritan evangelism also proclaimed the doctrine of Christ. "Preaching is the chariot that carries Christ up and down the world," wrote Richard Sibbes.[12] Preaching the whole Christ to the whole man,[13] Puritan preachers offered Him as Prophet, Priest, and King. They did not separate His benefits from His person or offer Him as a Savior from sin while ignoring His claims as Lord. The Puritans would stand aghast at the present trend in modern evangelism that seeks merely to rescue sinners from hell, postponing their submission to the sovereign lordship of Christ until later.

• *Puritan preaching was studiously symmetrical.* There was in Puritan preaching both well-roundedness and good balance. Puritan preaching achieved this symmetry in three ways.

First, it allowed Scripture to dictate the emphasis for each message. The Puritans did not preach sermons that were a balancing act between various doctrines. They preached a Bible text completely, whatever its theme, and so in time they were sure to address every major theme of Scripture and every major doctrine of Reformed theology.

Nothing was left unbalanced in the total range of the Puritans' frequent and lengthy sermons. In theology proper, they proclaimed God's transcendence as well as His immanence. In anthropology, they preached about the image of God in its narrower as well as its wider sense. In Christology, they exhibited Christ's state of humiliation as well as His exaltation. In soteriology, they presented divine sovereignty and human responsibility as doctrines that do not need to be reconciled by our finite minds, since, as Charles H. Spurgeon quipped, friends have no need of reconciliation. In ecclesiology, they acknowledged the high calling of special offices (ministers, elders, and deacons) as well as the equally high calling of the general office of all believers. In eschatology, they declared both the glories of heaven and the horrors of hell.

Second, Puritan preaching instilled appreciation for each scriptural doctrine. The typical member of a Puritan congregation could relish a sermon one week on Genesis 19:17 ("Escape for thy life") for its warning notes on fleeing wickedness and following God, and the next week savor a message on how difficult it is to follow God unless God draws us to Himself (John 6:44). Puritan pastors and parishioners alike treasured the full scope of God's biblical truth rather than just their favorite passages or particular doctrines by which they rated each sermon.

Third, Puritan preaching allowed for a wide variety of sermon topics. A carefully cultivated appreciation for all scriptural doctrine allowed the Puritans to cover nearly every topic imaginable. Modern evangelism, by contrast, is reductionistic—using only a few texts, expounding a limited range of themes, and bringing little if any doctrine to bear on the work of evangelism.

• *Puritan preaching was experimentally practical.* The Puritans explained how a Christian experiences biblical truth in his life. They expounded "the full range of Christian experience, and a developed experimental theology."[14] We can learn much from the Puritans about this type of preaching; however, as Paul Helm notes, we "must not deal in unrealities or treat congregations as if they lived in a different century or in wholly different circumstances. This involves taking the full measure of our modern situation and entering with full sympathy into the actual experiences, the hopes and fears of Christian people."[15]

Preachers therefore need to ask themselves whether their preaching, teaching, and evangelizing is thoroughly scriptural, holistically evangelistic, unashamedly doctrinal, studiously symmetrical, and experimentally practical.

THE METHOD OF PURITAN EVANGELISM

Although evangelism differs to some degree from generation to generation according to gifts, culture, style, and language, the primary methods of Puritan evangelism—plain preaching and catechetical teaching—can show us much about how to present the gospel to sinners. The Puritans employed:

• *Plain preaching.* The Puritan "plain style of preaching" avoided all that was not clear or perspicuous to an ordinary listener. The greatest teacher of this preaching style was Perkins. Perkins, often called the father of Puritanism, wrote that preaching "must be plain, perspicuous, and evident. . . . It is a by-word among us: It was a very plaine Sermon: And I say again, the plainer, the better."[16] And Cotton Mather wrote succinctly in his eulogy for John Eliot, a great Puritan missionary to the Indians, that his "way of preaching was very plain; so that the very lambs might wade into his discourses on those texts and themes, wherein elephants might swim."[17] The Puritans used the plain style of preaching because they were evangelistic to the core—they wanted to reach everyone so that all might know the way of salvation.

The first part of a Puritan sermon was exegetical; the second, doctrinal and didactic; and the third, applicatory.[18] The third part, often called the "uses" of the text, was quite lengthy and applied Scripture in various ways to various listeners.

Perkins gave distinct directions on how to shape Scripture's applications to seven categories of listeners: ignorant and unteachable unbelievers; teachable but ignorant people; knowledgeable but unhumbled people; the humbled who lack assurance; believers; backsliders; and "a mingled people"—those who are a combination of several categories.[19] Puritan preachers addressed all seven types of people over a period of time, but not in each sermon. Each sermon included at least directions to believers and unbelievers. The unbeliever was usually called to examine how he was living and what behavior needed changing; then he was admonished to flee to Christ, who alone could fulfill his needs. For the believer, "uses" usually contained points of comfort, direction, and self-examination.

Three characteristics associated with Puritan plain preaching need rediscovery by today's preachers. First, Puritan preaching addressed the mind with clarity. It addressed man as a rational creature. The Puritans loved and worshiped God with their minds. They viewed the mind as the palace of faith. They refused to set mind and heart against each other; instead, they taught that knowledge was the soil in which the Spirit planted the seed of regeneration.

Second, Puritan preaching confronted the conscience pointedly. The Puritans worked hard on the consciences of sinners as the "light of nature" in them. Plain preaching named specific sins, then asked questions to press home the guilt of those sins upon the consciences of men, women, and children. As one Puritan wrote, "We must go with the stick of divine truth and beat every bush behind which a sinner hides, until like Adam who hid, he stands before God in his nakedness." They believed that such an approach was necessary because, until the sinner is drawn from behind that bush, he'll never cry to be clothed in the righteousness of Christ.

Modern evangelism seems to be afraid to confront the conscience pointedly. We need to learn from the Puritans, who were solemnly persuaded that the friend who loves you most will tell you the most truth about yourself. Like Paul and the Puritans, we need to testify, earnestly and with tears, of the need for "repentance toward God, and faith toward our Lord Jesus Christ" (Acts 20:21).

Third, Puritan preaching wooed the heart passionately. It was affectionate, zealous, and optimistic. Puritan preachers did not just reason with the mind and confront the conscience; they appealed to the heart. They preached out of love for God's Word, love for the glory of God, and love for the soul of every listener. They preached with warm gratitude of the Christ who had saved them and made their lives a sacrifice of praise. They set forth Christ in His loveliness, hoping to make the unsaved jealous of what the believer has in Christ.

• *Catechetical evangelism.* Like the Reformers, the Puritans were catechists. They believed that pulpit messages should be reinforced by personalized ministry through catechesis—the instruction in the doctrines of Scripture using catechisms. Puritan catechizing was evangelistic in several ways.

Scores of Puritans reached out evangelistically to children and young people by writing catechism books that explained fundamental Christian doctrines via questions and answers supported by Scripture.[20] For example, John Cotton titled his catechism *Milk for Babes, drawn out of the Breasts of both Testaments*.[21] Other Puritans included in the titles of their catechisms such expressions as "the main and fundamental points," "the sum of the Christian religion," the "several heads" or "first principles" of religion, and "the ABC of Christianity." At various levels in the church as well as in the homes of their parishioners, Puritan ministers taught rising generations from both the Bible and their catechisms. Their goals were to explain the fundamental teachings of the Bible, to help young people commit the Bible to memory, to make sermons and the sacraments more understandable, to prepare covenant children for confession of faith, to teach them how to defend their faith against error, and to help parents teach their own children.[22]

Catechizing was a follow-up to sermons and a way to reach neighbors with the gospel. Alleine reportedly followed his work on Sunday by several days each week of catechizing church members as well as reaching out with the gospel to people he met on the streets.[23] Baxter, whose vision for catechizing is expounded in *The Reformed Pastor*, said that he came to the painful conclusion that "some ignorant persons, who have been so long unprofitable hearers, have got more knowledge and remorse of conscience in half an hour's close disclosure, than they did from ten years' public preaching."[24] Baxter invited people to his home every Thursday evening to discuss and pray for blessing on the sermons of the previous Sabbath.

The hard work of the Puritan catechist was greatly rewarded. Richard Greenham claimed that catechism teaching built up the Reformed church and seriously damaged Roman Catholicism. When Baxter was installed at Kidderminster in Worcestershire, perhaps one family in each street honored God in family worship; at the end of his ministry there, there were streets where every family did so. He could say that of the six hundred converts brought to faith under his preaching, he could not name one who had backslidden to the ways of the world. How vastly different was that result compared with those of today's evangelists, who press for mass conversions and turn over the hard work of follow-up to others.

DISCUSSION QUESTIONS

1. What was Puritan evangelism? What was it like?

2. What differences do you see between Puritan evangelism and modern-day evangelism? What can we learn from the Puritans in this matter?

3. What role did preaching play in Puritan evangelism?

4. Why is the heart attitude of the evangelist important?

NOTES

1 J. I. Packer, "The Puritan View of Preaching the Gospel," in *Puritan Papers, Vol. 1, 1956–1959* (Phillipsburg, N.J.: P&R, 2000), 263.

2 The best sources for a Puritan theology of evangelism and missions are Sidney H. Rooy, *The Theology of Missions in the Puritan Tradition. A Study of Representative Puritans: Richard Sibbes, Richard Baxter, John Eliot, Cotton Mather, and Jonathan Edwards* (Grand Rapids: Eerdmans, 1965), and J. I. Packer, *A Quest for Godliness: The Puritan Vision of the Christian Life* (Wheaton, Ill.: Crossway, 1990), chapters 2, 10, 17–19. Cf. Francis G. James, "Puritan Missionary Endeavors in Early New England" (M.A. thesis, Yale University, 1938); Ernst Benz, "Pietist and Puritan Sources of Early Protestant World Missions," *Church History*, 20, no. 2 (1951): 28–55; Johannes van den Berg, *Constrained by Jesus' Love: An Inquiry into the Motives of the Missionary Awakening in Great Britain in the Period Between 1698 and 1815* (Kampen: J.H. Kok, 1956); Alden T. Vaughan, *New England Frontier: Puritan and Indian, 1620–1675* (Boston: Little, Brown and Co., 1965); R. Pierce Beaver, *Pioneers in Mission* (Grand Rapids: Eerdmans, 1966); Charles L. Chaney, *The Birth of Missions in America* (South Pasadena, Calif.: William Carey Library, 1976); William S. Barker, "The Rediscovery of the Gospel: The Reformation, the Westminster Divines, and Missions," *Presbyterion*, 24, no. 1 (1998): 38–45. Most of this chapter is abridged from Joel R. Beeke, *Puritan Evangelism*, 2nd ed. (Grand Rapids: Reformation Heritage Books, 2007).

3 Richard Mitchell Hawkes, "The Logic of Assurance in English Puritan Theology," *Westminster Theological Journal*, 52 (1990): 247. Cf. D. Martyn Lloyd-Jones, "Puritanism and Its Origins," in *The Puritans: Their Origins and Successors* (Edinburgh: Banner of Truth Trust, 1987), 237–259, and Joel R. Beeke, *The Quest for Full Assurance: The Legacy of Calvin and His Successors* (Edinburgh: Banner of Truth Trust, 1999), 82ff.

4 Thomas Manton, *The Complete Works of Thomas Manton*, ed. T. Smith. (Worthington, Pa.: Maranatha, 1980), 2:102ff.

5 Edward Dering, *M. Derings Workes* (New York: Da Capo Press, 1972), 456.

[6] John Owen, *The Works of John Owen*, ed. William H. Goold (London: Banner of Truth Trust, 1965), 16:74.

[7] William Whately, *The New Birth* (London, 1618), and Stephen Charnock, "A Discourse of the Efficient of Regeneration," in *The Works of Stephen Charnock* (Edinburgh: Banner of Truth Trust, 1986), 3:166–306.

[8] William Perkins, *The Works of William Perkins* (London: John Legate, 1609), 1:10.

[9] William Ames, *The Marrow of Theology*, ed. John D. Eusden (Boston: Pilgrim Press, 1968), 77.

[10] Sinclair Ferguson, "Evangelical Ministry: The Puritan Contribution," in *The Compromised Church: The Present Evangelical Crisis*, ed. John H. Armstrong (Wheaton, Ill.: Crossway, 1998), 266.

[11] The classic work on God's attributes is Stephen Charnock's massive *Discourses on the Existence and Attributes of God* (1682; repr., Grand Rapids: Baker, 1996). See also William Bates, *The Harmony of the Divine Attributes in the Contrivance and Accomplishment of Man's Redemption* (Harrisonburg, Va.: Sprinkle, 1985).

[12] Richard Sibbes, *The Complete Works of Richard Sibbes*, ed. Alexander B. Grosart (1862; repr., Edinburgh: Banner of Truth Trust, 1977), 5:508.

[13] Thomas Taylor, *Christ Revealed: or The Old Testament Explained; A Treatise of the Types and Shadowes of our Saviour* (London: M. F. for R. Dawlman and L. Fawne, 1635), is the best Puritan work on Christ in the Old Testament. Thomas Goodwin, "Christ Our Mediator," vol. 5 of *The Works of Thomas Goodwin* (Grand Rapids: Reformation Heritage Books, 2006) ably expounds primary New Testament texts on the mediatorship of Christ.

[14] Paul Helm, "Christian Experience," *Banner of Truth*, no. 139 (April 1975): 6.

[15] Ibid.

[16] Perkins, *The Works of Perkins*, 2:222. Cf. William Perkins, *The Art of Prophesying* (1606; revised ed., Edinburgh: Banner of Truth Trust, 1996), 71–72, and Charles H. George and Katherine George, *The Protestant Mind of the English Reformation 1570–1640* (Princeton: Princeton University Press, 1961), 338–341.

[17] Cotton Mather, *The Great Works of Christ in America: Magnalia Christi Americana*, Book 3 (London: Banner of Truth Trust, 1979), 1:547–548.

[18] Perry Miller, *The New England Mind: The Seventeenth Century* (Cambridge: Cambridge University Press, 1939), 332–333.

[19] Perkins, *The Art of Prophesying*, 56–63.

[20] See George Edward Brown, "Catechists and Catechisms of Early New England" (D.R.E. dissertation, Boston University, 1934); R. M. E. Paterson, "A Study in Catechisms of the Reformation and Post-Reformation Period" (M.A. thesis, Durham University, 1981); P. Hutchinson, "Religious Change: The Case of the English Catechism, 1560–1640" (Ph.D. dissertation, Stanford University, 1984); and Ian Green, *The Christian's ABC: Catechisms and Catechizing in England ca. 1530–1740* (Oxford: Clarendon Press, 1996).

[21] John Cotton, *Milk for Babes, drawn out of the Breasts of both Testaments* (London, 1646).

[22] Cf. W. G. T. Shedd, *Homiletics and Pastoral Theology* (London: Banner of Truth Trust, 1965), 356–375.

[23] C. Stanford, *Joseph Alleine: His Companions and Times* (London, 1861).

[24] Richard Baxter, *Gildas Salvianus: The Reformed Pastor: Shewing the Nature of the Pastoral Work* (New York: Robert Carter, 1860), 341–468.

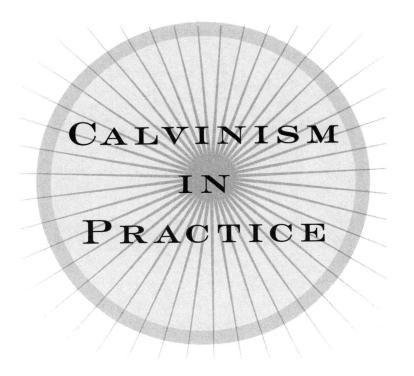

PART FIVE

CALVINISM IN PRACTICE

CHAPTER 22

A THEOLOGY FOR
ALL OF LIFE

Ray Pennings

There is not a square inch in the whole domain of our human existence over which Christ, who is Sovereign over all, does not cry "Mine."[1]

—ABRAHAM KUYPER

*P*aul told the Corinthians that everything in life, including eating and drinking, is to be done for God's glory (1 Cor. 10:31), and integrating this principle into theology has been a historical concern for Calvinism.

This chapter will identify various themes that have emerged in Calvinist history in regard to day-to-day living and conclude with suggestions for applying these themes in our time.[2]

MEDIEVAL DUALISM

Spirituality prior to the Reformation was attributed primarily to those who lived a contemplative life. Priests, monks, and others who could free themselves from the ordinary pursuits of daily life were believed best suited to serve God. Thomas Aquinas' perspective "that the contemplative life is simply more excellent than the active"[3] (based on the Luke 10 account of Mary's having made a better choice than did her sister Martha) pervaded the church. The logical consequence was that the ordinary things of life were deemed to have little religious importance. Belonging to the church and participating in her affairs were all that really mattered. The resulting practical dualism divided life into categories such as higher and lower, or spiritual and secular. The best ordinary believers could hope for was a second-class spirituality that gave little direction for how they were to live in the here and now.

The Reformation challenged this dualistic outlook. The doctrine of justification by faith alone challenged the church as the sole mediator and dispenser of grace. And the doctrine of the priesthood of all believers changed the understanding of how Christians related to God. These truths had implications not only for theology but for the social, cultural, and political arenas of life. Imagine having been raised with a dual perspective on life, only to become convinced of the truth as taught by Martin Luther: "However numerous, sacred and arduous [the works of monks and priests] may be, these works in God's sight are in no way whatever superior to the works of a farmer laboring in the field or of a woman looking after her home."[4] Suddenly, work, art, music, food, and the "stuff" of everyday life were understood differently. Ordinary believers and what they did every day were no longer considered second class before God.

Of course, radical paradigm shifts do not happen overnight or without controversy. Examining how Calvinists applied faith to the nonecclesiastical spheres forces us to contend with other views that emerged from the Reformation that dictated alternative, and sometimes competing, approaches.[5] Sorting out these views can be confusing indeed. This is understandable for several reasons.

First, the Reformation was primarily a religious movement. While the Reformers understood the broader implications of Calvinist theology, social or cultural change was not their primary motivation. This is not to suggest, however, that Calvinists thought of these areas of life as unimportant.

Second, some themes within Reformed theology seem to be in tension. On the one hand, the Reformers had robust doctrines of the goodness of creation and the fullness of redemption that could be developed into positive implications for living in this world. On the other hand, Reformed teachings on total depravity, the effects of the curse of sin, and the continuing hold of sin on believers suggested more negative implications. Depending on how these truths are presented in relation to one another, one can use Reformed doctrine to come to quite different conclusions on various issues.

Third, various eschatological views in Reformed thinking can have either positive or negative implications. The emphasis on a new heaven and new earth as the renewal of creation profoundly affects what happens outside the church.

Fourth, a five-hundred-year review of Calvinistic thought overlaps the pre-modern, modern, and postmodern eras, with all the philosophic, technological, political, and social changes that occurred in that time. A twenty-first-century analysis also uses contemporary words and frameworks, which create inherent confusion in the consideration of the past.

In spite of these challenges, we can develop a coherent theme regarding the comprehensive implications of Calvinism. Digging beyond the polemics of any specific issue, we find remarkable agreement within Calvinism regarding the underlying theological principles. Calvinists have always accepted the goodness of God's creation and its capacity to glorify Him. They also have been conscious of the effects of sin in polluting both the person and his ability rightly to understand and use God's creation, as well as of the structural effects of sin.[6] But they also have written much about the completeness of Christ's redemption, showing how it will be applied to all of creation in the fullness of time. The curse will be undone and the glories of the original creation will be exceeded in the new heaven and the new earth. Any debate within Calvinism usually concerns the translation of these theological principles into suitable norms and practices, not the principles themselves. Thus, Calvinism provides a consistent framework that answers the question "How must I live before God?" in a manner that contrasts sharply with the dualism offered by alternative systems.

HISTORICAL SAMPLING

The difficulty of overcoming this dualism was evident early in the Reformation. While Luther's "two kingdom" concept was developed primarily in political terms (due to the political disorder that occurred in the 1520s),[7] it had clear implications for understanding how faith applies to all spheres. Luther taught that Christians belong to the kingdom of God and are no longer slaves to the law because they are governed by the Spirit. God is their true master, and they have the freedom as well as the mandate to love God and their neighbors. By contrast, the kingdom of man is a realm of unbelievers to which the law applies. However, since the gospel is one of peace, we must live alongside unbelievers in the world, voluntarily working within the kingdom of man to promote God's law and order.

Two features of Luther's approach should be highlighted. First, at the heart of the discussion is the debate on the place of law in the life of the Christian. This was a significant theological question primarily argued in theological terms, though the results of that debate spilled over into other aspects of life. Second, Luther's approach was ethical. His teaching addressed practical questions about how believers should relate to their ungodly neighbors and their daily affairs. Luther had to contend not only with the legacy of Roman Catholic dualism, but also with Anabaptist arguments about withdrawing from society. In the context of theological and political controversy, he had no choice but to provide leadership.

Rather than placing John Calvin's more structured approach in tension with Luther's two-kingdom concept, let us examine Calvin's perspective as it developed.[8] He approached the questions foundationally rather than polemically, producing a more robust theology of man's responsibility in the context of revelation, creation, fall, and redemption.

In his *Institutes of the Christian Religion*, for example, Calvin explains wisdom as "the knowledge of God and of ourselves."[9] This knowledge of God is clearly a comprehensive view: Calvin says of the Creator God, "We must be persuaded not only that as he once formed the world, so he sustains it by his boundless power, governs it by his wisdom, preserves it by his goodness, in particular, rules the human race with justice and judgment, bears with them in mercy, shields them by his protection; but also that not a particle of light, or wisdom, or justice, or power, or rectitude, or genuine truth, will anywhere be found, which does not flow from him, of which he is not the cause."[10] Calvin started with God and His work, not man and his duty.

This framework acknowledges the positive aspect of various nonecclesiastical spheres. For example, Calvin did not begin with the medieval idea that church and state were in competition. He did not adopt Luther's opinion that the state was the kingdom of man to which Christians did not really belong. Neither did he accept the Anabaptist view that Christians should escape this sinful world and form their own communities. Rather, Calvin taught that government officials "have a commission from God, that they are invested with divine authority, and, in fact, represent the person of God."[11] This was radical teaching, indeed. In addition to the "ministry" inherent in government, Calvin acknowledged that manual and liberal arts should be recognized "as a special gift from God."[12] What happens in daily life matters not only in the context of survival or as a theater in which good and evil are carried out, but for its own sake. God is to be honored and respected by all of His creation; He takes an active interest in what goes on in our daily lives.

This view raises various questions, such as, "How can unbelievers who do not acknowledge God have proficiency and even excellence in various spheres?" Calvin addressed this directly, saying:

> How, then, can we deny that truth must have beamed on those ancient law-givers who arranged civil order and discipline with so much equity? Shall we say that the philosophers, in their exquisite researches and skilful description of nature, were blind? Shall we deny the possession of intellect to those who drew up rules for discourse, and taught us to speak in accordance with reason? Shall we say that those who, by cultivation of the medical arts, expended their industry in our behalf, were only raving? What shall we say of the mathematical sciences? Shall we deem them to be the dreams of madmen? Nay, we cannot read the writings of the ancients on these subjects without the highest admiration; an admiration which their excellence will not allow us to withhold. But shall we deem anything to be noble and praiseworthy, without tracing it to the hand of God? . . . Therefore since it is manifest that men whom the Scriptures term natural, are so acute and clear-sighted in the investigation of inferior things, their examples should teach us how many gifts the Lord has left in possession of human nature, notwithstanding of its having been spoiled of true good.[13]

With this perspective, Calvinists were motivated to pursue a remarkable range of initiatives. Historians will continue to argue about how church reform, political and economic reform, and popular reform relate within a single theological framework.[14] But this perspective made "comprehensive Calvinism" so natural that it is no surprise that Calvinist history includes extensive involvement in politics, the arts, education, economics, and science—to mention only a partial list.

Another question that arises has to do with the origin of the perception by some of Calvin as a "joyless killjoy, ruining peoples' lives in Geneva."[15] Likewise, until recently, the term *Puritan* has been widely understood as "an odd, furious, and ugly form of Protestant religion."[16] Where did such perceptions come from if Calvinism from the start was committed to the inherent goodness of creation?

One explanation is that, as noted earlier, the idea of creation's goodness existed alongside the doctrine of depravity and a keen awareness of Satan's desire to trip believers. There were also concerns within Calvinism about worldliness, the idolatry that accompanies extensive engagement in the nonecclesiastical spheres of life, and a desire to focus on spiritual needs. That led to a practical application of Calvinism that encouraged avoiding some spheres as being spiritually harmful for believers. Variations on the argument that "there is little use digging in a garbage can and getting dirty simply to retrieve a penny from the bottom" have been used to justify teaching that certain activities are not suitable for Christian involvement.

In some contexts, the lines were drawn even more boldly, especially in the area of arts and entertainment. In 1647, the English Parliament under Puritan influence banned all stage plays and interludes.[17] While some argued that acting itself was wrong, most suggested the theater was an unspiritual atmosphere. The content of many plays certainly contradicted biblical teachings on sexuality, language, authority, and attitudes toward God. Beyond the theater, the Calvinist interpretation of the second commandment restrained the development of religious art and destroyed much of the art of a previous generation.[18]

Luther and Calvin definitely varied in their view of the arts. Luther focused more on the beauty of the arts as reflecting the beauty of God, whereas Ulrich Zwingli and most of the Puritans stressed the abuses of art, especially religious art as a violation of God's commandments.[19] However, the Calvinistic repression of the arts did not diminish Reformed emphasis on the Word as the center of worship and of a culture in which education and literature flourished. Puritan authors, for example, contributed to a cultural milieu that produced writers such as John Milton and William Shakespeare. So while Calvinism repressed certain expressions of art, the underlying theology of the Calvinists percolated into the culture, influencing it in positive ways.[20] One might make similar observations regarding the contribution of the Reformation to "the golden age of music" in the sixteenth century.[21] The Calvinist emphasis on psalm singing in worship was part of "a substantial and broadly based artistic application of a Reformation worldview."[22]

Education was another sphere of life that Calvinism influenced. Historically, Calvinists have played a huge role in promoting education. Calvin was convinced that literacy and education were necessary for every person to rightly divide God's Word, so he promoted a universal education system. Geneva's education model, which started with an academy and led to a university, has been recognized as one of the finest in Europe at the time.[23] Modern historians credit the Puritans with promoting elementary and university education. New England Puritans established Harvard only six years after their arrival.[24]

Equipping students to read the Scriptures was not the only motivation for these efforts. As Leland Ryken notes,

> For the Reformers and their heirs the Puritans, no education is complete if it includes only religious knowledge. Samuel Rutherford said, for example, "It is false that Scripture only, as contradistinguished from the law of nature, can direct us to heaven; for both concurreth in a special manner nor is the one exclusive of the other." The General Court of Massachusetts went on record as believing that "skill in tongues and liberal arts" was "beyond all question not only laudable but necessary for educated people." Here again we see the Puritan unwillingness to set up a division between the spiritual and the natural.[25]

In the twentieth century, there is no better case study for the comprehensive reach of Calvinism and the issues it raises than that of the Dutch Prime Minister Abraham Kuyper (1837–1920).[26] It was Kuyper who wrote the famous words cited at the opening of this chapter: "There is not a square inch in the whole domain of our human existence over which Christ, who is Sovereign over all, does not cry 'Mine.'" His words and life demonstrate faith comprehensively applied. He was a pastor, academic, journalist, politician, and leader of the Christian school movement. He is commonly acknowledged as the inspiration for a movement known as Neo-Calvinism,[27] which focuses on "grace restoring nature"[28] and is characterized by four features: cultural mandate, common grace, antithesis, and sphere sovereignty.[29] In 1898, B. B. Warfield invited Kuyper to Princeton Seminary to deliver a series of lectures. These lectures, which produced the most authoritative text for Neo-Calvinism,[30] offered a thorough look at comprehensive Calvinism and its implications for life in modern society.

Calvinism emerged at the end of the medieval era when the religion of a monarch framed the religion of the people. Society was organized around a religiously informed and politically enforced moral consensus. Between the time of Calvin and Kuyper, the concepts of religious pluralism and toleration emerged,

along with an individual-rights-based society. Through the process, such basic
terms as *community, church, democracy, truth,* and *freedom* took on new meanings.
Today, technology has likewise redefined the framework of global information
and perspectives out of which day-to-day decisions are made. Although the context does not change the theological principles involved, it does require a different
application. So while Calvinism has changed little theologically through the ages,
it has changed practically, especially in the comprehensiveness of the questions it
faces because of the abundance of information that must be considered.

Kuyper saw himself as working from the same theological framework as Calvin. He thus writes:

> When the question is put, Who had the clearest insight into the reforma-
> tory principle, worked it out most fully, and applied it most broadly, history
> points to the Thinker of Geneva and not to the Hero of Wittenberg. Luther
> as well as Calvin contended for a direct fellowship with God, but Luther took
> it up from its subjective, anthropological side, and not from its objective,
> cosmological side as Calvin did. Luther's starting-point was the special sote-
> riological principle of a justifying faith; while Calvin's, extending far wider,
> lay in the general cosmological principle of the sovereignty of God.[31]

However, Kuyper was more like Luther in his polemical presentation. His
focus was on "the great and serious dangers" that modernism presented to Christianity. Thus, he wrote: "Two life systems are wrestling with one another, in
mortal combat. Modernism is bound to build a world of its own from the data
of the natural man, and to construct man himself from the data of nature; while,
on the other hand, all those who reverently bend the knee to Christ and worship
Him as the Son of the living God, and God himself, are bent upon saving the
'Christian Heritage.'"[32]

IMPLICATIONS FOR THE PRESENT

The Neo-Calvinist framework that emerged from Kuyper provides a helpful
paradigm for sorting the everyday issues of today's Christian.[33] Kuyper's cultural-
mandate interpretation of Genesis 1:28 provides a framework in which to make
occupational and vocational decisions. He developed Calvin's teachings into a

theology of common grace, which helps us sort through many issues regarding working with unbelievers. Neo-Calvinist work on the antithesis[34] is especially helpful in answering questions regarding apologetics, as well as understanding the structural implications of sin and the curse. Sphere sovereignty develops the creation principle of "after its kind" into a framework in which to understand the relationship between the various spheres of society. This provides an alternative to the left-right political divide that dominates contemporary political conversation.

While Kuyper's insights are often appreciated, the ways Neo-Calvinism has developed in the past century argue for caution. In the words of Cornelis Pronk: "Neo-Calvinists, with their emphasis on cultural, rather than missionary endeavor, tend to lose sight of the fact that believers do their work in the sphere and context of Christ's soteriological work. . . . [Kuyper's followers] were only too happy with [his doctrine of common grace] because it offered an escape from what they considered a too rigid view of the Christian's separation from the world. Common grace thus opened the door to worldliness."[35] The validity of this criticism has been acknowledged even by leading Neo-Calvinists. Albert Wolters writes: "Generally speaking, neocalvinists are more noted for their intellectual ability and culture-transforming zeal than for their personal godliness or their living relationship with Jesus Christ. This is of course not to suggest that there is some kind of inherent tension between intellectuality and spirituality, but only that the neocalvinist polemic against a pietistic otherworldliness can have the unfortunate effect of throwing out the godly baby with the pietistic bathwater."[36]

We may choose to dismiss this debate as the latest manifestation of a centuries-old discussion and retreat to the side we have chosen, there to reload our arsenal of arguments for the next stage of the battle.[37] But such resignation would deny the comprehensive claims of the gospel. It would result in either a this-worldly preoccupation with culture or an other-worldly focus that amounts to a utilitarian dualism. Such a choice is not available if we take seriously the call to live *coram Deo* ("before the face of God").

There is no simple formula for addressing the apparent tensions in applying the truths of Scripture to the various spheres of our lives. However, let me propose a synthesis that may help us move from the modern into the postmodern era. It is necessary to articulate a public theology that is rooted in orthodox doctrine, has a worldview robust enough to answer the real questions of everyday life, is applied with an ethic of integrity, and is lived out of a pilgrim spirit, recognizing that "here have we no continuing city, but we seek one to come" (Heb. 13:14).

When focusing on the comprehensive implications of our faith, it is tempting to downplay doctrine. Many attempts to "Christianize" nonecclesiastical spheres of life have become hopelessly muddled because doctrine has been downplayed and ultimately compromised. This is not to suggest that we need a sectarian or party spirit. However, we need to engage winsomely in dialogue that employs biblical truth as a basis for cooperation. This requires a nonpartisan spirit that can honestly acknowledge differences as well as similarities. The full orb of biblical teaching—including creation, fall, and redemption—must be applied carefully with biblical balance. And while this threefold summary is standard in worldview literature, a seventeenth-century, fourfold distinction of the same truths might be preferable. The advantage of dealing with primitive integrity, entire depravity, begun recovery, and consummate happiness or misery—to use Thomas Boston's words[38]—or creation, fall, redemption, and restoration or judgment, to frame it more cryptically, is that the fourth category reminds us to frame what appear to be temporal issues in the context of biblical teachings about eternity. Given that history shows how cultural engagement can result in misapplied priorities, including judgment would better equip us to balance the whole counsel of God.

Orthodox doctrine, however, must include practical implications for everyday life. Life is lived out of a worldview. Here we have much to learn from the Puritans. J. I. Packer writes: "There was for them no disjunction between sacred and secular; all creation, as far as they were concerned, was sacred and all activities, of whatever kind, must be sanctified, that is, done to the glory of God. So in their heavenly minded ardor the Puritans became men and women of order, matter-of-fact and down-to-earth, prayerful, purposeful, practical."[39] The Puritans did not reduce the sacred to a human level, cheapening the gospel. Rather, they raised the affairs of daily life to their rightful place before God.

Such a perspective is helpful in determining what we ought to do in our daily lives and how we ought to do it. High standards of conduct must be expected in our relationships in church life, but we should not accept "lower standards" for nonecclesiastical matters. The beliefs embodied in phrases such as "that's how business is done" and "it is just a game" can easily exempt certain corners of our lives from divine standards. While the argument is commonly made that an inconsistent ethic harms our witness (as it certainly does), it is even more fundamentally important that we see all of life as God-created and the object of Christ's redemption. God demands that we do our daily work well, not just because failure to do so harms our witness, but also because God loves a job well done.

The challenge is to live with a pilgrim mindset in which we seek a city to come. That city is not a place where a choir of disembodied spirits will gather for a perpetual concert; the groaning of creation will be answered finally in the unveiling of a glorious new creation in which God will be the focus of all things. What motivation! A pilgrim mindset allows the believer to reflect on how every activity and decision he makes will ultimately be perfected so that everything works for God's honor and glory, without decay, confusion, or selfish ambitions. We will not understand the full extent of God's sanctifying work until we see it with renewed minds in glory but, just as the sinful motives and tendencies of our hearts will be perfected in eternity, we know that leisure, work, fellowship, and enjoyment of creation will take on an unrecognizable hue and glory after the final judgment. "For of him, and through him, and to him, are all things: to whom be glory for ever. Amen" (Rom. 11:36).

DISCUSSION QUESTIONS

1. What is meant by the term *comprehensive Calvinism*?

2. What is medieval dualism? How did the Reformation challenge this view from the Middle Ages?

3. How did Martin Luther and John Calvin seek to overcome the dualism of the Middle Ages?

4. What was Calvin's view of the arts and education?

5. Abraham Kuyper wrote: "There is not a square inch in the whole domain of our human existence over which Christ, who is Sovereign over all, does not cry 'Mine.'" How does this statement serve as a summary of comprehensive Calvinism?

7. How does Kuyper's statement help us think about the arts, music, and literature?

NOTES

1   Quoted in R. C. Sproul, "A Free and Lasting Legacy," *Tabletalk*, 26, no. 10 (Oct. 2002): 6.

2   This chapter focuses on an overall framework for applying Calvinist thinking to the nonecclesiastical spheres of life. Given that other chapters in this book deal with the home (chaps. 23–24), the workplace (chap. 25), and politics (chap. 26), the examples selected in this chapter have been drawn primarily from other spheres, especially arts and culture.

3   Thomas Aquinas, "The active life in comparison with the contemplative life," *Summa Theologica*, II.ii.182, http://www.newadvent.org/summa/3182.htm.

4   Martin Luther, "Pagan Servitude of the Church" in *Martin Luther: Selections from His Writings*, ed. John Dillenberger (New York: Doubleday, 1961), 311.

5   It goes beyond our scope to deal with all aspects of debate that might be included here. To cite only two current, differing perspectives, Michael Horton's "Defining the Two Kingdoms: One of Luther's and Calvin's Great Discoveries" (*Modern Reformation*, 8, no. 5 [Sept.–Oct. 2000]: 21, 25, 28, interprets the relationship between Luther and Calvin's perspectives using historical and eschatological arguments that result in a "more Lutheran" conclusion. In a very different vein, writers associated with the Christian Reconstruction movement (also sometimes described as theonomy or "Dominion theology") proceed from a different application of the law to come to a very different conclusion. Prominent writers in this tradition include R. J. Rushdoony, Gary North, and Greg Bahnsen.

6   By structural effects of sin, I mean the nonpersonal or nonhuman impact of the curse that came as a result of the fall. The consequences described in Genesis 3:17–19 include thorns and thistles beginning to grow, work becoming toil, and childbirth becoming painful—all of which form part of the legacy of the curse that Paul describes as the "creation groaning" in Romans 8:22.

7   German peasants revolted against their feudal lords in 1524–25, led by various Protestants, including Thomas Muntzer. Eventually this stream of Protestantism became identified as "the Anabaptists." Critics of the Reformation were quick to cite the revolt as evidence of the disorder inherent in Luther's teaching, although Luther took a strong stand against the revolt. For more detail on this history, see George Hunston Williams, *The Radical Reformation* (Kirksville, Mo.: Truman State University Press, 2000), 137–174.

8   For the continuity between Calvin and Luther, see W. Andrew Hoffecker, *Revolutions in Worldview: Understanding the Flow of Western Thought* (Phillipsburg, N.J.: P&R, 2007), 227ff.

9   Inst. (Bev.), 1.1.1.

10 Inst., 1.2.1.

11 Inst., 4.20.4.

12 Inst., 2.2.14.

13 Inst., 2.2.15.

14 For example, Steven Ozment notes: "It is possible to distinguish three agents and levels of Reformation within the cities, each making an important contribution to the final shape of the reform. Preachers and laymen learned in Scripture provided the initial stimulus; ideological and socially mobile burghers, primarily from the (larger) lower and middle strata, created a driving wedge of popular support; and the government consolidated and moderated the new institutional changes" (*The Reformation in the Cities* [New York: Yale University Press, 1975], 131).

15 Cited as a common perception in W. Robert Godfrey, "John Calvin's View of Worship," in *Presbyterian and Reformed News*, 9, no. 1 (Jan.–March 2003): 3.

16 J. I. Packer, "Why We Need the Puritans," in Leland Ryken, *Worldly Saints: The Puritans As They Really Were* (Grand Rapids: Zondervan, 1986), ix. Packer credits the scholarship of Perry Miller, William Haller, Marshall Knappen, Percy Scholes, and Edmund Morgan, among others, for revamping this commonly held caricature.

17 A. W. Ward and W. P. Trent et al., *The Cambridge History of English and American Literature* (New York: G.P. Putnam's Sons, 1907–21; New York: Bartleby.com, 2000), www.bartleby.com/cambridge/--search for "Prohibition Stage Plays."

18 Iconoclasm refers to the deliberate destruction of religious art and artifacts. During the Reformation, iconoclast riots broke out in various Reformation cities, including Zurich, Geneva, and the Seventeen Provinces (what is now the Netherlands). Crowds would gather and smash various statues and works of religious art. Later, in seventeenth-century England, civil servants were commissioned to remove and confiscate art that included any portrayal of God.

19 For more on the Reformation's impact on the fine arts, see Lewis Spitz, *The Protestant Reformation, 1517–1559* (New York: Harper & Row, 1985), 367–371.

20 Hoffekker observes that the flourishing of the literary arts occurred in a cultural context dominated by the Reformation and its emphasis on the Word (*Revolutions in Worldview,* 236n).

21 Spitz, *The Protestant Reformation,* 371.

22 Hoffecker, *Revolutions in Worldview,* 236.

23 http://www.monergism.com/thethreshold/articles/questions/Calvin_bio.html.

24 Ryken, *Worldly Saints,* 157.

25 Ibid., 165.

26 English language biographies include Frank Vandenberg, *Abraham Kuyper: A Biography* (St. Catharines, Ont.: Paideia Press, 1978); R. Langley McKendree, *The Practice of Political Spirituality* (St. Catharines, Ont.: Paideia Press, 1984); Louis Praamsma, *Let Christ Be King: Reflections on the Life and Times of Abraham Kuyper* (St. Catharines, Ont.: Paideia Press, 1985); James McGoldrick, *God's Renaissance Man: The Life and Work of Abraham Kuyper* (London: Evangelical Press, 2000); and Joel R. Beeke, "The Life and Vision of Abraham Kuyper," *Banner of Truth,* no. 483 (Dec. 2003): 12–21.

27 The first known usage of the term "Neo-Calvinism" has been ascribed to Free University Professor A. Anema in an 1897 article. Cf. John Bolt, *A Free Church, A Holy Nation* (Grand Rapids: Eerdmans, 2001), 444n. A working definition of Neo-Calvinism has been offered by Dr. Gideon Strauss: "Neocalvinism is postmodern Calvinism. Neocalvinism is a global cultural movement that is the result of people motivated by the religious dynamic of the Reformation trying to get to grips with the historical consequences and implications of modernity." (http://en.wikipedia.org/wiki/Neo-Calvinism)

28 Drawn from Al Wolters, *Creation Regained: Biblical Basics for a Reformational Worldview* (Grand Rapids: Zondervan, 1985).

29 I have found these four concepts to be the most helpful in applying Neo-Calvinism to public square activities, and although these are all common terms that have widespread acceptance within the movement, I am not aware of any particular definition that explicitly utilizes these four as the defining features of Neo-Calvinism. They are essentially in line with, but more cryptic than, the "contours of the neo-Calvinist tradition" enumerated by Craig Bartholomew in his October 2004 lecture "Relevance of Neocalvinism for Today," available at http://kuyperian.blogspot.com/2004/09/relevance-of-neocalvinism-for-today.html. There are additional features of Neo-Calvinism that focus on the ecclesiastical sphere that are controversial.

30 Abraham Kuyper, "Lectures on Calvinism: The Stone Lectures of 1898," the Kuyper Foundation, http://www.kuyper.org/main/publish/books_essays/article_17.shtml.

31 Kuyper, Stone Lectures, "First Lecture – Calvinism as a Life System," http://www.lgmarshall.org/Reformed/
kuyper_lecturescalvinism.html.

32 Ibid.

33 Historian Mark Noll, in *The Scandal of the Evangelical Mind* (Grand Rapids: Eerdmans, 1993), lamenting
the lack of intellectual rigor among evangelicals in twentieth-century North America, highlights a Dutch
Reformed exception to his analysis, noting that "Reformed philosophers were a tonic—bold in confessing
historic Christian faith, expert in carrying on sophisticated philosophic argumentation, and far-reaching
in proposing new theories. . . . These philosophers pushed historic Christianity back into the arena of
modern philosophical debate" (235).

34 The antithesis is the idea that the struggle between the kingdom of darkness and kingdom of light takes
place not only in the hearts of individuals but also in the world of ideas.

35 Cornelis Pronk, "Neo-Calvinism," a speech to the Free Reformed Student Society published at http://
www.frcna.org/Data/StudentSocietySpeeches/Neo-Calvinism%20-%20Rev.%20C.%20Pronk.pdf,
accessed Nov. 21, 2006, p. 9.

36 Albert Wolters. "What is to be done . . . toward a neocalvinist agenda?" in *Comment* (Oct. 2005),
v.24.1.8

37 Already at the time of Kuyper, there was a debate between the "Old Calvinists" and the "Neo-Calvinists."
For a summary of the historical debate regarding Neo-Calvinism, see Appendix A, "The Debate about
Dutch Neo-Calvinism," in Bolt, *A Free Church, a Holy Nation*, 443–464.

38 Thomas Boston, *Human Nature in Its Fourfold State* (Edinburgh: Banner of Truth Trust, 1964). Boston
wrote this book in 1720.

39 Quoted in Ryken, *Worldly Saints*, xii.

CHAPTER 23

THE PURITAN
MARRIAGE

Before man had any other calling, he was called to be a husband. . . . First man must choose his love, and then he must love his choice. . . . The man and wife are partners, like two oars in a boat.[1]

—HENRY SMITH

There may be no better example of Calvinism in action than the lives of the Puritans at home. Their views on marriage and broader family life were biblical, positive, and lavish. Their writings[2] reveal this outlook, and many scholars have confirmed it through the years.[3] Therefore, in order to gain a better understanding of the Calvinistic idea of domestic life, I will focus on the Puritan view of marriage in this chapter and on the Puritan view of the family in the following chapter.

The Puritans had an astonishingly healthy view of marriage. Here is a description of marriage by Richard Baxter: "It is a mercy to have a faithful friend that loveth you entirely . . . to whom you may open your mind and communicate your affairs. . . . And it is a mercy to have so near a friend to be a helper to your soul and . . . to stir up in you the grace of God."[4] John Dod and Robert Cleaver put it this way: "Thy wife is ordained for man: like a little Zoar, a city of refuge to fly to in all his troubles: and there is no peace comparable unto her but the peace of conscience."[5] John Downame says that "God the Institutor of marriage, gave the wife unto the husband, to be, not his servant, but his helper, counsellor, and comforter."[6] And John Cotton writes, "Women are Creatures without which there is no comfortable Living for man: it is true of them what is wont to be said

317

of Governments, That bad ones are better than none." Though some call them "a necessary Evil," Cotton went on to say, they are really "a necessary Good."[7]

The Puritans built on Reformation teaching for their positive attitude toward marriage. In sermons and lengthy treatises, they set forth scriptural purposes, procedures, principles, and practices covering every point of marriage.

PURPOSES OF MARRIAGE

The Puritans agreed with the Reformers that Scripture sanctions three purposes for marriage, all of which aim for the higher good of the glory of God and the furthering of God's kingdom on earth. According to the *Book of Common Prayer*, the purposes of marriage are: (1) the procreation of children, (2) the restraint and remedy of sin, and (3) mutual society, help, and comfort. Some early Puritan works on marriage maintained this order, but the Puritans gradually moved the third purpose to first place, as was codified in the 1640s by the Westminster divines in the Confession of Faith (24.2): "Marriage was ordained [1] for the mutual help of husband and wife [Gen. 2:18]; [2] for the increase of mankind with a legitimate issue, and of the Church with an holy seed [Mal. 2:15]; and [3] for the preventing of uncleanness [1 Cor. 7:2, 9]."[8] Later Puritans focused more on the Genesis 2:18 mandate for marriage ("It is not good that the man should be alone; I will make him an help meet for him") than on the Genesis 1:28 command to be fruitful and multiply.

The first purpose for marriage, then, is to provide companionship and mutual assistance. Henry Smith says this is God's way "to avoid the inconvenience of solitariness signified in these words, 'It is not good for man to be alone'; as though he said, This life would be miserable and irksome, and unpleasant to man, if the Lord had not given him a wife to company his troubles."[9] William Gouge, whose hefty *Of Domestical Duties* became a classic among the Puritans as well as a common wedding gift, focuses more on the mutual assistance in marriage that flows out of companionship. This includes the tasks of childbearing, child-rearing, and family government, both in times of prosperity and adversity, and health and sickness.[10] Through such companionship, William Perkins says, "the parties married may perform the duties of their callings in a better and more comfortable manner (Prov. 31:11–13)."[11] All of this is to serve "for the benefit of man's natural and spiritual life," John Robinson writes.[12]

The second purpose of marriage is procreation and the building up of the church through godly child-rearing. The Puritans believed that having children is not simply a private matter to be decided between a husband and wife. Rather, from their perspective, children are a gift of God through which believers are to serve the family, the church, and the state. Gouge notes that Christians should have children so "that the world might be increased: and not simply increased, but with a legitimate brood, and distinct families, which are the seminaries of cities and the Commonwealths. Yea also that in the world the Church by an holy seed might be preserved, and propagated (Mal. 2:15)."[13]

The third purpose of marriage, as Gouge says, is for men and women to "possess their vessels in holiness and honour" and to avoid fornication (1 Cor. 7:2, 9). Gouge goes on to say, "Marriage is as an haven to such as are in jeopardy of their salvation through the gusts of temptations to lust."[14] Marriage is the best and most sanctified solution to the temptation of fornication.

In their emphasis on the physical purposes of marriage, the Puritans did not devalue its spiritual purpose. They stressed that marital love should remain subordinate to a loving God. John Winthrop, in a letter written to his wife shortly after their marriage, calls her "the chiefest of all comforts under the hope of salvation."[15] Cotton warns against "the error of aiming at no higher end" than marriage itself and encourages people to look upon their spouses "not for their own ends, but to be better fitted for God's service and bring them nearer to God."[16]

PROCEDURES FOR GETTING MARRIED

The Puritan procedure for getting married consisted of six steps. First was the period of getting to know, like, and love each other. This could be initiated by the couple themselves, by parents, or by friends. But wise young people would ask counsel both of parents and of friends concerning possible marital partners. Whatever the case, love is foundational in the Puritan view, for it encourages bonding. As Gouge says, "Mutual love and good liking of each other is as glue." This glue will sustain a couple through marriage, for "love will not easily be loosened by any trials."[17]

Second, there was a contract of espousals, which was a commitment to marry. This contract was more binding than our modern form of engagement. Gouge describes it this way: "This rightly made is a *contract*, which is the beginning of a marriage." While holding hands in front of witnesses, each party vowed: "I do faithfully promise to marry thee in time meet and convenient."[18] Biblical support for such a contract included the examples of Lot's daughters, who were "contracted to husbands [while] they are said to have known no man" (Gen. 19:8, 14), and Mary, who is described as "a virgin espoused" (Luke 1:27).[19]

Third, the contract was formally announced to the congregation on three successive Sundays. Those announcements provided an opportunity for any church member who had lawful objections against the marriage to voice them through proper church channels. If there were no objections, the church was assumed to have provided a "silent approbation" upon the marriage.

Fourth, the marriage was publicly solemnized in a religious ceremony, which consisted of the pastor administering the marriage vows and preaching a short sermon, followed by a civil celebration. Gouge describes the civil celebration as "all those lawful customs that are used for the setting forth of the outward solemnity [of the wedding], as meeting of friends, accompanying the Bridegroom and Bride both to and from the Church, putting on best apparel, seating, with other tokens of rejoicing: for which we have express warrant out of God's word."[20]

Fifth, after the service, there was feasting at the groom's home, where "witty questions and doubtful riddles may be propounded."[21] The questions and riddles that were entertained were wholesome and intellectually stimulating; nothing ribald was tolerated, in contrast with the often-suggestive comments and rituals that occur at many modern weddings.

Sixth and finally, the marriage was consummated through sexual intercourse.[22]

PRINCIPLES FOR MARRIAGE

The Puritans grounded marriage on two major scriptural principles: the Christ-church principle and the covenantal principle. These principles are perhaps the primary factors behind the orderliness, stability, and happiness of Puritan marriages.

• *The Christ-church principle.* Gouge's *Of Domestical Duties* is based on Ephesians 5:21–6:9, which describes the duties of husbands, wives, parents, children, masters, and servants. Prior to detailing these duties, however, Gouge gives an opening chapter of 133 pages that explains this scriptural passage phrase by phrase. He sets forth the major principle of marriage—that the husband is to love his wife as Christ loves the church, while the wife is to show reverence and submission to her husband as the church does to Christ.

The husband's headship over his wife parallels Christ's headship over His church (Eph. 5:23). As Christ loves His church, the husband must love his wife absolutely (v. 25), purposely (v. 26), realistically (v. 27), and sacrificially (vv. 28–29).[23] He must exercise a "true, free, pure, exceeding, constant love" to his wife, nourishing and cherishing her as Christ does His gathered people (v. 29).[24] Since Christ's love for His church is all-encompassing, a husband cannot love his wife adequately because, being a sinner, he will always fall short of Christ's perfect love (v. 25). But Christ's love to His bride must be the husband's pattern and goal.[25] Such love will serve "as sugar to sweeten the duties of authority which appertain to an husband," so that his loving wife may more easily submit to him.[26]

Given the modern caricatures of Puritanism, it is vital to note that Puritan husbands were rarely male chauvinists and tyrants. Modelling the husband's headship on Christ's headship of the church, Puritans understood that male authority was more a charge to responsibility than a ticket to privilege. Headship was leadership based on love (1 Peter 3:7).

Since the church humbly and unconditionally submits to Christ, the wife's submission to her husband means, according to Isaac Ambrose, that she should show reverence and "yield subjection" to her husband in all things, except when her husband acts contrary to God and His commandments (vv. 22–24). This principle holds true even if her husband is "a son of Belial" (1 Sam. 2:12)—i.e., of a difficult temperament. Ambrose writes, "A wife must be meek, mild, gentle, obedient, though she be matched with a crooked, perverse, and wicked husband."[27]

For the Puritans, submission was not so much a matter of hierarchy as of function. God assigns the role and duty of leadership to the husband not because he is superior to his wife, but simply because God delegates this authority to him and not to her. Robinson explained headship this way: "God created man and woman spiritually equal, and when both fell into sin she did not become more degenerated than he from the primitive goodness. Yet in marriage one of the two must have final authority, since differences will arise, and so the one must give way and apply unto the other; this, God and nature layeth upon the man."[28]

The Puritans believed that the wife must yield voluntary submission. If a husband compels submission, the battle is already lost. Submission is to be rendered by the wife as part of her obedience to Christ. Thus, it is her honor and freedom to acknowledge her husband as her head.

Both husband and wife should focus on their own duties, the Puritans said. If husbands show little love to their wives, they should not expect much submission and reverence from them; likewise, if wives show little reverence and submission to their husbands, they should not expect much love from them.[29]

• *The covenantal principle.* Flowing out of this principle of love and submission, the Puritans made much of the principle of marriage as a covenant (Mal. 2:14). Edmund Morgan summarizes their view:

> Every proper marriage since the first was founded on a covenant to which the free and voluntary consent of both parties was necessary. . . . Since time began no man and woman had ever been allowed to fix the terms upon which they would agree to be husband and wife. God had established the rules of marriage when he solemnized the first one, and he had made no changes in them since then. The covenant of marriage was a promise to obey those rules without conditions and without reservations.[30]

Morgan goes on to quote Samuel Willard: "Many other Covenants are bounded by the makers, but all the duties of this covenant [are] appointed by God. [Therefore] when husband and wife neglect their duties they not only wrong each other, but they provoke God by breaking his law."[31]

PRACTICES OR DUTIES OF MARRIAGE

The Puritans' concept of marriage was informed by the Bible. As J. I. Packer says, "They went to Genesis for its institution, to Ephesians for its full meaning, to Leviticus for its hygiene, to Proverbs for its management, to several New Testament books for its ethic, and to Esther, Ruth and the Song of Songs for illustrations and exhibitions of the ideal."[32] They let the practices, duties, and ethics of marriage flow out of the marriage textbook of Scripture. Edward Payson says that "the duties which they [husband and wife] bind themselves to perform [in marriage], are no more than God requires of them in his Word."[33]

The Puritans treated the duties of marriage, often at great length, in three sections: mutual duties, the husband's duties, and the wife's duties. All duties were to be done devotedly, kindly, and cheerfully.[34] Here is a brief summary of each type of duty:

- *Mutual duties.*[35] The foundational duty of marriage is love. Gouge writes, "A loving mutual affection must pass betwixt husband and wife, or else no duty will be well performed: this is the ground of all the rest."[36] "As for love," says William Whately, who wrote two books on marriage, "it is the life, the soul of marriage, without which it is no more itself, than a carcase is a man; yes, it is uncomfortable, miserable, and a living death." Whately describes marital love as "the king of the heart," so that when it prevails, marriage is "a pleasing combination of two persons into one home, one purse, one heart, and one flesh."[37]

Marital love must be *spiritual*, in Christ, and in accord with God's commandments. Love must be rooted in the experience of being equally yoked together spiritually. It must be built on a Christ-centered foundation and cemented with a mutual use of the means of grace. Husbands and wives must rejoice in humbly worshiping God together at church and in their homes.[38] They must read the Scriptures, sing psalms, observe the Sabbath, and partake of the sacraments together.[39] They must pray for and with each other.[40] Love that is built on physical appearance or human gifts rests on a sandy foundation and can easily be "blown down by some storm," Whately says, "but spiritual love, that looks upon God, rests upon his will, yields to his Commandment, and resolves to obey it, cannot change itself, because the cause thereof is unchangeable."[41]

Marital love must be *superlative*, so that a husband and wife love each other so dearly that both are persuaded that the other is "the only fit and good match that could be found under the sun for them," Whately writes.[42] Because of parental love, a godly parent would not trade his child for another parent's child, even if that child were better-looking and had more gifts; similarly, a godly husband and wife would not trade each other for a better-looking and more gifted spouse.[43] Whately quaintly concludes: "Marriage-love admits of no equal, but placeth the yoke-fellow next of all to the soul of the party loving; it will know none dearer, none so dear."[44]

Marital love must be *sexual*, so that both marital partners can give themselves fully to each other with joy and exuberance in a healthy relationship marked by fidelity. Reformers such as Martin Luther, Ulrich Zwingli, and John Calvin established this aspect of marriage by abandoning the medieval Roman Catholic attitudes that marriage was inferior to celibacy, that all sexual contact between marital partners was a necessary evil to propagate the human race, and that a procreative act that involved passion was inherently sinful.

This negative view was rooted in the ancient church and based on the writings of such notables as Tertullian, Ambrose, and Jerome, all of whom believed that, even within marriage, intercourse necessarily involved sin.[45] This attitude toward marital intimacy, which dominated the church for more than ten centuries, inevitably led to the glorification of virginity and celibacy. By the fifth century, clerics were prohibited from marrying.[46] Two classes of Christians emerged: the "religious" (i.e., the *spiritual clergy*), which included monks and nuns who vowed to abstain from all sexual activity, and the "profane" (i.e., the *secular laity*), who, being unable to rise to the noble heights of virginity or celibacy, were conceded the right to marry.

Puritan preachers taught that the Roman Catholic view was unbiblical, even satanic. They cited Paul, who said that the prohibition of marriage is a doctrine of devils (1 Tim. 4:1–3). Even the Puritan definitions of marriage implied the conjugal act. For example, Perkins defines marriage as "the lawful conjunction of the two married persons; that is, of one man and one woman into one flesh."[47] In contrast with Desiderius Erasmus, who taught that ideal marriage abstained from sexual intercourse, Cotton said in a wedding sermon that those who call for marital abstinence follow the dictates of a blind mind and not those of the Holy Spirit, who says that it is not good that man should be alone.[48]

The Puritans viewed sex within marriage as a gift of God and as an essential, enjoyable part of marriage. Gouge says that husbands and wives should cohabit "with good will and delight, willingly, readily, and cheerfully."[49] "They do err," adds Perkins, "who hold that the secret coming together of man and wife cannot be without sin unless it be done for the procreation of children."[50]

Perkins goes on to say that marital sex is a "due debt" or "due benevolence" (1 Cor. 7:3) that a couple owes to one another. That must be shown, he says, "with a singular and entire affection one towards another" in three ways: "First, by the right and lawful use of their bodies or of the marriage bed." Such physical intimacy by "holy usage" should be "a holy and undefiled action (Heb. 13:4) . . . sanctified by the word and prayer (1 Tim. 4:3–4)." The fruits of God-honoring, enjoyable sex in marriage are the blessing of children, "the preservation of the body in cleanness," and the reflection of marriage as a type of the Christ-church relationship. Second, married couples must "cherish one another" intimately (Eph. 5:29) rather than having sex in an impersonal way as an adulterer with a prostitute. Third, a couple should be intimate "by an holy kind of rejoicing and solacing themselves each with [the] other in a mutual declaration of the signs and tokens of love and kindness (Prov. 5:18–19; Songs 1:1; Gen. 26:8; Isa. 62:7)." In this context, Perkins particularly mentions kissing.[51]

Other Puritans stressed the romantic side of marriage as they compared the love of a husband to God's love for His own. Thomas Hooker writes, "The man whose heart is endeared to the woman he loves, he dreams of her in the night, hath her in his eye and apprehension when he awakes, museth on her as he sits at table, walks with her when he travels and parlies with her in each place where he comes."[52] He adds: "She lies in his Bosom, and his heart trusts in her, which forceth all to confess, that the stream of his affection, like a mighty current, runs with full tide and strength."[53]

The emphasis on romance within marriage (rather than in extramarital relations, as was common in the Middle Ages)[54] has often been attributed to the Puritans. Herbert W. Richardson writes that "the rise of romantic marriage and its validation by the Puritans represents a major innovation within the Christian tradition."[55] And C. S. Lewis says, "The conversion of courtly love into romantic monogamous love was largely the work of . . . Puritan poets."[56]

The Puritans took the matrimonial duty of sex so seriously that failure to extend "due benevolence" by either partner could be grounds for church discipline. There is at least one case on record in which a husband was excommunicated for "neglecting his wife" by not having intercourse with her for a long period of time.

Whately and Gouge also emphasize other mutual duties in marriage. A husband and wife must be faithful to each other and help each other in every conceivable way, including seeking each other's spiritual growth, healing each other's faults, and steering each other away from sin. They must pray for one another, compliment one another, appreciate one another, and "keep the unity of the spirit in the bond of peace" with one another. They must not speak harshly to or provoke each other, but must show kindness to each other and overlook each other's minor faults. They must cultivate true friendship and take an interest in each other. They must be sympathetic to each other in times of distress, sickness, and weakness. They must promote each other's reputation, never speaking ill of and weakness. They must promote each other's reputation, never speaking ill of each other in the presence of others. They must be confidential, not revealing each other's secrets. They must be industrious in their callings, working diligently as a team for each other, for their family, and in hospitality to others, especially the poor. For these reasons, they must manage their money judiciously.[57]

• *The husband's duties.* The Puritans were fond of enumerating each spouse's duties. They taught that in addition to loving his wife and fulfilling mutual marital duties, the husband must govern his wife—not tyrannically, but as an equal. A husband must strive to lead his wife spiritually for her betterment, taking charge of their mutual worship of God. Baxter says the husband is to be a wife's "teacher and guide in the matters of God."[58]

Husbands should delight in their wives (Prov. 5:18–19), esteeming them, respecting them, and seeking to please them, even to the point that others consider it "doting." Husbands should not allow blemishes in their wives to slacken their affection for them, either. Gouge says, "If a man have a wife, not very beautiful, or proper, but having some deformity in her body, some imperfection in speech, sight, gesture, or any part of her body," he ought yet be so affectionate to her, "and delight in her, as if she were the fairest, and [in] every way the most complete woman in the world."[59]

Then, too, a husband must provide for his wife in sickness and in health. He must particularly assist her when she is pregnant.[60] He must bestow favors, kindnesses, and gifts on her. He must never strike her or abuse her verbally or physically. As Smith says, "Her cheek was meant for thy lips, not for thy fist!"[61] At times, a husband may reprove his wife, but only in tender love and always to steer her away from sin. Reproofs, however, should be rare and administered in private with humility—never when his wife is angry.[62]

Finally, a husband must accept the functions that his wife performs. He must show his acceptance by his gratitude, by not demanding too much from her, and by giving her freedom to manage the affairs of the home. He must do all this cheerfully and tenderly.[63] Perhaps Matthew Henry summarizes a husband's duties best in saying that the woman is "not made out of his head to rule over him, nor out of his feet to be trampled upon by him, but out of his side to be equal with him, under his arm to be protected, and near his heart to be beloved."[64]

• *The wife's duties.* In addition to showing submission and reverence to her husband and fulfilling mutual marital duties, a wife has numerous unique him in a variety of ways, helping him "in business, in his labours, in his troubles, in his sickness, like a woman physician," according to Smith.[65] She should be content with her husband's work, social standing, and financial status.

Then, too, she should manage the affairs of the household effectively (Prov. 31). Such management includes helping her husband "establish Christ's glorious kingdom in their house"; being thrifty without being miserly; consistently persevering in completing her duties; and handling herself with sobriety, mildness, courtesy, obeisance, and modesty, as the Bible commands.[66] Thomas Gataker sums it up, saying that a good wife is:

The best companion in wealth;
The fittest and readiest assistant in work;
The greatest comfort in crosses and griefs;
The only warrantable and comfortable means of issue and posterity;
A singular and sovereign remedy ordained by God against incontinency,
And the greatest grace and honor that can be, to him that hath her.[67]

"NO SOCIETY . . . MORE DELIGHTFUL"

This study of the Puritans' view of marriage serves as a window for us to see how Calvinists brought all of life under the reign of Scripture. The Bible was the instruction manual for the purposes, procedures, principles, and practices of marriage. No doubt some Puritan marriages fell considerably short of the ideal; yet, the Puritans' view of an ideal marriage and their diligence, in dependence on God, to work toward that ideal made the foundations of their homes solid. They understood that the man who fears God in his own home normally will be blessed with a happy marriage (Ps. 128:3). As Thomas Adams writes, "There is no such fountain of comfort on earth, as marriage."[68]

Gataker says of marriage, "There is no society more near, more entire, more needful, more kindly, more delightful, more comfortable, more constant, more continual, than the society of man and wife, the main root, source, and original of all other societies."[69] And yet, keeping an eye on eternity more than anything else, the Puritans shared Gataker's longing that "having lived together for a time as *co-partners in grace* here, they may reign together for ever as *co-heirs in glory* hereafter."[70]

DISCUSSION QUESTIONS

1. The Puritans had a high view of marriage. What statements by the Puritans bear this out?

2. What are the three purposes of marriage? Where did the Puritans find these purposes in the Bible? Are there other purposes of marriage that are not listed here that are found in the Bible? If so, what are they?

3. What procedures for marriage were followed by the Puritans? What can we learn from the Puritans in this area?

4. What are two major scriptural principles on which the Puritans grounded marriage?

5. What did the Puritans understand by the concept of the wife submitting to her husband?

6. What responsibilities does marriage involve for the wife? For the husband? Which of these behaviors is most needed in today's evangelical culture?

7. Discuss this statement in light of the Bible: "The Puritans viewed sex within marriage as a gift of God and as an essential, enjoyable part of marriage."

8. The Puritans believed that "no society" was "more delightful" than the married estate. Do you agree? Why or why not?

NOTES

1 Quoted in John Blanchard, *The Complete Gathered Gold* (Darlington, England: Evangelical Press, 2006), 405.

2 Richard Adams, "What are the Duties of Parents and Children; and how are they to be Managed According to Scripture?" *Puritan Sermons 1659–1689* (Wheaton, Ill: Richard Owen Roberts, 1981), 2:303–358; Isaac Ambrose, *Works of Isaac Ambrose* (London: Thomas Tegg & Son, 1872); Richard Baxter, "The Poor Man's Family Book," in *The Practical Works of Richard Baxter* (Morgan, Pa.: Soli Deo Gloria, 1996), 4:165–289; Paul Bayne, *An Entire Commentary upon the Whole Epistle of St. Paul to the Ephesians* (Edinburgh: James Nichol, 1866), 491–563; Robert Bolton, *General Directions for a Comfortable Walking with God* (Morgan, Pa.: Soli Deo Gloria, 1995), 262–281; Thomas Boston, "Duties of Husband and Wife; Sermon XXIII," in *The Works of Thomas Boston*, ed. Samuel M'Millan (Wheaton, Ill: Richard Owen Roberts, 1980), 4:209–218; John Bunyan, "Family Duty," *Free Grace Broadcaster*, 170 (1999): 15–28; John Cotton, *A Meet Help: Or, a Wedding Sermon* (Boston: B. Green & J. Allen, 1699); John Dod and Robert Cleaver, *A Godly Form of Household Government* (London: Thomas Man, 1598); Thomas Doolittle, "How May the Duty of Daily Family Prayer be Best Managed for the Spiritual Benefit of Every One in the Family?" in *Puritan Sermons, 1659–1689*, 2:194–272; Thomas Gataker, "A Good Wife God's Gift," "A Wife in Deed," and "Marriage Duties," in *Certain Sermons* (London: John Haviland, 1637); Thomas Gataker, *A Marriage Prayer* (London: John Haviland, 1624), 134–208; William Gouge, *Of Domestical Duties* (Pensacola: Puritan Reprints, 2006); Matthew Griffith, *Bethel: or, a Form for Families* (London: Richard Badger, 1633); George Hamond, *The Case for Family Worship* (Orlando: Soli Deo Gloria, 2005); Matthew Henry, "A Church in the House," in *Complete Works of Matthew Henry* (Grand Rapids: Baker, 1978), 1:248–267; William Perkins, "Christian Oeconomy," in *The Work of William Perkins*, ed. Ian Breward (Appleford, England: Sutton Courtenay Press, 1970), 416–439; John Robinson, *The Works of John Robinson*, vol. 3 (Boston: Doctrinal Tract and Book Society, 1851); Daniel Rogers, *Matrimonial Honour.* (London: Th. Harper, 1642); Henry Scudder, *The Godly Man's Choice* (London: Matthew Simmons for Henry Overton, 1644); Henry Smith, "A Preparative to Marriage," in *The Works of Henry Smith* (Stoke-on-Trent, England: Tentmaker Publications, 2002), 1:5–40; William Whately, *A Bride-Bush or A Wedding Sermon* (Norwood, N.J.: Walter J. Johnson, 1975); and William Whately, *A Care-Cloth or the Cumbers and Troubles of Marriage* (Norwood, N.J.: Walter J. Johnson, 1975).

3 J. Philip Arthur, "The Puritan Family," *The Answer of a Good Conscience*, Westminster Conference, 1997 (London: n.p., 1998), 75–94; Lawrence J. Bilkes, "The Scriptural Puritan Marriage" (unpublished paper for Puritan theology class at Puritan Reformed Theological Seminary, Grand Rapids, Mich., 2002); E. Braund, "Daily Life Among the Puritans," *The Puritan Papers: Volume One*, ed. J. I. Packer (Phillipsburg, N.J.: P&R, 2000), 155–166; Francis J. Bremer, *The Puritan Experiment: New England Society from Bradford to Edwards* (New York: St. Martin's Press, n.d.), 176–180; Catherine A. Brekus, "Children of Wrath, Children of Grace: Jonathan Edwards and the Puritan Culture of Child Rearing," in *The Child in Christian Thought*, ed. Marcia J. Bunge (Grand Rapids: Eerdmans, 2001), 300–328; Ezra Hoyt Byington, *The Puritan in England and New England* (Boston: Roberts Brothers, 1897), 221–277; J. T. Cliffe, *The Puritan Gentry: The Great Puritan Families of Early Stuart England* (London: Routledge & Kegan Paul, 1984), 63–82; W. Gary Crampton, *What the Puritans Taught* (Morgan, Pa.: Soli Deo Gloria, 2003), 62–72; Gaius Davies, "The Puritan Teaching on Marriage and the Family," *The Evangelical Quarterly*, 27, no. 1 (Jan. 1955): 19–30; John Demos, *A Little Commonwealth: Family Life in Plymouth Colony* (Oxford:

Oxford University Press, 1970), 82–106, 181–190; Daniel Doriani, "The Godly Household in Puritan Theology, 1560–1640" (Ph.D. dissertation, Westminster Theological Seminary, 1985); Christopher Durston, *The Family in the English Revolution* (New York: Basil Blackwell, 1989); Alice Morse Earle, *Customs and Fashions in Old New England* (Detroit: Omnigraphics, 1990); "Form for the Confirmation of Marriage Before the Church," in *Doctrinal Standards, Liturgy, and Church Order*, ed. Joel R. Beeke (Grand Rapids: Reformation Heritage Books, 1999), 156–158; Philip J. Greven, "Family Structure in Andover," *Puritanism in Early America*, ed. George M. Waller (Lexington, Mass.: D. C. Heath and Co., 1973); William and Malleville Haller, "The Puritan Art of Love," *Huntington Library Quarterly*, 5 (1942): 235–272; Charles E. Hambrick-Stowe, "Ordering Their Private World: What the Puritans did to grow spiritually," *Christian History*, 13, no. 1 (1994): 16–19; Graham Harrison, "Marriage and Divorce in Puritan Thinking," *The Fire Divine*, Westminster Conference, 1996 (London: n.p., 1997), 27–51; Erroll Hulse, *Who are the Puritans: And What do they Teach?* (Darlington, England: Evangelical Press, 2000), 139–142; James Turner Johnson, *A Society Ordained by God: English Puritan Marriage Doctrine in the First Half of the Seventeenth Century* (Nashville: Abingdon, 1970); M.M. Knappen, *Tudor Puritanism: A Chapter in the History of Idealism* (Chicago: University of Chicago Press, 1965), 451–466; Edmund Morgan, *The Puritan Family: Religion and Domestic Relations in Seventeenth-Century New England* (New York: Harper & Row, 1966); Steven Ozment, *When Fathers Ruled: Family Life in Reformation Europe* (Cambridge, Mass.: Harvard University Press, 1983); J. I. Packer, *A Quest for Godliness: The Puritan Vision of the Christian Life* (Wheaton, Ill.: Crossway, 1994), 259–273, 355–356; Neil Pronk, "Puritan Christianity: The Puritans at Home," *The Messenger* (Sept. 1997): 3–6; Helen Ratner, "The Puritan Family," *Child & Family*, 9, no. 1 (1970): 54–60; Darrett B. Rutman, *Winthrop's Boston: A Portrait of a Puritan Town, 1630–1649* (New York: W. W. Norton Co., 1972); Leland Ryken, *Worldly Saints: The Puritans As They Really Were* (Grand Rapids: Zondervan, 1986), 39–54, 73–88; Levin Ludwig Schucking, *The Puritan Family: A Social Study from the Literary Sources* (New York: Schocken Books, 1970); Lawrence Stone, *The Family, Sex and Marriage in England 1500–1800* (New York: Harper & Row, 1977); and Margo Todd, "Humanists, Puritans and the Spiritualized Household," *Church History*, 49, no. 1 (1980): 18–34.

4   Quoted in Ryken, *Worldly Saints*, 42.

5   Dod and Cleaver, *A Godly Form of Household Government*, 125.

6   John Downame, *The Plea of the Poor* (London: Edward Griffin, 1616), 119.

7   Cotton, *A Meet Help*, 14.

8   *Westminster Confession of Faith* (Glasgow: Free Presbyterian Publications, 1994), 103. The Dutch Reformed liturgy of the late sixteenth century had already adopted the same order, though more descriptively: "The first reason is that each faithfully assist the other in all things that belong to this life and a better. Secondly, that they bring up the children which the Lord shall give them, in the true knowledge and fear of God, to His glory, and their salvation. Third, that each of them avoiding all uncleanness and evil lusts, may live with a good and quiet conscience." (*Doctrinal Standards, Liturgy, and Church Order*, 156). Cf. Ryken, *Worldly Saints*, 48.

9   Smith, "A Preparative to Marriage," in *The Works of Henry Smith*, 1:5.

10   Gouge, *Of Domestical Duties*, 152.

11   Perkins, "Christian Oeconomy," in *The Work of William Perkins*, 420.

12   Quoted from the *Works of John Robinson*, in Charles H. and Katherine George, *The Protestant Mind of the English Reformation, 1570–1640* (Princeton: Princeton University Press, 1961), 268.

13   Gouge, *Of Domestical Duties*, 152.

14 Ibid.

15 John Winthrop, *Life and Letters of John Winthrop*, 2nd ed., ed. Robert C. Winthrop (Boston: Little, Brown & Co., 1869), 1:159.

16 Cotton, *A Meet Help*, 12.

17 Gouge, *Of Domestical Duties*, 143.

18 Ibid., 144.

19 Ibid., 147. For a sample of a contract that includes a commitment to basic Christian doctrines and an exposition of the Ten Commandments in the context of marital duties, see Kenneth L. Parker and Eric J. Carlson, "A Treatise of a Contract Before Marriage," in *'Practical Divinity': The Works and Life of Revd Richard Greenham* (Aldershot, England: Ashgate, 1998), 339–348.

20 Gouge, *Of Domestical Duties*, 148–149.

21 Ibid., 152.

22 Morgan, *The Puritan Family*, 30–31; Arthur, "The Puritan Family," 79.

23 Ambrose, *Works of Isaac Ambrose*, 130.

24 Gouge, *Of Domestical Duties*, 31.

25 Ibid.

26 Ibid., 94.

27 Ambrose, *Works of Isaac Ambrose*, 133.

28 Quoted in Ryken, *Worldly Saints*, 76.

29 Gouge, *Of Domestical Duties*, 96–97.

30 Morgan, *The Puritan Family*, 30.

31 Quoted in Morgan, *The Puritan Family*, 30.

32 Packer, *A Quest for Godliness*, 263.

33 Edward Payson, *The Works of Edward Payson* (Harrisonburg, Va.: Sprinkle, 1988), 285.

34 Gouge, *Of Domestical Duties*, 85.

35 For an excellent summary by Richard Baxter of the mutual duties of husband and wife, see Packer, *A Quest for Godliness*, 263.

36 Gouge, *Of Domestical Duties*, 163.

37 Whately, *A Bride-Bush*, 7.

38 Baxter, *The Practical Works of Richard Baxter*, 4:234.

39 Payson, *Works of Edward Payson*, 3:288.

40 Ambrose, *Works of Isaac Ambrose*, 130.

41 Whately, *A Bride-Bush*, 7.

42 Ibid., 8.

43 Ibid.

44 Ibid., 9.

45 Packer, *A Quest for Godliness*, 261.

46 Ryken, *Worldly Saints*, 40.

47 Perkins, "Christian Oeconomy," 419.

48 Ryken, *Worldly Saints*, 42.

49 Quoted in Ryken, *Worldly Saints*, 44.

50 Perkins, "Christian Oeconomy," 423.

51 Ibid., 423–427.

52 Thomas Hooker, *The Application of Redemption* (London: Peter Cole, 1659), 137.

53 Thomas Hooker, *A Comment Upon Christ's Last Prayer* (London: Peter Cole, 1656), 187. I am indebted to Packer, *A Quest for Godliness*, 265, for the last two quotations.

54 William Haller, *The Rise of Puritanism* (New York: Harper, 1957), 122.

55 Herbert W. Richardson, *Nun, Witch, Playmate: The Americanization of Sex* (New York: Harper & Row, 1971), 69.

56 C. S. Lewis, "Donne and Love Poetry in the Seventeenth Century," in *Seventeenth Century Studies Presented to Sir Herbert Grierson* (Oxford: Oxford University Press, 1938), 75.

57 Whately, *A Bride-Bush*, 11–16; Gouge, *Of Domestical Duties*, 165–190.

58 Baxter, *The Practical Works of Richard Baxter*, 4:234.

59 Gouge, *Of Domestical Duties*, 260.

60 Ibid., 288.

61 Quoted in Arthur, "The Puritan Family," 81.

62 Gouge, *Of Domestical Duties*, 273–279.

63 Ibid., 263–297.

64 Matthew Henry, *Commentary on the Whole Bible* (McLean, Va.: MacDonald Publishing Co.), 20.

65 Smith, *Works of Henry Smith*, 1:28.

66 Ambrose, *Works of Isaac Ambrose*, 133; Baxter, *The Practical Works of Richard Baxter*, 4:235; Gouge, *Of Domestical Duties*, 198–200, 240–241.

67 Gataker, "A Wife in Deed," 166.

68 Quoted in George and George, *The Protestant Mind of the English Reformation*, 268.

69 Gataker, "A Wife in Deed," 139–140.

70 Gataker, "Marriage Duties," 208.

CHAPTER 24

THE PURITAN
FAMILY

A holy family is a place of comfort, a church of God. . . . Oh that God would
stir up the hearts of people thus to make their families as little churches, that
it might not be in the power of rulers or pastors that are bad to extinguish
religion, or banish godliness from any land![1]

—RICHARD BAXTER

The Christian's relationship with his family is inseparable from personal sanctification, according to the Puritans. The Scriptures set forth the ways in which we are to live righteously, and since the Bible takes great pains to teach how parents and children should relate to one another, these relationships are an index of sanctification. So it is of primary importance that Christians recognize that holiness begins at home and then extends to all of life.

Puritan pastors spent much time teaching fathers how to exercise spiritual leadership in the home. They also advised Christian mothers of their role in the biblical pattern, and they taught children to show proper respect for parents in service to God. In this family emphasis, they aimed to follow only the Bible, for, as they said, the Bible presents the family as the fundamental unit of human society.[2] The Bible tells us to glorify God by raising children for Him for the well-being of society, the church, and the family itself. As Richard Baxter puts it, "It is no small mercy to be the parents of a Godly seed: and this is the end of the institution of marriage."[3] According to Isaac Ambrose, parents have the task of "erecting and establishing Christ's glorious kingdom in their house."[4]

The Puritans, both in writing and by example, provide us with the ideal

Reformed Christian home, bequeathing it to us in a direct and substantive way. This chapter shows how they did that.

CHILDREN ARE GIFTS OF GOD

While most Puritans believed that the primary purpose of marriage was companionship, they also believed that having children was an expected consequence of marital love. Children were seen as blessings of the Lord. And apparently they were blessings that the Lord bestowed frequently and abundantly. Puritan families were large, with an average of seven or eight children. The infant mortality rate was also very high, however. Typically, of all the children born in a family, less than half reached adulthood.

Though they tended to have large families, Puritan husbands did not procreate without due concern for their wives. According to Allen Carden, it was common practice to space children—in many cases, two years apart—over a period of up to twenty years, with siblings varying widely in age.[5]

The Puritans were also keenly aware that children were a tremendous responsibility. Viewing their families as nurseries for church and society, parents were expected to do everything possible to make sure their children conformed to biblical norms and precepts, especially the commandment to obey their parents.

AUTHORITY IN THE FAMILY

The Puritans regarded the headship of husbands and fathers as a biblical command. They expected a man to exercise spiritual, social, and educational leadership for his wife and children, and to provide adequate support for his family.

Though a wife was expected to submit to her husband's authority, the husband's hierarchical headship did not imply that the wife was his servant.[6] Furthermore, the Puritans believed in spheres of responsibility in a family. The husband could delegate authority in some of these spheres to his wife, particularly in matters dealing with the children and household servants. According to Samuel Willard, "She is invested with an authority over them by God; and her husband is to allow it to her, for though the husband be the head of the wife, she is an head of the family."[7]

In areas where the wife was more capable than her husband, such as in managing family finances, it was common for him to delegate such responsibilities to her.[8] Also, the headship principle did not prevent a woman from religious teaching or spiritual admonition of a man. "Women may and must privately and familiarly exhort others," Samuel Torshell writes in *The Woman's Glory*. "They may also privately admonish men and reprove them."[9] Nicholas Byfield says the wife is not subject to the husband "in matters of her soul and religion when his will is contrary to God's will." He adds, "She is not so subject but she may admonish and advise her husband with certain cautions, if she be sure the thing she speaks against be sinful and hurtful."[10]

Even though, in the final analysis, the husband was the head of the family, the husband and wife shared the authority for the day-to-day oversight of the family, Leland Ryken says.[11] For example, the Puritans believed that the father bore the primary responsibility for the education of children, but because this duty was seen as the task of both parents, he often delegated much of that authority to his wife. An excellent summary of the mutual task and authority of Puritan parents toward their children is contained in the 1677 church covenant from the congregation in Dorchester, Mass., which required parents to vow "to reform our families, engaging ourselves in a conscientious care to set up and maintain the worship of God in them and to walk in our houses with perfect hearts in a faithful discharge of all domestic duties: educating, instructing, and charging our children and our households to keep the ways of the Lord."[12]

The Puritans extended the parent-child relationship to all of society, based on the fifth commandment (see Westminster Larger Catechism, Q. 124–133). As a child is to honor his parents who are placed in authority over him by God, so employees are to honor employers, students are to honor teachers, citizens are to honor magistrates, and church members are to honor church office-bearers. Each person must know his place—either of submission or authority—in every sphere of life. And all those in authority must exercise that authority in accord with the Bible and therefore under God, who gives the Scriptures and His Son, to whom the Father gives all authority in heaven and on earth.

PRINCIPLES OF CHILD-REARING

Although much of the writing about Puritan ideas of child-rearing seems familiar to us, some of their ideas were revolutionary at the time. Here are just a few of their contributions that promoted biblical child-rearing:

• *Child-rearing begins at conception.* Prospective parents had two major tasks
before a child was born. First, they were to pray daily for the salvation of their
child, since the child was conceived in sin (Ps. 51:5).[13] They also were to pray
daily for the protection of both mother and child. Richard Adams writes, "Whilst
it is yet but an embryo, there is not only requisite prayer, with thanksgiving for
the sanctifying [of] the fruit of the body, as Jeremiah and John were (1 Tim. 4:5;
Jer. 1:5; Luke 1:15), but also a tender care for the preservation of life."[14] Second,
since miscarriages were common, the health of the mother was to be carefully
protected. Husbands were expected to tenderly help their wives during pregnancy
and childbirth. If they failed to do so and the baby was lost, they were regarded
as "guilty of the sin, and liable to the judgment."[15] Pregnant mothers were not to
run or ride horseback. They were to watch their diets closely, not eating what was
harmful, and not eating too much or too little. If through carelessness a woman
contributed to the miscarriage of a baby, she was reckoned "guilty of the blood"
of their child, "at least in the court of conscience before God."[16] Parents who
aborted a child were guilty of "wilful murder" and were to be judged guilty and
"revenged" both in the court of God and the court of man.[17]

• *Mothers have the major role in caring for newborns.* The Puritans stressed
that a mother's responsibilities included breastfeeding, which ought not be delegated to a midwife or nanny. William Gouge wrote ten pages on why it was
important for the mother to breastfeed, answering twelve objections along the
way.[18] Husbands were to encourage their wives to breastfeed and to offer what
help they could in caring for the infant.[19]

• *Baptizing infants is part of parents' covenant obligations to God.* Puritan
child-rearing was rooted in the conviction that children belonged to the covenant God makes with believers (Acts 2:39; 1 Cor. 7:14), evident in baptism,
which, being a sacrament, is a visible sign and seal of God's invisible grace. Just
as the believing Israelite had to circumcise his son in the old covenant, so, in
the new covenant, believing Christians are to baptize children to confirm their
inauguration into the covenant of grace. Baxter says that God "ordained baptism
to be used as a solemn initiation of all that will come into his church, and enter
into the covenant of God."[20]

In baptism, Christian parents assume covenant responsibilities on behalf of
their children. God, therefore, claims these children as His own; parents are stew-
ards of their children on God's behalf. Thomas Watson goes so far as to say that

Christian parents "will endeavour that their children may be more God's children than theirs."[21]

Believing that their children belonged to God did not mean that the Puritans believed their children were saved from birth. Rather, they believed that all children, whether elect or not, entered the world in a depraved state. They were lost in sin until brought to faith in Christ. Thus, children were *in*, but not necessarily *of*, the covenant. They lived under the promises of the covenant, but they still needed to appropriate these promises through faith, evidenced by repentance, faith in Christ, and a holy walk. The Puritans were convinced that God has no grandchildren and that each generation has to experience conversion itself.

They believed, however, that God uses parents to bring their children to a personal conversion experience. Parents were regularly taught in sermons to bring up their children so that the covenant promises given them at baptism might be fulfilled and realized in their lives. The New England Puritan Thomas Cobbett writes, "The greatest love and faithfulness which parents as covenanters can show to God and to their children, who in and with themselves are joint covenanters with God, is so to educate them that the conditions of the covenant may be attended by their children and so the whole covenant fully effected."[22]

• *Children must be trained early in the nurture and admonition of the Lord.* The salvation and godliness of children is the main purpose of their education. That goal can be realized only through the Spirit's blessing of the Word of God (Rom. 10). The Puritans made it a law that parents must teach their children to read so that they could read the Bible and other religious material for their spiritual welfare.[23] Gaius Davies sums up the Puritan approach to teaching: "Education should begin as early as possible, and though it should be thorough, godliness is more important than learning, and schoolmasters must be chosen with this in mind. The aptness or gifts of children should be noted, that they might be trained for a suitable calling. The claims of the Christian ministry should be remembered, and where the ability exists, a son should be exhorted to enter it."[24]

Reading opened the world of doctrine to children. Even Puritan reading tools themselves, such as the *New England Primer* (1683), conveyed theology. From this primer, the theological ABCs were taught: from A, "In Adam's Fall, we sinned all," to Z, "Zacchaeus, he did climb the Tree, his Lord to see."[25]

These tools worked hand in hand with catechetical instruction. The Puritans taught their children catechism as soon as possible; most fathers catechized each child for one hour per week. To help them, Puritan pastors wrote books that explained fundamental Christian doctrines by means of questions and answers supported by Scripture.[26] Fathers explained the theological content of the questions and answers of these catechism books by illustrating them with Bible stories and dialoguing with their children.[27]

The goals of catechizing were to make sermons and the sacraments more understandable for covenant children, to prepare them for confession of faith, and to teach them how to defend their faith against error.[28] Then, too, children were taught that truth must be loved and lived. As the Puritan ministers' catechism books and sermons show, children were told the truth about matters such as the fall in Adam, sin, and condemnation, as well as salvation in Christ, His righteousness, and everlasting bliss. They also were invited, via appeals to their wills and hearts, to flee to Christ with their sins.[29] The ultimate goal was not simply a well-stocked head, but also a warm appreciation of the truths of God in mind and soul so that the child would lead a holy life. Baxter advises: "Let it be the principal part of your care and labour in all their education to make holiness appear to them the most necessary, honourable, gainful, pleasant, delightful, amiable state of life; and to keep them from apprehending it either as needless, dishonourable, hurtful, or uncomfortable. Especially draw them to the love of it, by representing it as lovely."[30] William Perkins advises that the "instruction of children in learning and religion, must be so ordered, that they may take it with delight."[31]

Parents were to nurture and train their children in godly ways not only by teaching, but, what was more important, by example. Richard Greenham writes, "Experience teaches us that children learn more by countenance, gesture, and behaviour than by rule, doctrine, precept, or instruction."[32] Likewise, it was recognized that a bad example would cause great harm. As Greenham says: "If parents would have their children blessed at church and at school, let them beware they give their children no corrupt examples at home by any carelessness, profaneness, or ungodliness. Otherwise, parents will do them more harm at home than both pastors and schoolmasters can do them good abroad."[33]

• *Family worship is the most powerful means for child-rearing.* Puritan families gathered for worship once or twice each day.[34] The Westminster Directory for Family Worship (1647), written by Puritans, states that "family worship, which ought to be performed by every family, ordinarily morning and evening, consists in prayer, reading the Scriptures, and singing praises."[35]

Typically, Puritan family worship included several elements. First, there was prayer. The Puritans believed that God would pour out His fury on families that did not call on His name (Jer. 10:25). Family prayer was both a domestic obligation and a privilege. Puritan fathers normally prayed for five to ten minutes. They aimed for simplicity without being shallow. They strove to glorify God in their prayers while being specific in their petitions. They confessed family sins, asked for family mercies, and offered family thanksgivings. Their prayers, which were natural yet solemn, often consisted largely of bringing God's own Word back to Him.[36]

Second, there was reading of Scripture. This was usually done by the father as head of the household, though some fathers delegated parts of it to family members who were capable of reading. The family usually read straight through the Bible, out of the conviction that God gave a whole Bible to make a whole Christian. On special occasions, such as the Lord's Supper, the death of a loved one, or a national day of prayer and fasting, the father would select an appropriate Scripture reading.[37]

Third, there was instruction from Scripture. In accord with Deuteronomy 6:6–7 and 11:18–19, the Puritans believed that the father should interact with his family about sacred truth on a daily basis by means of questions, answers, and teaching. Fathers should undertake this exercise diligently and with passion, the Puritans believed. The Directory for Family Worship provides insight into how they were to do this:

> The holy scriptures should be read ordinarily to the family; and it is commendable, that thereafter they confer, and by way of conference, make some good use of what hath been read and heard. As, for example, if any sin be reproved in the word read, use may be made thereof to make all the family circumspect and watchful against the same; or if any judgment be threatened or mentioned to have been inflicted, in that portion of scripture which is read, use may be made to make all the family fear lest the same or a worse judgment befall them, unless they beware of the sin that procured it: and finally, if any duty be required, or comfort held forth in a promise, use may be made to stir up themselves to employ Christ for strength to enable

them for doing the commanded duty, and to apply the offered comfort. In all which the master of the family is to have the chief hand; and any member of the family may propose a question or doubt for resolution.[38]

In leading the devotional time, the father aimed to remain pure in doctrine, relevant in application, and affectionate in manner. He asked and encouraged questions and, at times, lovingly examined the spiritual well-being of his children. Byfield says there are eight topics appropriate for family instruction: the fear of God, the meaning of the sacraments, the law of God, the consideration of God's judgments, God's great works on behalf of His people, how to hope in God, the general meaning of the Scriptures, and the reinforcing of what was preached in church.[39] Recent sermons (on which family members took notes), providential occurrences in the family, church, or nation, and pertinent illustrations were fertile fields for the father to plow as he sought to bring home to his family the truth about sin, Christ, grace, spiritual life, holiness, and scores of other doctrines and issues.

Fourth, there was praise in psalm-singing. Most Puritans believed, as did Philip Henry, father of the famed commentator Matthew Henry, that Psalm 118:15a ("The voice of rejoicing and salvation is in the tabernacles of the righteous") refers to daily singing in the tents of the Israelite families. By extension, Henry argues that the sound of rejoicing and salvation should rise from Puritan family homes through daily singing. In such singing, God is glorified and families are edified. It promotes devotion as it informs the mind and warms the heart. The graces of the Spirit are stirred up in us, and our growth in grace is stimulated (Col. 3:16). Singing must be biblical and doctrinally pure, and it must be done heartily and with feeling (Col. 3:23).[40]

Daily family worship was a necessity and a privilege in the typical Puritan home. It was viewed as a powerful tool to help parents rear children. Love for the glory of God and the welfare of His church called for family worship. Failure to lead the family in worship was failure to be a father, for no father could neglect family worship and keep a good conscience. William Whately says that a father who does not lead his household in the ways of God through family worship "keeps an household of fiends, a Seminary for the devil, a nursery for hell, and the kingdom of death."[41]

• *Discipline is an essential part of child-rearing.* Bringing up children in the fear of the Lord included firm discipline, the Puritans said. Such discipline involved more than teaching and modeling proper behavior. "Doctrine and example alone are insufficient," John Norton writes. "Discipline is an essential part of the nurture of the Lord."[42]

Reproof plus the rod gives wisdom, the Puritans said. When a child is disobedient, verbal reproof must be administered first. In this, the parent shows the child that he or she has committed sin against God and man, and must repent. If verbal reproof is ineffective, the rod must be used as "a means appointed by God," Gouge says, "to help good nurture and education of children. It is the last remedy that a parent can use: a remedy which may do good when nothing else can."[43] Spanking must be measured according to the offense committed, and must be done in a timely manner, with love, compassion, prayer, and self-control.[44]

Perkins warns against using excessive force in discipline, which will stir a child to wrath (Eph. 6:4), and against being too lenient, as Eli was with his sons (1 Sam. 2:23).[45] On the one hand, the child's naturally evil will must be broken. "Train them up in exact obedience to yourselves, and break them of their own wills," Baxter advises.[46] On the other hand, the Puritans did not want to break a child's spirit in the process of breaking his or her will, and they advocated that discipline be fair, gentle, and geared to the temperament of the child.[47] Parents were to see that their children's stubborn wills and selfishness were restrained and repressed, even as their attractive qualities were commended.[48]

Thus, the Puritans steered a balanced course between harshness and leniency. Despite their strong convictions about a child's inner depravity, they were optimistic that God would save that child, for they believed that God ordinarily works to save His covenant seed.[49] Cotton Mather says, "Young saints will make old angels; and, blessed be God, there are such young saints in the world." Recalling his own childhood, he says, "The great care of my godly parents was to bring me up in the nurture and admonition of the Lord: whence I was kept from many visible outbreakings of sin which else I had been guilty of; and whence it was that I had many good impressions of the Spirit of God upon me, even from my infancy."[50]

• *Children should welcome their parents' help in making major life decisions.* In the seventeenth century, young men and women prepared for a lifelong profession. The Puritans reasoned that God had foreordained a particular profession for every believer, through which he or she was to live and work to God's glory. As young people entered their early teens, their parents were expected to help them determine what those professions might be. Adams summarizes their task well: "Christian parents are concerned not only to train-up their children for business in the world, but to do what they can to provide an honest, fit, and useful calling or profession, wherein they may serve their generation according to the will of God (Acts 13:36), and the abilities he hath bestowed on them, and the inclinations he hath implanted in them, whereby they may mostly promote the kingdom of Christ."[51]

Similarly, Christian parents were to help their young people select a suitable mate for life. There were at least five major criteria parents considered, in the following order of priority: (1) Would the proposed spouse walk with their son or daughter with wisdom and genuine godliness in marriage? Such qualities were necessary for the marriage to be "in the Lord." (2) Would the proposed spouse fit the biblical description of what a marriage partner is to be? Does the proposed husband have good leadership skills and a loving demeanor? Does the proposed wife show submission and reverence to her own father? A biblical mindset about marriage and a character that reflected that mindset was of utmost importance. (3) Was the proposed spouse mature and properly motivated for entering into marriage? It was necessary to avoid marrying out of wrong motivations, such as the love of money or power. (4) Was the proposed spouse fairly equal to their son or daughter in terms of class and financial resources? It was necessary to avoid being "unequally yoked" culturally and socially, because people did not change classes often or easily three centuries ago. (5) Was the proposed spouse somewhat attractive in the eyes of their son or daughter? It was felt that there should be at least some romantic spark to begin with, though the Puritans taught that most romance would develop after marriage. Note that appearance was the last and least matter to be concerned about; marriages were built more on character than on appearance.[52]

Puritan pastors advised parents and children to avoid two extremes. First, parents were not to force their children into occupations and marriages to which the children were not attracted. "Though the match may seem meet [fitting] in the parents' eye, yet he may not force his children thereto," Gouge writes. "Though the authority of parents ought in this case to be inviolable, yet a middle course is so to be held, as the parties may willingly with a mutual consent join themselves together."[53] Second, children were not to dismiss their parents' advice because they were not immediately drawn to it.

Rather, they were to seriously consider that their parents had their best end in view, were wiser than their children, and often knew what was best for them. When parental advice differed substantially from a son's or daughter's desire, the young man or woman was expected to pray about the advice and consider it seriously before, if necessary, politely and reverently telling parents that he or she could not in good conscience pursue the recommended spouse or occupation.[54]

THOROUGH PARENTAL INVOLVEMENT

Many other notable tasks of Puritan parents—such as physical provision, recreational guidance, and preparing a will—cannot be addressed here. Suffice it to say that, from conception to marriage, parents were thoroughly involved in the lives of their children. In every area, the parental task was to lead children to God and to do His will. Puritan parents prayerfully awaited God's blessing on their endeavors. Blessing was measured primarily by their children's walking in communion with God, manifesting holiness in their lives, and exercising their gifts to the well-being of family, church, and society.

The Puritans scorned those who neglected the tasks of child-rearing, regarding them as fools and scoundrels. Puritan preachers frequently issued solemn warnings to parents who were neglectful in child-rearing. On the Judgment Day, Richard Mather says, there will be children who are condemned partly because their parents have neglected to bring them up in the fear of the Lord. These children will then accuse their parents in words like these:

> All this that we here suffer is through you; you should have taught us the things of God, and did not; you should have restrained us from sin and corrected us, and you did not; you were the means of our original corruption and guilt, and yet you never showed any care that we might be delivered from it. Woe unto us that we had such carnal and careless parents, and woe unto you that had no more compassion and pity to prevent the everlasting misery of your own children.[55]

With such warnings, Puritan parents generally performed their child-rearing duties with great seriousness, taking a theological, objective, and uncompromisingly biblical approach rather than a theoretical, subjective, and pragmatic approach. The result was that many families became like miniature churches. In his 1646 tract *The Character of an Old English Puritan, or Nonconformist*, the Puritan John Geree says, "His family he [the ideal Puritan] endeavoured to make a Church, both in regard of persons and exercises, admitting none into it but such as feared God; and labouring that those that were born in it, might be born again to God."[56]

According to the Puritans, the well-being of the local church and society depends on what children learn in the family.[57] Well-ordered families, Cotton Mather says, "naturally produce a good order in other societies." He concludes, "Families are the nurseries for Church and Commonwealth; ruin families and you ruin all."[58]

That the ideas summarized in this chapter are familiar to many of us is a testimony to the effect Puritan teaching had on later generations of educators. Ultimately, of course, their ideas were sound because they were drawn from Scripture. They were experts at combining personal piety with a comprehensive Christian worldview, one of the hallmarks of biblical Calvinism. Beginning with the premise that the Bible is a reliable repository of truth, they had a basis from which to apply their Christian faith to all areas of marriage and family life.

Packer concludes that the Puritans are "the creators of the English Christian marriage, the English Christian family and the English Christian home."[59] We need to recover their Calvinist vision, in the words of Philip Arthur, "by recovering their expectation that faithfulness to God in the commonplace things of life will be rewarded; that it is a high and noble aim to attempt the difficult balancing act of seeing that every relationship is honoured; that we meet our obligations to God, to the local church, community and Commonwealth, that we honour and serve spouse, parents, children, employers and employees, in other words that we do the ordinary things well in dependence on God knowing that he honours those who honour him."[60] Here is solid, honorable, practical Calvinism, worthy of emulation and sorely needed in our day of self-gratification and disrespect for authority, a day in which every man does that which is right in his own eyes.

DISCUSSION QUESTIONS

1. What did the Puritans think about the relationship between husbands and wives? How does their view challenge the thinking of today?

2. How should we view children? Why?

3. How should children be raised? Give biblical support for your answer.

4. The Puritans thought that child-rearing ought to begin at conception. Why did they think this?

5. What did baptism mean for the Puritans?

6. What is catechizing? Why is it vital for child-rearing?

7. *Discipline* is a negative word in modern culture. How did the Puritans regard the use of discipline in the raising of children? What can we learn from them in this regard?

8. How were Puritan parents involved in the marriages of their children? Is this practice biblical? Why or why not?

NOTES

[1] Richard Baxter, "The Poor Man's Family book," in *The Practical Works of Richard Baxter* (Morgan, Pa.: Soli Deo Gloria, 1996), 4:230–231. For much of what follows, including several quotations, I am indebted to Leland Ryken's excellent chapter on the Puritan family in his *Worldly Saints: The Puritans as They Really Were* (Grand Rapids: Zondervan, 1990), 73–90, and to Neil Pronk for freedom to use several thoughts from a lecture that he gave on "The Puritans at Home," most of which was later published in *The Messenger*, 44, no. 8 (Sept. 1997): 3–6.

[2] Ryken, *Worldly Saints*, 74.

[3] Quoted in John Halkett, *Milton and the Idea of Matrimony* (New Haven: Yale University Press, 1970), 20.

[4] Quoted in R. C. Richardson, *Puritanism in North-West England: A Regional study of Chester to 1642* (Manchester: Manchester University Press, 1972), 105.

[5] Allen Carden, *Puritan Christianity in America: Religion and Life in Seventeenth-Century Massachusetts* (Grand Rapids, Baker, 1990), 174.

[6] Ibid.

[7] Quoted in Ryken, *Worldly Saints*, 78.

[8] Edmund Morgan, *The Puritan Family: Religion and Domestic Relations in Seventeenth-Century New England* (New York: Harper & Row, 1966), 43.

[9] Quoted in Richardson, *Puritanism in North-West England*, 106.

[10] Quoted in Ryken, *Worldly Saints*, 78.

[11] Ibid.

[12] Ibid., 80.

[13] William Gouge, *Of Domestical Duties* (Pensacola: Puritan Reprints, 2006), 364.

[14] Richard Adams, "What are the Duties of Parents and Children; and how are they to be Managed According to Scripture?" *Puritan Sermons 1659–1689* (Wheaton, Ill.: Richard Owen Roberts, 1981), 2:324.

[15] Gouge, *Of Domestical Duties*, 368.

[16] Ibid.

[17] Ibid.

[18] Ibid., 368–377; cf. Lawrence Stone, *The Family, Sex and Marriage in England 1500–1800* (New York: Harper & Row, 1977), 426–432.

[19] Ibid., 368, 376–377.

[20] Baxter, *The Practical Works of Richard Baxter*, 4:179.

[21] Quoted in Ryken, *Worldly Saints*, 79.

[22] Ibid.

[23] Morgan, *The Puritan Family*, 88.

[24] Gaius Davies, "The Puritan Teaching on Marriage and the Family," *Evangelical Quarterly*, 27, no. 1 (Jan. 1955): 19.

[25] Charles E. Hambrick-Stowe, "Ordering Their Private World: What the Puritans did to grow spiritually," *Christian History*, 13, no. 1 (1994): 18.

[26] See Ian Green, *The Christian's ABC: Catechisms and Catechizing in England, ca. 1530–1740* (Oxford: Clarendon Press, 1996); George Edward Brown, "Catechists and Catechisms of Early New England" (D.R.E. dissertation, Boston University, 1934); P. Hutchinson, "Religious Change: The Case of the

English Catechism, 1560–1640" (Ph.D. dissertation, Stanford University, 1984); R. M. E. Paterson, "A Study in Catechisms of the Reformation and Post-Reformation Period" (M.A. thesis, Durham University, 1981); Timothy Sisemore, *Of Such is the Kingdom: Nurturing Children in the Light of Scripture* (Ross-shire, U.K.: Christian Focus, 2000), 93–94.

27 For contemporary books that will help you recover this lost art of home-catechizing, see Joyce M. Horton, *How to Teach the Catechism to Children* (Jackson, Miss.: Reformed Theological Seminary, 1979); Starr Meade, *Training Hearts, Teaching Minds: Family Devotions Based on the Shorter Catechism* (Phillipsburg, N.J.: P&R. 2000); and Donald VanDyken, *Rediscovering Catechism: The Art of Equipping Covenant Children* (Phillipsburg, N.J.: P&R. 2000). VanDyken includes a thorough, annotated bibliography.

28 Joel R. Beeke, *Bringing the Gospel to Covenant Children* (Grand Rapids: Reformation Heritage Books, 2004), 28–32; Morgan, *The Puritan Family*, 98–100.

29 For a largely negative but informative study of Jonathan Edwards' sermons to children, see Catherine A. Brekus, "Children of Wrath, Children of Grace: Jonathan Edwards and the Puritan Culture of Child Rearing," in *The Child in Christian Thought*, ed. Marcia J. Bunge (Grand Rapids: Eerdmans, 2001), 315–317.

30 Baxter, *The Practical Works of Richard Baxter*, 1:451.

31 William Perkins, *The Works of William Perkins* (Cambridge: J. Legatt, 1606), 1: 694.

32 Quoted in Ryken, *Worldly Saints*, 83.

33 Richard Greenham, *The Works of Richard Greenham* (New York: De Capo Press, 1973), 162.

34 For an excellent treatment of family worship by a Puritan, see Obadiah Heywood, "The Family Altar," in *The Works of Oliver Heywood* (Morgan, Pa.: Soli Deo Gloria, 1999), 4:294–418.

35 *Westminster Confession of Faith* (Glasgow: Free Presbyterian Publications, 1994), 419.

36 See Thomas Doolittle, "How May the Duty of Daily Family Prayer be Best Managed for the Spiritual Benefit of Every One in the Family?" in *Puritan Sermons 1659–1689*, 2:194–271.

37 Cf. George Hamond, *The Case for Family Worship* (Orlando: Soli Deo Gloria, 2005).

38 *Westminster Confession of Faith*, 419–420.

39 Nicholas Byfield, *A Commentary on the Epistle to the Colossians* (Stoke-on-Trent, England: Tentmaker Publications, 2001), 42.

40 Cf. Horton Davies, "Puritan Family Worship," in *The Worship of the English Puritans* (Glasgow: Dacre Press, 1948), 278–285.

41 William Whately, *A Care-Cloth or the Cumbers and Troubles of Marriage* (Norwood, N.J.: Walter J. Johnson, 1975), 16; cf. Matthew Henry, "On Family-Religion," *Complete Works* (Grand Rapids: Baker, 1997), 1:254–257, and Joel R. Beeke, *Family Worship* (Grand Rapids: Reformation Heritage Books, 2002.

42 Quoted in Ryken, *Worldly Saints*, 80.

43 Gouge, *Of Domestical Duties*, 403–408.

44 Ibid., 406; cf. John Dod and Richard Cleaver, *A Plain and Familiar Exposition of the Ten Commandments* (London: Thomas Man, 1632), 179–180.

45 Perkins, *The Works of William Perkins*, 1:694; cf. Thomas Lye, "What May Gracious Parents Best Do for the Conversion of Those Children Whose Wickedness is Occasioned by Their Sinful Severity or Indulgence?" in *Puritan Sermons 1659–1689*, 3:154–184.

46 Baxter, *The Practical Works of Richard Baxter*, 1:450.

47 J. Philip Arthur, "The Puritan Family," in *The Answer of a Good Conscience*, Westminster Conference, 1997 (London: n.p., 1998), 85.

[48] John Robinson, *The Works of John Robinson* (Boston: Doctrinal Tract and Book Society, 1851), 1:247; cf. Arthur Hildersham, "Disciplining Children," in *The Godly Family*, ed. Samuel Davies (Morgan, Pa.: Soli Deo Gloria, 1997), 104–137.

[49] Ryken, *Worldly Saints*, 84; Herman Witsius, *The Economy of the Covenants Between God and Man* (London: R. Baynes, 1822), 2:442.

[50] Quoted in Ryken, *Worldly Saints*, 84.

[51] Adams, *Puritan Sermons 1659–1689*, 2:338.

[52] Gouge, *Of Domestical Duties*, 410–413.

[53] Ibid., 412.

[54] Morgan, *The Puritan Family*, 79.

[55] Quoted in Ryken, *Worldly Saints*, 84.

[56] Quoted in Gordon S. Wakefield, *Puritan Devotion: Its Place in the Development of Christian Piety* (London: Epworth Press, 1957), x.

[57] Ryken, *Worldly Saints*, 74.

[58] Quoted in Carden, *Puritan Christianity in America*, 175.

[59] J. I. Packer, *A Quest for Godliness: The Puritan Vision of the Christian Life* (Wheaton, Ill.: Crossway, 1994), 341–342.

[60] Arthur, "The Puritan Family," 91.

CHAPTER 25

WORKING FOR
GOD'S GLORY

Ray Pennings

Every age has tended to make its view of work conform to prevailing social practices. In a society based on slavery, Greek thinkers decided that work was beneath the dignity of free people. In an era when the clergy dominated society, people were content with a two-track view of work that made ordinary work second best. As Western civilization drifted from its Christian roots, its work ethic became decidedly secular and devoid of a religious base. It should be clear, therefore, that a genuinely Christian view of work must be based on something (the Bible) more authoritative and transcendent than mere human thinking, no matter how helpful that thinking is.[1]

—LELAND RYKEN

*A*ttitudes toward work help define societies. For instance, the ancient Greeks believed that "work was a curse and nothing else."[2] Their society thus supported slavery so that free men, like the gods, could pursue contemplation and immortality. But basic perceptions regarding work are important not only for understanding societies; they also practically affect how most people experience life.

Calvinism is associated with a particular view of work. The familiar term "the Protestant [work] ethic" is defined by the *Encyclopedia Britannica* as "the value attached to hard work, thrift, and efficiency in one's worldly calling, which,

349

especially in the Calvinist view, were deemed signs of an individual's election, or eternal salvation."[3] Although the term was popularized by the 1905 publication of Max Weber's *The Protestant Ethic and the Spirit of Capitalism*,[4] some have argued that "for the past three centuries Western civilization has been dominated by a secularized perversion of the original Puritan work ethic."[5] Even contemporary literature links Calvinism (or Puritanism, in a North American setting) with various aspects of our political and economic systems. Secular critics use this work ethic to critique religious involvement in the public square. Some blame the legacy of Puritanism for lifestyles "that are damaging to people and the environment."[6] The Puritan heritage has been linked to versions of "health and wealth" theologies,[7] a work-life imbalance and lack of leisure in society,[8] and even the obsessive use of company fitness programs.[9]

This chapter evaluates the origins of the caricature of Calvinism that gave rise to these critiques, then summarizes the main themes in Calvinism regarding work and vocation. It concludes with some suggestions for applying Calvinist principles to our contemporary situation.

WEBER'S CARICATURE

Weber, a German sociologist with Marxist leanings, saw a correlation between the predominance of Calvinism in a country and that nation's subsequent economic prosperity. In contrast with his contemporary, Karl Marx, who explained the development of capitalism in terms of class, Weber suggested that religion created "the psychological conditions which made possible the development of capitalist civilizations."[10] Weber started with the premise that a Calvinist could never really know whether he was saved, since salvation was a result of God's decree. A "conviction of salvation," Weber's term for assurance, comes from seeing good works in one's life. However, individual good works do not merit salvation; rather, the God of Calvinism demands a life of good works from those He saves.[11] The burden of this requirement affected how an individual approached his work, Weber said, because "the process of sanctifying life could thus almost take on the character of the business enterprise."[12]

Weber's thesis continues to be widely debated today.[13] One contemporary Reformed author on work conspicuously ignores what he calls the "dreaded Weber thesis," saying it is unhelpful for a "discussion of the Protestant concept of vocation to be dominated by a speculative thesis which, in my estimation, has rightly lost its credibility."[14] But even though few Calvinists view work as Weber did, his thesis remains influential—particularly so for those who study Calvinism in a secular academy, where Reformed Christianity is seen as an individualistic religion in which everything is understood in the context of how it affects personal salvation.

An individualistic view of Calvinism profoundly influences the perception of work. Election contributes to a believer's sense of duty to acquiesce when one's role is prescribed by God. Thus, the believer strives to carry out his responsibilities with excellence and dedication. So election not only motivates good works as a means of assurance, it also results in the economic class system that often derives from market economies.[15] One can see how, with arguments for private property that derive from the eighth commandment and with the notion of political accountability to God, Puritanism has been used to defend what would commonly be referred to in the popular press as a "right wing market agenda"[16]—an acceptance that there will be economic winners and losers. Variations on this approach have been used by critics who wish to discredit market economics as theologically and politically misguided, as well as by defenders who suggest that the Puritan legacy is essential to understanding America's historical tradition.

To be sure, election, calling (or *vocation*, to use the historic word), a view of work as good, and the promotion of thrift, stewardship, and private property all are supported in Calvinist and Puritan literature. Consequently, it is not difficult to offer an impressive argument with supporting quotations that uses Calvinist ideas to defend the prosperity theology[17] that is promoted by a "large and visible segment of American evangelicalism."[18] While most who argue this way would not identify themselves as Reformed, some covenant views are taught in ways tantamount to a version of prosperity theology. For example, children are taught that by walking in the Lord's ways, practicing good stewardship, and diligently using their gifts they may expect a life of relative prosperity. Later, I will examine the Puritan understanding of *promised blessing*, since the potential for misapplication of this teaching is real. Also, there are Reformed churches where people who do not achieve economic success are marginalized. More than once, the Puritans have been cited to support "the American dream"[19] as a consequence of an orthodox religious framework. It is possible that the thinking of many Reformed young people has been shaped by exposure to Weber's caricature of

Calvinism during their study of business, economics, political theory, and sociology in secular settings.

A POSITIVE FRAMING

Given these misunderstandings, there is an obvious need for the teachings of Calvinism to be applied properly to issues of work and vocation. But in order for this to happen, several themes emerging from Calvinism must be grasped:

• *View of work.* The Reformers considered work to have intrinsic dignity. John Calvin wrote, "No work will be so mean and sordid as not to have a splendor and value in the eye of God."[20] Hugh Latimer linked the dignity of work to the dignity of Christ. "This is a wonderful thing, that the Saviour of the world, and the King above all kings, was not ashamed to labour; yea, and to use so simple an occupation," Latimer wrote. "Here he did sanctify all manner of occupations."[21] John Cotton noted, "Faith is ready to embrace any homely service his calling leads him to, which a carnal heart would blush to be seen in."[22]

Reformed teachings regarding work can be summarized in the following points:[23]

1. God works, and we are called to bear His image.

2. God derives satisfaction from His work.

3. God provides for us through our work.

4. God has commanded man to work, and to work within the framework of His commands.

5. God holds us accountable for our work and expects to be acknowledged through it.

6. God provides particular gifts designed to meet particular needs in the advancement of His kingdom.

7. The fall radically affected our work. Work became toil; thorns and thistles frustrate our efforts; fallen man seeks to glorify himself rather than his Creator through work.

8. Work is an individual as well as a social activity.

9. God takes pleasure in beauty, and the Scriptures do not focus simply on the functional and utilitarian aspects of work.

10. Christ worked as part of His active obedience, and the believer's work through Christ is part of obedience.

- *Vocation.* The most influential Puritan writing on vocation is a 1603 sermon by William Perkins titled "A Treatise of the Vocations or Callings of Men."[24] Basing the sermon on 1 Corinthians 7:20, "Let every man abide in the same calling wherein he was called," Perkins defines vocation as "a certain kind of life, ordained and imposed on man by God, for the common good." He uses military and clock metaphors to show how the callings of individuals relate to one another, suggesting that "no more may any man leave his calling, except he receives liberty from God." This is because the purpose of a calling is not individual accomplishment but the "common good, that is, . . . the benefit and good estate of mankind," he says. "The common good of men stands in this, not only that they live, but that they live well, in righteousness and holiness and true happiness. And for the attainment hereunto, God hath ordained and disposed all callings, and his providence designed persons to bear them."

Perkins distinguishes between general and personal calling. General calling is "the calling of Christianity." In that context, a believer should carry out his or her personal calling. Personal calling includes "the execution of some particular office," with distinctions in work arising from the application of different gifts. There is a "diversity of gifts that God bestows on his Church, and so proportionally in every society," Perkins says. There is also a distinction so "that in every society one should be above or under another, not making all equal, as though the body should be all heading and nothing else."

Our gifts are not just for ourselves but also for service to church or society. As Perkins argues: "Every particular calling must be practiced in and with the general calling of a Christian. It is not sufficient for a man in the congregation, and in common conversation, to be a Christian, but in his very personal calling, he must show himself to be so. For example, a Magistrate must not only in general be a Christian, as every man is, but he must be a Christian Magistrate, in bearing the sword." Perkins concludes that the benefits of our callings are not the real purpose for them: "Some man will say perchance, 'What, must we not labour in our callings to maintain our families?' I answer, this must be done, but this is not the scope and end of our lives. The true end of our lives is to do service to God, and in service of man: and for a recompense of this service, God sends his blessing on men's travails and allows them to take for their labours."

In contrast to medieval dualism, which viewed contemplation as the best way to worship God, the Reformers emphasized how all work activity can be viewed as worship. Calvin says God is not "the vain, indolent, slumbering omnipotence," as the Sophists portrayed Him, but "vigilant, efficacious, energetic, and ever active."[25] As Lee Hardy notes, "It follows, on Calvin's view, that we express the image of God within us, that we become most Godlike not when we turn away from action, but when we engage in it."[26]

• *The promise of blessing.* While the Puritans would not have denied that believers can expect blessing on their work because of God's covenant faithfulness, citing such passages as 2 Thessalonians 3:10, their early literature does not support the notion that wealth is to be regarded as a sign of God's favor.[27] The more common theme in their writings is the spiritual danger inherent in the possession of wealth. Richard Baxter warns, "Remember that riches do make it harder for a man to be saved,"[28] and the Puritan Samuel Willard notes, "As riches are not evidences of God's love, so neither is poverty of His anger or hatred."[29]

Calvin also notes the difference between merit and reward, saying that whatever blessings come our way are rooted in the goodness and graciousness of God:

> A reward is promised, not as a debt, but from the mere good pleasure of God. It is a great mistake to suppose that there is a mutual relation between Reward and Merit; for it is by his own undeserved favor, not by the value of our works, that God is induced to reward them. . . . Whenever we meet with the word *reward*, or whenever it occurs to our recollection, let us look upon this as the crowning act of the goodness of God to us, that, though we are completely in his debt, he condescends to enter into a bargain with us.[30]

VOCATIONAL CALVINISM FOR OUR TIMES

Resolving the tension between critiques of the Protestant work ethic and the concept as it was proposed in the original sources reveals practical lessons for today.

Weber relies extensively on Baxter's "eminently practical and realistic attitude"[31] to present a methodical formula of dos and don'ts for Puritan life. Weber quotes Baxter to bolster his assertions that Calvinists promote menial physical labor,[32] sexual relations within marriage only for purposes of procreation,[33] and selecting and sticking to an occupation.[34] What Weber misses, however, is the explanation that the Christian life is lived out of gratitude for the deliverance provided in Christ rather than as a means of proving one's salvation. In the introduction to *The Saints' Everlasting Rest*, Baxter positions his arguments in the context of "enjoyment of God." "Doubtless as God advances our senses, and enlarges our capacity, so will he advance the happiness of those senses, and fill up with himself, all that capacity," he writes. "Certainly the body would not be raised up and continued, if it were not to share in the glory."[35] Baxter and other Puritans were not motivated by the desire to merit salvation or to be assured of it; rather, they offered ways to live the Christian life that flowed out of the experience of salvation. We may fault Weber for misunderstanding the heart of Calvinism, but those within the church today can easily make similar errors.

Thus, one lesson we can learn from this discussion is that literature dealing with the practical issues of the Christian life should proceed from the essence of the gospel. The work of Christ is what makes it possible for sinners to live doxologically and work in obedience to God. This view does not mean that questions such as "How should I choose a job?" or "What is a Christian attitude toward work?" can be answered only with a sermon on justification. It does suggest, however, that elements of a life of sanctification should organically connect with the entire corpus of biblical truth.

In his sermon on vocation, Perkins provides an example of the Puritan approach. Proceeding from a text that is eminently practical, he develops principles, points, and subpoints that expand the biblical notion of calling. Throughout, he ties together general calling and personal calling, and presents an experiential approach to the question that involves body, mind, and soul.

A second lesson we can learn is a communal perspective on vocation. Today it is common, even in Calvinist churches, to hear questions of vocation addressed primarily in personal terms. Careers are viewed in the context of personal gifts and passions, as well as the rewards and opportunities those occupations provide. What is missing from such an analysis is the weight of the "common good." Calvin employs the "body" language of the New Testament not only to speak of the church, but also to describe the Christian obligation to neighbors and society at large. In a sermon on 1 Timothy 6:17–19, he speaks of "the fraternal affection which proceeds from the regard that we have when God has joined us together and united us in one body, because he wants each to employ himself for his neighbor, so that no one is addicted to his own person, but that we serve all in common."[36] The Puritans approached the question of what vocation to pursue not simply by asking what would be best for them and their families, but also by asking how the gifts God had given them could be used best for the glory of His name in a broader context.

It is important to note that the Calvinistic view of work did not consume all of life and that vocation was not understood only in the context of occupation. The Puritan John Preston warned against "too much business or intending it too much or inordinately."[37] Richard Steele criticized those who were seeking to "accumulate two or three callings merely to increase [their] riches."[38] The Scottish divine Robert Woodrow commented, "The sin of our too great fondness for trade, to the neglecting of our more valuable interests, I humbly think will be written upon our judgment."[39] The Puritans cited the dangers of an excessive focus on work and promoted the enjoyment of other facets of life. In so doing, they followed the lead of Calvin, who wrote, "Let this be our principle, that we err not in the use of the gifts of Providence when we refer them to the end for which their author made and destined them, since he created them for our good, and not for our destruction. No man will keep the true path better than he who shall have this end carefully in view."[40] Calvin then listed things that believers ought to enjoy, such as food, clothes, flowers, and other created gifts.

While we hesitate to draw the kinds of conclusions that Weber did, we do admit that some criticism of the Puritan work ethic is warranted. Calvinist societies have not always been characterized by satisfying jobs and balanced lives. The association of the Protestant work ethic with "workaholism" and the disapproval of leisure activities is not without historical foundations. This can be explained as a combination of ideals falling short and a desire to avoid common recreational pursuits that were considered spiritually harmful. The result was that "the Puritans valued hard work, were suspicious of much recreation, and made no attempt to conceal their scorn for lazy and idle people."[41] One historian quipped that in the Netherlands, the "industrious revolution" preceded the "industrial revolution."[42]

Although the matter of material possessions and appropriate use of them falls beyond the scope of this chapter, attitudes and motivation toward work are inevitably affected by what we do with our earnings. Thus, the Puritan notion of thrift influenced their understanding of vocation. Baxter says, "Frugality or sparing is an act of fidelity, obedience, and gratitude, by which we use all our estates so faithfully for the chief Owner, so obediently to our chief Ruler, and so gratefully to our chief Benefactor, as that we waste it not any other way."[43] The thrift of the Dutch and the Scottish is sometimes mocked, but this image is based on historical attitudes toward work and possessions. This focus on thrift was imported to America by the Puritans and is evident in their writings. It appears that much of this legacy in America, however, has been overshadowed by the materialism of North American culture. While the Netherlands, Scotland, and the United States have a similar legacy of views regarding work, vocation, and thrift, it is telling that the phrases "being Dutch" and "being Scotch" evoke thrift, while the phrase "being American" suggests the acquisition of possessions.

The Calvinist perspective on work and vocation challenges many perspectives on occupation, career choices, and workplace ethics in the church today. It provides a clear alternative to the self-affirming, be-everything-you-can-be-and-enjoy-the-rewards approach of our materialistic age. It challenges us to view our work as good because of what it is, not what it makes us. Just as God delights in His work, His image-bearers should delight in their vocations. The notion of calling and God's sovereignty prompts us honestly to evaluate the gifts we have been given and ask how we might best use them in His service: these gifts were given to us not for personal gain but to enable us to carry out our God-given roles in church and society.

Above all, our callings should be viewed in the context of God's glory, which is His sovereign purpose for the world. While we by nature would place ourselves in the center and measure our success by our accomplishments, a biblical sense of vocation brings us back to our general calling to "glorify God and enjoy Him forever," in the words of the Westminster Shorter Catechism. From this general call emerges our particular calling. Equipped with our God-given talents and committed to serving Him with our whole heart, we can go to work each day and delight in the creations of our hands. Good work will contribute to the glory of God and the well-being of our fellow man. Work then will be part of our worship.

DISCUSSION QUESTIONS

1. What is the Calvinistic view of work?

2. Who was Max Weber? How did he caricature the Calvinist view of vocation?

3. Historically, what is meant by *vocation*?

4. What should mark a Calvinistic understanding of Christian vocation in our day?

NOTES

1 Leland Ryken, *Work and Leisure in Christian Perspective* (Eugene, Ore.: Wipf & Stock, 1986), 76–77.

2 Adriano Tilgher, *Work: What It Has Meant to Men Through the Ages* (New York: Arno Press, 1977), 3.

3 *Encyclopaedia Britannica Online*, s.v. "Protestant ethic," http://www.britannica.com/eb/article-9061605/Protestant-ethic (accessed Jan. 8, 2008).

4 Max Weber, *The Protestant Ethic and the Spirit of Capitalism* (New York: Charles Scribner's Sons, 1958).

5 Leland Ryken, *Worldly Saints: The Puritans as They Really Were* (Grand Rapids: Zondervan, 1986), 23.

6 Molly Scott Cato, review of *Selling the Work Ethic: From Puritan Pulpit to Corporate PR*, by Sharon Beder, *The Ecologist*, May 2001, http://findarticles.com/p/articles/mi_m2465/is_4_31/ai_74583532.

7 Ibid.

8 "The Puritan hyper-work ethic of America, which, especially in Stelzer's mind, views leisure as an odious word, is so deviously effective because it is self-insulating" (David A. Schneider, "(The Lack of) Leisure in America," October 2003, http://daschneider.wordpress.com/2007/12/22/the-lack-of-leisure-in-america-october-2003/).

9 Peter Mudrack, "'Work' or 'leisure'? The Protestant work ethic and participation in employee fitness programs," in *Journal of Organizational Behavior*, 13, no. 1 (1992): 81–88, http://www3.interscience.wiley.com/cgi-bin/abstract/113471292/ABSTRACT?CRETRY=1&SRETRY=0.

10 R. L. Tawney in his foreword to Weber, *The Protestant Ethic*, I(b).

11 Weber, *The Protestant Ethic*, 117. Weber includes footnote references to Obadiah Sedgwick in support of this point. He also utilizes extensive quotes from Richard Baxter, *The Saints' Everlasting Rest*.

12 Ibid., 125. Weber cites the Puritan proclivity for using commercial rather than legal metaphors in their sermons as further evidence of the mindset that emerges from a Calvinist framework, quoting as evidence, among others, Matthew Henry's sermon on "The Worth of the Soul" (238n).

13 A summary of these critiques can be found in Sandra Pierotti, "Backup of the Protestant Ethic and the Spirit of Capitalism: Criticisms of Weber's Thesis," http://www.csudh.edu/dearhabermas/weberrelbk01.htm.

Michael Novak, a prominent Catholic theologian who specializes in matters relating to work and calling, provides a more nuanced religious critique of Weber in "Max Weber Goes Global," *First Things*, April 2005, http://www.firstthings.com/article.php3?id_article=180.

14 Lee Hardy, *The Fabric of This World: Inquiries into Calling, Career Choice and the Design of Human Work* (Grand Rapids: Eerdmans, 1990), xviii.

15 To oversimplify, market economies usually end up with three clear class categories: an "upper class," members of which own the capital and live from the profits of that capital; a "middle class," those who sell their labor and use their earnings to purchase homes and a living; and a lower class, people who usually sell their labor and rent their homes. The hard work and diligence motivated by a believer's sense of duty to God are seen to have religious rewards, but they also reinforce this economic reward system.

16 I use American examples since it is there that the issue has been most pronounced in contemporary debate, but similar discussions have taken place in Canadian and European contexts. Recent scholarship has demonstrated how this is accurate in neither a historical nor a contemporary sense. See Donald E. Frey, "Individualist Economic Values and Self-Interest: The Problem in the Puritan Ethic," *Journal of Business Ethics*, 17, no. 14 (Oct. 1998): 1573–1580. Damon Linker suggests that the modern "religious right" movement in the United States most often identified with these perspectives emerges more from the application of Catholic natural law theology than historic American Puritanism (*The Theocons: Secular America Under Siege* [New York: Doubleday, 2006]).

17 By "prosperity theology," I mean a range of theological perspectives that link Christian obedience with an expectation that it will result in relative earthly economic prosperity and physical health.

18 Randy Alcorn, *Money, Possessions and Eternity* (Wheaton: Tyndale House, 2002), 75. Alcorn provides a helpful compilation of the various biblical passages typically used to defend a prosperity theology in chapter 6, "Prosperity Theology: The Gospel of Wealth."

19 "But there has been also the *American dream*, that dream of a land in which life should be better and richer and fuller for every man, with opportunity for each according to his ability or achievement" (James T. Adams, *The Epic of America* [Boston: Little, Brown & Co., 1931], 404).

20 Inst. (Bev.), 3.10.6.

21 Quoted in Ryken, *Worldly Saints*, 25.

22 Ibid.

23 For a more detailed development of these ten principles, see Ray Pennings, "Work and Vocation," in *Work and Leisure in the Life of a Christian*, ed. Cornelis Van Dam (Burlington, Ont.: Burlington Reformed Study Centre, 2004), 1–18.

24 William Perkins, "A Treatise of the Vocations or Callings of men, with sorts and kinds of them, and the right use thereof," in *Working: Its Meaning and Its Limits*, ed. Gilbert Meilaender (Notre Dame: University of Notre Dame Press, 2003), 108–114. The subsequent quotes from this sermon are taken from this edition.

25 Inst. (Bev.), 1.16.3.

26 Hardy, *The Fabric of This World*, 57.

27 Ryken, *Work and Leisure in Christian Perspective*, 91. No such reserve was expressed by Reformed writers regarding the blessings on nations as a sign of God's favor. Abraham Kuyper may have been enthusiastic but is not unrepresentative in his assertion that "Calvinism has liberated Switzerland, the Netherlands, and England, and in the Pilgrim Fathers has provided the impulse to the prosperity of the United States" (quoted from Kuyper's Stone Lectures in John Bolt, *A Free Church, A Holy Nation: Abraham Kuyper's American Public Theology* [Grand Rapids: Eerdmans, 1981], 158).

28 Quoted in Ryken, *Work and Leisure in Christian Perspective*, 91

29 Ibid.

30 *Commentary* on Luke 17:7–10.

31 Weber, *The Protestant Ethic*, 155.

32 Ibid., 158.

33 Ibid., 158–159.

34 Ibid., 160–161.

35 Richard Baxter, *The Saints' Everlasting Rest* (Ross-shire, U.K.: Christian Focus, 1998), 31–32.

36 Quoted in Hardy, *The Fabric of This World*, 63n.

37 Quoted in Ryken, *Work and Leisure in Christian Perspective*, 88.

38 Ibid.

39 Quoted in Ryken, *Worldy Saints*, 33.

40 Inst. (Bev.), 3.10.2.

41 Ryken, *Worldly Saints*, 19.

42 Jan DeVries, quoted in Philip Benedict, *Christ's Churches Purely Reformed: A Social History of Calvinism* (New Haven: Yale University Press, 2002), 538.

43 Quoted in Theodore Malloch, *Spiritual Enterprise: Doing Virtuous Business* (New York: Encounter Books, 2008).

CHAPTER 26

POLITICAL MINISTERS
OF GOD

Ray Pennings

Mr. TAFT cannot get away from the idea, drummed into the heads of people during seven years by the President, that we are a Nation of transgressors. The bulk of his speech consists of advocacy of new laws of penalty and restriction. Of helpful counsel, of encouragement, of opportunity sought out and indicated, we find very little. Of appeal for new laws to punish transgression there is much. The candidate has worked himself into a stern and Calvinistic temper. He applies the doctrines of Calvinism to our political and economic problems. Fashioning his thought upon the thought of MR. ROOSEVELT, he persuades himself that the American people are given over to sin. As CALVIN taught that fallen man is incapable of voluntary repentance, so Mr. TAFT holds with Mr. ROOSEVELT that our corporations must be cudgeled into salvation.[1]

—*New York Times*, July 29, 1908

he label *Calvinist*, when used in today's political arena, is usually intended as an insult, as it was in the editorial quoted above. The term evokes images of moralistic legalism. Calvinists are suspected of harboring secret desires to use state power to restrict freedom and to support a particular theology. The term provokes debate in academic circles as well, with various approaches attempting to understand the political theory and practical implications of Calvinism. And the confusion is not limited to critics; on the front lines of contemporary political life are those who appeal to Calvinism but argue contradictory positions on issues.

Sorting through this muddle is a tall order. To do so, we should ask to what extent Calvinism has contributed to the emergence of modern democracy. The scope of Calvinism's influence on the political realm can be debated, but its historical significance cannot. John Calvin's thought undoubtedly contributed to the development of political theory, particularly in the English-speaking world. Even the philosopher Rousseau acknowledged Calvin's significance: "The editing of our wise laws, in which he had a large share, does him as much honor as his *Institutes*."[2] Johannes Althusius, the father of federalism, also supported a position implied by Calvin's political views.[3] Those who support a Calvinist influence argue that "the Reformed tradition frequently emboldened resistance to unjust authority and that the congregational, consistorial and presbyterial-synod forms of church government found within the Reformed tradition offered lay participants in these systems a useful apprenticeship in self-government."[4] And in B. B. Warfield's words, "The roots of Calvinism are planted in a specific religious attitude, out of which is unfolded first a particular theology, from which springs on the one hand a special church organization, and on the other a social order, involving a given political arrangement."[5]

In this chapter, I will explore some relevant themes in Calvinist thought, then briefly describe four cases in which Calvinism was applied to the political sphere. My goal is to identify practical lessons[6] that are useful to people in Western democracies for applying a Calvinist perspective to political activity today.[7]

MAJOR THEMES

Calvin's writings must be considered in their sixteenth-century context, which was the age of the Holy Roman Empire. Within the political structures of that time, monarchies were exercising influence in ways that were reducing the emperor's power. New ideas were being tried. A series of riots, including an Anabaptist revolt, was raising fundamental questions about freedom, order, and authority.[8]

Calvin's insights were influential not only because of his position and theological acumen, but also because of the breadth of his thinking. He blended "patristic, scholastic, and Lutheran theological elements with ideas and methods drawn from classical political philosophy, and humanist literary, historical and legal scholarship."[9]

His views clearly changed throughout his career, as revealed by significant differences among the 1536, 1543, and 1559 editions of the *Institutes of the Christian Religion* on matters of political and ecclesiastical governance.[10] Calvin's awareness of these changes helps explain his arguments for contextualization in the matter of church government. He writes, "Because things of this nature are not necessary to salvation, and, for the edification of the church, should be accommodated to the varying circumstances of each age and nation, it will be proper, as the interest of the Church may require, to change and abrogate the old, as well as to introduce new forms."[11]

John Owen's views went through a similar development. The great English Puritan, best known for his theological writings, was a political adviser to Oliver Cromwell. As one writer said, "Owen not only embraced the collective theology in its revolutionary form before 1643, . . . he gave it apocalyptic overtones in 1649 when most Presbyterians were in full retreat."[12] After 1652, Owen began advocating policies related to both church government (he supported the Independent and Nonconformist movements) and state government that shaped an "overarching unity that bound the rapidly changing country together as a nation. . . . It was, surprisingly perhaps, the unity of a modern pluralistic state, rather than that of a Puritan commonwealth, that he was helping to establish."[13]

If these giants of Calvinism found themselves adapting their positions as circumstances changed, we should not simply promote orthodox-sounding approaches drawn from previous generations as "the Christian answer" to a particular issue. Rather, we should approach issues with humility and not expect to derive from political Calvinism a series of specific policy prescriptions applicable for all times and places. We also should exercise charity when critiquing Christian political leaders. In our concern for orthodoxy, we might be tempted to view arguments for contextualization as compromise or even the abdication of principles. But although we cannot retroactively question Calvin or Owen, or know with certainty when and under what circumstances they changed their minds, we can be sure that they faced pressures on all sides of the issues as do our own leaders.

However, contextualization arguments should not be used to suggest that there are no enduring themes that characterize political Calvinism. Clearly, Calvinists have a positive view of government. In contrast with the Anabaptist view that the magistrate was "carnal" and "outside of the perfection of Christ,"[14] Calvin viewed magistrates as having a commission from God, as being invested with a divine authority, and as representing "the person of God, as whose substitutes they in a manner act."[15]

What about rulers who fail to govern in a way that reflects God's laws? In his writings, Calvin usually recommends subjection. In a sermon on Titus 3:1, Calvin saw resistance to magistrates as evidence of the sinful human nature, since "no one is willing to submit himself to another."[16] Commenting on Jeremiah 29:7, Calvin noted: "For if it was the duty of the Jews to pray for the well-being of the Chaldeans for this reason, because they were for a certain time under their authority, there is no excuse for us, when we live under any legitimate prince, and that not only for a few days, unless we testify our voluntary submission before God, and he who prays to God for the happy state of the country in which he lives, will not surely neglect his other duties."[17] Calls to obey authorities and warnings against civil disobedience are clear throughout Calvin's writings, often directed forcefully against the Anabaptists of his day.[18]

However, Calvin did permit resistance to the tyrannical abuse of power: "Far am I from forbidding those officially to check the undue license of kings, that if they connive at kings when they tyrannize and insult over the humbler of people, I affirm that their dissimulation is not free from nefarious perfidy, because they fraudulently betray the liberty of the people, while knowing that, by the ordinance of God, they are the appointed guardians."[19] The quoted paragraph refers to a specific situation in Calvin's own time, so the conditions under which he approved the overthrow of tyrants are unclear. But Calvin did favor a limit on the absolute power of kings: "In this especially consists the best condition of the people, when they can choose, by common consent, their own shepherds: for when anyone by force usurps the supreme power, it is tyranny: and when men become kings by hereditary right, it seems not consistent with liberty."[20] Furthermore, in a sermon on Ephesians 6:5–9, Calvin describes the institution of the bondservant as "totally against the order of nature."[21]

Later Reformed thinkers developed these seeds of protest into comprehensive agendas for social reform. The Puritan Thomas Case told the English House of Commons in 1641: "Reformation must be universal. Reform all places, all persons, and callings: reform the benches of judgments, the inferior magistrates. . . .

Reform the universities, reform the cities, reform the countries, reform the inferior schools of learning, reform the Sabbath, reform the ordinances, the worship of God. . . . You have more work to do than I can speak."[22]

Until recently, most Reformed believers accepted civic activism as a religious duty. Today, however, some leaders advise against it. For example, John MacArthur cites four reasons for discouraging Christian political activism. He says political activism (1) denigrates the sovereignty of God over human history and events, (2) promotes biblical values in a culture through fleshly, selfish means, (3) creates a false sense of morality, and (4) risks alienating unbelievers by casting them as political enemies rather than as a mission field. MacArthur concludes: "I believe America's heart can be turned toward God, but only through the power of the Spirit, one person at a time. And you and I have at our disposal the only means to bring genuine, lasting change: God's good news of salvation. So use it for the glory of God's kingdom."[23]

MacArthur likely is responding partly to the stridency that often characterizes the conduct of politics today. This stridency is not unprecedented; the arguments of Martin Luther, Calvin, or the Puritans against their political foes were hardly winsome or gentle. However, the context of those arguments is significant. During the time of the Reformers, religious arguments in the public square were normal. There was an ongoing debate about established religion. Likewise, in the early days of the United States, religious arguments took place in a context of a public Christian religion. That context has changed significantly in the past few decades. MacArthur is right in saying that the conduct of our lives and the tone of our conversation shape how the gospel is understood and received today. Here the Savior's recommendation to be "wise as serpents, and harmless as doves" (Matt. 10:16b) is relevant.

To discourage any form of civic involvement, however, is to depart from a rich Reformed heritage. Jonathan Edwards pressed the Christian citizen to "full and responsible participation in the civil community for the purpose of improving its quality of life."[24] Dr. D. Martyn Lloyd-Jones even argued, in contrast with MacArthur's fourth point, "that a lack of political and social concern on the part of Christians can very definitely alienate people from the Gospel and the Church."[25] Yet Lloyd-Jones was conscious of the imperfections of politics and warned: "The Christian must act as a citizen, and play his part in politics and other matters in order to get the best possible conditions. But we must always remember that politics is 'the art of the possible': and so the Christian must remember as he begins that he can only get the possible. Because he is a Christian he must work for the best possible and be content with that which is less than fully Christian."[26]

One other defining theme of political Calvinism needs to be considered, especially today, when the political methods of Islam are compared to the political methods of Christians. Calvin argued that church and state have separate responsibilities and that each is directly accountable to God. Calvin focused the church on spiritual matters and the state on temporal matters. Subsequent Calvinists expanded those notions to devise systems in which different levels of government have different responsibilities. In consideration of the doctrine of depravity (as it applies to rulers, who more easily abuse power as they gain more of it), Calvinists tended to emphasize clear limits on a government's power by means of a system of "checks and balances," both within and among governments.

The Calvinist system applies beyond government to other spheres of life, such as family, business, church, and community, each having their own responsibilities. The diversity of God's creation, in which He made things "after their kind," is another important theological principle invoked here. As political philosopher Oliver O'Donovan notes, summarizing the thinking of Althusius on this subject, society is composed of a single order or framework. However, that order is made up of a series of "intersecting covenantal associations." All of those, whether they be the family, the church, or other social institutions, of necessity have within themselves a unique balance of order and freedom, the nature of which differs according to their purpose.[27] The notion of federalism, then, is not only applied to the political division of powers between governments. A similar notion applies between the institutions that make up the different spheres of society.

The continuing application of the moral law, most commonly understood as the Ten Commandments, is a theme of Reformed theology. So the question naturally arises, what is the role of the state in enforcing the first table of the law, which concerns man's responsibility toward God? A related question concerns the state's role in protecting the church. Because of the medieval legacy in the sixteenth century, state churches developed in countries where the Reformation achieved dominance. In many European countries, the resources of the state were used to promote religion through churches, even while a form of pluralism was tolerated. In America, the heirs of the Puritan tradition worked with other leaders in a process that led to a constitution in which the principle of "separation of church and state" ultimately prevailed.[28]

Thus, differentiated responsibilities, checks and balances, and avoidance of the concentration of power in any one body are features of Calvin's thinking on ecclesiastical as well as civic governments. These principles have been expanded in subsequent centuries of political theorizing. With these principles, Calvinism frames the connection between faith and politics in a different way than do most other religious traditions.

A HISTORICAL SAMPLING

These theological principles of Calvinism were not simply debated by academics and theologians but were applied directly to issues of the day. The following examples illustrate four ways that these ideas were put into practice in different contexts. There is little reason to question the sincerity of these efforts, even though the results were mixed, at best. Where good was achieved, it was relatively short-lived, showing how the personal and structural effects of sin influence the most devoted human efforts. Like other aspects of sanctification, progress is continually challenged by the sin that remains in us. So there are pages in this history we would prefer to skip, but we cannot do so if we are to be biblically obedient and avoid hagiography. History contains valuable insights to consider as we carry out our civic responsibilities.

Cromwell (1599–1658) was the first well-known political leader to integrate Calvinistic principles. He was elected to Parliament in 1628 and became the leader of an independent Puritan party. The monarch at the time, Charles I, exercised his executive authority without calling Parliament for eleven years. Cromwell sought to check this abuse of executive power and to abolish episcopacy. From 1642 to 1649, a civil war ensued, ending with the execution of Charles I and the establishment of the Commonwealth.

Cromwell recruited a loyal army of godly men, whom he led to Ireland and Scotland, where they used force, with considerable loss of life, to restore order. He then became the lord protector of the Commonwealth. His focus was on political, moral, and spiritual reform. He died in 1658 amid political confusion and instability. The monarchy was restored in 1660 with the crowning of Charles II, thus ending Puritan rule.

How did devout, spiritual men justify a revolution of such bloody and massive dimensions? Peter Lewis notes various factors that help us understand this history.[29] The Puritans did not view their actions as civil disobedience or revolution; rather, they were convinced they were defending the legitimate authority of Parliament against the absolutism of the Stuart monarchy. They believed that the king was the tyrant and they were on the side of freedom. They cited passages pertaining to Old Testament Israel to support their contention that England had a special place in God's providential plan. When we combine this thinking with some private political interests, the inevitable influence of money, and naïveté on the part of some who participated in the process, we can begin to make sense of a time when so much happened that seems to contradict the ideals of Calvinism.

Not all Puritans agreed with these revolutionary tactics. Rather than fight political abuses, they left England. While Cromwell sought to reform England (after wondering himself whether it might be preferable to make the trip to New England),[30] some twenty thousand Puritans traveled to Massachusetts to establish a third English colony in the New World. The citizens of the Massachusetts Bay Colony envisioned their community as "a city upon a hill," that is, a model for the whole world.

Other Calvinists used different tactics. Thomas Chalmers (1780–1847), a Scottish mathematician who became a leader in the Free Church of Scotland, was instrumental in applying a parish approach to the social and political issues of his time. Chalmers was convinced that the physical needs of people had to be addressed along with their spiritual needs. He set up a system in which elders and deacons teamed to visit every one of the eleven thousand homes in Glasgow. He resisted the prevalent taxation approach of his day to provide resources to help the poor and relied instead on voluntary gifts. Within a short period of time, poverty was significantly alleviated and an ambitious program of education implemented. Ecclesiastical reform accompanied political reform, with Chalmers becoming one of the leaders of the Free Church movement.

A century later in the Netherlands, education and poverty were the platform for Abraham Kuyper (1837–1920) and his Anti-Revolutionary Party. Rejecting the Enlightenment liberalism of Dutch society, Kuyper formed an explicitly Christian political party in 1878, and, from 1901 to 1905, he served as the prime minister of the Netherlands. Kuyper championed working-class issues and promoted the equal funding of faith-based institutions.

In each of these examples, basic Calvinist themes appear. A more detailed study would offer positive lessons from each. However, few would recommend for our times a Cromwellian effort to establish a kingdom by force, the pioneering of a Puritan society on a distant continent, the parish-based model advocated by Chalmers, or Kuyper's democratic efforts. Each of these approaches proved to be relatively short-lived. Furthermore, had they lived to see the results, the leaders of each of these movements would have been greatly disappointed regarding their legacy and impact.

These are valuable reminders that God's kingdom will not be established through political means. Political Calvinism must be pursued in the context of an eschatology that is essentially pessimistic regarding earthly success. The argument can be made that a nation that lives according to God's laws can expect more stability and prosperity than those who do not, but that success often comes in spite of, not because of, the efforts of Christians to influence the public square.

LESSONS FOR TODAY

As we examine how political Calvinism has been implemented in different settings, several lessons for today emerge.

The obvious one is that civic engagement is not optional. The paradox of political Calvinism is that, while we must admit that many attempts to apply it historically have been short-lived, that is no reason to abandon our responsibilities to be involved. While we cannot transpose the opportunities for citizen involvement of our own generation with those of others, it seems reasonable to conclude that most Calvinists in previous generations would have found it unthinkable not to vote or follow the political news of the day. These events are God's workings in providence, and obeying and responding to His works is a basic element of Christian living. The motive for political engagement is obedience to God and a desire to serve Him in every area of our lives. As Micah 6:8b says, "What doth the LORD require of thee, but to do justly, and to love mercy, and to walk humbly with thy God?"

Apart from whatever good our involvement may accomplish, there is a more fundamental reason for civic engagement: it gives us the opportunity to glorify God in the public sphere. We are called to praise God in everything we do and in all aspects of His creation.

A second lesson is that there is no common blueprint that can be implemented whatever our circumstances. No matter how we pursue matters, we must strive for

Christian charity, grace, and humility in the political sphere. Lloyd-Jones warns against three dangers. The first is that Christians will become mere defenders of the status quo. When Christianity becomes "a middle-class movement . . . (the temptation) confronting the Christian is to become a political conservative, and an opponent of legitimate reform, and the legitimate rights of people,"[31] he says. The second danger is the opposite extreme—a radicalism focused on political reform. Although the bias of Calvinism has been to stress order over liberty, a danger still exists that we will define success in terms of "Christianizing" the various spheres of life or liberating people through an antinomian spirit of lawlessness.[32] The third danger is "complete other-worldliness. . . . It is the duty of the Christian always to be concerned about these matters and have a world-view."[33]

Third, while politics is usually discussed in terms of current issues, it is fundamentally a debate about ideas and direction. Previous generations understood this fact well; people in the nineteenth and twentieth centuries were well aware that the ideas of the Enlightenment and the French Revolution ran counter to biblical thought. That's why Kuyper's party was named the Anti-Revolutionary Party. By contrast, many people today, even in the church, have unwittingly adopted the two-realm theory of truth that modernism has recommended. We accept a divide between facts and values, working with frameworks that accept the proof of the scientific method as reflecting truth of one type, while the proof of faith results in something that is less publicly true. We resent the secularists' insistence that religion is private, but nonetheless adopt their individualist framework.[34] We can readily see how our faith gives us something to say on certain moral issues such as abortion and marriage, but we are hard pressed to see the relevance of our faith for an urban development plan, taxation strategy, or foreign policy. When Reformed Christians live with a private faith that affects only parts of their lives, they have lost a great part of the richness of the Puritan legacy.

Politics cannot save us. Those who caution against the excesses of political promises and the necessity of individual conversion and living a life of sanctification are right. However, the desire to avoid excess does not justify neglect. Calvinists see government as accountable to God like any other sphere of life, and righteousness and justice in that sphere give God the glory He deserves. This required as much energy yesterday as it does today. As Samuel Rutherford observed, "Without running, fighting, sweating, wrestling, heaven is not taken."[35]

Few have seen this truth with greater clarity than did Edwards. In a series of sermons on 1 Corinthians 13, preached in Northampton, Mass., in 1738,[36] Edwards said that the reason God created the world was for His glory. Therefore, God was not indifferent to what happened to this world. In the eighth sermon, on 1 Corinthians 13:5, "[Charity] seeketh not her own," Edwards makes the call to public-mindedness a logical expression of Christian love: "A man of right spirit is not a man of narrow and private views, but is greatly interested in and concerned for the good of the community to which he belongs, and particularly of the city or village in which he resides, and for the true welfare of the society of which he is a member."[37] The implication for all those who hold public office was also clear in Edwards' mind, and ought to be also in ours: "And so, whatever the post of honor or influence we may be placed in, we should shew that, in it, we are solicitous for the good of the public, so that the world may be better for our living in it, and that, when we are gone, it may be said of us, as it was so nobly said of David (Acts 13:36), that he 'served our generation by the will of God.'"[38]

DISCUSSION QUESTIONS

1. Why did Calvin and other Christian theologians change their views on political matters during their lives?

2. What is the significance for us of their openness to changing their political views?

3. What are some enduring principles when it comes to a Calvinist perspective on political thought?

4. Is it right to contemplate revolution against a government? Who in the history of Calvinism thought armed revolt was legitimate? Why? Is there biblical warrant for this position?

5. What is civil activism?

6. What three dangers does D. Martyn Lloyd-Jones warn us against when it comes to politics?

NOTES

[1] Editorial, "Political Calvinism," *New York Times*, July 29, 1908, http://query.nytimes.com/gst/abstract.html?res=9507E4DC123EE233A2575AC2A9619C946997D6CF (accessed Jan. 10, 2008).

[2] Quoted in H. Henry Meeter, *The Basic Ideas of Calvinism* (Grand Rapids: Baker, 1975), 94.

[3] Carl J. Friedrich, preface to the English translation of Althusius's *The Politics*, available online at http://www.constitution.org/alth/alth_pr0.htm (accessed Jan. 11, 2008). The translator, Frederick Carney, details Calvinism as one of eight categories of writings that informed Althusius's thought. He suggests that Calvinist writings regarding concepts of justice and piety as well as ecclesiastical order and the role of the law played a particularly significant role. Althusius served as the rector of the Reformed Academy at Hebron, an institution whose first rector was Caspar Olevianus, co-author of the Heidelberg Catechism.

[4] Philip Benedict, *Christ's Churches Purely Reformed: A Social History of Calvinism* (New Haven: Yale University Press, 2002), 533.

[5] B. B. Warfield, *The Works of Benjamin B. Warfield* (Grand Rapids: Baker, 2003), 5:354.

[6] The principles and practical lessons emerge from the author's study of history and from his personal experience, namely, twenty-five years of active involvement in Canadian electoral politics at the municipal, provincial, and federal levels; work as a policy analyst making regular submissions to government on behalf of labor and industry groups; and work for a Christian think tank with regular opportunity to serve as a commentator in the mainstream media. Applications made in this chapter are intended to suit a broader context and are not peculiar to the Canadian setting.

[7] Given the range that is being covered in a short chapter, I neither define nor make the distinctions between terms that those familiar with the literature might expect.

[8] For a summary of the political structures and dynamics that set the context for the Reformation in Europe, see Lewis W. Spitz, *The Protestant Reformation 1517–1559* (New York: Harper & Row, 1985), 36–48.

[9] Oliver O'Donovan and Joan Lockwood O'Donovan, eds., *From Irenaeus to Grotius: A Sourcebook in Christian Political Thought 100–1625* (Grand Rapids: Eerdmans, 1999), 662.

[10] Ibid., 663.

[11] Inst. (Bev.), 4.10.30.

[12] Lloyd Glen Williams, "Dignatus Dei: God and Nation in the Thought of John Owen" (Ph.D. dissertation, Drew University, 1981), ix.

[13] Ibid., xiv.

[14] "The Schlietheim Confession," 1527, Article 6, in William Lumpkin, *Baptist Confessions of Faith* (Valley Forge, Pa.: Judson Press, 1959), 27–28.

[15] Inst. (Bev.), 4.20.4.

[16] Quoted in Graham Harrison, "Luther and Calvin," in *The Christian and the State in Revolutionary Times* (London: The Westminster Conference, 1975), 22.

[17] Ibid., 23.

[18] Cf. Willem Balke, *Calvin and the Anabaptist Radicals* (Grand Rapids: Eerdmans, 1981).

[19] Inst. (Bev.), 4.20.31.

[20] Quoted in Harrison, "Luther and Calvin," 21.

[21] John Calvin, *Sermons on the Epistle to the Ephesians* (Edinburgh: Banner of Truth Trust, 1973), 634.

[22] Quoted in Lee Hardy, *The Fabric of this World* (Grand Rapids: Eerdmans, 1990), 66.

23 John MacArthur, *Why Government Can't Save You: An Alternative to Political Activism* (Nashville: Word, 2000), 192.

24 Gerald R. McDermott, *One Holy and Happy Society: The Public Theology of Jonathan Edwards* (University Park, Pa.: Pennsylvania State University Press, 1992), 137.

25 D. Martyn Lloyd-Jones, "The French Revolution and After," in *The Christian and the State in Revolutionary Times* (London: The Westminster Conference, 1975), 106.

26 Ibid., 108.

27 O'Donovan and O'Donovan, *From Irenaeus to Grotius*, 758.

28 The clause preventing Congress from making a "law respecting the establishment of religion, or prohibiting the free exercise thereof" is part of the First Amendment, adopted in 1791. The popularized, shorthand phrase, "separation of church and state," was first used by Thomas Jefferson in a Jan. 1, 1802, letter to the Danbury Baptists ("Jefferson's Letter to the Danbury Baptists," Library of Congress, http://www.loc.gov/loc/lcib/9806/danpre.html).

29 These arguments are drawn from Peter Lewis, "Puritan England," in *The Christian and the State in Revolutionary Times* (London: The Westminster Conference, 1975), 60–75.

30 Mark Noll, *A History of Christianity in Canada and the United States* (Grand Rapids: Eerdmans, 1992), 32.

31 Lloyd-Jones, "The French Revolution and After," 103.

32 Ibid., 104–105.

33 Ibid., 105.

34 A helpful work on this subject is Nancy Pearcy, *Total Truth: Liberating Christianity from Its Cultural Captivity* (Wheaton, Ill.: Crossway, 2004).

35 Quoted in Ryken, *Worldly Saints*, 212.

36 Jonathan Edwards, *Charity and Its Fruits* (Edinburgh: Banner of Truth Trust, 1969).

37 Ibid., 169.

38 Ibid., 171.

CHAPTER 27

CALVINIST ETHICS

Nelson Kloosterman

Adam was at first created in the image of God, so that he might reflect, as in a mirror, the righteousness of God. But that image, having been wiped out by sin, must now be restored in Christ. The regeneration of the godly is indeed, as is said in II Cor. 3.18, nothing else than the reformation of the image of God in them. But there is a far more rich and powerful grace of God in this second creation than in the first. Yet Scripture only considers that our highest perfection consists in our conformity and resemblance to God. Adam lost the image which he had originally received, therefore it is necessary that it shall be restored to us by Christ. Therefore [Paul] teaches that the design in regeneration is to lead us back from error to that end for which we were created.[1]

—JOHN CALVIN

$\mathcal{T}$he early Reformers did not separate "ethics" from "dogmatics." Doctrine and life were one: biblical doctrine was rightly thought to be the necessary foundation and source of Christian living, and holy living was the necessary implication of sound doctrine. Thus, initially, the discipline of ethics was embedded in every form of doctrinal teaching, including confessions and catechisms, sermons, and treatises. Within the context of teaching, the Reformers explained human moral conduct in terms of divine revelation and applied the great truths associated with *sola Scriptura*, *sola gratia*, *sola fide*, *solus Christus*, and *soli Deo gloria*. Thus, although John Calvin himself neither taught ethics nor wrote a treatise on it, his teaching helped to shape the tradition of Reformed ethics.[2]

BIBLICAL AND THEOLOGICAL BACKGROUND

The first word that comes to mind as we seek to explain Calvinist ethics is *theo-centric*. God-centeredness characterizes everything associated with Calvinism. Divine sovereignty marks the beginning, the middle, and the end of all reality, all history, and all existence. The glory of God as the goal of all things, especially of Christian living, is the comprehensive theme of Reformed ethics. Celebrating the comprehensive power, wisdom, and knowledge of God, the apostle Paul sings, "For of him, and through him, and to him, are all things: to whom be glory for ever. Amen" (Rom. 11:36).

If God and His sovereignty are the heart of Calvinist ethics, the believer's union with Christ is its bloodstream (Rom. 6:1–14; 2 Cor. 12:9; Phil. 2:12–13; 4:13). Union with Christ begins with the Holy Spirit's work of faith and regeneration within people's hearts, whereby they are grafted into Christ and His living body, the church. By the Holy Spirit, Christ dwells in His people and nourishes them with the gospel through preaching and the holy sacraments so that by grace they may live to please God. Justification and sanctification, then, undergird all of Calvinist ethics.[3]

The restoration of God's image in those united to Christ is the goal of the gospel, the purpose of salvation, and the full expression of the Christian life. This image is displayed most perfectly in the person and work of the God-man, Jesus Christ. As new creatures in Christ, believers are being renewed in knowledge, righteousness, and holiness according to the image of their Creator and of their Lord Jesus Christ (Col. 3:9–10; see also especially Rom. 8:29 and Eph. 4:24). To follow the pattern established by Christ, then, is the essence of Calvinist ethics. This "Christo-morphic" pattern involves dying to sin and living in grateful obedience to God (Rom. 6:1, 4–6; 8:13; 12:1; Col. 2:20; 3:1–17). Until Christ returns in glory, the shape of Christian living is cross-like (Gal. 6:14): believers die to self and sin as they deny themselves and bear the persecution and hardship furnished by divine providence, especially trials endured for the sake of the gospel. Because physical death is not the end of existence and because this world is not all that is, believers live with double vision, attending to today's tasks while meditating on the blessedness of future life with Christ. Moreover, believers are encouraged to persevere in faith and affliction by the real prospect of divine rewards upon their obedience. These rewards are entirely due to the grace of God and are bestowed in proportion

to the believers' love for that grace (Matt.16:27; Luke 17:10; Rev. 22:12; Belgic
Confession, Art. 37; Heidelberg Catechism, Lord's Day 24, Q/A 64).

Calvinist ethics emphasizes the need to live fully before God (*coram Deo*)
in this world in the station and calling (*vocatio*) furnished by divine providence.
Christ's redemptive work not only obtains forgiveness of sins for believers, but
just as importantly, His redemption restores them to their original calling to serve
God with obedient faith in every part of life.

Grace is not designed as an alternative or supplement to nature, but as a
means to restore nature; redemption does not bypass creation, but will one day
purify it. Reformed ethics recognizes believers' calling to exercise dominion and
stewardship over creation as servants of God, followers of Christ, and laborers
together with the Holy Spirit (on this last point, see 1 Cor. 3:9).

Hence, God calls believers to use creation and its gifts with moderation and
freedom. First, moderation is needed because sin produces unrestrained passions
and excessive desires within the human heart, which lead to the misuse of creation's
gifts. Believers also are called to moderation so that our enjoyment of creation's
gifts will be regulated and we will be directed to contentment. Such contentment
yields patience in adversity and humility toward God and our neighbor.[4] Second,
Christian liberty is a precious commodity, or, in the words of Calvin, "a thing
of prime necessity," because ignorance of it renders the conscience fearful and
wavering.[5] This liberty consists of three parts: (1) freedom of conscience, since
Christ has liberated believers from the curse and condemnation of the law; (2) the
freedom of children obeying their heavenly Father without fear of recrimination
or judgment; and (3) freedom in the use of creation's gifts, serving neighbors in
love rather than satisfying personal lusts of indulgence and luxury.

THE LAW OF GOD

The law of God is the standard for Christian conduct. It reveals the character of
God and His perfect righteousness. The origin of the law is the will of God, which
is neither arbitrary nor capricious. Because the law expresses God's unchangeable
holiness and righteousness, it endures forever. The law exerts its authority in every
human conscience, bearing witness to good and to evil. Even moral principles of
justice and equity (think of the Golden Rule or the obligation to give everyone
their due) require the light of special revelation in order to be properly inter-

preted, comprehended, and followed. Fallen sinners need the Holy Spirit to lead them through the Scriptures to a proper understanding of God's will. We cannot rightly understand or obey any of God's commandments apart from the covenant of grace in Christ. That is because Christ is the "end" of the law (Rom. 10:4).

Scripture reveals three types of divine law: ceremonial, judicial, and moral. These distinctions became necessary with the progress of salvation history. Jesus Christ fulfilled every aspect of the law of God revealed in the Old Testament. He did this in two ways: He perfectly performed the demands of the law and He realized the promises of the law. In Him, the law reached its fullest purpose. Therefore, for the New Testament believer, every biblical prescription and duty finds its root and substance in the person and work of the Savior. Jesus Christ is the foundation, source, and norm of the Christian life.

Calvinist ethics also recognizes three uses of the divine law. First, like a bridle, the law restrains the wickedness of unregenerate people. Second, like a mirror, the law shows people their sin and their need of Jesus Christ. Finally, like a map, the law guides God's redeemed children along the way of living faithfully before Him. Throughout its history, Reformed ethics has stressed the positive use of the law in the Christian life in teaching believers grateful obedience to God.[6]

Jesus Christ is the best interpreter of the law. In the Sermon on the Mount, Jesus taught the extent of the law's righteousness that God requires. He also modeled the law in His righteousness, both toward His Father and toward others, and in His love, the heart of the law.

Commentators have drafted the following rules to explain the law in the context of Scripture, both the Old and New Testaments:

1. The Decalogue must be interpreted spiritually, since only Christ perfectly fulfilled the law and since God will not be satisfied with external conformity. In the law, God seeks our hearts.

2. The negative commandments include positive requirements, and vice versa.

3. Each commandment must be interpreted *per synecdoche*: the mention of a particular sin covers the range of related sins.

4. Commandments dealing with love toward God are weightier than commandments dealing with love toward our neighbor.

5. The starting point and goal of every commandment is love.[7]

These guidelines are important reminders that God's law is comprehensive; in it, God seeks the love of our hearts, souls, minds, and strength. Moreover,

Calvinist ethics does not separate the two tables of the law, insisting that love for our neighbor arises only from our love for God, and love for God necessarily shows itself in love toward our neighbor.

CASUISTRY AND CONSCIENCE

From its beginning, Calvinist ethics included casuistry, or the application of biblical principles to concrete situations, usually in the context of pastoral care. In letters, tracts, commentaries, and treatises, the Reformers addressed a wide variety of moral questions in the light of Scripture and church history. These questions pertained to engagement, marriage, and divorce; the right of revolution; the allowance of monetary interest; church struggles of various kinds; and myriad other topics.[8]

In personal ethics, Calvinists recognize the importance of the human conscience in moral reflection and evaluation. The conscience is a person's capacity for moral self-accountability, an internal authority that approves or disapproves of one's actions. In children, this capacity must be developed; in many habitual criminals, it seems to be repressed; and, among unbelievers, its testimony is regularly suppressed (Rom. 1:18–23).

The human conscience functions like a judge sitting in a courtroom. Conscience either accuses us of wrongdoing or approves of our doing right. But because sin affects the conscience by limiting its accuracy, the human conscience must be renewed by God through regeneration and conversion. The conscience cannot function as a reliable moral guide apart from the Word of God. True faith and a clear conscience function together, while unbelief functions with a torn or seared conscience.

The Bible speaks of a *good* conscience or a *clear* conscience, one that renders no accusation against a person before God and before other people. Think of the apostle Paul, who sought to maintain a pure and undefiled conscience before God and others (Acts 23:1; 24:16; Rom. 9:1; 1 Tim. 1:5; 3:9; 2 Tim. 1:3). Yet the apostle acknowledged that his conscience was not the highest norm; rather, the judgment of God conclusively establishes a person's innocence, purity, and uprightness. When we are converted, purified, and renewed by God's Word, our conscience is purified, for the Holy Spirit "beareth witness with our spirit, that we are the children of God: and if children, then heirs;

heirs of God, and joint-heirs with Christ" (Rom. 8:16–17a).

The Bible also speaks of a *weak* conscience (1 Cor. 8:7)—specifically, the conscience of a believer that is unable to grant the moral permissions that other believers enjoy.[9] Both in Romans 14 and in 1 Corinthians 8–11, Paul urges us to care for weaker believers, even to the point of renouncing our freedom in certain activities for the sake of others. As 1 Corinthians 8:13 says, "Wherefore, if meat make my brother to offend, I will eat no flesh while the world standeth, lest I make my brother to offend." Rather than viewing Christian liberty as being limited by others, we should see it as freedom to serve a neighbor in love. As Calvin says, "We have due control over our freedom if it makes no difference to us to restrict it when it is fruitful to do so."[10]

The Bible also speaks of a *seared* conscience (1 Tim. 4:2), in which the conscience's judgment concerning wrong is resisted and silenced. By its very nature, sin denies that we are created to obey God's law. Sinners without Jesus Christ stifle the truth with every kind of unrighteousness (Rom. 1:18). God's law is written deep in the heart of every human being (Rom. 2:15), but unregenerate fallen man attempts to excuse his unwillingness to avoid what he knows to be evil and to pursue what he knows to be right.

Calvinist ethics deeply respects the authority of a Bible-formed conscience without ascribing to it infallibility or universal authority. This ethical system also resists the binding of a person's conscience, particularly in the worship of God, with requirements that either exceed or violate what is revealed in Scripture.

THE KINGDOM OF GOD

Calvinist ethics teaches that believers are restored in Christ to their true calling in the world. To flee from engaging with the world is to betray one's God-given calling. However, Christian living is not limited to this world. Calvinism reminds us that Christians live as pilgrims who may have a home on earth but who are never entirely at home in the world.

Fulfilling a calling in the world is not an individual endeavor but a communal activity. Geographically, the community of believers reaches around the world; historically, it stretches far back into salvation history. Its center is Jesus Christ and its circumference is cosmic. Reformed confessions and theologians speak of this as the kingdom of God.

The kingdom of God is the rule and reign of God in the world. This domin-ion was present at Creation, has been opposed since the fall, and is being restored by the victory of Jesus Christ over sin, Satan, and hell. Entering the kingdom of God requires regeneration and faith-wrought holiness (John 3:3; Matt. 7:21).

God's kingdom causes tension in this world, since the two are opposed to each other. This tension is intensified because although God's kingdom is already pres-ent in the world—if not, how could we speak of Christian living in this world?—it is not yet full and perfect. The kingdom of God is fundamentally related to Jesus Christ. He is its King; His will, its polity; His disciples, its citizens; and His righ-teous rule, the content of gospel preaching. The tension between what we see now and that which is yet to come is alluded to in Hebrews 2, where we read:

> Thou madest him a little lower than the angels; thou crownedst him with glory and honour, and didst set him over the works of thy hands: Thou has put all things in subjection under his feet. For in that he put all in subjection under him, he left nothing that is not put under him. (vv. 7–8a)

This "already" kingdom was ushered in by the victory and enthronement of King Jesus. But then we read about the "not yet," the still-to-be-accomplished kingdom:

> But now we see not yet all things put under him. But we see Jesus, who was made a little lower than the angels for the suffering of death, crowned with glory and honour; that he by the grace of God should taste death for every man. (vv. 8b–9)

The "not yet" kingdom will be complete when Christ returns again to rule His kingdom in all His glory.

This present and future work of Jesus Christ offers both challenge and certainty to Christians in this world. The challenge is the ongoing struggle for supremacy against sin and Satan. The certainty is the reality of Christ's victory in His resurrection and ascension, which is celebrated each Lord's Day in the church's public worship as a foretaste of the eternal Sabbath. Calvinist ethics inte-grates daily living in the world with this view of the end times, supplying biblical motivation for holiness, clear-mindedness, and self-control (cf. 1 Peter 4:7–11).

According to Calvinist ethics, believers neither "bring in" the kingdom of God nor "extend the lordship of Jesus Christ." Rather, in praying "Thy kingdom come," we ask that we may submit ourselves more and more to God and His will so that He will preserve and increase His church and destroy the works of the Devil and every power exalting itself against Him until the perfection of His kingdom arrives, when He will be all in all (Heidelberg Catechism, Lord's Day 48). The coming of God's kingdom is not due to our effort or zeal, but to God's own work.

THE ETHICS OF THE WORD OF GOD

Calvinist ethics is fundamentally the ethics of the Word of God, beginning by acknowledging the sovereignty of God. The Holy Spirit energizes the church's obedience by applying to her the lasting benefits of Christ's work through the Word. Divine sovereignty includes human responsibility; hence, we must promote a wholesome biblical emphasis on human holiness and obedience in a world governed by divine providence. Moreover, Calvinist ethics acknowledges that human sin, though pervasive and fatal in the world, does not have the last word. We await the full manifestation of Christ's victory over sin and Satan, a victory already experienced by the church in spiritual birth and in progressive sanctification.

DISCUSSION QUESTIONS

1. What does it mean to live *coram Deo*?

2. What is Christian liberty?

3. What role does the law play in Calvinistic ethics?

4. Why is the conscience an important factor in thinking about ethical issues?

5. What is the kingdom of God from the Calvinistic point of view?

NOTES

1   *Commentary* on Ephesians 4:24.

2   Donald Sinnema, "The Discipline of Ethics in Early Reformed Orthodoxy," *Calvin Theological Journal*, 28, no. 1 (April 1993): 10.

3   Guenther H. Haas, "Calvin's Ethics," in *The Cambridge Companion to John Calvin*, ed. Donald K. McKim, (Cambridge: Cambridge University Press, 2004), 94.

4   Ibid., 96.

5   See Inst., 3.19.1–16.

6   The sixteenth-century beginnings of Calvinist moral teaching were followed by the systematic formulation and development of Calvinist ethics in the seventeenth century. Early examples of Calvinist ethics include works by Lambert Daneau (1530–1595) and Bartholomaeus Keckermann (1572/3–1609). The abbreviated title of Daneau's work was *Ethices Christianae III* (Geneva: Eustathius Vignon, 1577), and Keckermann's work was titled *Systema Ethicae tribus libris adornatum et publicis praelectionibus traditum in gymnasio Dantiscano* (Hanau, 1607). Other main works of Calvinist ethics appearing during this period were treatises by Andreas Hyperius (1553), Peter Martyr Vermigli (1563), William Perkins (in 1596 and 1606), Amandus Polanus (1609), and Antonius Walaeus (1620). To this period belongs also Wilhelmus à Brakel (1635–1711), whose treatment of the Decalogue (in *The Christian's Reasonable Service*, written in 1700) has supplied generations of believers with a reliable compendium of Calvinist ethics (*The Christian's Reasonable Service*, vol. 3, trans. Bartel Elshout, ed. Joel R. Beeke [Pittsburgh: Soli Deo Gloria, 1994], 35–242).

Preeminent in the eighteenth century was Jonathan Edwards (1703–1758), who defended historic Calvinism within the context of challenges from Enlightenment thought, and whose ethical treatises include *Charity and Its Fruits* (1738), which originated as sermons on 1 Corinthians 13; *Religious Affections* (1746), dealing with genuine Christian spirituality; and *Two Dissertations* (1765), which includes *Concerning the End for Which God Created the World* and *The Nature of True Virtue* (the sermons and two dissertations are reprinted in *The Works of Jonathan Edwards*, vol. 8: *Ethical Writings*, ed. Paul Ramsey [New Haven: Yale University Press, 1989]).

In the nineteenth century, American Presbyterian Robert Dabney wrote *The Practical Philosophy* (1897), his last book, of which Part IV treats applied ethics, although Part I offers a useful discussion of the psychology of human feelings, including aesthetic sensibilities, the love of applause, and the love of power (reprinted as *The Practical Philosophy. Being the Philosophy of the Feelings, of the Will, and of the Conscience, with the Ascertainment of Particular Rights and Duties* [Harrisonburg, Va.: Sprinkle, 1984], Part I, 1–135, and Part IV, 320–521).

The twentieth century saw significant contributions to Reformed ethics from W. Geesink (*Van 's Heeren ordinantiën*, 4 vols. [Kampen: J. H. Kok, 1925] and *Gereformeerde Ethiek*, 2 vols. [Kampen, J. H. Kok, 1931]); John Murray (*Principles of Christian Conduct: Aspects of Biblical Ethics* [Grand Rapids: Eerdmans, 1957]); Carl F. H. Henry (*Christian Personal Ethics* [Grand Rapids: Eerdmans, 1957]); and J. Douma (a fifteen-volume series titled *Ethische bezinning*, two volumes of which are translated as *The Ten Commandments: Manual for the Christian Life*, trans. Nelson D. Kloosterman [Phillipsburg, N.J.: P&R, 1991], and a third volume of which is translated as *Responsible Conduct: Principles of Christian Ethics*, trans. Nelson D. Kloosterman [Phillipsburg, N.J.: P&R, 2003]).

7   See Inst., 2.8.10; Francis Turretin, *Institutes of Elenctic Theology*, trans. George Musgrave Giger, ed. James T. Dennison, Jr. (Phillipsburg, N.J.: P&R, 1994), 2:34–36; Westminster Larger Catechism, Answer 99; summarized in J. Douma, *The Ten Commandments: Manual for the Christian Life*, 12.

8   In England, William Perkins, often called "the first Reformed casuist," published two works offering pastoral advice regarding cases of conscience, works that were quickly translated into Latin, German, and Dutch, thereby helping to define Calvinist ethics for generations. Comparable influences on Calvinist ethics were the writing and teaching of Gisbert Voetius (1589–1676), often called "the standard bearer of the Further Reformation," a Netherlander famous for his opposition to Arminianism at the great Synod of Dort (1618–1619) and against the philosophy of Descartes. Voetius was influenced by Willem Teellinck (1579–1629) and William Ames (1576–1633), both of whom also sought to apply biblical principles to specific questions of Christian living. For a contemporary discussion of casuistry as part of Reformed ethics, see Nelson D. Kloosterman, "Casuistry as Ministerial Ethics: A Plea for Rehabilitating Moral Nurture in the Church," in *Nuchtere Noodzaak. Ethiek tussen navolging en compromise. Opstellen aangeboden aan Prof. Dr. J. Douma*, ed. J. H. F. Schaeffer, J. H. Smit, Th. J. M. Tromp (Kampen: J. H. Kok, 1997), 106–116.

9   For a broader treatment of the subject of offending the weaker believer, see Nelson D. Kloosterman, *Scandalum Infirmorum et Communio Sanctorum: The Relation Between Christian Liberty and Neighbor Love in the Church* (Neerlandia, Alberta: Inheritance Publications, 1991).

10   Inst., 3.19.12.

PART SIX

CALVINISM'S
GOAL

CHAPTER 28

DOXOLOGY

Sinclair Ferguson

Praising God is one of the highest and purest acts of religion. In prayer we act like men; in praise we act like angels.[1]

—THOMAS WATSON

*T*o set the scene for the conclusion to this book, let me invite you to take a simple word-association test. The usual procedure for such a test is that the administrator says a word and the subject responds with the first word that comes to mind. Thus, the word *horse* might immediately prompt the word *cart* from some people, but *race* (as in horse race) from others.

Here, then, is the word-association test:

Calvinism _____

Did the noun *doxology* or the adjective *doxological* come to mind? If so, would it have come to mind apart from the title of this chapter? The terms *Calvinism* and *doxology* are not ordinarily associated with each other, even by Christians. Yet it is the overall contention of both this volume as a whole, and of this conclusion in particular, that Calvinism is *always* doxological—otherwise it cannot be either truly biblical or truly Calvinistic, and therefore, at the end of the day, cannot be true theology. For true theology always leads to doxology.

Doxology is, literally, a word or words of praise. Doxologies punctuate the Bible because they punctuate the life of faith.[2] This at least was Paul's understanding of the life of Abraham: "he was strong in faith, giving glory to God" (Rom.

4:20). The rhythm of the Christian's life is always determined by the principle that when the revelation of God in His glory is grasped by faith, the response is to return all glory to God.

Paul himself summarizes this truth at the climax of three chapters of the most tightly woven theology found anywhere in Scripture. In Romans 9–11, he traces God's ways in faithfulness to His Word, in divine election, and in distinguishing grace (chap. 9); in gospel proclamation (chap. 10); and in sovereign, divine providence toward Jew and Gentile (chap. 11). Then he draws the conclusion: "For of him, and through him, and to him, are all things: to whom be glory for ever. Amen" (Rom. 11:36).

What is being underlined here is, surely, that the knowledge of the sovereignty of God exercised in all of these spheres leads to a single response from the heart of faith: "Glory to God forever," or, in the familiar Latin words by which the teaching of the Reformation is often summarized, *soli Deo gloria*—to God alone be the glory!

These considerations notwithstanding, the expression *doxological Calvinism* may seem strange to many people—an oxymoron or even a straightforward contradiction in terms. Whether one thinks of the so-called five points of Calvinism (in terms of their origin, more accurately labeled "the five corrections to Arminianism"), of the much larger vision of John Calvin himself, or of the teaching of his followers, such as John Knox and the Puritans, *doxology, praise, worship*, and *adoration* may not be words that come to mind in any word-association test.

But if with B. B. Warfield we consider Calvinism to be no more and no less than biblical theology expressed in its fullest and richest way, we readily see that the effect of such theology will indeed be doxology. That is true because Reformed theology emphasizes doxology-evoking *biblical teaching*, it is illustrated in the expressions of *Calvinistic singing* we find in church history, and it is evident in the *Christian experience* of those who have embraced the Reformed faith and lived it out as a lifestyle.

BIBLICAL TEACHING

Perhaps the historically best-loved gospel invitation in the New Testament is found in the so-called "comfortable words" of Christ: "Come unto me, all ye that labour and are heavy laden, and I will give you rest. . . . Take my yoke . . . ye shall find rest unto your souls" (Matt. 11:28–29). Here is rich grace; here is an open-hearted, genuine invitation to all in need to come to Christ. Here, too, the Lord Jesus is God's yes and amen to all His promises (2 Cor. 1:19–20)—the rest in God that was symbolized (but rarely experienced) in the old covenant is now realized in the shed blood of Jesus Himself in the new covenant.

But what lies behind these words? Surprisingly to those who are familiar with these words only apart from their context in Matthew 11, they follow a most remarkable outburst of praise from the heart of the Lord Jesus: "I thank thee, O Father, Lord of heaven and earth. . . ." But for what reason does Christ express such worship? It is "because thou hast hid these things from the wise and prudent, and hast revealed them unto babes. Even so, Father: for so it seemed good in thy sight. All things are delivered unto me of my Father: and no man knoweth the Son, but the Father; neither knoweth any man the Father, save the Son, and he to whomsoever the Son will reveal him" (Matt. 11:25–27).

Jesus' invitation to trust Him emerges from His praise to His Father. That praise is predicated on the distinguishing election of God: in sovereign fashion (His gracious will, Matt. 11:26), God has hidden His truth from some and revealed it to others; only the electing grace of the Son opens the way to the knowledge of the Father. Here the praise of Jesus *presupposes* human depravity and helplessness (the Father is not known by men naturally); it *rests on* a divine choice in which God both hides and reveals; and it *affirms* God's sovereign good pleasure in irresistible grace. What strikes most readers as so remarkable is that Jesus does all this within the context of the clearest, sweetest, most gracious invitation to sinners to come to Him for rest.

It should be no surprise that it was a Calvinist, Horatius Bonar, who penned the famous hymn lines:

> *I heard the voice of Jesus say, "Come unto Me and rest;*
> *Lay down, thou weary one, lay down thy head upon My breast."*
> *I came to Jesus as I was, weary and worn and sad;*
> *I found in Him a resting place, and He has made me glad.*[3]

The rooting of doxology in divine sovereignty, glory, grace, and freedom—in a word, in God's "Godness"—is a pattern we find regularly repeated in the New Testament. And it is not in the more recondite texts of the New Testament that we find doxology closely linked with the truths that "Calvinists" affirm, but in those passages that are the commonly loved property of all believers.

What Christian has never found consolation in the comfort of Romans 8:28—surely one of the all-time-favorite texts of Scripture? Everything works together for our good. Yes, but how do we know that everything works together for good for those who love God? We have this assurance: because we are called according to His purpose. And where is that purpose rooted but in the sovereign, pre-temporal disposition of God: "For whom he did foreknow, he also did predestinate. . . . Moreover whom he did predestinate, them he also called: and whom he called, them he also justified: and whom he justified, them he also glorified" (Rom. 8:29–30).

Paul's repeated and consistent use here of the aorist tense for his main verbs underscores the certainty and the definitiveness of God's sovereignty; nothing can ultimately resist His will. Moreover, these truths stimulate Paul to speak with a doxological heart and a confident—indeed, exuberant—lyricism in the face of all that might oppose God's work for and in him. These truths are the marrow of Calvinism and give to true Calvinism the same lyrical and doxological spirit.

The point could be illustrated from a variety of other passages. The doxology of Ephesians 1:3ff ("Blessed be the God and Father of our Lord Jesus Christ . . . to the praise of the glory of his grace . . . to the praise of his glory . . . unto the praise of his glory") is rooted in the sovereign, loving election of God and in His equally sovereign outpouring of all spiritual blessings on us. Faith receives these blessings, but it is not their cause.

In the same way, the doxology that opens Peter's first letter expresses the praise of those who have been chosen by God; brought into new life by sovereign, spiritual new birth; and persevere because God perseveres with them (1 Peter 1:1–5). Faith grasps this, but is not its origin. Rather, we "are kept by the power of God [a present *passive* participle] through faith."

This point, then, should be beyond dispute. Praise to God in Scripture results from the sense that we are depraved and can contribute nothing to our salvation—yet, God has been pleased to save us. He has chosen us; Christ's blood has atoned for us; the Spirit has worked irresistibly in us (despite our initial resistance) to give us new life; and we persevere as saints because of the perseverance of God with us. This biblical teaching is precisely what later came to be described as Calvinism.

CALVINISTIC SINGING

The wonderful, albeit absentminded, "Rabbi" John Duncan (1796–1870), professor of Hebrew at New College, Edinburgh, once read out the words of Charles Wesley's hymn "And Can It Be That I Should Gain":

Long my imprisoned spirit lay
Fast bound in sin and nature's night;
Thine eye diffused a quickening ray;
I woke, the dungeon flamed with light;
My chains fell off, my heart was free;
I rose, went forth, and followed Thee.
My chains fell off, my heart was free;
I rose, went forth, and followed Thee.[4]

Duncan commented quizzically, "Where's your Arminianism now, friend?" The Wesley brothers were indeed Arminian in theology (despite their conviction that many of their views were "within a hair's-breadth of Calvinism"[5]). But at this point, Charles Wesley's expressions of praise are rooted in a theology borrowed from his Calvinist friend George Whitefield's preaching on the new birth.

Wesley bids us sing praise to God for His sovereign, liberating, prevenient, divine work on the soul that both awakens us and delivers us. When he does so, he is forced to borrow a Calvinistic frame of reference. A moment's reflection will underline how contradictory it would be to sing praise to God for something He had not done. Of course, hymns may be written to parody Calvinistic doctrine, and on very rare occasions one hears songs that celebrate "free will." But the great hymns of ages past, like their predecessors in Scripture, praise God for being God, for being sovereign, for being a saving and keeping God. To cast a critical glance sideways in the contemporary evangelical world, it is difficult to imagine what hymns of adoration and praise might be written by Open Theists (whose chief enemy appears to be Calvinism). Do we praise God for being like us in that He is neither sovereign over all things in the present nor aware of what will unfold in our future?

Most of the old hymns underscore the point that Calvinism is in its very nature doxological, and that all doxology, in fact, depends on such biblical theology. Here, for example, is the best-known hymn of Augustus Montague Toplady (1740–1778):

> *Not the labors of my hands*
> *Can fulfill Thy law's demands;*
> *Could my zeal no respite know,*
> *Could my tears forever flow,*
> *All for sin could not atone;*
> *Thou must save, and Thou alone.*
>
> *Nothing in my hand I bring,*
> *Simply to Thy cross I cling;*
> *Naked, come to Thee for dress;*
> *Helpless look to Thee for grace;*
> *Foul, I to the Fountain fly;*
> *Wash me, Savior, or I die.*[6]

This is Calvinism in poetry: such is our depravity and helplessness that "Thou must save, and Thou alone." Only these emphases that are characteristic of Calvinism can give birth to such theology as poetry. Granted, the Calvinism is more pronounced and more deliberately articulated with some hymn writers. But these same truths come to expression in the more pastoral spirit of a John Newton and his "Amazing Grace!" What makes grace so amazing is precisely that it sovereignly frees and sovereignly saves from first to last. Since every stable doctrine of providence stresses God's absolute sovereignty over the details of life, robust singing on providence is characteristically well-rooted in this Calvinistic emphasis.

It is no surprise, therefore, to discover that at the time of the Reformation, while Ulrich Zwingli, despite his own musical accomplishments, resisted singing in worship, Calvin insisted on it. Not only so, but while Calvin was in Strasbourg, he himself put into verse a number of the psalms for congregational singing, and later he encouraged others to do so in Geneva. We still use many of these tunes. Doxology sits comfortably within Reformed theology; in fact, it is required by it as a logical and spiritual necessity.

CHRISTIAN EXPERIENCE

Calvinistic theology has always placed great emphasis on biblical and doctrinal knowledge, and rightly so. We are transformed by the renewing of our minds (Rom. 12:1–2). This transformation is a prerequisite for our worship, since it is by the Spirit's illumination of our minds through Scripture that we gain understanding of God and His ways. But Calvinism—at least in its consistent forms—has never been merely cerebral. The history of Reformed Christianity is also the story of the highest order of spiritual experience. Calvinistic doctrine expressed in God-exalting words of praise leads to a distinctive Christian experience. The melody that is composed intellectually in Calvinistic theology and sung enthusiastically in Reformed worship also can be heard in the lifestyle and experience of Reformed Christians.

The seriousness of the Reformed world and life view means that, even when the melody is played in a minor key, it remains a melody. Indeed, to use a metaphor of Calvin, as this melody is played in the church, it becomes a glorious symphony[7] blending the following motifs:

- Trust in the sovereignty of God.
- The experience of the power of God's grace to save hopeless and helpless sinners.
- An overwhelming sense of being loved by a Savior who has died specifically and successfully for one's sins.
- The discovery of a grace that has set one free to trust, serve, and love Christ while yet not destroying one's will.
- The quiet confidence and poise engendered by knowing that God has pledged Himself to persevere with His people "till all the ransomed church of God is saved to sin no more."[8]

These motifs all conspire to give God alone the glory.

The essence of the Calvinistic life is living in such a way as to glorify God. This, after all, is the burden of the answer to the opening question of the Shorter Catechism written by the Westminster Assembly of Divines: "Man's chief end is to glorify God, and to enjoy him for ever." Here is the ultimate surprise in Calvinism for many people: the glory of God and the enjoyment of man are not antithetical, but are correlated in the purposes of God.

The view that God's glory diminishes man and robs him of pleasure is, in the light (or should one say "darkness"?) of Genesis 3, the lie about God that was exchanged for the truth (Rom. 1:25). It is satanic theology that plays God against man.

In sharp contrast, biblical theology that exalts God in His sovereign grace and glory opens the door for man to enter into a quite different order of reality. Here is offered the experience of, and delight in, the rich pleasures of restoration to fellowship with God, transformation into the likeness of Christ, and anticipation of being with Christ where He is in order to see Him in His glory (John 17:24). This, at least, was the view of Isaac Watts:

> *The sorrows of the mind*
> *Be banished from the place;*
> *Religion never was designed*
> *To make our pleasures less.*
>
> *Let those refuse to sing,*
> *Who never knew our God;*
> *But favorites of the heavenly King,*
> *May speak their joys abroad.*
>
> *There we shall see His face,*
> *And never, never sin!*
> *There, from the rivers of His grace,*
> *Drink endless pleasures in.*
>
> *Yea, and before we rise,*
> *To that immortal state,*
> *The thoughts of such amazing bliss,*
> *Should constant joys create.*
>
> *The men of grace have found,*
> *Glory begun below.*
> *Celestial fruits on earthly ground*
> *From faith and hope may grow.*

The hill of Zion yields
A thousand sacred sweets
Before we reach the heav'nly fields,
Or walk the golden streets.[9]

It is surely this outlook that Warfield had in mind when he described the fruits of doxological Calvinism in a story he relates in his essay, "Is the Shorter Catechism Worthwhile?"

We have the following bit of personal experience from a general officer of the United States army. He was in a great western city at a time of intense excitement and violent rioting. The streets were over-run daily by a dangerous crowd. One day he observed approaching him a man of singularly combined calmness and firmness of mind, whose very demeanor inspired confidence. So impressed was he with his bearing amid the surrounding uproar that when he had passed he turned to look back at him, only to find that the stranger had done the same. On observing his turning the stranger at once came back to him, and touching his chest with his forefinger, demanded without preface: "What is the chief end of man?" On receiving the countersign, "Man's chief end is to glorify God and to enjoy him forever" — "Ah!" said he, "I knew you were a Shorter Catechism boy by your looks!" "Why, that was just what I was thinking of you," was the rejoinder.[10]

That is doxological Calvinism—a melody played in the midst of a world of chaos, a life lived in the knowledge that God is the Lord, that the Savior is also the Creator who sustains all things, so that I can be assured,

That I with body and soul, both in life and death, am not my own, but belong unto my faithful Savior Jesus Christ; who, with his precious blood, hath fully satisfied for all my sins, and delivered me from all the power of the devil; and so preserves me that without the will of my heavenly Father, not a hair can fall from my head; yea, that all things must be subservient to my salvation, and therefore, by his Holy Spirit, he also assures me of eternal life, and makes me sincerely willing and ready, henceforth, to live unto him.[11]

This is doxological Calvinism—and when we see and hear it, we are never in any doubt that we have seen Christianity in its finest flower.

DISCUSSION QUESTIONS

1. What is meant by the term *doxological*?

2. What is doxological Calvinism?

3. How is worship viewed from a doxological Calvinistic point of view?

4. How does doxological Calvinism play out in human experience?

NOTES

[1] Quoted in I. D. E. Thomas, *The Golden Treasury of Puritan Quotations* (Chicago: Moody Press, 1975), 209.

[2] See, for example, Gen. 24:27; Ex. 18:10; 1 Chron. 29:10–13; Luke 1:68; Rom. 9:5; 2 Cor. 1:3–4; Eph. 1:3; Rev. 5:12.

[3] From the hymn "I Heard the Voice of Jesus Say" by Horatius Bonar, 1846.

[4] From the hymn "And Can It Be That I Should Gain" by Charles Wesley, 1738.

[5] From *Minutes of Some Late Conversations between the Rev Mr Wesleys and Others*, Conversation II, August, 1745, Bristol, in *The Works of John Wesley* (Grand Rapids: Baker, 1979), 8:284.

[6] From the hymn "Rock of Ages, Cleft for Me" by Augustus M. Toplady, 1776.

[7] John Calvin, *Commentary on the Book of Psalms*, trans. and ed. James Anderson (Edinburgh: Calvin Translation Society, 1845), 5:178.

[8] From the hymn "There Is a Fountain Filled with Blood" by William Cowper, 1771.

[9] From the hymn "Come, We That Love the Lord" by Isaac Watts, 1707.

[10] B. B. Warfield, *Selected Shorter Writings*, ed. John E. Meeter (Nutley, N.J.: P&R, 1970), 383–384.

[11] The Heidelberg Catechism, Answer 1.

INDEX OF SUBJECTS AND NAMES

INDEX OF SCRIPTURE

ABOUT THE AUTHOR

Dr. Joel R. Beeke is president and professor of systematic theology and homiletics at Puritan Reformed Theological Seminary, pastor of the Heritage Netherlands Reformed Congregation, editor of Banner of Sovereign Grace Truth, editorial director of Reformation Heritage Books, president of Inheritance Publishers, and vice president of the Dutch Reformed Translation Society, all in Grand Rapids, Mich. He has written, coauthored, or edited fifty books (most recently, *Meet the Puritans*, *Reformation Heroes*, *Walking as He Walked*, and *Striving Against Satan*) and contributed fifteen hundred articles to Reformed books, journals, periodicals, and encyclopedias. His Ph.D. is in Reformation and post-Reformation theology from Westminster Theological Seminary. He is frequently called on to lecture at seminaries and to speak at Reformed conferences around the world. He and his wife, Mary, have been blessed with three children: Calvin, Esther, and Lydia.

CONTRIBUTORS

Dr. Sinclair B. Ferguson is senior minister of the First Presbyterian Church, Columbia, S.C., and distinguished visiting professor of systematic theology at Westminster Theological Seminary.

Dr. James M. Grier is the distinguished professor of philosophical theology at Grand Rapids Theological Seminary, where he served for sixteen years as academic dean and vice president. Previously he served as associate professor of philosophy at Cedarville University. He is an adjunct professor at Puritan Reformed Theological Seminary, Asia Baptist Theological Seminary, and London Reformed Baptist Seminary.

Dr. Michael A. G. Haykin is professor of church history and biblical spirituality at the Southern Baptist Theological Seminary in Louisville, Ky., as well as the director of the Andrew Fuller Center for Baptist Studies, based at the Southern Baptist Theological Seminary.

Dr. Nelson D. Kloosterman is a minister of the gospel among the United Reformed Churches in North America, professor of ethics and New Testament studies at Mid-America Reformed Seminary in Dyer, Ind., coeditor of the *Mid-America Journal of Theology*, and secretary of the Dutch Reformed Translation Society.

Rev. Ray B. Lanning is minister of First Reformed Presbyterian Church, Grand Rapids, Mich., and an instructor in homiletics at Puritan Reformed Theological Seminary.

Dr. Robert W. Oliver is a Reformed Baptist pastor who served the Old Baptist Chapel, Bradford on Avon, U.K., for thirty-five years. He is currently a lecturer in church history and historical theology at the London Theological Seminary and at the John Owen Centre for Theological Studies.

Ray Pennings is the vice president of research for the Work Research Foundation (www.wrf.ca), a Canadian think tank dedicated to cultural renewal. He serves as a teaching elder in the Free Reformed congregation of Calgary, Alberta, and is chairman of the board of governors of Redeemer University College. He is a regular public affairs commentator in the Canadian media and has authored numerous monographs and articles in both the public and church press.

Dr. Derek W. H. Thomas is a professor of systematic and practical theology at Reformed Theological Seminary, Jackson, Miss., an adjunct professor at Puritan Reformed Theological Seminary, the minister of teaching at First Presbyterian Church, Jackson, and the editorial director of the Alliance of Confessing Evangelicals.